HORARY
ASTROLOGY

Books by Marc Edmund Jones

HOW TO LEARN ASTROLOGY
THE GUIDE TO HOROSCOPE INTERPRETATION
HORARY ASTROLOGY
ASTROLOGY, HOW AND WHY IT WORKS
SABIAN SYMBOLS IN ASTROLOGY
ESSENTIALS OF ASTROLOGICAL ANALYSIS
OCCULT PHILOSOPHY
GANDHI LIVES
GEORGE SYLVESTER MORRIS
THE SABIAN MANUAL
THE SCOPE OF ASTROLOGICAL PREDICTION
MUNDANE PERSPECTIVES IN ASTROLOGY

DR. MARC EDMUND JONES

HORARY ASTROLOGY

PRACTICAL TECHNIQUES
FOR PROBLEM SOLVING

WITH A PRIMER OF SYMBOLISM

AURORA PRESS

P.O. BOX 573 SANTA FE, N.M. 87504

© The Marc Edmund Jones Literary Trust, 1993

Library of Congress catalog number: 78-149643
ISBN: 0-943358-39-6

No part of this book may be reproduced by any mechanical, photographic or electronic process, or in the form of a phonographic recording, nor may it be stored in a retrieval system, transmitted, translated into another language, or otherwise copied for public or private use, excepting brief passages quoted for purposes of review without the permission of the publisher.

First published in 1993 by:
Aurora Press
P.O. Box 573
Santa Fe, N.M. 87504

Printed in the United States of America

CONTENTS

Foreword 7

INTRODUCTORY

Chapter		
One	What Is Horary Astrology?	13
Two	Significant Sensitiveness	22
Three	Charting the Pertinent Moment	37

THE FOUNDATION OF HORARY ART

Four	Putting Experience in Place	63
Five	The Planets	107
Six	Phrasing the Question	122
Seven	Locating the Question	131

THE METHOD OF HORARY INTERPRETATION

Eight	The Yes-and-No Technique	233
Nine	Testing the Grain of a Chart	268
Ten	The Time Measure	293
Eleven	Planetary Dynamics	303
Twelve	The Judgment Chart	322

THE RAMIFICATIONS OF HORARY ART

Thirteen	The Use of Natal Methods	337
Fourteen	Multiple Questions	377
Fifteen	Parallels of Declination	385
Sixteen	Inaugural Horoscopes	390
Seventeen	Special Fields of Judgment	399
Eighteen	The Method of Birth Planets	406

APPENDIX

Primer of Symbolism	411
Index to Main Text	453

THERE IS ...
> A time to keep,
> And a time to throw away.

Ecclesiastes, 3:6
Translation by J. M. Powis Smith

FOREWORD

ALTHOUGH preceded by two smaller manuals, published in response to an immediate and specific demand (*How to Learn Astrology*, Philadelphia, 1941, and *The Guide to Horoscope Interpretation*, same year), this book represents the first of a projected series of volumes in a research project that was launched in December, 1928, when the results of investigation up to that time were made available in a preliminary mimeographed form. The present book was not originally scheduled as the first in the series, and its place in that position has been determined entirely by considerations of supply and demand.

The author first investigated horary astrology in the winter of 1913-14. The mechanisms and materials of analysis were shared originally with small private groups, as they were developed, and the techniques were subjected to continual test and refinement. The mimeographed sheets have been distributed rather widely among astrological practitioners and students, and the actual writing of these pages was preceded by several years of intensive classwork as a means for determining the best presentation of the principles from a teaching and learning standpoint.

The materials are presented as interestingly as possible, in a step by step unfoldment designed to give the book a simple readability, and the more difficult sections are set in a compact form of type in order to encourage the newcomer or casual reader to pass over them until ready to undertake a measure of serious study. For the student and teacher—as well as the practitioner who needs the text as a reference—an exceptionally ample index is arranged in topical form. Without a continual employment of this index, the full value of the volume will be lost, at least in the case of most of those who in the preliminary judgment of the author might be expected to purchase it.

If the volume were to have a dedication it should be inscribed to Dane Rudhyar, who early took an interest in the mimeographed materials and who insisted upon giving credit in print to the whole research project and thereby unwittingly destroyed the anonymity that the author had felt would better serve the purposes in view. It is thanks to Rudhyar primarily, who through the years has remained a friend in his own maturing as the philosopher as well as the artist, that the astrological materials conveniently labeled Sabian in their totality were brought to the attention of the general astrological public.

Very grateful acknowledgment must again be made to Margaret Morrell and Mathilde Shapiro for the embarrassingly generous editorial assistance given earlier in the case of the two preliminary manuals. Elizabeth Aldrich and Joyce Mayday were kind enough to read the manuscript critically, and to make suggestions. Miss Dale Adams made the drawings. The book owes much to the conscientious attention to its details on the part of the author's secretary, Miss Elsie Boyle.

New York City, December 22, 1942 (abridged)

FOREWORD

THE REVISED EDITION

Few developments in human affairs have been as curious as the fact that astrology, coming down into modern times as hardly more than a medieval superstition and one that perpetuated itself for the most part as a particularly fascinating form of fortunetelling, has survived and now and suddenly has achieved a very wide if casual respectability. The reason for its acceptance would seem to be that, in spite of much illogical explanation and gratuitous assumption, it has succeeded in making some very real sense in everyday application.

Indeed, there is a hard core of sheer demonstrable performance provided by its more expert practitioners. More importantly however, following its popularization by the pioneer souls of its new image together with a fresh and fundamentally valid investigation reaching full tide within the present century, it has shed much of the earlier aura of magic that could not but thoroughly disqualify it in modern scientific circles. Incompetence and superficiality remain a primary handicap to its full recognition, but these are factors that impede human progress in every area of man's specializations. Any ultimately adequate organization of the illimitable potentials, of what is still a very nascent astrological science, may of course lie far in the future.

What can be done at the present time must of necessity be tentative. If in later perspective it proves to have been no more than earnest spadework, the effort is no less a contribution. Here is the one sure justification of this series of textbooks. In the *Scope of Astrological Prediction* it was necessary to formulate a set of "essential principles" since without them, as explained in that volume, the writing could not have been brought to logical focus and thus in any way have been completed effectively. But as also suggested, it is necessary to realize that the formulation might be a tour de force, of value only in serving the preliminary purpose. At the point now in the author's contribution-in-work to astrology it might be well to remember that the fundamental scheme of horoscopic operation, given its exposition as a primer of symbolism, may no less turn out to be a trail-breaking tour de force such as dramatizes the remarkable mirror-image relationship between chance and certainty in the structure of a horoscope.

Stanwood, Washington, March 6, 1971

Introductory

Chapter One

WHAT IS HORARY ASTROLOGY?

Some years ago a man sat at his portable typewriter in a Midwest hotel room on a Sunday afternoon. He was a motion picture director who had gone out from New York on short notice to produce a number of comedies. Now he was preparing his script for the next morning's work, but the intrusion of some vague element into his consciousness interrupted the smooth flow of his ideas.

He stopped his typing, to look at his watch. Tired after several hours of concentrated effort, he interpreted the stirring within himself as a desire to go to church, for the evening music. There was little else for a stranger to do on this day, and he had not attended a religious service for many months. He shaved, dressed and at length walked down to a cathedral-like edifice which he had noticed nearby. On arrival in front of the building, however, he felt a distinct disinclination to enter. Not giving much thought to his feeling, and observing the spire of another church in the distance, he decided to go there. On walking the several blocks, he found himself once more of no mood to go in.

These vagaries of impulse rather amused him now. When he crossed to a third place of worship, a little further on the other side of the street, but again did not feel inclined to enter, he decided he was getting temperamental. Better that he return to his room, and do some more work on his script! He started back, still on foot. Approaching a hotel, within perhaps fifty feet of the entrance, he glanced up just in time to observe a car with California license plates, as it drew up to the curb. Two old intimates from the Coast emerged, and he was close enough to hail them, and thus to begin an interesting evening.

This sort of thing, in one form or another, happens to everybody at fairly frequent intervals. The motion picture director, in the particular case, knew that his friends intended to drive from Los Angeles to New York, but he had no idea when. His friends expected to see him at the end of their journey, but had no intimation of his presence in the Middle West. The tie of relationship between them, through a thoroughly roundabout operation of his mind, brought him to leave his own hotel, and to wander here and there more or less at random, until his arrival on a given spot at a moment which, to be effective, had to be exact to within some sixty seconds at least.

Many explanations are offered for such an occurrence. It will be said to be coincidence, but this simply contributes a name for the event, and does not yield any clue to its nature. Of the same piece of cloth is its identification as intuition, which still leaves the "intuition" unexplained. Occultists may recognize these things as the evidence of an "astral world," and others will resort to means of explanation which may well have philosophical value. However, the suggestions are usually of little help to the layman. To remove something from ordinary reality is certainly no aid when it comes to making the best use of this ordinary reality.

WHAT IS HORARY ASTROLOGY? 15

No confusion can arise over these "coincidental" manifestations of relationship, either in life or in thinking about life, if the nature of time is understood. Time is the integrating dynamic in experience, but it is usually taken for granted. A man goes to catch a train, and regards it as nothing particularly remarkable when he is able to get to the station a few minutes before the train leaves. True, he has consulted a timetable, and has guided his actions by the movement of the hands on the face of his watch, but this only means that he has taken charge of the particular integration of events. The average individual, as a matter of fact, exercises this control over events during most of his waking hours.

Few people realize how large a content of human experience is made up of conventions and agreements by which the acts and responses of men and women are arranged, deliberately, for mutual convenience. Thus business is conducted on weekdays, more or less universally, with Sunday set aside for relaxation. In those lines of effort where the work of some is an immediate necessity for the relaxation of others, as in the case of various public services, simple but special adjustments are made for those who must labor while their fellows play. This is accomplished, without difficulty, through a manipulation of the time factor in experience. No mystery is recognized in any of this, with the result that no one finds himself unable to order his business activity to any reasonable degree.

There is another large segment of total human experience where the organization of events in time is equally deliberate, but more indirect, and usually without any conscious control of circumstances. This is illustrated in the field of romance. The boy and the girl meet, and soon find themselves quickening to the mutual interest which will culminate in a lifelong partnership. The occasion of meeting seems very exciting to them, but actually it is a mere matter of normal pointing in time. They are two individuals who have come together in a context which offers them an adequate prophecy of their capacity for mutual experience. Their initial great moment is a simple reflection of this potentiality in some situation which, in its turn, reflects a maturing point in the lives of both. In their minds the event dramatizes the consummation in a very colorful fashion, and this is healthy self-discovery through the very fact that it seems wonderful to them.

It is only the extreme case of a reflection in consciousness of this pointing in events, such as is less universally recognized as an ordinary part of experience, that is commonly rationalized and made something of a mystery. When a celebrity, about to board an airplane, changes his mind on a "hunch" and goes by train, he seems to give testimony to a greater or unknown "reality" if the plane crashes, and he proves to have saved his life by following his intuition. However, to find life mysterious in cases of this sort is simply to destroy all chance for the control of events, since the "real" becomes remote and beyond human knowing. "Hunches" of this sort are actually a commonplace, and for the one person who alters his plans, and so escapes danger, there are uncounted hundreds who turn about-face in similar circumstances with results that are not significant, or that even prove disadvantageous.

What happened in the celebrity's case was that the whole context of relations, in which he was about to leave

WHAT IS HORARY ASTROLOGY?

for his given destination by plane, was sufficiently unsatisfactory in its general integration, somewhere below the level of normal consciousness, to bring about his refusal to participate in it; as a conscious but as yet unrationalized act. There is always danger in this blind a response to the sense of potentiality in a total situation, but nonetheless this instinctive sensibility is the bottom factor in all conscious judgment; no wise man ignores it even if he may move most infrequently upon its prompting. No individual can be very successful in business unless he possesses this intuitive capacity for recognizing the undercurrents and unsuspected facets of his environment, throughout the passing and fluid kaleidoscope of events.

Life is "organic" in the sense that there are continual and exceedingly complex adjustments of act to situation, with the vast bulk of these occurring below the conscious level. What is involved is not a mystery, but rather is the simple phenomenon of selection, or the method by which existence gives a knowable pointing to reality, and so carries the thread of any given relation through the totality of all relationship. Intelligence, in the broadest possible definition, is sensitiveness to this individual pointing of things, primarily in time and secondarily in space. The only approach to a greater intelligence, either for an individual or for all individuals together, is an increased knowledge of the converging factors in any given kind of situation. This may be developed below the conscious level, as the enhanced sensitiveness which has its spectacular demonstration in the form of clairvoyance, but far more wonderful refinements of human capacity are provided in the course of normal everyday experience. These are the means for utilizing the common persistency in the relations of things to each other, as this may be controlled from a focus in time.

The development of mathematics, as an impartial measure for the relationship in any given pointing of existence, has provided the foundation for man's mechanical civilization; far outstripping the powers in animal instinct or savage intuition. Because fine-tooled parts can be manufactured to an accuracy within less than thousandths of an inch, engineers can predict the function they will perform with absolute confidence. This is more startling than anything Nostradamus ever did, since a thousand schoolboys can be taken almost at random, and trained to produce equally dependable results. As for Nostradamus, he remains unique. The interpretations of his *Centuries* vary to an extent that clouds every serious claim made for his prophetic ability. By contrast the "physical sciences" all together have piled up a colossal store of carefully verified facts, so that the ramifying persistency of characteristics in almost all known substances can be charted, tabulated and made available in books. Biological science has applied modern exact measurement to the phenomena of living things. Psychology has begun to bring this same torch of scientific enlightenment to the examination of probabilities in human action, and to the discovery of methods for the control of conscious life and social eventualities.

Of all forms of psychology which, through human history, have attacked this general problem of establishing a control over events on the social level, or in conscious realms, astrology stands apart because it antedates all the other sciences in its antiquity and because, in its major

WHAT IS HORARY ASTROLOGY?

methods of operation, it has squared its theories with many long centuries of valid if not always well-organized verification. Astrological practice has suffered under a tremendous overriding burden of superstition and incompetence, and this has put up a screen which all too few scientifically-trained minds have been able to penetrate. Astrology has survived and is increasingly effective, however, primarily because it charts everything in terms of time, or the focal pointing by which the underlying pertinency of phenomena is best disclosed for analysis. The effectiveness of this procedure will be demonstrated amply in the following pages.

One particular department of astrology has specialized in the control of ordinary or everyday phenomena, as encountered at random but as found to be significant or critical in the terms of an immediate and practical human need. This is known as "horary" astrology, from the Latin word for "hour," and the name has its origin in the importance of anything as this may be identified—or as its focus in time and space may be traced out through various potential ramifications in a general way—by taking the exact moment at which some phase of experience becomes pertinent within a recognizable or measurable context, and by making this minor focus in time the foundation of a highly revealing analysis.

Just what does this use of an "exact moment" mean in common everyday terms? Why is time more important here than space? The general difference between these two modes of approach to reality is that time is more the measure of internal existence, and space more the yardstick of external activity. While any "present moment" is shared in some respect by everyone everywhere, time other than in this present moment is distinctly a personal matter. The line of the past and also of the future, in any genuine reality of experience, exists either in memory or in anticipation; or is what history on the one hand, and potentiality on the other, become in an individual consciousness. A person's actual relationship with others is entirely in a "now," since it is his option to forget or remember, and to reject or accept his experience, both past and to come, with far less actual limitation than the average man realizes. The present moment is not only the coincidence of these relations in the sharpest possible focus, but it is also the point of greatest real or effective co-operation with society and with the trend of events.

The horary figure of the heavens maps out the significance of such a present moment as it becomes focal first of all in the experience of a given individual, relative to some problem which he faces, and also as it is found significantly central in the general experience of all men, relative to the special case in a way illuminating to the astrologer as he in turn is able, on his part, to identify its indications as a basis for his judgment. All astrology fundamentally applies itself to charting the processes by which these significant moments sort out the potentialities and probabilities of experience, and the horary technique is of special value because it normally does this in complete independence of the place, date and hour of birth, which are the necessary foundations for the more familiar natal horoscope.

Here is an example horary chart, in the form most commonly employed by professional astrologers.

WHAT IS HORARY ASTROLOGY?

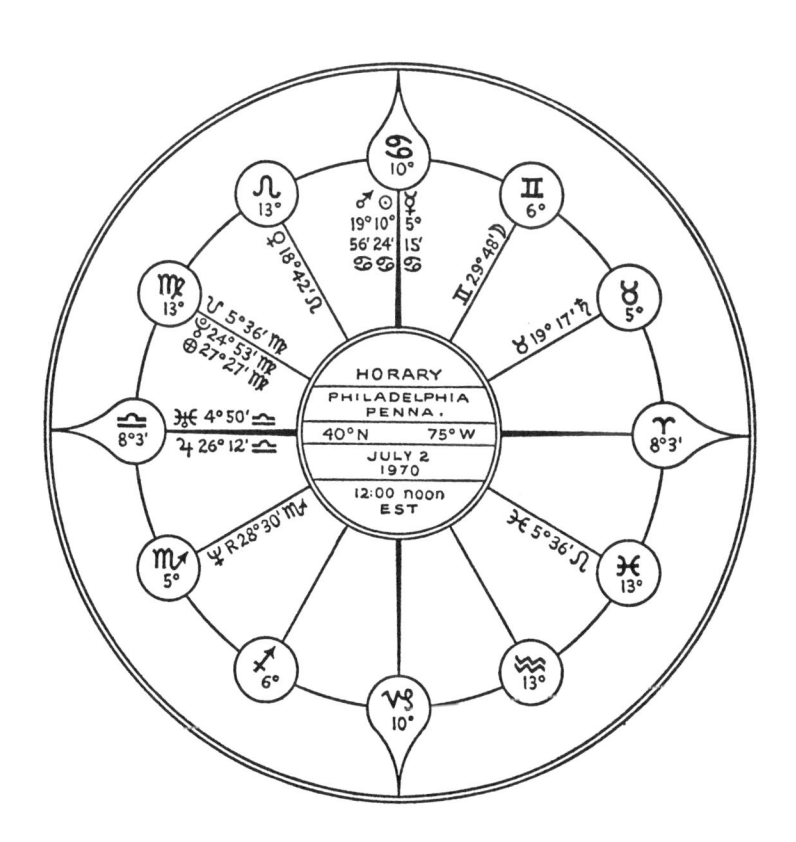

HORARY
PHILADELPHIA PENNA.
40°N   75°W
JULY 2
1970
12:00 noon
EST

Chapter Two

SIGNIFICANT SENSITIVENESS

The primary characteristic of every living creature is sensitiveness. Even the most simple cell has the power to become aware of its environment, and to respond to various stimuli. This is very necessary to organic continuity. Unless life can protect itself from threatened harm on the one hand, and can reach out to know and acquire what it needs for itself on the other, its course of existence becomes exceedingly hazardous. Therefore it can be said that man, with all of his complexity, is at root still sensitive above everything else.

This characteristic is obvious enough in the case where an individual sees an automobile coming, and steps out of the way; or where an "empty feeling" suggests that he go for lunch. What is less evident is the important fact that little of this human sensitiveness reveals itself on the conscious level. Personality exists in a broad and continually shifting complex of relations, through an infinity of responses to various factors in every direction of reality. They may be remote stimuli, as illustrated by the mother who knows "intuitively" when something happens to her child many miles away, or by the ridiculous commonplace when some man forecasts a change in weather from the sensation in callouses on his feet. They may be direct, as especially revealed in conscious act or choice. In either case intelligence is nothing but an ordering of these fac-

SIGNIFICANT SENSITIVENESS

tors of sensitiveness in experience, and an employment of them for the benefit of the organism. This is no less true when the sensitive impulse, as often, is a response to the relations between present events and past experience.

Thus an expert in any field of human effort is an individual who is able, out of his resources of prior knowledge, to be sensitive or "intelligent" in some specific or special regard. The automobile mechanic will know something is wrong with a motor when the average motorist may be blissfully insensible to trouble ahead. There are innumerable ways in which this intelligent or intuitive alertness of an organism can be classified, but at no time is it ever evident, subconsciously or otherwise, unless it amounts to a pointing of some given relationship in space and time. Horary astrology operates under the universal presence of these time and space factors, in any situation requiring conscious act or choice, by combining them in a science of logical judgment. It becomes a true "science" because all scientific knowledge is a generalization of experience in one way or another, and horary astrology, by exact definition, is the generalization of the abstract potentiality in any given set of human relations. It depends upon the simple but true observation, attributed to King Solomon by the Bible, that there is a time for all things, according to their own particular nature and place.

If a man wishes to catch a train, he must conform to its moment of departure. Solomon might as well have said that there is a time for all trains to start. This would mean that the movement in the given direction can be taken at the moment when the vehicle for such a movement is ready to move. Modern civilization has made the proposition somewhat more complex with the development of the automobile, but also has provided a better illustration for the principle. The traveling salesman who formerly was dependent on trains, and a consequent rather rigid schedule, does not now have to lose perhaps as much as a day in order to have the extra half-hour necessary to close a deal with Mr. Smith. He can drive from east town to west town entirely at his own convenience. However, if he selects an hour which presents a peak of traffic, he may have a real problem in covering a given space in a given interval. In no less true although considerably more complicated fashion, there is still a "time" for driving from east town to west town, bearing in mind what this "driving" means in the terms of any individual convenience.

The matter of Solomon's "time for all things," therefore, begins to identify itself as the coincidence among the converging lines of relationship in human situations, disclosing the "moment" as not only pertinent in the given individual experience but as convenient also for other factors of vital concern, many of them utterly unsuspected. Life reveals a complex world, but one which may be brought to operate according to any person's desire at the "proper time" simply because the special needs of his existence must sort out ultimately in an orderly relation to the special needs of everyone else.

Individual differences are real. However, they are a part of the totality of all things, and so must contribute to the convenient orderings of many phases of reality other than the individuality in question. Thus the young lady wishes to be an actress, and this she accomplishes because her fresh youth and particular talent afford pleasure, or are a

SIGNIFICANT SENSITIVENESS

"convenience" to the audience. The players and playgoers in a true sense make each other possible, requiring only that the pointing in time and space be instrumental in events common for both. The "normal curve" in statistics shows that the exceptional single instance finds its place in the average of the whole. The unusual event has a special pertinency in time and space, even if only that it extends the possibility of experience. Things happen according to usual expectation in a predominant percentage of cases, and this fact constitutes "convenience" in terms of a cosmic order. At the same time, the novel event of "little expectation" will no less demonstrate that these new infinite ramifications of the expected take place in an orderly scheme. The line of the "normal curve" never reaches the base of the graph, and so never shuts out the most remote possibility of difference.

The universe is orderly because it holds a place for anything at all, according to the particular time and space requirements of whatever general and specific relations are brought together in experience; that is, given a focus in an identifiable situation. Horary astrology takes the moment of an event in the ordering of the universe, which is provided quite literally for all human beings by the celestial motions of the earth, and measures the relations of these heavenly movements with that horizon on the earth's surface which, in its turn, is established by the place of the event. The seasons, and the succession of days, generalize the basic relations of man's existence and—as a similar phenomenon of the same cosmic order, which operates without any by-your-leave on the part of man's intelligence—the celestial motions which produce summer and winter, and day and night, can also, in astrological technique, identify the potentials of special significance among the many shifting constants of this same human experience in any particular case. The astrological chart itself offers only abstractions, or "expectations" of statistical probability, but, to the degree that any one fact in the given complex is known objectively and individually, other relative and equally tangible possibilities become intelligently deducible.

The power of the astrological analytics is due to a strict employment of heavenly motions which, while they are independent of human affairs, yet are an integral part of the general energy system in which humanity has its existence. There is nothing mysterious about astrology. Horary practice is not a hocus-pocus, but is rather an art of judgment. It only differs from the ordinary wisdom of a businessman—who from his charts of sales can analyze the pertinent factors in his own field of effort and predict correctly the quantities of a given product he will need—in the fact that it deals with general potentialities, such as can be applied to any given case. This is possible because the root of any matter is taken, astrologically, in the moment of time which has become pertinent, and so constitutes a basis for analysis.

The way in which time may be the key to judgment is illustrated by the case of a certain clever sales manager, under consideration by a group of his friends who are engaged in organizing a nation-wide enterprise. Because he is inclined to talk too much, they wish to keep him in ignorance of the project, at least until they are ready to make him a proposition. Unknown to these men, the sister

SIGNIFICANT SENSITIVENESS

of one of them, while on a trip, has met the sales manager in his own city, and for conversation has told him of the new plans in some detail; not realizing her brother wants him kept in ignorance. He sees the possibilities in this opening for himself, greatly bettering his present position, but he has decided not to admit that he knows anything, in his business and social contact with these others, believing he can drive a better deal if he does not speak up prematurely, or seem too eager. He is watching events carefully, waiting for some real clue as a guide to action.

When he receives a telegram to meet one of the organizers at a local hotel, in connection with a different matter, and concurrently is advised in a letter from a second member of the group that this individual will be in town, "quite by chance," and would like a social get-together, the moment gains significance. The third organizer lives in the same city as the sales manager, and the fact that all three are here at an identical time suggests some activity in connection with the new enterprise. When none of the three mention it to him, even casually or indirectly, he assumes that no real progress has been made; that things are still at the preliminary stage. The basis of his judgment is the point in time, giving its special focus to the rather long and intimate tie of friendship among the four men. Horary astrology operates in precisely the same fashion, but is able to go much farther in its deductions because it distributes relationships in a greater independence of the "accidents" of conscious knowledge pertinent to the particular issue.

Everything in life is given its significance by the impacts it receives from everything else. It is much easier to chart these impacts in general, as a means for the particular deduction, than to trace them out laboriously in the special case, as the basis for an isolated judgment. Astrology organizes the "putting two and two together" of all human deduction by illuminating the specific meaning of events within a frame of general relationships, on the pattern employed by life itself through innumerable examples in which the ordinary simplicity of a moment's focus in relations is immensely revealing, often without any conscious analysis at all.

Thus a charming widow graces a house party. The hostess, although almost Mid-Victorian in her standards, is happy to welcome one of such vivacity. Another guest is a successful author, especially noted for his sophisticated stories. The hostess, in talking with him, expresses her admiration for his work, but at the same time remarks that she does not approve of life as he portrays it. She asks if his portrait is not largely untrue, a fictional exaggeration. "On the contrary," he explains, "life beneath the surface, if anything, is even more degraded than I paint it. Indeed, when I first came east, with high ideals and out of an environment that gave me little preparation for the undercurrents of a big city, I was offered hospitality in a home of my father's fraternity brother. First thing I knew, I was caught in the old drama of Potiphar's wife, and when I had no idea how to deal with a persistent and dissolute lady."

The hostess, still somewhat unbelieving, had some moments later with the vivacious widow. Conversation turned to the author, and the other laughed. "He's a dear boy! When he first came from the West, he was a guest in our

SIGNIFICANT SENSITIVENESS

home. His father and my husband had gone to college together, and I tried hard to help him get started as a writer." What the hostess now knows is not actually communicated to her, but is knowledge that results from pertinent relations brought to a focus in time and space. All events similarly illustrate, to some degree, how moments become significant.

Everything in horary astrology depends, fundamentally, upon the correct selection of a pertinent point of experience in time and space, as the basis for analysis. The factor of space more or less takes care of itself, however, since it merely provides the place for which the horary wheel is erected. This leads to simplicity, in identifying the critical pointing of a situation, by reducing everything at the beginning to a recognition of the proper time. One branch of horary art avoids every further difficulty here because it operates on the basis of a horoscope set up for the moment of some actual event, along the lines of a natal horoscope for the birth of a child. A man opens a store, or starts out on some adventure. An astrologer, interested in his success, makes a careful note of the exact minute the doors are unlocked or the trip is begun, and prepares an astrological chart for this significant instant. The technique is often particularly valuable for beginners because there is no question of the time factor, either its exactness or its reliability.

Closely related to the procedure, but requiring more skill than the astrological neophyte may be able to muster, is an exactly reversed application of this horary analysis of single fixed events, or what is known as the astrology of "elections." Here an astrologically minded individual, determining to open a store or seek adventure, asks in advance for the proper time to start, in order to guarantee himself a favorable outcome. The astrologer erects tentative horoscopes, or takes various possibilities of planetary relations into account, until he finds the most favorable moment, at which instant the doors are unlocked or the journey is begun.

Horary astrology is employed most commonly, however, for gaining a real perspective on some proposition, in the face of a necessity to form a judgment or reach a decision. A letter or telegram is received by a client, and the question asked the astrologer is whether an offer is advantageous, or whether it is wise to respond to some given demand. A careful note is made of the time such a message arrives, and a chart is put up for this significant moment, at the place of receipt, as the basis for proper guidance. Because few people can be depended on to note and report the exact instant of events, since they are always more interested in the content of a telegram than the minute of its arrival, professional astrologers usually operate from the moment the problem is presented to them, or make use of the time it becomes significant as an astrological query. It makes no difference whether a client brings his question, asks it over the telephone, or sends it by wire or mail. The hour and minute when the astrologer understands the situation is the point of its impact on his consciousness, and is the proper basis for the astrological wheel he will employ in suggesting a solution for any difficulty.

What always puzzles some younger students is the fact that this moment of impact, by a mere fragment of intelli-

SIGNIFICANT SENSITIVENESS

gence on an outsider's mind, can yield any significant insight into a matter brought up for analysis. The actual start of an enterprise by comparison will seem as tangible as the birth of a person, with the chance for something close to a natal horoscope. The time when a person, who must come to a conclusion or make a move, receives the proposition or the request for action may seem almost as tangible as such an event, because his concern is definitely personal; something has happened to him! But in the case of the astrologer the moment obviously takes on significance through what by comparison is quite an oblique relationship.

There is no real difficulty here, as will be evident if consideration is given to the parallel instance of a doctor or lawyer. The physician consulted in a case of sickness is certainly a factor in a very tangible chain of activity. He will assume control of the general situation involving the ill-health. Not only will he act, but he will dictate action. The same result follows, almost as obviously, when a lawyer is engaged in connection with some dispute. What must be realized is that there is just as much decisive "act," or as tangible a move for a given individual by the "proxy" provided through the personality of an expert in a given line of action, when consultation is purely intellectual, or advisory, in this more abstract way. In all these instances the outside party consulted for judgment, whether this leads to literal supervision or not, is a partner in acting; at least to the extent of the given issue which requires immediate decision or ultimate solution. Under the general economy of the total world in which events have come to some point of crisis, consultation is as significant in terms of time and place as any other type of action.

Horary astrology presents something closer to genuine difficulty when it comes to the case where a horoscope is erected by an individual for guiding the judgment of his own mind. The old traditional rule is that such a chart should be made for the time and place of his impulse to ask the question of himself, and this is the correct procedure, provided it is understood properly. A person whose thinking has not been made unduly introspective by any of the modern intellectual disciplines of science and philosophy, particularly by the many quarreling psychologies, is capable of a sharp or identifiable "impulse" in this sense. The normal analytical mind, however, frequently finds itself in an argument with itself as to when the impulse "is" an impulse. Granting the impulse to posit the question, when did it really take form in the mind? More narrowly, the correct time for casting a horary wheel is when an individual first realizes that a given matter, or phase of the matter, is critical. This can come about in two ways.

First and simplest is the welling up in consciousness of an overlooked or hitherto unsuspected consideration, which is easy enough to identify. Either the moment of conscious realization is used, or else the subsequent moment when the individual thinks to employ the horary technique. This can be a day or so later, but usually, in the case of any astrologically minded person, it is a matter of minutes. The second and ultimately more satisfactory way to identify significance in the time and space pointing is to utilize the moment of a definite development in the given matter; that is, to wait until something happens, so

SIGNIFICANT SENSITIVENESS

that the point in time is always an actual occurrence of the sort evident to the external senses.

Horary art is a mechanism of judgment. This means, in simple terms, that what a horary chart measures is the contents of a given mind. What it does not mean, however, is that "mind contents" are something mysteriously different from the rest of life. Often horary astrology will be said to depend on the "birth of an idea," which merely dramatizes the fact that a coincidence of relationships has become momentarily significant, and that this pointing in time makes it possible to chart them for the purpose of intelligent deduction. Any more elaborate explanation rather "paints the lily," if it does not add confusion to ignorance.

The actual procedures of horary astrology stem from the work of William Lilly, an English astrologer (1602-1681), who achieved his greatest prominence in his own day through his successful prediction of the great London fire of 1666. His pioneer work, together with the very few and sometimes surprisingly inconsequential books on the subject written since his day and employed by recent generations of astrologers, are listed in the brief bibliography at the end of the chapter. In addition to this material, outlines of horary astrology are included in a number of general texts, and there are some special courses of instruction. The practice of astrology from the days of Lilly—and John Gadbury, his most prominent disciple—has contributed to a considerable measure of confusion between natal horoscopic and strictly horary art. The tendency in modern times, however, has been to sharpen the distinction, which on the whole is a healthy tendency.

Since horary astrology is more an application of astrological science to the contents of the mind than to definite lives (that is, to the whole contexts of personal experience) constant attention must be given to particular psychological necessities, such as do not enter into the analysis of an ordinary horoscope. Most importantly, the mind must be provided by horary technique with some way for rejecting, subconsciously, the tendency it exhibits, consciously, to reflect surface limitations, or to conform to temperamental distortions. In other words, intelligence must have a mechanism for protecting itself against its own wishful thinking. The means by which mind is able to order itself in the terms of its deeper rather than its more superficial sensitiveness is established by the so-called "considerations before judgment." If the moment identified as significant by the conscious mind does not meet certain tests, the fact is an indication that, from some deeper frame of reference, the time is not correctly taken, and that any attempt to proceed will result in error.

The next particular psychological necessity in horary practice is a means for a widening reference. When the first time selected fails to meet the test of the "considerations before judgment," use must be made of another. Many astrologers ask the clients whom they serve by mail to put the moment of completing a letter below the signature. This can be used for a horary chart, since it represents the focus of issue established in the content of the inquirer's mind, and the practitioner can then assimilate it to his own. While it gives a narrow point of view, this fact can be taken into account in any interpretation. When there is an interval between the receipt of a message and

SIGNIFICANT SENSITIVENESS

the occasion when it is possible to erect the horary wheel, the astrologer, in a case when the first time is not acceptable, may consult his watch and thereupon use the hour and minute of his attack upon the problem for the horoscope. In every such case, when a second-choice moment is taken, an extra factor enters into the matter, and it is an indication most fundamentally that the message or inquiry concerns more ramifications of the given matter than might be suspected on the surface of things.

The novice must be extraordinarily careful in his recognition of significant moments. He will be much safer if he refuses to proceed with any matter, whenever a chart does not conform to the standards put down in the "considerations before judgment." If he wishes to proceed he must be familiar with the general principle dramatized at this point. Expressed most simply, it is the fact that the refusal of the mind to form an integrated conception of a given set of relations, on the basis of the problem as presented to it on the conscious level, is an indication of its sensitiveness to some necessary deeper consideration or hidden factor, which must then be taken into account. Whenever there is a retreat from the first selection of a time to a second, to meet such an issue, some extra factor of consideration in the matter must be identified, whether by judicious questioning, careful investigation, or other means. If on rare occasions there is a necessary retreat to a third significant moment, a second additional relationship must be traced out; and so on.

BIBLIOGRAPHY

Lilly, William, *An Introduction to Astrology* (incorporated in "Christian Astrology"), London, 1647; edited by Zadkiel (Richard James Morrison), London, 1852; popular edition, "Bohn's Scientific Library," London, 1865, reprinted by Dorothy Hughes, soft covers, 1967

Simmonite, William Joseph, *The Prognostic Astrologer*, London, 1851; new edition, *Horary Astrology*, by John Story, Sheffield, 1896; reprinted in soft covers by American Federation of Astrologers, 1952

Raphael (Robert Cross), *Horary Astrology*, London, 1883

Leo, Alan, *Horary Astrology*, London, 1907

Zain, C. C. (Elbert Benjamine), *Horary Astrology*, three manuscript lessons, Los Angeles, 1920; combined with further material and issued in hard covers, 1931

Jones, Marc Edmund, *Divinatory Astrology*, in mimeographed lesson form, Hollywood, 1930-1

DeLuce, Robert, *Horary Astrology*, Los Angeles, 1932; enlarged edition, 1942, available in soft covers

Davis, Geraldine, *Modern Scientific Textbook on Horary Astrology*, Los Angeles, 1942

Jones, Marc Edmund, *Problem Solving by Horary Astrology*, Philadelphia, 1943, now revised in this present new edition

Goldstein-Jacobson, Ivy M., *Simplified Horary Astrology*, offset typing in hard covers, 1960

Chapter Three

CHARTING THE PERTINENT MOMENT

The underlying responsibility of mathematical science for every wonder of modern civilization has been suggested in the opening chapter. This reference is not to "mathematics" as intricate computation—as a drudgery of figures or a hopeless complication of abstract symbols—but rather as an identification of a method for viewing life in the terms of its uncompromising order, or of whatever in experience is absolute in its dependability. Horary astrology enters the realm of mathematics when it identifies the significant moment in experience, and then proceeds to locate this same moment as a particular point of time and space in the celestial mechanism. The identification of such a "significant moment" in terms of the heavenly motions is a way of generalizing it, or taking it out of the experience of one individual, or some single group of people, and bringing it into the broader experience of everyone. All prediction of probability is dependent on the recognition of a correspondence between the particular case and the general tendency, and astrology—to the extent it does this—differs in no great respect from any other form of scientific judgment.

As a matter of mathematical technicality, which the average student of astrology needs to understand only in bare principle, the identification of any significant moment in astrological terms is merely the location of the precise position of the earth in the heavens at the given point in time, in the terms of an observation taken from a point in space upon the earth's own surface. This pointing in time and space is then compared with equivalent situations of the earth at other moments, from the same or similar points of observation, on the basis of the positive correlations that have been found between details of human experience and these phases of heavenly positions. Such positive correlations have been the means for all astrological deduction, whether in horary, natal, or any other branch of the stellar art, throughout the ages of recorded history.

The specter of mathematical requirements has closed the doors of astrology to many interested people whom the natal horoscope or horary chart would have served very well, and this has all come about through a needless apprehension. The more difficult operations in mathematics, without exception, may be avoided by the use of special tables, easily available, and described for the newcomer at proper points in the present text. Nothing is really needed, for normal horary practice, except the ability to add and subtract.

However, there are many explanations of particular technical value to the astrologer or investigator with specialized mathematical or statistical and other background, but of questionable worth to the general reader or new student. They are printed in a more compact form, as here, so that they may be skipped if desired. This procedure will help the neophyte to escape any discouragement before he is fairly started, since he will not miss anything essential to his progress by omitting these sections.

A fundamental realization of astrology is that the earth is moving in the heavens, and that it establishes the positions of the other heavenly bodies in reference to itself, as

CHARTING THE PERTINENT MOMENT 39

far as they are seen from the earth's surface, quite independently of the fact that these other bodies all have motions on their own account. Because the observer is situated on the earth, that body, in terms of his particular concern, is standing still. Its own motions have to appear somewhere, and they are translated, in actual experience, to the heavens. The whole astrological language is based upon this simple state of affairs. As a result astrology is much more consistent with everyday experience than the usual astronomical point of view, and in consequence becomes much more valuable for the analysis of ordinary life. Astrologers quite properly identify a daily "movement" of the whole heavens, and they always chart the particular motion of certain bodies in the heavens, in contrast to the relative fixity of most stars or star-groups, according to the apparent changes in position exhibited by these bodies when they are observed from the earth.

The most important motion in the heavens is the regular rising and setting of the stars and planets, because this becomes day and night, and occurs more frequently than the seasonal changes brought about by the annual journey of the sun through the zodiac. The daily "apparent" movement, as closer to commonplace affairs in this way, is made the primary basis of horary astrology; and of other branches of astrological art to only an appreciably lesser degree. The significant moment of an event, therefore, is first charted according to the twenty-four-hour rotation of the entire celestial sphere.

The identification of any point in the heavens is made possible by the positions of the so-called "fixed stars," because they can be grouped together conveniently by the eye in recognizable patterns. Perhaps the best known of these is the Big Dipper, familiar to everyone in northern latitudes. The fact that this artificial grouping is also known as the Great Bear does not take away from the fact that it is easy to see in the skies. There are twelve such patterns, of basic concern to astrologers, which are exceptionally useful in delimiting various sections of the heavens, not only for the purpose of telling what part of the great celestial sphere is here or there, but also for describing the special positions of the moving bodies of the solar system; specifically the sun, moon and eight true planets used commonly in astrology. These twelve stargroupings are known collectively as the "zodiac," more technically as the "constellations of the zodiac" and sometimes loosely as simply the "constellations."

Enemies of astrology sometimes suggest that there is no truth in astrological theory because the zodiacal groups or star-patterns, originally described by various arbitrary figures,[1] do not now correspond to the sections of the heavens they once designated. Reference in this criticism is to the precession of the equinoxes, a very slow backward crawling of the astronomical or mathematical points set up by the earth's two principal motions in reference to the distant fixed stars, as these are seen from the earth. Here is an attempt to quarrel over an entirely technical matter of little possible importance. It is simply more convenient to retain the ancient names for the mathematical trisections of the heavenly quadrants, set up at the equinoxes and solstices, than to regroup the stars in the zodiacal band, and attempt to modify a symbolism which has crept into literature and poetry everywhere.

The actual constellations served a very useful purpose in earlier ages when books were awkward collections of clay tablets, or had to be put on expensive parchment and

[1] Mostly animals, hence leading to the word "zodiac," which means "circle of the animals."

CHARTING THE PERTINENT MOMENT 41

fragile papyrus. For the purposes of rough-and-ready calculation it was only necessary to memorize these star-patterns, and then to go out and look at the heavens in order to know where the planets were, or to determine what section of the heavens rose and culminated. The point in the astrological description of a focus in time is not that the heavens of themselves have some particular mysterious meaning or power, but only that various moments in human experience are comparable to each other through their degree of mutual positive correlation with the patterns of cycles and position in a cosmic system of energy. The meaning of everything in astrology comes, not from the empyrean blue or some remote spiritual revelation, but out of human experience. Events in human affairs which are alike in certain particulars have correspondence to patterns of cosmic energy which exhibit a similar likeness among themselves. Any form of astrology identifies the heavenly factors, not as any supposed manifestation of a literal cause and effect, but in their relationship to human affairs, through this concordance of parallel activities.

A horary chart has its origin most fundamentally in a simple observation, which reveals how the whole revolving celestial sphere is situated in relation to the ground or plane of a particular experience. In other words, where do the heavens lie in relationship to the level or plateau of a given event? More technically, where is the immediate horizon located in heavenly terms?

In an earlier age, the astrologer had to go out and examine the sky, to see this. Because the stars are invisible through the daylight hours, and because storm and clouds interfere with the star-gazer's view during many nights in the year, it was necessary to establish tables by which, instead of examining the heavens, it would be possible to look at a book. This book is known in the present day as an "ephemeris" (plural, "ephemerides"). The information on the position of the celestial vault, relative to the horizon, comprises a single but very important column, and consists of one mathematical notation for each day of the year. It is the first factor needed for the making of any horoscope, and it is identified, somewhat unfortunately for anyone without a knowledge of astronomy, as "sidereal time." It is given daily for the case of a person standing on the meridian at Greenwich (a borough of London), and either at midnight or noon, depending upon the particular tables consulted.[2]

It will be obvious to anyone thinking about the matter that to make tables for every different spot on the globe, for every different moment of the day, would not only be a tremendous amount of work, at prohibitive cost, but would be highly inefficient. A number of clever labor-saving devices are employed to meet this difficulty. The first of these takes care of the adjustment due to the spherical (really spheroid) shape of the earth itself. When the horizon for the place where a moment becomes significant is taken in reference to the whole daily turning of the heavens, the geographic latitude is a primary controlling factor. This is the simple phenomenon known to everyone,

[2] *Raphael's Ephemeris* has been published for the years 1800 to date and is calculated for noon at Greenwich. *Die Deutsche Ephemeride* covers the years 1850 to date for noon at Greenwich through 1930 and for midnight thereafter. The *Simplified Scientific Ephemeris* of the Rosicrucian Fellowship embraces the years 1900 to date for noon at Greenwich but is not adequate for very precise work. A new *Golgge Ephemeris* begins with 1961 and is calculated for midnight at Greenwich. Midnight of course means the 0ʰ starting the day. More comprehensive Tables of Houses than found in some ephemerides are the *American Astrology Tables of Houses* by Hugh S. Rice (1944) and the *Spherical Basis of Astrology* by Joseph G. Dalton (1893).

CHARTING THE PERTINENT MOMENT 43

the increasing variation between day and night during most of the year at points moving away from the equator towards either pole. In the Arctic regions the days grow in length during the summertime until, for a short period, there is no darkness at all, just as the exact reverse is true in winter, with the so-called long night.

Astrologers avoid the major complications resulting from this influence of geographic latitude, and a necessarily tilting horizon, by calculating the position of the ambient or heavenly sphere from the meridian, or the point overhead, rather than from the "ascendant," which is the name given in astrology to the horizon where it rises in the east. The meridian is not affected by geographical position north or south from the equator, and thus is the same at a given time of any day for every spot between the two poles. Thus every ephemeris identifies the position of the great sphere relative to the "midheaven," as astrologers term the meridian in a horoscope, rather than the much more individually varying ascendant or eastern horizon. In order to learn the position of the all-important ascendant, relative to a given midheaven, the astrologer has recourse to usually separate Tables of Houses that give him the ascendant for any required geographic latitude, once the position of the midheaven is known.

The use of "sidereal time" for identifying the position of the heavens as they rotate from day to day is a long-established tradition, rooted originally in some astronomer's idea of convenience. Any circle can be described as accurately by twenty-four hours as three hundred and sixty degrees. The only trouble is that in such a case the hours, minutes and seconds of circle division are known as "time." Here the word does not refer to any passage of events in sequence, which is the meaning of the "time" shown by a clock, but rather identifies a measure of motion in a system of energy. Thus the sidereal time used to locate the midheaven for an astrological chart has nothing to do with the clock, or the ordinary measure of duration in any direct sense.[3] The young astrologer saves himself many puzzled and unhappy moments by just remembering this fact. The ephemeris, showing the "sidereal time" for each day, is thus indicating the position of the midheaven in an astrological horoscope or map for the geographical meridian at Greenwich long used as a basic one, either at midnight or noon, for some one calendar date. To proceed from this point, in the study and use of horary astrology, therefore, an ephemeris for the current year is required, together with a Table of Houses including the latitude of the place or places where horoscopes will be erected.

A second labor-saving device developed by astrologers involves "time" in the everyday sense of that word. Exactly as prohibitive expense would be involved in presenting the sidereal time of the horizon for every terrestrial latitude from the equator to the poles, so also the listing of the position of the heavenly sphere for midnight or noon at all the meridians around the globe in geographic longitude, or even for all places that have a different kind of time by their clocks, would mean an equally unfortunate cost. Civilized man discovered long ago that he must have an easy reconciliation of time differences for everyday intercourse, and for better than a half-century he has standardized the clock according to various zones.[4] This was a development made particularly necessary by the growth of railroads, since even so simple a matter as the publication

[3] Technically, sidereal time is the exact equivalent of "right ascension," which is the same measure of the heavens' diurnal rotation when given in degrees. This, of course, is from the astrological and psychological point of view. Astronomers set up a system of absolute relations which demand a sharp distinction between the measurement of duration and of distance in arc, but "time" as duration in this sense has no practical implication in man's normal or everyday experience. The "sidereal clock" of the astronomer is the means for a very specialized measure.

[4] Usually established on the basis of meridians east and west from Greenwich at multiples of the fifteen degrees which correspond to even hours, although this is not universally true. In the United States the time meridians are centered on 75° west longitude for Eastern Standard Time, five hours earlier than London; 90° for Central Standard Time, or six hours earlier; and so on at 105° and 120° west for Mountain and Pacific Standard Time, respectively seven and eight hours earlier.

of timetables was impossible with every town and city operating on its own local hour basis. Standard time, however, as now shown by all clocks, is of no particular help to astrology, since it identifies the heavenly correlations inaccurately except for communities fortuitously situated on a standard-time meridian.[5] Anywhere else, it is necessary to translate "standard" into "local mean" time. Whenever the clocks are changed arbitrarily, as for "daylight saving," "summer" or "war" time, a further adjustment must be made.

There is no difficulty in identifying the proper meridian for the time shown by a given clock, since this is usually stated if there is any chance of misunderstanding, but the correction to local mean time produces a result not shown by any clock. Students of astrology sometimes have trouble at this point in deciding whether the correction is an addition or a subtraction. It is easy to remember, however, that it is always later at the place where the sun arrives first, i.e., to the east. The comparison, of course, is between the local meridian and that particular time meridian to which the clocks normally conform. If the time meridian is to the west, the local time is later. Since fifteen degrees correspond to one hour of time, each single degree of difference means four minutes change in time. Any atlas, of course, will give the latitude and longitude of the location where the astrologer is at work, and for which he will calculate his horary chart.

The labor-saving device in this connection, used by navigators and astronomers as well as astrologers, is a further development of the standard meridian idea, and is the employment of a single basic meridian for the entire globe instead of one for each fifteen degrees of longitude, as in standard time. This single ephemeris-meridian was first taken from Greenwich, since terrestrial longitude itself is indicated in terms of distance in degrees from the London

[5] Moreover, a community may not use the expected or nearest meridian for its time basis, as in Michigan where gradually Eastern Standard Time has been legalized and established virtually statewide.

longitudinal line, and it has become customary to have all calculation of the midheaven sidereal time and the planetary places and allied information in the published astrological ephemerides on the basis of the 0° longitude of such a universal meridian of reference.

The result of all this is that one daily identification of position for the whole turning heavens is adequate in astrology for any geocentric latitude, providing the sidereal time of the midheaven rather than the eastern horizon is taken, and also adequate, by the same token, for any terrestrial longitude on the globe, if only the two necessary adjustments or corrections are made; that is, for the difference in longitude of a birthplace other than on the meridian at Greenwich or east or west of it in each case, and for the difference in hour and minute of birth, in terms of the local mean time, if birth has not taken place at the midnight or noon of the tables employed. Any difference in terrestrial latitude, controlling the tilt of the horizon in reference to the heavenly motion, is expressed in astrological factors taken from the Tables of Houses, but the differences in geocentric longitudes are entirely a matter of time, requiring a very simple calculation on the astrologer's part.

A largely predominant growth of astrological interest in the New World led to an ambitious but abortive attempt to provide an ephemeris for Philadelphia or 75° west. In the meanwhile a different change from noon to a midnight base has come to broad acceptance of its reasonableness even if it was confusing to many students at the start. For long years the noon positions have been a commonplace, probably due to the early necessity in navigation for working entirely from the sun's apparent time, but noon as a dividing point makes an artificial division in the ordinary waking day. The midnight positions are gradually coming to be preferred, although many astrological ephemerides have clung to noon even after the nautical almanacs changed to midnight as their base.

CHARTING THE PERTINENT MOMENT 47

Whether one or the other is used, no difficulty whatsoever arises as long as the astrologer remembers from which he is working. To erect a horoscope, he must know the distance in sidereal time the heavens have turned between the given midnight or noon and the local mean time for which the horary chart is calculated. The heavens rotate once, approximately, in the course of a day. In view of the fact that any given position of the ambient is identified in terms of hours and minutes of sidereal time, and that the turn takes place, approximately, in twenty-four hours measured by a clock, it is only necessary to adjust the sidereal time of the midheaven by adding or subtracting the hours and minutes before or after noon or midnight, as the case may be, in order to find just how the heavens lie. Thus the calculation of the position of the ambient would be utterly easy, except that some slight corrections have to be made. Even at that, the arithmetic is quite simple.

The corrections arise from the fact that "noon" or "midnight" are moments established by the position of the sun.[6] The sun moves through the heavens by an annual motion which produces the seasons, and this means that while the day is the interval between two successive transits of the sun over the upper or lower meridian the interval does not correspond to a complete revolution of the heavens because, in a sense, the sun has moved to meet itself. It goes forward in the zodiac about a degree a day, but it is also lifted up backwards and carried around with the rotation

[6] To be precise, this is what astronomers term the "mean sun." The actual movement of the sun through the year is not quite even, since it leads or trails its fictitious counterpart by a deviation from average, twice during the course of a year, close to fifteen minutes in time. To build clocks to measure time accurately enough to take this annual wobble into account would be expensive, and also more or less useless. Nothing would be gained in most areas of life by having twelve o'clock correspond exactly to the actual position of the sun on the meridian. The movement of the sun is averaged, and time is taken on the basis of the interval from mean midnight to mean midnight, or mean noon to mean noon, thus giving a time hour of equal length throughout the year. "Mean time" is thus the only sort any individual is ever apt to encounter, unless he owns a sundial.

of the heavens in each twenty-four hours, with the result that the four minutes required for a degree's rotation are not used in any actual matter of duration or elapsed time. If a chart is cast for any moment other than the midnight or noon of the tables used, the hours of difference as shown by a clock are of a different length, so to speak, and they must be adjusted. This is what is known technically as the "correction from mean to sidereal time." What it amounts to in practice is that an approximate ten seconds must be added to each hour, or hours, of mean time before any such hour, or hours, can be added to or subtracted from the sidereal time taken from the ephemeris for the purpose of identifying the position of the midheaven, horizon and whole rotating ambient.[7]

In the case of a difference in terrestrial longitude, between the place for which an astrological chart is cast and the meridian at Greenwich, there is the same problem of the slight difference between successive mean midnights or mean noons. The column of sidereal time in any ephemeris shows this increment from day to day. In other words, the heavens are in one position when it is midnight or noon at Greenwich, but when it has become midnight or noon five hours later in Philadelphia, the midnight or noon designation of the heavens, created by the position of the mean sun, is somewhat different because the sun obviously has moved a little during the turning of the heavens, in order to make it midnight or noon at Philadelphia rather than Greenwich. The correction here, of course, is the same sort as that for mean to sidereal time, since it is caused by the same phenomenon. It is added for places west from the prime meridian such as Philadelphia, but is subtracted similarly for all places east, because the sun in the former instance has the ground to cover, and in the latter has not come as far. In astrological practice this "cor-

[7] In very fine work this correction is 9.86s, rather than the even 10s, and the best Tables of Houses provide a tabulation which will give the correction exactly for any combination of hours and minutes up to one full day.

CHARTING THE PERTINENT MOMENT 49

rection for longitude" is usually made first, with the corrections for local time following.

There is an additional labor-saving, or perhaps error-saving, device rather universally recommended to astrological students. Experience shows that it is always conducive to accuracy and ease of effort if a series of routine operations can be standardized, and that in consequence, in making a horoscope, it is always better to work from a midnight or noon previous to the given time of a birth or query. When this is done the correction from midnight or noon to local mean time is always an addition. The use of subtraction, of course, is quite as accurate, but in such a case the correction from mean to sidereal time has to be added to the interval in hours before this interval in turn can be subtracted from the basic sidereal time, which is apt to be confusing to the non-mathematician. This is especially true in cases where he has had to subtract the correction for longitude, or when the horoscope is for points east of Philadelphia or London.

The first step in calculating a horoscope is to take the proper sidereal time from the ephemeris, to correct this for any difference in longitude from the ephemeris meridian, according to the rules given in any competent Tables of Houses, to correct it further for any difference between the local mean time and the basic noon or midnight of the ephemeris, according to these same rules, and then to draw out the "houses" of the chart, as they are given for the terrestrial latitude in the Tables of Houses.[8]

[8] This can be illustrated in the case of the example chart on page 21, where the computations are as follows:

	h	m	s
Sidereal time of 0ʰ, Greenwich mean time:	18	38	29
Correction for longitude (mean to sidereal time):			49
Correction for mean time of horoscope:	11	59	
Its correction (mean to sidereal time):		1	58
Sidereal time of horoscope midheaven:	6	40	16

The simple situation of the ascendant, in its relation to the whole heavens, provides the first key-indication in a horary chart. Thus it is possible to begin the evaluation of the significant moment even in the initial procedure of charting it. Attention has already been directed to the necessity for some mechanism to protect the astrologer's conscious judgment by permitting the significant moment, in response to deeper relationships, to cancel itself, or invalidate itself by failing to provide a valid horoscope. The "considerations before judgment" are a very important and a long-established factor in all horary astrology, and the first of them is the determination whether or not an astrological chart is "radical," or "fit to be judged," on the basis of the ascendant's strength. If any of the first or the last three degrees of a sign of the zodiac are "rising," or correspond to the eastern horizon, the horary figure is characterized as incompetent by these traditional rules, and it is only to be interpreted very exceptionally.[9]

This matter of a "radical ascendant" at once brings up the whole question of the signs and houses. What are they, and what is the difference between them? It has been explained that the constellations of the zodiac were originally a means for identifying the position of the whole celestial vault in reference to the earth, or in locating the place of the moving bodies of the solar system as they are seen from the earth in their geocentric relationships to each other and to the ambient. By a very happy fact the satellites of the sun all move around that body in a close approximation to a single plane. Their orbits, taken all together, constitute a sort of gigantic saucer in the heavens. The calcu-

[9] As when a very obvious prematurity or an evident exhaustion of all potential, respectively, is the real heart of the matter.

CHARTING THE PERTINENT MOMENT 51

lation of their positions is thus, for all ordinary practical purposes, in two dimensions only, whereas, if their orbits inclined away from each other to any great degree, the measure of relationships would become so highly complex that none but exceptionally well-trained mathematicians could ever hope to be astrologers. With these movements virtually in the one single plane, they can all be taken in the terms of the earth's own orbit, and this is done. In a loose but entirely accurate and practical sense, the zodiac is the orbit of the earth.

The sun acquires the earth's own motion, and moves around the zodiac regularly during the year, creating the seasons. While the moon circles around the earth directly in its own special path, its motion yet conforms largely to that of these other bodies in the zodiac, and its cycles are described in zodiacal terms as handily as in the case of the true planets. Contrariwise, the earth's daily rotation is defined in quite a different plane, set off from the other one at an angle of about twenty-three degrees. The net result is that the moving bodies of astrology travel in one path, while the whole heavens turn in another. This means there are two great primary circles in the celestial sphere. The one in which the whole heavens move around the earth, due to the earth's rotation, is measured in what is known as the celestial equator because it is, to all intents and purposes, an extension of the earth's equator. Position around this first circle is measured in sidereal time, and reference has been to this equatorial factor in any identification of the meridian or midheaven of the horoscope, and of its eastern horizon or ascendant. The other circle is the zodiac, taken mathematically as round rather than elliptical.

The practical result of the angle between these great circles is that the horizon of the horoscope, established in the celestial equator by the diurnal rotation of the earth, does not lie at any point fixed in its correspondence to the zodiac where the planets have their places, due to its usual tilted position on the surface of the earth. Reference has been made to this fact, in drawing attention to the necessity for taking geographical latitude into account when erecting a horoscope. The astrological consequences of the distortion is that the distance from the midheaven to the ascendant is always represented by an even six hours or ninety degrees in the celestial equator, but almost never by the corresponding ninety degrees or exact quarter of the circle in the zodiac. Here is an important source of the almost infinite possibility of variation in astrological charts, and a most vital root of effective difference in astrological indication.

The equatorial factors in astrology, particularly the ascendant or horizon, are the basis for measuring the individual against the group experience, of which he presents only single facets, while the planetary cycles in the zodiac are the foundation for all astrological charting of the group potentials, that is, the accumulated race experience against which any estimation of the individual is possible. One celestial plane delineates the "little man" of every day, and the other the "great man" in whom all humanity is patterned. Here are two different elements that must be brought together in some practical way for daily use. Either the position of the heavens in terms of the equator and ascendant must be charted in the zodiac, or the zodiacal place and movement of the sun, moon and planets must be indicated in the circle of the ascendant and midheaven.

This means simply that either one of these two systems of relationship must be expressed in the terms of the other in order to have a horoscope, and to get it down on a piece of paper. Because there are ten planets moving in the zodiac, all in different and changing positions with continually shifting relations to each other, and because the structure of midheaven and ascendant, or what astrology knows as the "houses," is a single pattern for the place of the self in the cosmos as a general whole, it is easiest to translate the latter into the terms of the former. Thus astrology may

CHARTING THE PERTINENT MOMENT 53

be said, in its practical form, to be "zodiac minded," and to be inclined to see its roots in the twelve signs, and in the actual geocentric motion of the planets through them.

An astrological chart, whether for horary or natal astrology, is arranged in the form shown on page 21, now generally employed by astrologers everywhere. The midheaven and ascendant are already printed or drawn on the blank paper used for the horoscope, and the correspondence to the zodiac of these and other points in the basic wheel is shown by writing the equivalent zodiacal sign at each important point, together with the degrees and perhaps minutes of correspondence. This interrelationship, of course, is very real. In a way, the point of view is that of someone far off in the heavens able to see the planets as they lie in both great circles at once, and as the two circles themselves are mutually disposed over each other.

The astrologer is under the necessity of knowing the names and symbols of the twelve signs into which the zodiac is divided, as well as the order in which they come, and their relations to each other. In particular he must know which signs lie opposite to each other because Tables of Houses give only the correspondence of six of them to six of the equatorial houses, including the midheaven and ascendant. The other correspondences are exactly the same, except at directly opposite points in the great circles, so that they are filled in easily and without calculation.

Position in the zodiac is described in terms of degrees, and is known as celestial longitude. Instead of presenting these degrees from 0° to 360°, as in astronomical practice, the astrologers find it more convenient to use the twelvefold divisions of thirty degrees each, and to identify each group by the constellations which originally occupied the same areas in the heavens. The names and symbols of the signs, placed as they lie opposite each other, are as follows:

♈ Aries	♎ Libra
♉ Taurus	♏ Scorpio
♊ Gemini	♐ Sagittarius
♋ Cancer	♑ Capricorn
♌ Leo	♒ Aquarius
♍ Virgo	♓ Pisces

Each one of these thirty-degree divisions of the zodiac has a particular power or potency, because these areas of the heavens mark points emphasized in human experience by the four seasons, together with the waxing and waning of this seasonal influence. In horary astrology, the principal significance of the signs lies in the fact that, since each represents an area of the heavens which can be used to define a particular phase of experience, and since horary technique primarily separates or draws out various phases of experience for precise analysis in connection with specific difficulties, their boundary lines have an exceptionally heightened symbolism. It will become increasingly evident that this branch of stellar art differs widely, in its approach to human problems, from the natal horoscope with its broader involvements in the complex of a whole life.

Horary delineation is especially sharp or incisive in its methods, as indicated already in the first "consideration before judgment." If the ascendant of a chart lies in the first or last three degrees of a zodiacal sign, the matter at issue is taken as not centered thoroughly enough in the

CHARTING THE PERTINENT MOMENT 55

one given area of experience to afford a reliable judgment. Astrologers, after three centuries of horary practice, are a unit in considering three degrees or less of a sign on the ascendant as an indication of a premature matter, or something as yet without definite form, and the last three degrees as a testimony of a proposition long neglected, or a potentiality which has thinned out and so lost its vitality.[10]

Sometimes the condition shown by a horary chart, when it is not "radical," will prove to be an accurate description of the issue or situation which is the basis of inquiry. The first three degrees of a sign may rise when the concern is over some spontaneous notion; or when the query is about an enterprise just about to be launched, or an idea which is barely projected. Again, the final three degrees may appear on the ascendant when some delayed or drawn-out affair, or a matter long under consideration, is brought forward for examination. In such circumstances the horary figure becomes "radical" in a very special sense. What otherwise indicates its rejection as "unfit to be judged" becomes a marked testimony to its astrological competency. Such cases demonstrate the most important principle in all horary astrology, the essence of which is that nothing is to be brought into a given consideration at any time except as it "makes sense" in some definite or individual way. There are a series of basic or fundamental principles, on the order of this first "consideration," to which the astrologer conforms normally, and there are the exceptional conditions which not only allow him to proceed but which actually give an added significance to the horoscope.

[10] This, of course, applies to normal horary practice; not to horoscopes put up for actual events, for the start of an enterprise or for the launching of some specific project.

Whenever it is possible to proceed with the analysis of a chart, despite its initial failure to meet the special requirements of horary practice—as in the case where the particular form of this failure especially illuminates the given issue—the astrologer continues at once, but he only does so as he is able to add an additional factor to the consideration, or as he can find an extra and often unsuspected element of importance in the matter brought before him. The rule is that, for each additional detail of exceptional significance uncovered in the chart itself, one additional facet of necessary emphasis must be identified in the circumstances inquired about.

In the language of modern science this is the measure of the "degrees of freedom" in any given problem, or is the expanding capacity of a situation for modes of variation or new lines in development as these are matched, point by point in horoscope interpretation, by a regression from one to another potentiality of astrological significance. The horary practice outlined in this text presents a program of simple one-to-one correspondences established between any matter of inquiry and its astrological diagram. This normally reveals a straight relationship, such as produces immediate "yes" or "no" judgments. It also provides for the progressive increase in factors of pertinent concern as these are identified in the supplementary correlations between the querent's affairs and the horoscope wheel. As a consequence of this approach to the interpretation of experience in its narrow or immediate focus of the moment, horary astrology may be seen to be almost diametrically opposed to the best techniques employed for natal analysis. The whole chart is taken into account in the latter case, with all possible factors brought into a clear synthesis, whereas the horary astrologer properly gives attention only

CHARTING THE PERTINENT MOMENT 57

to those astrological indications which acquire pertinency through their relation to the ascendant or eastern horizon.[11] Astrology thus reflects the important difference found in life between an issue of the moment, to be analyzed more or less in a pattern of straight lines of consequence, and a living personality, to be seen in its total ramification throughout a social complex.

There is another way in which the presence of the first or final degrees of a sign on a horary ascendant can be significant, and this was commonly advanced to the status of a normal expectation by many astrologers of a former generation. They took the position of the rising sign and degree as necessarily duplicating the natal chart of their client, so that a man with two degrees of Libra rising could actually be expected to call on them at the time of day when that point was again on the eastern horizon. The limitations of this procedure are obvious, since this client would have to forego consulting astrology in August and September, or else make his calls in the "wee small hours" before dawn. However, the broader principle that the horary ascendant must describe the querent, or person making inquiry about his problems, is definitely valid in a more general fashion. The degree of a person's sun or moon, or some section of the zodiac particularly indicating him through the current place of the planets in the heavens, will often be rising in the east at any moment of really serious inquiry. When the first or last three degrees of a sign, turning up in this fashion, are definitely suggestive, the astrologer proceeds with

[11] The offshoot branches of horary art, however, represented by the charts for the actual time of starting an enterprise, and so on, whether taken afterwards or selected in advance by an "election," have a closer conformity to natal astrology in demanding more consideration of the whole chart, as suggested in the footnote on p. 55.

his analysis, but he also remembers that this special illumination of the client's personality has some extra dynamic significance in the matter at hand.

The question often raised by a non-astrologer is the practical proposition: how can this patterning of some trivial life situation have its reflection in the heavens? The answer is found in the general concordance of events in an orderly universe or integral energy system. After all, horary astrology operates by reflecting the consciousness of the person who practices it. The chart, in the case of a question, patterns a matter resident in some individual's mind, and the content of that mind is also contained in the general social complex—along with everything else—and hence under as real a necessity to operate in concordance with universal order. This leads to the rule that anyone who practices horary astrology must be very definite in everything he does, not hesitating to express his own individuality. Every good practitioner makes modifications in the techniques according to his own tastes, because his private universe of thought has its own specialized way of ordering things. It is in accordance with the general reality, of necessity, but it is also necessarily personal in all respects.

This explains the fact that some astrologers can make certain horary procedures "work" for them, although these may be of little use to anyone else. Obviously there is much greater possibility for variation in the patterning of ideas than in the social flesh-and-blood existence of the tangible creatures analyzed by natal astrology. Even in the case of as carefully prepared a manual as this, it is necessary to suggest that any student make whatever modifica-

CHARTING THE PERTINENT MOMENT 59

tions are compatible to his own modes of thinking. All that is done here is to hold to practices which are of the widest desirability; or suitable for the greatest range of difference in individual temperament, because they are in the closest possible accord with the best insights of modern psychology. Therefore many recommendations, positive or negative, while amply justified in general, may have no validity in a given case. The wise investigator of horary art will ultimately set up his own rules and standards. What is put down in definite form for all people may remain the best basis for instruction, or classwork, but it can hardly ever be a complete guide for any one astrologer.

In one fashion or another, therefore, the ascendant of a horary chart always describes the person who asks a question. While the eastern horizon is significant in a special way when the first or last three degrees of a sign are ascending, it no less provides an initial confirmation of the chart's radical nature in every case. The recognition of this rapport between the querent and the astrological wheel is a necessary first step in charting the significant moment, and the signs of the zodiac are especially valuable for this purpose as they chart the functional scope of the planets they contain. Effective use may be made here of the tabulated astrological "appearance" indicated by signs and planets, appearing more properly at a later point in the text,[12] but it must be remembered that such indications yield the suggestiveness of appearance in the light of some given or immediate problem; in other words, the correspondence may be highly illuminating while not at all correct in any literal or photographic sense.

[12] See p. 286.

the foundation of horary art

CHAPTER FOUR

PUTTING EXPERIENCE IN PLACE

THE foundation of all interpretation in horary astrology is through the "houses" of the heavens. These are established by extending the horizon (of the place of an event or situation on the surface of the earth) out towards the farther limits of the universe, and projecting the midheaven meridian out among the stars in the same way, thus dividing the entire knowable cosmos into four great quarters, each of which is then trisected.[1] This means that the plane of the horizon is always at right angles to the plane of the meridian. The lines representing these two planes become the basic axes of the houses in all astrology, and are the means by which the general experience of man is given its most detailed charting in the heavenly generalization, or the universal synthesis, from which the astrologer derives his judgments. The conventional form of horoscope, showing these houses, has been presented on p. 21.

The twelve houses which are provided by the trisection of four quadrants are related to each other, primarily, through their grouping in the regular triangles which can be described from each of the four points established by the horizon and midheaven on the equator. These threefold groups, which will be shown by diagram and given

[1] The division is made, mathematically, in the earth's daily rotation on its axis, so that the horizon in the east and west is taken as a point on a circle which, if not the equator itself, lies in a plane parallel to the equator, and so is identical with it in the given motion.

further explanation in a few pages, are the foundation of the most simple astrological generalizations. While they appear only in cross section when the wheel is seen on a piece of paper, it must be remembered that these houses, all together, comprise the complete extent of the cosmos as it has been divided from the earth as a center of observation. The twelve segments, marked off around the celestial equator, can be likened to a sort of gigantic orange, since every star in the skies must lie in one or another of them, whether near the equatorial plane or far around in the area of the poles.[2]

The very great initial problem, in understanding horary or any other form of astrology, is the seeming lack of any real or valid connection between the astrological factors and the events or situations with which they have significant relation. There is no difficulty in seeing that moments which are alike in some certain respect might have a correspondence to events with similar likenesses in some respect, but just how is this to be expressed in the details of a horoscope?

The answer is simple. Astrological factors acquire meaning in exactly the same manner as experience. The basis for any significance in events is the ground on which they are experienced, the place of their occurrence in time and space relative to other experience, and the source of any

[2] The divisions of the zodiac into twelve signs is exactly the same proposition except that the quartering of the heavens, and the trisection of each quarter, is in the other great circle, established by the earth's annual revolution around the sun. Thus the astrologer operates with a combination of two twelvefold divisions of the entire cosmic sphere. The two schemes of measurement are completely interpenetrating, and every star in the sky also lies in one or another of the signs which, like the houses, appear only in cross section when indicated on the horoscopic chart. The zodiac in astrology, therefore, is not limited to the traditional 16° band.

PUTTING EXPERIENCE IN PLACE 65

paralleling astrological significance in events is the ground on which a similar time and space focus of horoscopic relations can be established. This "ground" of pertinent correlations in astrology has already been identified as the horizon, and it has been pointed out that the tilt of the horizon's plane is a very fundamental factor in producing the individuality of a horoscope, that is, in charting individual human differences for the purpose of analysis. In consequence of this, the horizon at its rising or "active" edge, which is the ascendant or first house in the astrological chart, is made the foundation for everything else in horoscopy. It represents the personality, or the total individuality, in natal astrology. It reveals the whole matter inquired about, or the immediate state of affairs characterizing a given issue, in horary art.

The midheaven is the point on the circle of the houses which intercepts the meridian passing directly overhead at that place on the globe where some horizon of the moment becomes significant. It describes a pertinent over-all influence and is, most simply, the superior in life. It may be the state or government, and show the demands upon a native by the community in which he lives, or it may identify the corporation for which he works, or any individual in a position to give orders to which he may conform, such as a parent, a teacher or a supervisor. Here is not only the authority which an individual must recognize, but whatever skills, refinements or social talents enable him to gain and hold a position of superiority among others with whom he shares experience. This position may be held as the result of special training, as in the case of a definite profession, or be merely a "fortunate situation" as the result of inheritance, large resources, and the like. Exactly as the ascendant charts the present status of particular affairs, or the general ground for experience in a given aspect, the midheaven affords the clue to the particular importance of this larger state of things. All other astrological meaning or significance of the houses is derived from these two factors.

A philosophical difficulty confronts the average trained mind at this point, when it encounters the astrological mechanism for the first time. The student who is uncritical, in a technical or scientific sense, is not at all disturbed, since he has the simple criteria of demonstration and practice. He soon discovers that, when handled properly, astrology "works." The more academically conditioned inquirer, however, finds himself unable to get beyond a certain metaphysical "why." He fails to realize that he has set up a straw man, or that he is facing a dilemma rooted in his own presuppositions rather than in any situation of true facts. He jumps to the assumption that astrology deals with lines of cause and effect. Indeed, he finds many accounts of their own art by the astrologers who attempt to find the foundation for their belief in the various hypotheses of the physicists of each generation; who seek to gain scientific "regularity" by an unintelligent aping of scientific methods. The astrological chart is a mode of psychological measurement, and what it measures is a concordance in events and not any sort of physical cause, or even any actual functional relations in nature as such.

Thus, on the basis of an idea of "cause," it would be exceedingly difficult, if not grotesque, to find any way to explain why the meridian for a given time at a given place will make a man a banker, or give him a red-headed parent, and why her horizon in the stars will equip a young lady with the "skin you love to touch." The operation of

PUTTING EXPERIENCE IN PLACE 67

"concordance" in the universe is merely the tendency expressed crudely in the "survival of the fittest" and evident in psychology through the positive correlation of desirable traits. There is no "cause" in the fact that certain factors gravitate to common complexes, but merely the operation of convenience. Whether desirable elements are positive in their convenience to each other because they are "desirable," or are "desirable" because they are convenient, is a metaphysical question at best. Life displays these aggregations, and the similar aggregations of elements in the heavenly mechanism—naturally expressing a different sort of concordance when seen in their own terms—provide patterns which have an over-all parallel with the factors of experience, and hence can be used to chart them. The reliability in this charting is high, in a statistical sense, but there is no more certainty in a single astrological indication than in a single statistic.

The houses in astrology are numbered, in contrast with the signs of the zodiac, known by names and arbitrary symbols. While the signs are fixed in the heavens, always measured from the vernal equinox and so turning with the stars in the daily rotation of the heavens, the houses are fixed in relation to a given moment and place on the surface of the earth; although the celestial equator, in which they are established, turns in the same way and to the same extent as the zodiac. The houses are identified in terms of the latter circle, or in degrees of celestial longitude, in order to focus attention on their relation with the signs and planets, but their numbers run consecutively from one to twelve, beginning at the ascendant and moving around counterclockwise through the others. They are taken in the order in which the heavenly segments, and significant bodies found within them, will rise over the eastern horizon in the course of any given next twenty-four hours.

Each house represents an actual twelfth part of the entire universe, with every celestial entity other than the earth placed in one or another of them. An even thirty degrees of right ascension, or two hours of sidereal time, constitute each in order. However, all reference to a particular house, or all consideration of its meaning—except only in determining what bodies or points it contains—is taken from its first or leading edge, as this faces clockwise or in the motion of the heavens by which they rise in the east and set in the west; that is, reversing the normal direction of planetary movement in the zodiac. This "leading edge" of a house is known as the cusp. It is identified by the degree and sign of the zodiac to which it corresponds by projection over from the equatorial circle in which it is established, and it is neither necessary nor common for houses and signs to correspond exactly. Indeed thirty degrees of one are seldom equivalent to the same span in the other.

The sign correspondences of the houses, therefore, are taken on the basis of these cusps, and never the whole houses. New students are confused sometimes because the house cusp will be identified by the very last degree of a sign, with the result that the house contains most of another sign—or all of it, and more—and so only matches the sign with which it is said to have correspondence to a minimal degree. There is no difficulty here when it is realized that the cusp is like the front of the building. It represents the whole, whether a given sign lies almost entirely in front, or almost entirely behind.

PUTTING EXPERIENCE IN PLACE   69

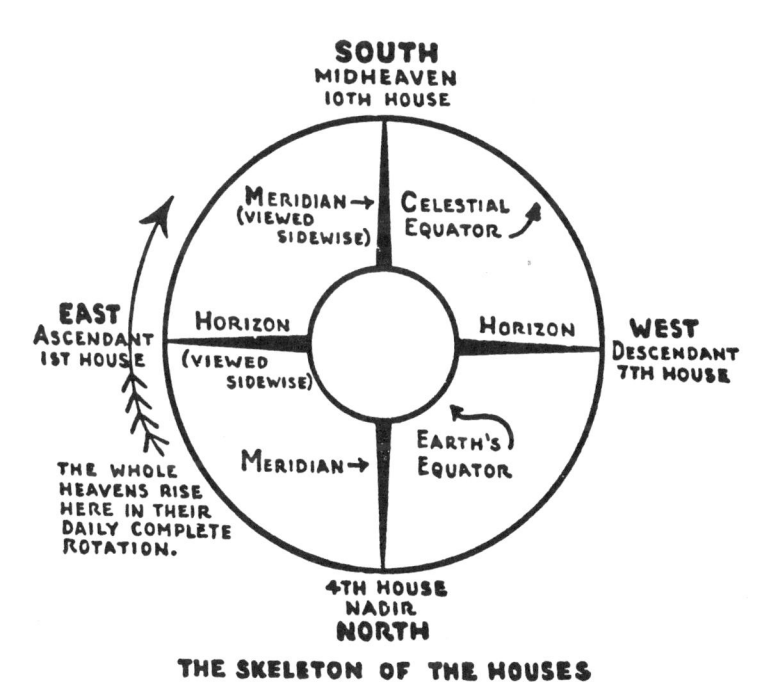

THE SKELETON OF THE HOUSES

Diagram labels: SOUTH / MIDHEAVEN / 10TH HOUSE; MERIDIAN→ (VIEWED SIDEWISE); CELESTIAL EQUATOR; EAST / ASCENDANT / 1ST HOUSE; HORIZON (VIEWED SIDEWISE); HORIZON; WEST / DESCENDANT / 7TH HOUSE; THE WHOLE HEAVENS RISE HERE IN THEIR DAILY COMPLETE ROTATION.; MERIDIAN→; EARTH'S EQUATOR; 4TH HOUSE / NADIR / NORTH

The horizon not only establishes a house cusp where the heavens rise at its eastern intersection of the equator, but it also cuts the equator on the descending side, there marking off what astrologers sometimes call the "descendant;" a cusp much more commonly known by the number of the house, namely, the seventh. Astrological reference to the ascendant always means exactly the same thing as reference to the "first house," and the indication in either case may be to the cusp or to the whole area in the heavens. In the same fashion the terms "midheaven" and "tenth house"—as well as "nadir" and "fourth house"—are interchangeable in ordinary astrological usage. "M.C." and "I.C." are abbreviations of the Latin terms for midheaven and nadir, respectively, often employed to designate the cusps of the meridian circle.

The next step in deriving astrological meaning for the houses of a horoscope from the celestial mechanism is a consideration of the other poles of the basic house axes, i.e., the descendant and nadir. The first house, ascendant or eastern horizon represents the ground of being on the positive side of selfhood, or reveals the emergence of the various primary factors in experience as they rise to attention above the threshold of conscious identity, or as the individual displays his basic initiative by his first, simple and continuing attack on life in each special aspect. The seventh house represents the same fundamental ground of existence as a corresponding more negative relationship of individuality to its whole complex, and is best understood by continuing the contrast with the ascendant. Thus the day begins, in literal fact, when the sun rises in the east, and a moment is significant when some potential rises, as it were, on the horizon of experience. This phenomenon of "origin," as an emergence into pertinent relations, is the positive ground for anything that may be "experienced." When the sun sets, contrariwise, the day is over and when, in a concordant descriptive symbolism, events drop below the horizon, they are dismissed, in the broadest sense, to other responsibility.

PUTTING EXPERIENCE IN PLACE

There is an important distinction here between the conscious act or positive impulse of life, at its point of direct and unconditioned impact, and the complementary type of relatively indirect action, which is no less a basic part of existence. Man actually has a limited initiative in any one particular line of activity. This varies with the individual as well as with the particular set of circumstances, and experience may take its form from the freedom evident within this "limitation," or from the constriction which keeps any such "freedom" within the convenience of cosmic order. Neither freedom nor limitation is an absolute reality, but each contributes to the other in the give-and-take process which creates conscious reality. Thus one person may be free to take a five-mile walk, in order to join his cronies at the club for an afternoon's game of chess, while another, who has fallen down a dry well and does not possess the means or ability to clamber out, can walk only in an exceedingly limited area, if at all; and must devote his energies to crying out, or scheming some way to extricate himself from his predicament, rather than to the enjoyment of a contest with the chessmen. The second man is equally "free" however, in a very true fashion, to take primary action in his own interest. He will walk five miles on another day. His chess is merely displaced in time.

It should become increasingly apparent that the symbolism of astrology is very simple indeed, or essentially naïve. What "comes up" in the heavens corresponds to what "comes up" in experience, and so on through relations which to the non-astrologer may at times seem to be derived from the most farfetched suggestiveness. The symbols, however, represent a most profound insight. The general concordance of the universe not only comprises the physical orderliness of heavenly movements on the one hand, and of terrestrial events on the other, but also the materials and structure of the language and thinking by which any parallel between them is determined, becoming the basis of astrological analysis. The very unconditioned simplicity of these symbolical distinctions holds astrology close to its universal reference at all points.

While the first house in the horoscopic mechanism indicates the potentialities of act, it does not show the compass of action, since it emphasizes the emergence of the factors in experience, or charts their appearance at the horizon of objective realization and conscious thought. Initiative is one thing, but effective co-operation with the initiative by the general situation is something else. In other words, there is the ground for action and there is also the ground for its possible continuance to some degree of achievement. This latter factor is indicated most significantly by the seventh house, or the descendant; that is, by the emphasis on the horizon at the point where experience passes from direct initiative. Responsibility is shifted to others, and activity can only continue through co-operative relationships. Man has made his contribution, and events must demonstrate its worth. As a result, in horary astrology, the seventh house rather than the first becomes the crux of any given judgment. It shows the element of "carry on" in any particular case.

In natal astrology the seventh house is important as the indicator of partnerships, or those joint relations with other people which dramatize a limitation rather than the relatively untrammeled impulse or free act evident at the ascendant. Man lives in a social world, and therefore can only act by himself, or without reference to other people and things, in very limited areas. The descendant represents the people he selects, out of his total existence, for a real intimacy in the experience he will make especially his

PUTTING EXPERIENCE IN PLACE

own. In primitive relations this indicates the mate; a husband or wife. With the organization of a human society it means a partner in business, or in any type of joint enterprise. It also identifies not only established associations of this sort, but any particular person with whom the native sets up a momentary balance in special act. This includes a lawyer or a physician, an escort or a social companion, as well as any out-and-out or public enemy; that is, anyone with whom the native interacts in conflict rather than in a more literal "co-operation."

The descending horizon in horary astrology thus corresponds to every element in life that can be brought to a point of particular co-operation, or direct and effective opposition, in connection with any given act or projected action. This most simply is the basic tête-à-tête relationship in experience; i.e., co-operative contact with no subordination of any one factor to another. The house is described most completely in natal astrology as the ruler of opportunity, or of the explicit "permissions" which lead to this directness of unprejudiced touch or contact in experience. The opportunity may result from the possession of very special personal skills. These create the "fine arts" which are always indicated by this house, and which have the greatest possible degree of "carry on" when it comes to the survival of the efforts and works of a person beyond his own immediate or first-house efforts. More frequently, however, the effective agency of this opportunity is the personality of others who in some pertinent way are led to embody the interests of the native in their own life and activity. The process is illustrated most perfectly in the "ideal marriage," or the totally understanding partnership sometimes found in business. "Opportunity" is the infective momentum of individual desire, as this becomes a practical potential in experience on its own account. It is the degree of partnership a man may establish with life or cosmic reality as a whole. In horary astrology it is the most direct indication of immediate promise in any matter at definite issue.

A chemical curiosity, introduced to students very early in school laboratories is provided by litmus, a substance which conveniently turns red when touched by a solution with an excess of acid, and blue when the balance is on the alkaline side. A fascinating game is to get a given solution at the very point of balance, and to observe how only a single drop of acid or alkali is necessary to reverse this reaction. The point of view in astrology is fully as sensitive as litmus in its capacity for reversal, and astrological skill is greatly dependent on the practitioner's ability to see relations in either of two directions, according to the moment's necessity, and to do it without mental confusion.

Most importantly, this is the proposition of clockwise or counterclockwise perspective.[3] All individual movement of astrological significance in the heavens is of the latter sort —that is, forward in the normal order of the zodiac— whereas all group activity, or larger, superior and transcendental relationship is measured clockwise, as just illustrated in the discussion of the horizon's general significance. Because the turning of the whole heavenly sphere is brought about by the counterclockwise rotation of the earth on its own axis, the ambient's movement is clockwise. Astrological symbolism in consequence is clockwise in its root philosophy, expressing the fundamental relations set up by a horizon according to a clockwise perspective. Thus the eastern horizon of the horoscope is said to demark the realm "above the earth."

[3] The point of view is from the north celestial pole.

PUTTING EXPERIENCE IN PLACE 75

The first house as a segment of the heavens is actually below, and the seventh above, the plane in question. No difficulty arises here if it is remembered that the hemisphere above the horizon represents the area of experience faced or confronted by the personality, which is indicated by the ascendant as such. Personality seen exteriorly from itself, as in the judgment of a horoscope, is subjective—that is, centered within itself and so having the nature of "below the earth" reality—but when personality acts or shows initiative it obviously must move out of the center in itself to the open or free world of experience, which extends "above the earth." By the same token the whole subjective area of experience "below the earth," which lies clockwise before the seventh house, shows the general potentiality of those advantages to self which are administered by circumstances and people other than the self, or by factors which are necessarily charted or identified in the great objective or "above the earth" area of experience where the house itself lies.

The midheaven or tenth house represents the zenith point in life for the individual, or his touch with the authoritative factors pertinent to the significant moment. The nadir or opposite fourth house charts the corresponding bottom factor in experience. These indications hold for both natal or horary astrology. The idea of the fourth house as the ruler of foundations, or underlying ultimate relations, is in contrast with the immediateness of public advantage or necessity shown at the upper meridian. The most simple antithetical relation here is between the outer or social world and the inner or private domain of self. Thus the most familiar rulership assigned to the tenth house is "business," and to the fourth house is "home." The commercial or professional aspect of life is the individual's contact with his whole group, while the intimate and hidden emphasis is his activity through that part of the general milieu he has made particularly his own.

The fourth house rules all the ramifications of man's especially private universe of experience. Astrologers employ it to indicate the soul, or the psychological anchorage of life in contrast with the tenth, which reveals the purely practical situation of the native among everyday affairs in general. The home represents a retreat and a sanctuary, or the place to which an individual retires at the end of his public work for the day. By extension it becomes his final resort, after the complete cycle of incarnation, and thus the ultimate home, or the grave.

The first and seventh houses, taken together as originating in the horizon, have a distinctly personal reference and are said by astrologers to indicate the individual or essentially human side of life. The tenth and fourth houses, by contrast, have a more remote impersonal or social application. While commercial and professional relations, under tenth house rulership, may certainly be very "personal" and immediate in their details, what they actually reveal is the necessary conformity of some person to a group convenience. The tenth house always identifies superiors, or measures the imposition of requirements from a larger complex of reality. The midheaven, it is true, shows a native's position in life, and thus provides an intimation of his possible achievements and standing, but in all his accomplishment here he simply demonstrates his success in assimilating group functions to himself.

Similarly, the privacy of the home and the ultimate self-realization of the soul, ruled by the fourth house, seem to

PUTTING EXPERIENCE IN PLACE 77

constitute a very "personal" field of interest until it is realized that any real home comprises a group of individuals welded together in a genuine group entity, even in the transient relations and grudging intimacies of a hotel or boardinghouse. Man's "soul" is social in this same sense, since his inner life keeps him forever linked with his race and blood, with those of his intimates and fellows who have shared his values or made them real, and with God and every spiritual experience that marks his group or social existence on invisible planes. The fourth house always reveals the persisting integrity of the family or clan, and so particularly indicates estates and all the fruits of special privilege and luxury, for better or worse; such as parks, public no less than private grounds and preserves, fine buildings, and the "home" for any or every phase of large group experience as well as for the least of single persons.

The distinction between the axes formed by the horizon, on the one hand, and the midheaven meridian, on the other, while fundamentally between these immediately personal matters and the more ramified group concerns, is a mode of differentation which is seldom obvious in ordinary experience. Astrologers, in consequence, sometimes draw the line on the basis of "simplicity" as in contrast with "complexity," or else teach that the horizon axis indicates the "physical" factors, and the midheaven-nadir line the "spiritual" elements, in everyday affairs. These are relations which will be traced out in great detail, with much further explanation.

The eight houses other than the axial points are created by the trisection already explained, and their meanings are derived from the ascendant, descendant, midheaven or nadir. The four primary houses represent the focal or "angular" aspects of experience. Those which lie behind them in the order of the normal movement of the planets through the zodiac, or which define the segments in the heavens that rise immediately ahead of the angles, are known as the cadent houses. They are the third, sixth, ninth and twelfth. Those that lie ahead of the angles, counterclockwise, or describe heavenly areas immediately behind the angles from the clockwise point of view, are known as the succedent houses. These are the second, fifth, eighth and eleventh.

The rulerships of the "minor" houses, as they are designated in astrology, arise from their relations in counterclockwise order, as given a common expression in the time-sequence of daily life. Thus the angles represent the present moment, or the points of crisis and critical relationship established primarily at the horizon and midheaven meridian. The cadent houses, as lying "behind" the angles, represent the past (the meaning conveyed by the word "cadent"), while the succedent houses in corresponding fashion give an indication of the future, or the immediate dynamic of promise and potentiality. The house schematism sets up four groups of three, in interlacing triangles.

The philosophy of number has held an exceptional fascination for the human mind, from the days of Pythagoras and before, with a particular appeal to the Greeks and modern occultists. Extremists among the devotees of numerical speculation have made actual entities out of abstract number values, a tendency reflected in the effort of some writers to explain various astrological relations by the supposed power of the "three" or "four" *per se*. Fourfold structures are found commonly enough in all nature, largely because the intersection of any two lines of influence at once produces quarters, and by this same convenience of actual facts the "three" is a commonplace of thinking, reflected in the famous dialectic process developed by Grecian philosophy and implicit fundamentally in the act of placing a point of emphasis on any line of sequence. This is familiar to everyone in time, or in the "present" as related to a "past" and a "future."

Immanuel Kant's identification of space as an exterior sense, and time as an interior one, emphasizes the spatial ramification either in the simple two dimensions of "self" and "other," or in the complex fourfold patterns of common experience. The action of time in bringing existence into the more constricted line of personal experience, or individual consequences, is the root of the similar but less literal threefold organization of reality. By and large, the general fact of experience has "existence" in an objective and fourfold nature, and the corresponding specific fact in the antithetical subjective and essentially threefold activity of personal concern. How astrology first came to use this triad of individual differentiation, to break up each heavenly quarter into three segments, is unknown to history. Through many ages it has remained a convenient and effective means for indicating how experience may be "realized," or how its relations to space—that is, to broad cosmic generalization—may be recognized at some point of individual manipulation in terms of change, choice and chance.

The astrological trisection of the heavens charts the cycles of events in a rhythm of before-now-and-after emphases.[4] The "present" of each angle is sustained in a

[4] Actually astrology is only charting everyday experience as it exhibits, at every point of emphasis, a punctuation of some line of sequence in other experience, but the "three" idea is clearer in time symbolism.

"past" and "future" created at the opposing ends of the other house axis. This is the way each quarter in experience is active, or has practical meaning as it subordinates its own simple antithesis in order to function in co-operation with the other set of opposing relations that cut across it. Here is the astrological process by which the "three" activates the "four." In their relation to the ascendant the tenth house establishes the ninth, and the fourth sets up the fifth; a simple psychological patterning which is repeated at each angle. What is contributed to house meanings can be given in summary, with the house names in italics in order to emphasize the relations.

Thus *personality* (first house) discovers its past through *life position*, and its future through *end values*. These *end values* find their past through *personality*, and their future through *opportunity*. This *opportunity* depends on the past established in *end values*, and has encouragement for the future through *life position*. The *life position* rests on the past that has been *opportunity*, and has promise for the future through *personality*. The implication of this schematism is shown by the arrows in the diagrams for the four triads, and it must be remembered that houses also give meaning to adjacent houses, or gain meaning from them, over and above all the primary significance arising at the angular points.

The Ascendant Triad

The group of houses focused through the ascendant is particularly useful, in natal astrology, for describing the individual and his simple act of self-being and, in horary astrology, for identifying the query or querent, as well as for indicating the simple purpose and nature of the enterprise or situation about which inquiry is made. The as-

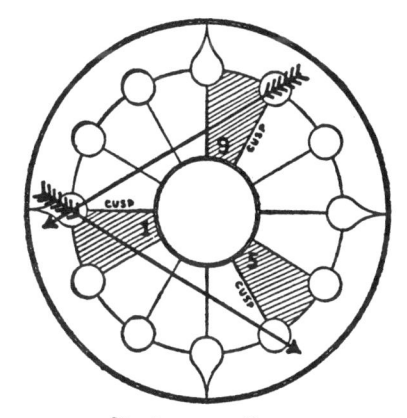

THE ASCENDANT TRIAD

cendant, or first house, has already been presented as the ruler of any proposition in general.

The ninth is the related cadent house, revealing the pertinent influences out of the past. The root signification of this ninth house in the astrological tradition is "higher mind," or man's true thinking processes, together with all their fruits, as well as all possibility for an individual's relationship with things at a distance or remote in experience. Thus the house is said to identify knowledge; language, which makes possible the preservation of knowledge; books, in which thinking is communicated and knowledge is recorded; science, as the organized procedure of using thinking or broadening knowledge; religion, as the process of thought applied to the examination of the universe and a determination of its meaning; conscience, as the application of conscious realization to the estimation of judgments upon a given event or situation; long journeys, distinguished from the shorter trips or moves around in the immediate environment for practical and transient orientation, and seen as an individual's intellectual capacity for relating things at a distance; and so on indefinitely. In all these indications the reference is to the simple existence of an individual, and to details of his free act of being on his own account.

The fifth or related succedent house is the same factor of simple individuality in its projection towards the future. Thus it reveals, primarily, the simple out-spilling of self, or the pursuit of pleasure. It also includes the prodigal expression of the same impulse, and so indicates dissipation, or every possible capacity for self-wastage. It shows talents in this naïve individual sense, and so has been seen to rule creativity in all its immediate or common and tangible aspects. It rules the unfoldment of self into the future in the domain of intellectual life, or is the total of preparation for what in the ninth house ends up as knowledge and wisdom; hence embracing everything in connection with schools, the process of learning or training, discipline and the like, including teaching in every aspect. It charts this projection of self in a perfectly literal or physical sense, thus identifying offspring, either in the form of actual children or of special works and enterprises of some definitely private sort.

Every particular ramification of these basic relations is included in the fifth house's general rulership. Thus it indicates courtship, or the relationship with a potential life-partner up to that point where the individual still reserves to himself the right to withdraw and go seeking elsewhere. It rules entertainment, not only as amusement but as an actual wooing of some potential associate in a business deal or other intimate tie. It embraces sex indulgence in a purely animal sense; i.e., where the creative impulses are reduced to this point of pure self-indulgence or dissipation. It covers all direct organization of amusements and sports, as well as all actual participation in them, so that anything in connection with the theater is found at this point. While research, or the refinement of knowledge, is a matter of analysis in the light of the past, and belongs to the ninth house, the tentative expression of self or the dilettante outreaching of the mind is found here as long as the values involved are of the future, that is, as long as the self is projecting its underlying energies out on and beyond its normal periphery of being in order to touch something as yet not a true part of itself.

The Midheaven Triad

The group centering at the midheaven is particularly useful in natal astrology for describing the individual's social place, or his general relationship with his group, and in the horary branch it gives a general clue to his broader relations with the particular community in which he is functioning, or within which the particular question or issue has arisen. The distinctions again can be seen most clearly through the abstract time distinction, with the tenth house revealing the present situation of some specific matter in its general context, the sixth similarly representing the past or what are distinctly contributory circumstances in the given group relationship, and the second house indicating the future aspect in the form of an accumulation of resources which will be available, or of value, in the settling of the particular problem.

The tenth house in horary astrology most importantly represents authority. This may be an individual person who is a superior with the right to give orders, such as an employer, or an officer of higher rank in a company or an organization. In such a case this individual represents the group interest. The tenth house particularly shows this element of authority, however, as it takes political or a definable community form. This means government in any aspect in which it is known, and comprises the towns or cities, counties or parishes, states or provinces, principalities or nations, in which the native or querent dwells, or to which he is subject. It indicates both the smaller and larger jurisdictions. More specifically, it represents the "police power," the magistrates or other agencies that establish or enforce discipline in any way. Hence the house can represent the principal or dean in a school or college, and so on. When a horary question concerns trade and commerce, the house identifies the given business world in which transactions take place or questions arise, or the prevailing economic "authority." This is usually expressed by saying that the tenth house rules "business," although a question about a given or specific business as a project or matter of concern, in contrast with the recognition of a pertinent authority, would be referred to the first house primarily.

It is essential to remember, at this point, that astrological rulerships depend on what things mean, or what they do, and not on what they are called. Words like "business" have different implications in different situations, but the

PUTTING EXPERIENCE IN PLACE 85

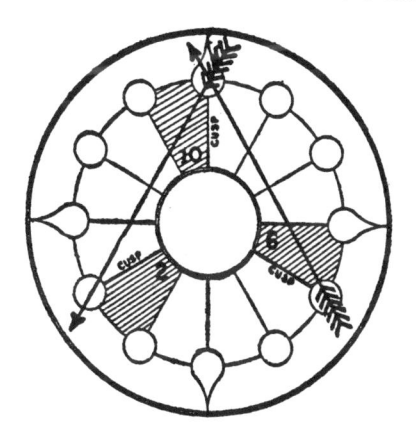

THE MIDHEAVEN TRIAD

young astrologer will never encounter any difficulty if he keeps the general principles of astrological rulership perfectly clear in his mind. When a question is asked about a specific "business," reference is to a body of interests and relationships which, all together, constitute a sort of "entity," and are to be considered as a person—i.e., an individualized group activity—for the purposes of horary analysis. The tenth house only rules business as a contact when the inquiry concerns the acts of some individual within its pattern of relation, never when the business as a whole is seen to act; that is, when it is taken as an integrated organism.

The great power of horary astrology lies in the fact that the astrologer sees life as essentially organic at every point of analysis. In other words, each organism constitutes a part of some larger entity, and at the same time comprises innumerable others within its own completeness of make-up. The living cells in any physical body are "organisms" on their own account, and the physical body itself is like a larger "cell" of this sort in the social community which, again in its turn, has as definite an organic existence as the body in question. The orderliness of the world is evident continually in the fact that every part of existence not only functions on its own account but also affords a context for the operation of smaller factors within itself, and additionally and at the same time carries out activities useful or essential to the greater complex of relations which constitute an integrated existent from another and larger point of view.

Profound philosophical analysis is challenged by the descending and ascending hierarchies of nature. Unquestionably any speculation upon the infinite potentiality of nesting considerations is not only fruitless, but upsetting to reason itself. Fortunately, in practical fact, life brings the individual face to face with problems which, in an everyday sense, concern him alone. His worry may be the necessity for getting or holding a job, which represents a relatively individual matter; or a concern over the danger that the corporation for which he works may not survive the current complex of conditions within which it functions as an entity, which is a definite group crisis. His wife may be sick, or difficulties in his church or some social organization may make an important impact on his life. By the same token, and perhaps simultaneously, the city in which he resides may face a serious shortage in its water or power supply, or the government may encounter emergencies on the ever-enlarging scale.

Horary astrology is not concerned with these dimensions of experience as such. It places any matter inquired about into the pattern of the houses on the basis of the fundamental entity involved, and the tenth house, together with the two others related to it, primarily show the superior frame of reference, or the simple and general context in which a difficulty must be met. The first house, with the ninth and fifth, are a triad revealing the immediate status of affairs in some given matter, as this is seen at a point of organic activity thereby focused in a critical

PUTTING EXPERIENCE IN PLACE 87

moment of time. The tenth house and its related pair constitute a trinity of houses which show the immediate but general and larger total circumstances of the situation or problem, or reveal the focus by contrast at the critical point in space. The distinction is the one already made in terms of simplicity versus complexity.

The tenth house not only rules the authority exercised over any person by others, but also that which he is able to establish over himself by virtue of special skills and capacities. The house in this sense is said to rule profession, and it charts the detailed compulsions which such a state puts upon the individual. Thus the doctor is subject to call at any hour of the night, and so on. In a broader social way this factor of "authority" ramifies out to less tangible compulsions, as in the case of any person achieving some position of prominence among his fellows. Consequently the house is said to rule honor, and to show the requirements of attitude and act which, while not "imposed from above" literally, are to all intents and purposes a rigid social limitation because the individual becomes a living embodiment of the ideals quickened in his fellows, and must act according to the rule he has made real for himself, whether or no. This is simple dignity.

The sixth house is related to the tenth as the support given out of the past to the general larger situation. Since the purpose in any astrological chart is to map the potentialities in a given matter, this past is never examined merely to discover what went on at some prior time, but rather is studied to determine in what manner this past, or its influence, still operates in the present. If the tenth shows the superior situation in general, then the sixth indicates the procedures by which this general situation was given its particular set or direction. This means the attitudes and established ways of acting by which any social or group advantage has been achieved, as well as the tendencies towards that failure to act, or to act properly, by which desired advantages are not gained. It is the house of struggle for place, position and focus in life's total reality, and in the present moment this means primarily the labor or hard work required by the particular situation. It does not imply competition, or contest. Most simply, it identifies the deference that must be paid to others because they occupy a better position in the world, together with the same deferring to self that may be compelled from whoever occupies an inferior position. This makes the house most commonly the ruler of service and servants, or of adjustment in the general relationships of society at large.

The same idea of fundamental social orientation applies within the economy of self, revealing the attention that must be given to certain parts or functions of the organism, together with what co-operation may be had from them in any special degree at any particular time. Ordinarily this means sickness, indicating the general pattern under which the organism gets out of harmony with its general situation, and so requires attention. Also it charts the special self-mobilization possible under unusual stimulus and emergencies. In the broadest sort of way the sixth house is the place in the astrological chart at which the problems of general adjustment are brought to a focus in self-consciousness. These include every possible social relationship which can or must operate through a non-family disparity of some sort, as in the dealings with superiors and inferiors already pointed out. There is much more to the matter, however, since the house not only shows sickness and social inadequacies in a physical sense, but maladjustments of a definite psychological sort. This commonly includes business in the occasional case where a person is wholly a misfit, or where he must perform work which he distinctly dislikes. It indicates effort under circumstances when the individual is exceptionally unable to control his actions, with outstanding examples in the army and navy, and common illustration in any enterprise where he is under constant and detailed domination by superiors, or where regimentation is very marked.

The house rules farming and the production of the raw materials of food and clothing in every ordinary sense, because the worker on the land must adjust himself constantly to the convenience of the weather, the caprice of natural forces and other factors almost entirely beyond his control. Here is a link with the cooking, sewing and other services normally performed by menials, or by the socially underprivileged. While modern scientific methods may change the picture of an agriculture at the mercy of chance, there is no astrological difficulty in any special case since any highly organized or large-scale scientific farming becomes a business, and is then quite distinct from the individual linked to his soil, or held rigorously at the service of his fields and cattle. Food products are included here, whether plant or animal. Useful pets, such as dogs employed for watching the premises or helping control the various other livestock on the farm, are ruled by this house, as are all the "small animals" of the older astrological books. This means the beasts that can be domesticated or controlled in a household or farm economy, and even the pet which becomes a pure parasite, since he serves his master psychologically.

By contrast the animals allowed to roam at large, or those that have to be handled with special precautions because never thoroughly trained or domesticated, are found in the twelfth house, but all matters concerning food and its controlled sources are located in the sixth because all problems of commissary concern inferiors, either workers in the larger sense or the detailed functions of an organism more specifically. Another important distinction is between children, ruled by the fifth, and the other helpers in a strictly family or agricultural economy. The boys and girls raised on the farm have a burden of labor unknown by city youngsters, and the work they do is as much a matter of the sixth house as any other effort belonging there. Because the worker has no relation to a given matter except through his work, however, he is found, both in his function and in his person, in the sixth.

The second house, also linked with the tenth, represents the future potentiality of the individual's social place in life. In the same way that any analysis of the past is futile except as an indication of a present realization, so the examination of this "future" merely discloses the influence in the same present of some special freedom or pertinent capability. The general potentials of any given social situation have expression in the resources and accumulations available for immediate use, so that the second is primarily the place of money or its equivalent.

All three houses focused at the midheaven reveal the situation in which a question is asked, or a life is lived, in terms of a superior-inferior relationship of some sort. Money, astrologically, is an agency for social change, or for manipulating the pertinent factors in a given matter, and this means not only possessions in a static sense but also resources as they particularly are associated with an individual's move upward or downward in the social scale. Here money is shown as it identifies human achievement, in a normally continuous fluctuation. This idea was expressed by the older astrologers when they said that the house ruled loss and gain, or the improvement or degeneration of a situation in the broad terms of its total potentiality.

The Descendant Triad

The houses focused at the descendant are like the three established by the ascendant, for the obvious reason that their foundation is in the horizon, or the fundamental ground of the particular matter in the case of each horoscope. Rather than showing social or group relationships, as the midheaven triad, they indicate personal lines of action and reaction, on the order of the ascendant's triangle. This individuality is not self-centered, however, as at the eastern horizon, but these three houses instead reveal the bridging activity between the individual and the group. Here is the function of direct co-operation with other individuality, as already outlined at some length.

From the philosophical point of view there are three simple stages in understanding a universe characterized by both free will and uncompromising order. The first is to realize that everything has existence in its own terms, through a basic continuance of its own nature. This phase of reality is charted by astrology through the first house. The second stage in understanding is the realization that everything exists in the terms of everything else as well as itself, or through the universal concordance by which it is enabled to be what it is in definite time and space relations. Here is the focus of group reality which the horoscope reveals at the midheaven. The third stage in understanding requires an appreciation of the fact that some active connection must exist between the individual and the group, or between one person and another.

This is the philosophical explanation of the phenomenon by which "existence" becomes "experience." Thus a man has other men around him, and he comes to know himself, in any conscious sense, by his co-operative activity with them. He can have ideas because he can exchange them, compare them, try them out, and so make them his own. He discovers that some traits are of value, and others worthless, to the degree he can exhibit them or see them in others, and thereby increasingly becomes acquainted with himself through this immediate response from the world of events in which he has existence.

The seventh house primarily rules simple co-operative relation in partnership. These ties, however, no matter of what nature or duration, are more than a mere linking of factors in some form of tête-à-tête interaction. They are always the means for joint activity as an act of self-discovery, or an increase in the effective dimension of selfhood. Hence the seventh house does not fundamentally show marriage, as an example, in the physical or mating sense, although it includes this in every essential feature. Rather, it charts the challenge which comes to any entity or organism when it is obliged to share its experience, or to

PUTTING EXPERIENCE IN PLACE

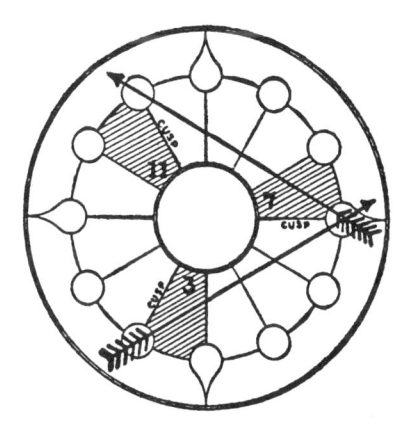

THE DESCENDANT TRIAD

grasp its opportunity for continual self-realization among equals, that is, with persons of comparable experience and capacity. Astrological "marriage," in consequence, consists at times of intimate relations between men and women when there is no legal tie and, by the same token, the partnership may be legal without normal physical relations. In cases where a sex intimacy is the sole basis of relationship, even when sanctioned by an actual wedding, the sharing of experience in any true sense is absent, and the result is a self-indulgence which puts the matter in the fifth house.

Mere mutual convenience is thus never partnership, which is a relation based on an effort to expand rather than indulge the self. The principle is well illustrated in the case of artistic effort so intensified in a given life that the individual becomes, in a sense, "wedded to his art." While creative expression ordinarily is a simple self-centered activity, charted through the fifth house even if quite exalted in vision, a whole life may yet be bent to the achievement of a certain beauty or of particular skills that must perforce carve out an exceptional opportunity. When what has been a private interest becomes a public responsibility, and when a sense of major esthetic partnership with the whole cultural tradition gives a new and unique dimension to the artist's talents, the result is the "fine arts" over which this house has long had rulership.

While the tenth house rules professional excellency, the seventh indicates the direct employment of anyone who possesses special skills or capacities of this sort, whether as a consultant to whom appeal is made for advice, or as an expert retained for guidance or direction in the solution of some problem. This does not include mere workers or agents, but means the "professions" generally. Thus the seventh rules the astrologer in horary art, and every practitioner should consult this house in order to have light on his own individual competency in the particular case; as well as to gain an index of the chances that his advice will be accepted and understood. In this way he minimizes the possibility of getting enmeshed in the "psychological fallacy" (that is, seeing another's problems through his own colored glasses).

The third house is related to the seventh in terms of the contribution of past general experience to the present moment. In a horary chart, it primarily indicates all the elements which give incidental or taken-for-granted support to the immediate opportunity. Natal astrology puts less emphasis on the transient aspect of gadgets or superficial conveniences, and stresses personal relations of this

PUTTING EXPERIENCE IN PLACE 95

contributing sort, as illustrated by brothers, sisters and the family background of blood ties. It is the house of the immediate environment in all cases, including the climate of opinion or body of notions found associated with a given problem or issue, and so the indicator of everything that has been said or brought to attention in connection with a particular matter, not excepting gossip or even outright misrepresentation. This category comprises all forms of communication, from conversation and speech to letters, telephone, telegraph, radio, and so on. Equally important is the rulership over all pure instrumentalities, simple tools, or whatever is handy or useful in an immediate or trivial way for the move towards some opportunity.

There is considerable contrast here between these conveniences and the concern of men with the machines of an industrial age, or the technical tools which are the necessities of real labor or routine work indicated by the sixth house. The third reveals the commonplace manipulation of people and things in circumstances where no creative attention is required, or where no specific skills are called into conscious being. This means general routine activity of the sort that is never a burden, and it includes the normal moving about of self, such as any traveling around in the immediate community in what astrological tradition describes as "short journeys."

The three houses linked through the descendant have a special importance in natal astrology which is equally vital although less emphasized in horary art. They reveal man's dismissal of responsibility to others in special degrees of the increasingly close personal relations between an individual and those with whom he shares fellowship as equals in his own world. The seventh house shows such relationships as fundamentally in the process of becoming permanent, or else breaking up to make way for other ties. Thus marriage, despite what is wittily termed modern man's consecutive as against concurrent polygamy, is idealized as "made in heaven." In principle, at least, it is not to be broken except by death. Even business partnerships have an ideal measure of permanency. An individual is expected to have a regular lawyer, physician, and so on. However, with the continual self-reconstruction of all human character, changes are inevitable in the special case, producing the crisis and realignment which the seventh house charts most directly.

The third house indicates these relationships as they are found in their state of permanence, or when no further responsibility is taken for them. They may be established quite literally in the blood, as in brothers and sisters specifically, and all relatives in general. Particular sibs, or cousins, and the like, may be traced out into other houses by the special horary technique to be illustrated in a following chapter—when the house-meanings are given a much greater ramification of detail—but they are always charted here also. The only blood relatives not ruled by the house are children and parents, in which case there is a social or disciplinary disparity, as well as a very definite and continuing responsibility, which places the rulership in the fifth for the inferior, and in the tenth and fourth, for the superior direct generation.

The eleventh house represents the unlimited potential of tête-à-tête relations and hence indicates friends and acquaintances. These are the "equals" in experience when

PUTTING EXPERIENCE IN PLACE

the relationship is especially tentative, or on the whole a matter of experiment with others and a least-responsible contact. As an extension of this function the house rules objectives in general—that is, the visualization of them—or what the old astrologers always knew as "hopes and wishes." Of all twelve houses, this usually proves to be the easiest to understand, since it has the least ramification of indication. It does not represent the opportunity confronted immediately, or that specific situation shown at the seventh house, but rather the remote contingency or the more general potentiality. This has its present significance in the form of plans, detailed outlines of projects and intentions, and those who co-operate with the various aspects of man's "day-dreaming" capacity.

The house thus shows the possibilities of strictly vicarious experience, or the tentative use that may be made of imagination and analytical qualities in facing any given moment in experience. Here is an unconditioned employment of imaginative and subjective factors in the practical world of everyday, but never any experience of these inner or psychic realities on their own account; which is an eighth-house phenomenon. The eleventh primarily shows the ordered anticipation of experience, the scheduling of conscious act in advance of the action.

There is a vital but very subtle distinction here between the eleventh and ninth houses, but this should involve no difficulty because the latter indicates the total of possessed knowledge, wisdom, and the like, together with a native's sensitiveness to the values and implications of situation and act, whereas the former shows the capacity for reaching out ahead of experience, and getting light upon it by a trial and error experience wholly within the imagination. In the case of thought and thinking in the ninth house, reference is to a content of experience built into the self as knowledge. In the eleventh house the rulership is over potentials as apart from the real limitations of a wisdom already possessed.

By the same token there is another exceptionally refined distinction between the eleventh and twelfth houses, but again there need be no trouble because the eleventh deals with an inner manipulation of experience on the tentative side as this is under the continual control of the consciousness, whereas the process of inner and subjective experience, as ruled by the twelfth house, is entirely as this lies beyond control, or has been dismissed to automaticity.

It must be realized, in connection with these distinctions, that no one house can be discussed adequately, or understood, apart from the others. It may be noted that the reference to various houses increasingly occurs under the heading of other ones, and that the meanings are expanded through tracing out lines of relationship and distinction at that point where the particular consideration lends the greatest clarity to the general analysis. Astrology is an organic whole, and it cannot be learned, or employed with any skill, if the newcomer attempts to master its elements in separation, or in disregard of each other. They cannot be put together, as the bricks of a building in a purely exterior assembly, because they are the parts of an organism. They arise from an interior integration which is "whole," even in what might seem to be a preliminary assembling.

The Nadir Triad

The three houses established at the nadir provide the same contrast with the midheaven triad that is evident in

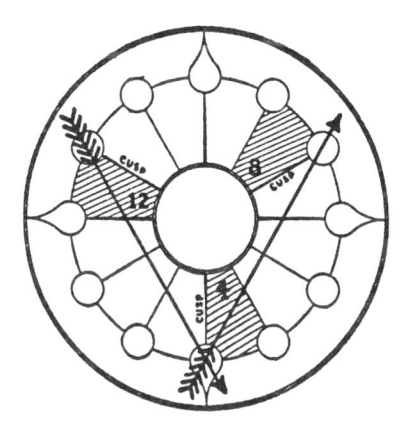

THE NADIR TRIAD

any comparison of the descendant group with the ascendant. They represent the working out of group relations in a new dimension, exactly as the third, seventh and eleventh houses show the expansion of responsibility exhibited by the individual factor (the immediate situation in a given case). The houses of the nadir group, however, present considerable difficulty to the layman or young enthusiast, both in natal and horary astrology, because they reveal affairs which are in no way as tangible as those ruled by the other nine divisions of the heavens. An earlier generation of astrologers made a great mystery out of this nadir triangle, and many older books exhibit a distinct fear of whatever is shown here; especially in the case of the eighth and twelfth houses.

By comparison the functions of the seventh and allied houses are easy to grasp because they deal directly with the special or quite individual matters brought to analysis at the ascendant, and chart the general adaptation that must be made to the broad opportunity of the moment, or the co-operation needed on the personality side by a particular enterprise. The fourth-house group is not hard to understand if it is remembered that these houses show the necessities involved in the enlistment of group interests, that is, a different and indirect sort of co-operation with the problem at issue, or with the person whose horoscope is under examination.

The nadir triangle, most fundamentally, establishes the pattern by which the general reality, or the impersonal whole of all things, can be helpful to individual efforts and desires, and in consequence one of the most serviceable meanings for the fourth house is "the end of the matter." Unfortunately, in much astrological literature, this takes a literal and macabre overemphasis as the tomb, monuments, and the physical end of living experience. Thus it has long been observed in natal astrology that the ascendant has a definite rulership over the beginning of life, and so can be said to indicate the early environment, whereas the fourth house shows the declining years and the similar environment of old age.

The simple idea behind all rulership of the fourth house is the more important service of the whole group to its individual members while they are alive. This most immediately is the point of privacy or safety for individual existence; i.e., the "home" as the place of residence in a physical sense, as the point to which retreat is made for rest and psychological self-rehabilitation, and in general as the special circumstances under which a man may actually experience his wholeness of existence. Here he is not chal-

PUTTING EXPERIENCE IN PLACE   101

lenged in any way that makes him uncomfortably "more" or "less" than his own basic self-content, since the totality of the universe sustains him in a total moment all his own, and so affords him a real experience or knowledge of "soul" as such.

The general idea of the pertinency of old things as a basic fourth-house rulership may be spun out to include inheritance, family background, and the tradition of the clan or the race. The idea of inheritance is only found in this house when it is in a sense entailed, that is, when the given person receiving it is under obligations to pass it on unimpaired to his successors in turn. Rather than his property, in any real sense, it is in legal terminology a usufruct. The idea is embodied in the astrological books as estates, grounds, preserves, and the like, and the house not only rules these as private domain but also as public reservations such as parks, community buildings,[5] museums and galleries; together with cemeteries and all other specially dedicated public areas.

The twelfth house represents the concept of the past in this service of the total context of existence to the individual existent, and it becomes most simply the house of institutions. The term ordinarily means hospitals and welfare agencies such as clinics, emergency shelters established for air raids in wartime, and the like. Thus the twelfth is the house of confinement in a very real sense. It rules establishments where liberty is curtailed both for the sake of the individual, to compel his restraint, and for the safety of society also; as in the case of penitentiaries, jails, insane

[5] Distinguished from third-house "premises" when entirely public in support or upkeep, as well as in use or supervision, either in essence or in fact.

asylums, reformatories, concentration camps and all compulsory rehabilitation agencies. In the broad application of this function, the rulership comprises the aspect of home in a protective or involuntary sense, as when the individual is immature or incompetent, or when he requires protective custody in any respect, identifying orphan asylums, juvenile detention homes, and so on. More pleasantly, it indicates unexpected help, or assistance on the constructive side of things. This is an indication badly neglected by older astrologers, who often saw only the destructive side in hidden enemies and unsuspected misfortunes.

What the twelfth house actually indicates, in its "destructive" functioning, is the point of basic inadequacy in the individual life, or where personal initiative is lost to the extent that the general situation must provide the administration or stimulus of events. The manner in which the group control is exercised is not fundamentally inimicable to the existence of self, but rather is disciplinary or ordering. When the agencies are actual events of a repressive sort, the result obviously appears unfortunate to the individual, but when he is sensitive to the disciplinary elements he also instinctively senses the manner in which he will be protected or guided, and this is manifest through his subconscious sense of things. More importantly than anything else, therefore, the house rules the basic subconsciousness, or the undercurrents in experience by which a real personality is able to guide itself, or work in line with the greatest degree of group or social co-operation. The twelfth house shows, in consequence, the conscious or deliberate as well as unwitting or compelled dismissal of various psychological functions to that automaticity by which

PUTTING EXPERIENCE IN PLACE 103

the dynamic or control is placed in group rather than individual factors.

The eighth house represents the future aspect of the total situation's link to individual activity, and this is manifest in many important details of everyday life. First of all, the house indicates death, or the point of complete future supervision of the individual, i.e., the cancellation of objective individuality as such. This seldom becomes death in a literal sense, in astrological practice, but more often means merely the complete termination of some particular cycle or aspect in relationship. The house, as a result, is also the point of regeneration or re-establishment. This may refer directly to the individual, or to the particular matter at hand, and it may also indicate particular phases of total-group co-operation in terms of resources and potentials. Thus the eighth house indicates legacies and minor inheritance, in the sense of gifts or endowments which are available in full support of individual effort.

The fourth house is the direct outcome of the tenth-house stress of individual activity in group terms, or the direct consequences of honor and achieved professional excellency. The tenth is the authority in a given life, as this is imposed upon the individual or as he imposes it upon himself for the sake of some particular goal, and the fourth is a purely private enjoyment of the achievement, and the final establishment of some outer symbol of what has been gained. Up to the time of an individual's maturity, this intimate relation between the midheaven and nadir is expressed through the situation of the parents or family, since he is unable to go out to create a world of his own.

The child, during his early years, has the same home as his parents, and whatever business or profession he may have is fitted into the setting of this parental scheme of things, and so will be shown at the tenth. Life as such has begun in the womb, which is ruled by the fourth, and of which the home is a continuing symbol, hence this place of residence is a welcome retreat whenever any self-gathering is necessary. The active direction or compulsion of the life remains at the midheaven always, which normally rules the mother as the personality charged with maintaining the home for the child; i.e., at first the womb, then the cradle, and finally the institution of which she has immediate charge. Thus astrology identifies the tenth with the "close-link parent," usually the woman.

This rulership is long-established in the astrological tradition, although a recent generation of astrologers has assimilated the idea of business to the father, and the idea of home to the mother. The reversed house designations will be encountered in many books. Not infrequently the actual father will be the "mother" to all intents and purposes, and with the complexity of modern society the distinction of identification at this point is not as sharp in practice as in theory. As a consequence, in natal astrology, it is necessary to analyze every horoscope separately. In horary astrology, however, the rulerships must be sharp. While the inverted assignment of parents will work perfectly in the case of an astrologer who adopts them—if he remains adequately consistent throughout his practice—[6] the traditional identification has the advantage of the weight of long practice, as well as of a correct theoretical substantiation.

[6] The function of psychological adaptation, since the horary chart reflects the mind of the practitioner, but a frail reed that should not be leaned upon too heavily.

The fourth house shows the end of the matter, and this has particular association with the father because normally he is charged with the duty of sustaining the family tradition, giving it a renewed point in a social recognition or total group regard. To the child in the womb, the father is distinctly remote, and at the nursing and cradle stage almost equally so. The individual's tie with his mother has the physical basis which strikes deep and is fundamentally real. The respect for the father comes out of conscious experience in a common sharing of the family values, and the cycle has its proper completion or genuine fullness as the individual, whether boy or girl, grows to the point of appreciating the family honor, or the worth of the general estate, and becomes willing in turn to contribute to it and give it, if possible, an enhanced reality. Hence the house is said to rule the "remote-link" parent, usually the man.

There is some possibility of confusion, in horary astrology, between the seventh house as the immediate outcome of any given matter, and the fourth house as the ultimate end of things. This may be avoided by realizing that the seventh shows the direct consequences of individual act, whereas the fourth house shows the more remote results of an inflexible demand on the individual by the total group situation. The question may well be asked, "If the fourth house shows an inevitable outcome, how then can the seventh house show a result which follows from the exercise of choice and free will?" The answer is that the "inevitability" of the fourth house is in terms of what the group or total compulsion means to the individual, whereas the seventh house shows the contribution that the individual may make to group affairs and so, in passing, to himself. The general pattern of life, the skeleton of existence, does not change, but the flesh that is put upon it, and the conscious significance that it gets, are subject to continual alteration and revision. Man goes home sooner or later, in the sense that he returns to the basic anchorage of his own pattern, but he may do so filled with the substance of a real contribution to his fellows, or in relative defeat in order to achieve safety and a restrengthening of his own determination.

The fourth house is always the larger frame in which individual affairs are worked out ultimately, and in horary astrology it offers a convenient broader view for any given matter. It does not cancel out free will, but instead it reveals the ordering in which, by the paradox, free will is possible. Any difficulty in understanding at this point is a philosophical one, with no real parallel in actual life. The newcomer to astrological law may eliminate every possibility of conflict by recognizing the fact that there is always an immediate and a remote consequence in things; that the seventh house shows the immediate and the fourth the remote consideration. Both are necessary, and both are available. The concentration of attention in practice is on the former, while the latter is employed as a general rectification to take care of the occasionally broader considerations in judgment.

Chapter Five

THE PLANETS

A HOROSCOPE, whether in natal or horary astrology, would be meaningless if there were no factors other than the twelvefold division of the heavens. This mode of charting human experience in the celestial expanse has produced the houses, the implications of which have been traced out in considerable preliminary detail, and when the same division is made on the basis of the earth's annual rather than daily motion, the result is the zodiac with its twelve signs. However, even with these houses and signs together, the horoscope is incomplete and therefore ineffective. The houses distribute the heavenly relationships according to the individual horizon of the person, event or problem, and the signs according to the general or common necessities of existence—in other words, as already indicated, the two circles provide a particular focus in contrast with a universal one—but these distributions, by themselves, are static and unable to give any insight into a living situation. They must be linked in a dynamic relationship, a functioning pattern. This need creates the role of the planets, and explains the rulerships given to them in the astrological mechanism. The horoscope must now be approached as a means for charting events, and controlling them, in a system of unceasing movement and change.

The whole idea of astrology is that any given point in time and space has dependable significance if it can be identified recurrently in both human affairs and heavenly motion. This identification is easier on the heavenly side, because man's ramifying ties with his fellows, and with his whole immediate world of experience, are so infinitely kaleidoscopic in nature that they can never be analyzed except through the generalization of important or recognizable features. The celestial situations, contrariwise, are sufficiently simple so that all the ramifications can be scheduled without difficulty, and so become available to use for screening out or sorting human events. The basis of such a screening process is primarily the houses, with the help of the signs, but this is only a static preliminary, as has been stated.

The constants in the correspondence between human events, as they are brought to a generalized "focus of the particular" in experience, and the various heavenly emphases of relationship, have been discovered and described through uncounted centuries of actual astrological practice. The fact that these basic correspondences should exist is no philosophical or scientific difficulty, since everything has its being in the one self-sufficient energy field of the solar system. What affects anything at one point must, to some degree, affect everything else. No idea of cause or direct influence is involved, necessarily, although most attempts at explanation have been of such an order. Rather, any condition of stress in the general system, as this is particularly recurrent, must have some general concordance with the recurrence of similar aspects of strain in typical smaller areas or subsidiary relationships.

The state of affairs in the general energy system is shown by the time and space positions of the bodies which com-

THE PLANETS

prise it, in any physical or objective sense; namely, the sun and its planets, with the attendant satellites, comets, meteors, and fragments. Of these bodies, the earth is only one, but its activities—that is to say, its motions—are nonetheless the sole means by which the ambient can be divided for man. The charting of the heavens through the houses affords a primary ordering of individual affairs in reference to the cosmic pattern of energies, but it remains the ramification of relations from one heavenly mass taken apart from the others. Of equal importance are the activities of the other bodies, as their time and space relations provide dynamic constants of stress on the heavenly side to aid further in mapping the individual situation. The astrological significance of any matter about which a question is raised, or of any event such as the birth of an individual, is determined by the relationship of the factors in the life situation—as they are distributed by the earth through the houses primarily and the signs secondarily—to the paralleling situation in the whole heavens, and is shown entirely by the planets through their time and space arrangement in connection with each other.

The establishment of an astrological chart, therefore, is a twofold problem. The first part is to divide the heavens on the basis of a given event, through the horizon which identifies its ground of being; and this procedure has been explained in detail. The other part is to chart the general energy situation, as this is shown by the position of the various bodies relative to each other.

The system of celestial mechanics, as recognized from a center taken at the point of man's experience on the earth, has been given every description essential for the astrologer's understanding. The pragmatic perspective means that the positions of the planets are charted in celestial "geocentric longitude," as in distinction from the "heliocentric longitude" of their actual places in their own orbits (that is, as viewed from the sun). An astrological ephemeris always gives geocentric longitude and this is easily converted into right ascension or the corresponding measure in the celestial equator when this is needed. Recent work of an experimental nature—and possibly of ultimate great importance—is based on a use of right ascension rather than celestial longitude, and there is also a small body of astrologers who have continued to use the heliocentric positions, either alone or in combination with the geocentric places, ever since the publication of Hiram E. Butler's *Solar Biology* in 1887. Contemporary practice in horary astrology has little if any practical concern with these deviate methods, since they offer a difference rather than a supplementation or expansion of analytical potentials.

The houses in astrology take on particular or personal meaning as the planets are situated in them. In order to determine which planets lie in each of the twelve places, it is only necessary to find out where they are in celestial longitude. Thus if the ascendant or eastern horizon, as a case in point, is situated at Aries 10°, and the sun is found in Aries 12°, the sun is just below the ascendant and is said to be in the first house. If the sun is in Aries 8° instead, it has already been carried up above the horizon, out of the first house, by the rotation of the whole heavens, and is said to be in the twelfth.

There are two points of view here, both of which are used in astrology, and it is very easy for the novice to confuse them. Thus the planets themselves move through the zodiac, as the sun from Aries 8° to Aries 10° or Aries 12° in the illustration above. Hence they can be said to move from house to house, counterclockwise, through the zodiac. However, the turning of the whole heavens, in which these planets are moving, is a speedier motion, and one more primary in human experience, so that in many respects it is more correct to say that the houses put the planets in their horoscopic places. This means that the houses, aided by the signs, distribute the dynamic planetary indications.

Finding the place of the planets according to their positions in the signs by geocentric longitude is very simple, because the time of a given event or birth represents a fractional part of the twenty-four hours from the midnight to midnight, or noon to noon, of the ephemeris giving the planetary positions. Each planet will have moved a proportionate section of the whole distance it covers in the particular twenty-four hours. The procedure in determining this can be illustrated by example.

If an infant is born in London at 4:00 A.M., Greenwich mean time (generally abbreviated as G.M.T.) and if an ephemeris is used that shows the planetary positions for midnight at Greenwich, the calculating formula is as follows: four hours is to twenty-four hours as the required motion of the planet is to its total motion. If the birth takes place on one of those few days of the year in which the sun's motion is an exact sixty minutes, the calculation for the horoscopic position of that one of the ten "planets" would depend on the proportion:

$$4 : 24 :: x : 60$$

Since four hours is a sixth of the twenty-four, the motion of the sun, in arriving at its place in the chart, is one-sixth of the sixty, or ten minutes of longitude. This is added to

HORARY ASTROLOGY

the position of the sun as given in the ephemeris for the midnight at which the given day begins.

Of course, the relationship is not always as simple. In consequence, it is necessary to know how to use simple proportion, or the "rule of three." In the proposition above the product by multiplication of the outside figures (that is, the extremes) is always equal to the product by multiplication of the inside figures (the means). When only three of the four quantities are available, the two that constitute either the means or extremes are multiplied. This would also be the product of the other two, of which one is missing, and therefore the missing figure is found by dividing the product by the figure which is known. Thus four times sixty is two hundred and forty which, divided by twenty-four, yields ten.

If the G.M.T. of birth or event is 2:00 A.M., the formula is: two is to twenty-four as x is to sixty. Two times sixty is one hundred and twenty which, divided by twenty-four, is five. Obviously two hours out of twenty-four are one-twelfth, and one-twelfth of sixty is the five obtained by this proportion.

In the case of noon tables calculated for the Greenwich or London meridian, the proposition is exactly the same. However, here or in any case where the time shown by the clocks is different from the time of the meridian used for the ephemeris, one must be translated into the other. 4:00 A.M. E.S.T. is 9:00 A.M. in Greenwich Mean Time (usually abbreviated to G.M.T.) and 2:00 A.M. E.S.T. is 7:00 A.M. G.M.T.[1] If the G.M.T. of a significant moment is 3:00 P.M., three out of the twenty-four hours from noon have elapsed, and since three is one-eighth of twenty-four, the answer, in the case of a sun moving sixty minutes a day, would be one-eighth of sixty, or seven and a half degrees. The formula would run in figures:

$$3 : 24 :: x : 60$$

[1] These time adjustments have been discussed at length; see pp. 44 ff.

THE PLANETS

Three times sixty is a hundred and eighty which, divided by twenty-four, yields seven and a half.

Calculation in the case of uneven factors would be quite a puttering matter if done exactly by this straight proportion, and altogether a baffling matter for many people who either are not mathematically minded or else long ago dismissed their mathematics with a sigh of relief on leaving school. The problem might be particularly acute in the case of the moon, which on an average moves thirteen degrees and ten minutes in twenty-four hours. Thus a question might be asked at 5:00 P.M. by G.M.T. and the moon might be moving twelve degrees and twenty-one minutes in the twenty-four hours.[2] This would make the formula, if midnight tables for G.M.T. are used:

$$17h \quad : \quad 24h \quad : : \quad x \quad : \quad 12°27'$$

The multiplying by seventeen hours (though an even number) of twelve degrees and twenty-seven minutes would stop the average hopeful neophyte in his tracks at this point. "How can I ever do that?" he might well remark.

Going back now, and observing the several examples of the astrologer's use of the "rule of three," where the formula is put down in figures, it will be noted that the factor of twenty-four hours always appears. The persistent presence of this twenty-four gave an idea to an unknown genius some generations ago.

"You are always dividing by twenty-four, aren't you?"

"Necessarily!"

"Well, suppose special numbers were to be provided, each of which in a sense is 'predivided' by the twenty-four. Then you would only have a single operation—one multiplication—for your answer."

"That is right!"

The anonymous benefactor of astrology thereupon proceeded to develop a means for calculating this relationship with the greatest simplicity, through special logarithms.

[2] As in the example chart on p. 21.

Logarithms provide a way of multiplying by adding, of dividing by subtracting. Thus, the first formula above ran as follows: 4 : 24 : : x : 60. The multiplication of 4 by 60, and the division of the product by 24, can be repeated by regular logarithms (such as appear in Chamber's *Mathematical Tables* and similar general compilations) quite easily. The logarithm for four is 0.6020600, and for sixty is 1.7781513. The sum of these is 2.3802113, which is the logarithm for two hundred and forty. Subtracting the logarithm for twenty-four, which is 1.3802112, the result is 1.0000000, which is the logarithm for ten, or the answer required. (The slight differences here in the seventh decimal place will disappear if eight-point logarithms are used.)

The new and special logarithms, which provide the "pre-division" of every number by the twenty-four factor, are known as "diurnal[8] proportional logarithms," and are found in practically every ephemeris. By their use it would have been only necessary to add the logarithm for four hours to the logarithm for sixty minutes in order to obtain the logarithm for ten minutes. Thus 0.77815, added to 1.38021, yields 2.15836, which gives ten minutes by these tables.

Since hours and degrees both divide into sixty minutes, the logarithms may be used for either, and so for both of them together. They are only printed up to fifteen degrees (or hours) and fifty-nine minutes in the older tables, in order to cover the extremes of the moon's possible motion, but the more modern ephemerides provide the full twenty-three hours and fifty-nine minutes needed when calculation is made consistently from a previous noon or midnight.

It is a waste of time to use logarithms in so simple a proportion as illustrated above, but in the other case, with an interval of seventeen hours from midnight when the moon during the day moves twelve degrees and twenty-one min-

[8] The word "diurnal" refers to the twenty-four factor.

THE PLANETS

utes, the logarithmic method is the most simple of all. The logarithm for the hours from midnight is .14976, and for the moon's daily motion is .28504. Added, they give .43480, showing eight degrees and forty-nine minutes of movement by the moon from its position at midnight to its place in the astrological wheel.[4]

The accuracy of the results obtained in this fashion by logarithms can always be double-checked fractionally by using a simple fraction increased or decreased by a fraction of itself, but this procedure may not lie within the range of skills possessed by the average adult. He will have to rely on ordinary carefulness, and a repetition of his operations, for surety of work. In the case of planets which move very slowly, such as Saturn advancing perhaps five minutes in twenty-four hours, or Jupiter twice that far, the use of ordinary proportion, as illustrated in the sun's case, is quite the easiest technique.

The best practical method for determining the planetary positions in an astrological chart is to use logarithms for the moon always, and also for Mercury, Venus, the sun and Mars when the proportionate distance cannot be approximated without uncertainty. This degree of accuracy is more than adequate for normal horary interpretation.

Actually the greatest source of confusion on the part of a neophyte, or one who attempts the mathematics of a horoscope at infrequent intervals, is a failure to remember that the calculation of the wheel is directly from local mean time, after the sidereal time has been corrected for longitude, while the determination of the planetary positions requires a translation of the local or standard hours and minutes into the corresponding Greenwich mean time!

The planets used in astrology consist of ten bodies, or the sun and moon with the eight best known solar satellites

---

[4] Computations from both noon and midnight for check on each other may show discrepancies due to the moon's nonuniform motion during any given day or to rounded numbers in the tables, but they are inconsequential.

other than the earth itself. These have symbols, which are used in all horoscopes, and they are taken in the order of particular astrological significance, primarily based on their relative swiftness of motion.

The names and the symbols employed are as follows:

> ☽ Moon
> ☿ Mercury
> ♀ Venus
> ☉ Sun
> ♂ Mars
> ♃ Jupiter
> ♄ Saturn
> ♅ Uranus
> ♆ Neptune
> ♇ Pluto

Of the planets, Uranus is known also as Herschel, and Pluto has the additional symbols ♇ and ♂.

These planets have some very important individual meanings in the more detailed stages of horary practice, but initially—in every consideration—they have equal status, with no particular distinction one from the other. It is unnecessary for the present to give attention to their individual implication, although their symbols must be known in order to place them in the chart. One factor of immediate importance, however, involves the later implication of a single one among them.

In addition to the fact that an astrological chart must be radical, by having more than three or less than twenty-seven degrees of a sign rising, an important "consideration before judgment" involves Saturn. This planet was regarded as particularly evil by the ancients, and the rule is that a horary chart should not ordinarily be judged, or analyzed, when Saturn is found in the seventh house.[5] As has been explained, the seventh house rules the astrologer, or the person who is asked to judge the chart, and the presence of Saturn here is apt to impede or cloud his judgment. It is only safe to proceed if this particular placing of the planet has special significance, through revealing an extra consideration in the matter, or affording a pertinent and important description of the given issue.

The signs of the zodiac have no immediate individual import in horary astrology, in the most simple forms of its practice, but instead merely identify the cusps of the houses, and the positions of the planets. However, they not only give these locations in a mathematical sense, but they distribute the significance of relationships among the planets and the houses because they establish the former as the all-important rulers of the latter, based upon the underlying function of the planets as lords of the signs. The planetary rulerships of the signs are as follows and it will be noted that, except in the case of the sun and moon, each planet is put in charge of two.

Cancer ♋	☽ Moon	
	Sun ☉	♌ Leo
Gemini ♊	☿ Mercury ☿	♍ Virgo
Taurus ♉	♀ Venus ♀	♎ Libra
Aries ♈	♂ Mars ♂	♏ Scorpio
Pisces ♓	♃ Jupiter ♃	♐ Sagittarius
Aquarius ♒	♄ Saturn ♄	♑ Capricorn [6]

[5] A possibly necessary warning in popular or superficial astrology.

[6] The newly discovered planets, Uranus which has been available for astrologers since 1781, Neptune which has been located since 1846, and Pluto, which was identified in 1930, have been assigned rulership, giving Uranus to Aquarius, Neptune to Pisces, and Pluto to Scorpio. These rela-

The planet which rules the sign found on the cusp of the house is the lord of that house. This holds whether the cusp lies at the beginning point of a sign, or in the middle, or at the very end, and to the same degree. Attention already has been directed to the fact that it is not the sign or signs lying within the boundaries of a house that are most significant in reference to the house in question, but rather that the one of them in which the cusp itself lies is the salient factor in analysis.

The affairs of the houses in horary astrology are almost entirely distributed by the relationships among them, as this is patterned through the planets which become their lords. Thus if the ruler of the ascendant, which indicates the querent, is favorably related to the lord of the tenth, which indicates the authority under which the querent operates, the indications are that the fears he entertains—to the effect that he will lose his job—are probably quite unfounded. Horary interpretation may seldom be as simple as this, in any literal fashion, but in an appreciable percentage of cases it can hardly be said to be any more difficult.

Horary astrology primarily requires (1) an ability to calculate the chart itself, and then (2) a fluid mastery of the meaning and implication of the houses, accompanied by (3) a knowledge of the planets as rulers of the houses and (4) a grasp of the special relations among the ten bodies in question. These planetary relationships in astrology are

tions are very significant in natal astrology, in reference to those phases of human experience which parallel the discovery of the planets, and the skilled practitioner will sometimes make use of these rulerships in horary art. However, the secret of success in the use of a horary chart is the absolutely rigorous use of fixed rules and practices, since it is entirely a symbolical art, and it is recommended to the newcomer, or occasional practitioner, that he hold at all times to the older so-called Chaldean rulerships, given in this tabulation.

known as aspects. Five of them are normally used in horary practice, but many more are employed in the natal art, and so sometimes are given a supplementary role in the more intricate horary procedures.

The conjunction is the case where two planets are found at the same point in the zodiac. This means that they have the same celestial longitude, as this is expressed in terms of signs, degrees and minutes. After the conjunction, the most important major aspect is the opposition, when two planets lie exactly across from each other in the zodiac.

The other three of the aspects utilized at all times by horary astrology are established by the positions of planets at those points of the zodiac which become sensitive to each other because they divide the circle on the basis of inscribed equilateral figures. Thus two planets are in trine when they rest at points where the circle is divided into three equal parts, or where they lie a hundred and twenty degrees from each other. Planets are square when they mark two of the four points of an inscribed regular square, or are found ninety degrees from each other. They are sextile when they emphasize two adjacent points of an inscribed regular hexagon, or stand sixty degrees apart.

An aspect in actual practice will seldom be exact. Hence, the question of orbs arises, particularly in natal astrology. How far away from the precise points of aspect can two planets lie, and still be considered to have this relationship?[7] Orbs never enter the picture in the first stages of horary analysis, since every initial consideration is of planetary movements into or out of relationship. The problem

[7] The most generous allowance is 17° when the sun is involved, 12°30′ if the moon is one of the planets in the aspect, and 10° for all other cases. More conservative practice limits all orbs of aspect to 6°.

is not so much the strength of aspect as the time of its maturity. When do the two planets consummate the relationship? This is the important clue to the significant moment, relative to a given problem or issue, and so is the basis for the horary timetable to be presented at a later point.

In horary astrology the opposition and the square are classified as "bad aspects," marking afflictions in the horary figure. The trine and sextile represent "good aspects," and are interpreted as uniformly favorable. The conjunction is taken as "good" also in horary practice, up to that point where the individual meanings of the planets become significant, at which time its favorable or unfavorable nature is determined by the particular case.

One basic rule of exceptional importance in horary astrology is that no planet can ever move out of one sign, into another, to make an aspect of significance in reference to the given question or matter for which the chart is erected. This rule gives rise to the next, or the third, of the preliminary "considerations before judgment." The moon, because of its swiftness of motion, and its consequent significance in indicating the superficial focus of a given issue, must make some major aspect to at least one of the other planets before it leaves the sign in which it lies at the moment of issue. Otherwise the chart is not valid because the moon is "void of course."[8] There is then a definite lack of pertinent dynamic in the situation, and judgment will be unsound unless the static nature of the circumstances have a special meaning in the given case.

It has been pointed out that the chart should not be judged if Saturn is found in the seventh house. Many prac-

[8] An example of this is provided by the specimen horary chart on p. 21.

THE PLANETS

titioners also refuse to judge if Saturn afflicts the lord of the seventh. This can now be seen to mean that if Saturn is in the seventh house, or is in square or opposition to that other planet which becomes the lord of the house, it may be unsafe to proceed.[9]

Three additional factors, commonly employed in horary astrology, and in many respects treated as planets, are explained at a later point in the text, but their names and symbols are as follows:

⊕ Part of Fortune
☊ Dragon's head
☋ Dragon's tail

The calculation of the first of these is a special technique which will be given in connection with the explanation.[10] The dragon's head is the moon's ascending or north node, which is found in the ephemeris, and its position is corrected in the same way as that of a planet. The tail lies at a point in the zodiac exactly opposite the head. These two nodes are used by horary astrologers in the regression to natal methods.[11]

---

[9] This expansion of the warning is not recommended in modern practice. It represents the medieval perspective, which at its worst and perhaps in an instinctive compensation for the greater number of planets discovered and found effective today but unknown and ineffective then, is always hovering at the edge of indications regressing to infinity. The whole matter of "affliction" and "bad aspects" has by now been found an oversimplification of little help in the broadened horoscopy.

[10] See p. 280.

[11] See p. 363.

Chapter Six

PHRASING THE QUESTION

Horary astrology has been developed primarily for answering definite inquiries—that is, for direct problem-solving—although it is equally useful for gaining an insight into the probable outcome of specific events, as well as for determining, in advance, the most advantageous time for starting things. These other adaptations of the horary technique run much closer to natal astrology than the analysis of questions, but they are quite distinct from ordinary horoscopy. They are a legitimate branch of horary art, which must be outlined before the conclusion of the present volume. Horary procedures fundamentally deal with the queries of people in trouble, however, and the most important step in proceeding to the details of interpretation, following upon a recognition of the proper time for which the chart will be erected—a matter already covered at length—is to make sure that the inquiry is properly phrased.

Thus a romantic adolescent might come to some young horary astrologer with the question, "Does Mary love me?" This enthusiastic neophyte might glance at the clock, and then proceed to erect a chart for the time and place at which the inquiry was made. With the chart erected, his next problem would be to determine its meaning; which really is impossible because there is no astrological configuration that specifically and always means "being in

PHRASING THE QUESTION 123

love." Venus, which from time immemorial in astrology has taken on the aspect of the goddess, and like Aphrodite herself has had a very particular connection with romance, might show a trine aspect to Jupiter, which by an equally venerable tradition indicates expansion. This could suggest the expansiveness of love, but would it apply to Mary? The boy who asked the question was caught up in something of this sort, otherwise the inquiry would not have been made. Mary may well be "in love," since at her age she may be presumed to gravitate around that state of feeling with a fair regularity and an even variety, but is her kittenlike affection directed towards this eager soul awaiting astrology's answer?

It is obvious that innumerable questions cannot be answered by a horoscope. Thus the query, "What is the price of sugar?", or, "What is the weight of my new automobile?" are wholly beyond the scope of stellar art. The fact which goes unrealized, often by practitioners who have used astrology for many years, is that at root no reply can be given to queries concerning simple static facts. An astrological chart works, after all, because it gives a measurement of human events parallel to the movements of the heavenly bodies. Since the measure is provided by motion, what is measured must be, psychologically if not actually, likewise a matter of moving or action. This ultimately comes down to the fact that what may be determined by horary astrology is never more than the result of act or decision. To ask the question, therefore, "What is Mr. Smith's financial rating?" is silly, but the query, "Will Mr. Smith be able to finance the venture?" is quite legitimate. Moreover, the latter inquiry is something that can be charted with high accuracy if the rules are observed.

The young man who wanted to know about Mary's love really desired to learn whether Mary would go to the senior prom with him, or perhaps whether she would wear his fraternity pin. Nothing in life is understandable, in any dependable or practical sense, except in the form of the action it takes, or can take. Astrology is successful because it holds to this basic realization, and thereupon measures things in the terms either of what they do, or what they might do. This is as true of natal astrology as the horary branch, because the measuring of a life represented by the birth horoscope is simply a charting of that progression of acts and decisions which, when taken collectively, constitute the given personality.

It is essential in horary astrology, therefore, to make sure that all questions are phrased in the terms of action or motion. When this is done, whether explicitly or implicitly, it is possible to read the chart. It is true that the older practitioners do not bother to get this dynamic factor down in words, but it is obvious that the young astrologer should have any problem so stated that he will be able to interpret the horoscope when it is cast. The most simple and wisest rule of horary art, in connection with the phrasing of the question, is to insist that it be expressed along the following lines: what will be the result of doing thus and so, or of making such and such a decision, or of taking or holding this or that attitude? If necessary the inquiry should be reworded, until it definitely asks about the consequences of something. A more general expression that is always useful in this connection is, "What will be the outcome of. . . ?"

PHRASING THE QUESTION

The whole analysis in natal astrology concerns the outcome of a person's persistent effort to continue to exist. Everything else is subordinate to this fundamental urge-to-life, and the nativity techniques are constructed accordingly. In the subordinate forms of horary astrology—dealing with the probable end of an enterprise already started, or of an event which already has taken place; or with the election in advance of the most advantageous time to do something—there is no problem of a question to be phrased. However, there is the assumed if not expressed necessity to act in a certain way. The clearest possible analysis, even in the case of an event definitely occurring, or a situation already precipitated, is gained when the querent approaches any matter concerning him on the basis of the results he may expect from his own continued act or reaction. Thus a business is started. The chart might be erected for the moment of opening the doors, to give an idea of the probable course of events, but by the same token a partner or the proprietor might ask the astrologically sound question, "What will be the consequences of continuing according to our present program?"; or from another view, "What will be the results of changing our plans in such and such a fashion?" The only difference between an attack upon a given problem through the fundamental horary technique, and an analysis of the situation through events which actually have taken place, is that the former method is more fluid. It provides an approach to the problems of existence entirely from the view that they can be controlled through proper and adequate decision.

The horoscope for a definite occurrence is always valid, disclosing the structure of relations under which subsequent events will operate. It is in the same category as the natal chart, where the basic pattern of the life continues, or is effective, no matter what a native may do with his opportunities. Thus a natal wheel provides the pattern of success, but when the individual is not successful it presents the same general set of relationships as an equally convenient pattern for the failure. The horoscope for a given event, or even the chart for a time selected in advance, operates in the same way. It reveals the pattern which holds throughout the given chain of events while what is done with these events still remains a matter of choice. Life always supports free will, or sustains difference, even as it maintains the underlying order. The great strength of basic horary art—the analysis of questions—is therefore to be found in the fact that the particular outcome of definite choices is made the guide in approaching the problems of any given situation, thereby building upon free will rather than limitation. All this leads to the most important principle of horary astrology, which may well be put in italics for emphasis.

The state of affairs indicated by a horary chart holds only as long as the act or choice, which it measures, goes unchanged.

In other words, a man may ask the question "What will be the results of closing the business deal?", and the astrological wheel may show a period of two years marked by great financial difficulty, inharmony and general frustration. All this is predicated, however, on the fact that he actually does go ahead. It is his equal privilege to turn down the proposition, in which case nothing revealed by the chart will apply. The only exception to this is a result

PHRASING THE QUESTION

of the general concordance in human events, or what may more simply be described as the basic orderliness of the universe. The fact that a man may be contemplating such a deal shows that his own prior acts and decisions, together with the pattern of his life, have drawn him to the threshold of this possibility. This means that some general situation of this sort has come to the forefront of his experience, and must take some particular form.

The man's true problem is to find out how to use the general development constructively, or to apply the drift in his affairs towards the attainment of whatever he may desire. The ultimate purpose of horary astrology—of all astrology for that matter—is to assist him in doing this. The horary chart is exceptionally helpful because it reveals the specific outcomes of very definite acts and decisions. The fact that it also reflects the general state of affairs, to a very considerable degree, is no less important, but this is never its main function. The determination of the secondary reflection of a querent's circumstances is the basis of many details worked out in the technique, but these are not dependable except in the narrow context; they are at no time an adequate substitute for the natal horoscope. The primary light upon the immediate problem is the first consideration, at all times, and now it must be realized that this direct implication of a horary wheel is wholly tentative, or is entirely contingent upon free will and choice. It is in this respect that the true horary figure differs most radically from the natal horoscope.

The horary chart, in its most simple and direct form, not only answers any questions as to the results of act or decision, but it ordinarily does so in the case where the querent has a definite option of decision or act. If he likes the consequences revealed by the horoscope, he is able to go ahead, whereas if he does not like them, he may refrain from proceeding and so escape them entirely. Actually the inquiries in horary astrology may be divided into two sharply distinguished groups. They may be classified as these normal or "option questions" on the one hand— where there is complete freedom either to proceed or not —and the less common "orientation questions," where there is no option in any direct sense but where the problem rather is to make the best of affairs which have been given a special form or set by action already consummated, or by decision already made.

Thus the inquiry, "What will be the result of going to Florida for the winter?," is a simple option matter. If the outlook in Florida seems disadvantageous, the querent can go to California, stay at home, or turn to any other alternative. An orientation question is the case when a querent telephones his astrologer excitedly to say, "I lost my temper and resigned my job; where am I going to go now?" When this latter query is twisted around into its better form of "consequences" it becomes, "What are the results of quitting my position?" There is no direct option here because, even if the outcome shows up as bad, the individual can hardly undo his act. If he is sorry he lost his temper, and is of a mind to go back to his ex-employer, to make his peace and get his job back, then the question is properly an option one and should take the form, "What are the consequences of asking for my position again?" In this attack upon the problem he has a real choice because he may not like the results of going back, perhaps to be treated

PHRASING THE QUESTION

differently because of a certain psychological advantage lost in burying his pride now or in displaying his hot-headedness before; and so decide not to do so.

In every case where an individual has already acted or decided, but where he has a well-defined idea of something to do as a result—such as a move for the rectification of affairs—the situation really involves an option query, and the question should be put in that form. The most effective horary procedure is to handle every inquiry in the question form if possible, and to put this question on the basis of an option whenever it can be done. The advantages are obvious. When the probable results are adverse, the projected move can be abandoned, and another or alternative attack planned to meet the difficulty. When a new suggestion is well worked out in mind, a separate horary figure can be used for the analysis of its possibilities.

All human knowledge at base is derived from a process of trial and error. Only when experience is generalized, so that principles can become the basis of expectation, is abstract analysis or the purely intellectual judgment a possibility. For most of life, the way to wisdom is experiment. This means that if something is suggested, man's impulse is to try it, and see what happens.

It is not only legitimate but distinctly advisable to use horary astrology as an adjunct to the trial-and-error solution of human problems, or to the experimental efforts made for the enrichment of human lives. This suggests that the option question is the soundest technique at root. The purpose of the horary chart in the case of the orientatation question, however, is not to say "yes" or "no" to a projected course of act or choice, but instead is to reveal what changes in the situation must be utilized for the querent's benefit. The result is some rather distinct differences in technique, which will require special exposition, but for the major part the consideration may rest upon the option type of inquiry, as the most effective guide to conduct in the normal problems of everyday life. The next step, in employing this simple analysis of free choice, is the classification of the various possible forms of options in experience. This must be preceded by a necessary and long intervening chapter, completely outlining the distribution of all experience, as such, through the houses.

Chapter Seven

LOCATING THE QUESTION

There are two invariable rulerships in a horary chart, to which reference already has been made. The first house of the wheel as it is erected always represents the person who asks the question, or the general situation responsible for the inquiry, and the seventh house, among its other functions, always rules the astrologer. These indications have to be remembered, although in many actual cases no direct use may be made of either. Sometimes a person able to erect and interpret his own horoscope will both put and answer a query, and in this case he will find the chart referring to himself in two respects. As the one who asks the question, he is shown by the first house, and as the one answering or judging it, he is described in the seventh. Here is one of the oddities of horary art. The way in which any consideration may be divided up or distributed through horary astrology, at times almost without end, is an important factor in the astrologer's very great powers of analysis.

Life is an extraordinarily complex phenomenon, no matter how it is viewed philosophically, and any problem that arises in the course of experience must be seen in a pertinent distinctness from surrounding or allied phenomena, if a proper course of action is to be determined. Some questions may have a number of different facets or phases, but all these may be located and handled separately in the horary chart. However, the whole consideration must be kept in mind, and it must be seen in terms of the situation under which both the querent and the astrologer operate, in order to guard against the "psychological fallacy," i.e., thinking about the difficulties of one person in the perspective of another. The first and seventh houses are of primary significance at all times, although often in the background.

One of the most valuable rules of procedure in horary astrology, adopted in the practice of many experts, is to keep the focus of the matter of inquiry out of the first house whenever possible, and to avoid placing it in any other angle if this can be done. The elimination of all four angles is impractical in better than half of the questions asked any particular astrologer, but the effort to carry the focus on into the subordinate houses is an aid in getting the best possible distribution of each problem as it is brought to analysis. Probably it will be well for a beginner to regard the first house as that one in which a question is put only when it cannot be located anywhere else. This would dramatize the fact that, when a question is at focus on the ascendant, not all the factors involved have been taken into consideration; resulting in a basic inadequacy of perspective. The querent, of course, as a person, is described by the first house, irrespective of the particular questions asked.

The first step in any judgment by a horary chart is to locate the question or pertinent problem in the house which describes its focal potentiality. Little is accomplished, by and large, if the given difficulty is regarded as a sort of "person" shown at the ascendant, and if the chart is then interpreted after the fashion of a natal horoscope;

LOCATING THE QUESTION

although there are occasions when recourse to this technique is very effective in the hands of a practitioner with sufficient skill. The genius of horary art, however, offers much more simple procedures, producing spectacularly direct results with much less effort in the great majority of possible cases. These require, primarily, a careful tracing out of those chains of relationship in which a given issue has arisen. The laws of horary astrology have to be very strict at this point, but they may be formulated in different ways; and it must be recognized in fairness that there are many horary astrologers with successful practices who will differ from the point of view adopted here, and who will succeed in obtaining accurate results. The present method, rapidly coming into favor throughout the astrological world, has the benefit of initial simplicity, and also of a standardization of technique which contributes to accuracy, ease of instruction and a common interchange of results; i.e., it is more "scientific" in the basic sense of that word.

The principal school of thought, among the horary astrologers who do not employ the focal distribution suggested by Lilly's original work and now expanded in the technique presented by this text, makes use of the general mental synthesis developed by the natal astrology of an earlier generation. The fact that this method dominated the horary field a generation ago, and that it does produce results, suggests the question, "Why wasn't this general practice recognized, and its canons adopted for everyone?" The answer is that the conclusions resulting from a completely subjective synthesis, or "intuition," are apt to be erratic, since they are dependent upon a pattern of intangibles in the temperament. To put the matter another way, while use is made of the mathematical operations of a pure astrology at base, in this method a psychic or intuitive factor is involved, which means that horary art in such an instance, to varying degrees, is removed from the category of a science and made more an intuitive operation, such as lies outside the possibility of scientific test.

To keep astrological practice within the limitations of a true science, the cycles in the heavens must be seen as no more than convenient norms for a measurement of events on earth. A horary chart is a pattern of relationship as this is identified in or through some person or active factor definitely concerned in a particular situation. To the degree that this relationship to the querent, or to the issue for which a horoscope is cast, can be traced through the distribution of the houses, the horary chart will operate scientifically. By "scientifically" at this point is meant no more than that any one competent investigator—astrologer, student or critic—will arrive at practically the same judgment as any other.

The first of the rigid rules in an adequately "scientific" horary art is that a horoscope is not dependable if it is erected for a question or issue concerning which the querent or proponent has no responsibility, or no direct concern. Thus the overly enthusiastic or hopeful soul who makes a chart for the altogether general question, "What will be the outcome of the present war?," must be placed in the same category as the psychic who consults an invisible guidance, the spiritualist who goes into a trance, or the fortune-teller who uses any other psychological mechanism as the basis for prognosticating the outcome of remote affairs. This is not denying the value of a genuine seership, nor refusing to admit its spectacular validity in the occasional case, but is the necessary recognition that

LOCATING THE QUESTION

horary astrology is something of quite a different sort. Carrying the principle a step further, this means that a horary chart cannot be regarded as scientifically dependable when used in connection with any matter about which the given individual is unable to do anything.

As has been pointed out at the beginning, and cannot be reiterated too often, astrology operates because it takes advantage of the general concordance in a single and self-contained system of energy, that is, correspondences between action or movement at one place and independent but corresponding action or movement in another place. In this proposition of war outcomes—which is the sort of widely generalized inquiry always springing into mind among the neophytes of astrology—the newcomer might well ask, "Suppose the ruler of a country, who has full responsibility in making or terminating hostilities, propounds such a question?" Horary astrology can then operate successfully, and accurately. The query becomes, "What would be the result of my taking this given action?," and the potentialities of the situation, as it took form in the experience of the ruler, would be revealed by the resulting figure.

Much thinking about astrology is muddled to a serious extent because the relationships of acts and choices are traced out on too specific or literal a level of facts. Thus a man in financial difficulties might face eviction from his home, and ask an astrologer what the results would be of his latest attempt to avoid such a crisis. The interpretation of the resulting horary chart depends entirely upon the meaning of events to the querent. If his problem is one of relief from the pressure of this issue, an extension of time in which to meet his obligations would be no different from receiving the money enabling him to pay the amount due, or a part of it sufficient to satisfy the immediate demand. The actual result in any one of these possible developments in his situation would be the same, namely, relief from pressure.

On the other hand, the center of interest in this case might be pointed entirely to the permanent solution of the difficulty. Subconsciously, if not consciously, the querent might wish to escape a complex of relations which continually produces issues of this sort. When he has not been harassed one way it has been another, so that the actual loss of his home might contribute to such circumstances as would be, in roundabout fashion, the answer to his desire. This would mean a train of events, of course, that would leave him neither homeless nor embarrassed.

Thus his purchase of the home might have been under an arrangement whereby the difference between the actual cash he has had to pay each month as owner, for purchase or maintenance, and the much larger outright rental he formerly paid, as merely a lessee, might have at length cancelled out his "down payment" in cash, made when he became an "owner." If he can now drop the proposition without facing any deficiency judgments or penalties, he actually loses nothing in "losing" the house, but instead gains a psychological freedom he did not have the acumen to seize. Simply by giving up his "title," and considering that he has been paying rent, withal some of it all at once in advance, he stands in no different position than had he paid his "rent" monthly in larger amounts under the more simple arrangement. This would be an extreme case, but it illustrates the general principle. Successful horary astrology at all times is dependent on an accurate tracing out of these lines of relationship in a situation, according to their actual importance or implication in experience.

The basic meanings of the houses have been given in Chapter Four, and these must now be expanded according to their potential ramification in everyday human re-

LOCATING THE QUESTION

lationships. Every possible line of connection, of course, begins at the first house, which shows the person asking a question or the situation raising an issue or precipitating a crisis. If the querent inquires about his home, the question is located in the fourth house; if he wants to know about his wife, the consideration centers at the seventh; or if the query concerns problems in his general business situation, the pertinent house is the tenth. These simple relationships involve no difficulty at all. A letter is placed in the third, a child in the fifth, a servant in the sixth, a friend in the eleventh, and so on.

Many actual relationships are much more complex, however, and have to be traced out step by step, through a simple procedure which has acquired its name from the old game, ring-around-a-rosy. Thus a typical question might be, "What will be the result of the present treatments for the illness of my cousin's baby?," an unusual query which becomes pertinent because a line of blood relationship has developed a considerable intimacy, and a consequent responsibility. It is necessary to trace the connections from the querent in detail to get a dependable answer. Therefore he is asked, "What do you mean by cousin?" He explains, "She is the daughter of my father's sister," which provides the following steps in locating the question. The querent is taken in the first house, hence the querent's father is found in the fourth. The father's sister is the third of this fourth, which is the sixth house of the original chart. The sister's daughter is the fifth of this sixth, or the initial tenth house. The child who is sick is the fifth of this fifth, which is the second of the basic chart. The matter of the sickness is the sixth of this last fifth, or the seventh of the original wheel. The question of this special sickness, therefore, is located in the seventh rather than sixth house of the primary figure.

It is to be noted, in tracing out these house relationships in astrology, that the counting is according to the ancient rather than modern fashion, and that the last number of one sequence is the first of the next. Thus the father of the querent is ruled by the fourth house of the first. This is not the fourth "from" the ascendant, which would make it the fifth house. In similar fashion, the sister of the father was the third of that fourth, and not the third from it, or was taken as the sixth and not the seventh. The most widely familiar example of this method of counting is found in the Bible in connection with the crucifixion of Jesus, when the statement is made that He rose from the dead "on the third day." His death took place on Friday, and His resurrection on Sunday, so that the modern way of reporting this would be to say that He rose on the second rather than third day. It is exceptionally important for the beginner to watch himself in using the ring-around-the-rosy technique, to make sure he does not go one house too far at one or another of his steps.

The purpose of the ring-around-the-rosy technique is not to equip the astrologer for handling bizarre cases, but rather to give him a procedure of orientation by which he can make sure that every situation is reflected in the heavenly cycles with the greatest possible degree of accuracy. If both the person who asks the question and the question itself are established at one place, in the first house, there is hardly the same degree of perspective, or psychological anchorage in the cycles, as occurs when the querent is described at the first, and the question is located somewhere else. When an inquiry has several aspects,

LOCATING THE QUESTION

then additional houses of the horary chart are involved, under the proper location of each, and this distribution provides a further degree of perspective in the great cycles; thereby strengthening the potentialities for an accurate astrological judgment.

The multiple question, in consequence of all this, is desirable rather than the reverse. Thus his client might ask the astrologer, "What will be the results if I apply for the position; if I name the salary I want rather than letting them make an offer; if instead of applying directly I ask my friend to go after it for me?" In this case the querent would be in the first house, and the potential position or opportunity in the seventh. The question of the salary, if this is to be raised as a feature of the application, would be the second of that seventh, or the original eighth. The question of moving through a friend would make the eleventh from the same seventh, or the original fifth, the dynamic point of the opportunity.

A number of details of importance now come up for consideration, and become the real basis of this chapter in contrast with the Fourth. There the houses are seen, more or less, in their simple case, but here they have to be presented in their genius for revealing the individual and exceptional potentiality, or the immediately significant shading of relationship. The newcomer may well ask, "The question above concerned a position, and a man's business is ruled by his tenth; why do you use the seventh?" True, the tenth house rules an individual's social situation in life, which means profession, business, position, or everything except a mere job or undistinguished hard labor. However, it rules these social advantages as they are possessed. When it comes to obtaining a position, this "position" before it is obtained is not an actual social place or prerogative, but only an opportunity, and as such it lies in the seventh.

Similarly, when the position-seeker is operating through a friend, the dynamic in the given case is not the friend (original eleventh) but the opportunity to be grasped (original seventh) as especially carried on to another special point by the ring-around-the-rosy chain of relations. The eleventh house not only rules friends in the static sense of having them (the original eleventh) but rules the use of them, or the development of wholly tentative procedures that seek to develop new or "friendly" ties or connections. In distinctions of this sort it is only necessary to ask the simple question, "What comes first in the given case?" The man is not hunting a job because he has friends; but he is using a friend because he is hunting a job. It is literally true in the particular instance that his friend is not so much his "friend" as an all-important friend of the job-getting potential. Obviously it is impossible, and unnecessary, to anticipate all possible ramifications of relationship in this fashion, but there is much that should be put down, out of horary art's rich tradition of successful practice, by way of detailed and valuable light on the more speciffc significance of the houses.

The First House

The first house is the general situation in the given specific case, or it is the totality of everything that cannot be traced out more definitely, or "distributed" in terms of

LOCATING THE QUESTION

some immediately pertinent problem. Hence it is the "masses" in an older literature. It rules everything of which there is any appreciable doubt, or over which there is real concern, prior to the more definite location of the matter and its relationships as a step towards understanding; that is, before the resolution of difficulty in the form of some action that can be taken or of some choice that can be made. Thus the first house never indicates anything about which there is genuine certainty.

In natal interpretation this means the personality, which is not a static or fixed and limited entity but rather is a living and changing potentiality, or is human character as fundamentally unpredictable except in those few given or known chains of relationships which come to common attention. In horary astrology this means the issue of the moment, or that focus of perplexity in the mind which makes a horary chart possible.

One of the most vital developments in astrological opinion during the past century has been given all too little attention by recent writers and teachers, with the result that many newcomers approach these techniques with a complete misapprehension of the powers and limitations of horoscopic analysis. Also, critics of astrology often concern themselves over what is really old straw left from the threshing of astrological theories a generation or more ago. Most fundamentally this is the question whether the stellar art is magic or science, and it comes down to the question whether its normal employment is for the purpose of bringing freedom or limitation to everyday experience. Many astrologers will still hold the idea that their task is to provide the determining factor in all judgment, rather than the supplementary agency necessary for intelligent act and choice in the exceptional case. They fail to understand that their true service begins with the appearance of definite problems or crises, such as extend the relations and potentials of a given issue out and beyond the resources of normal intellectual capacity.

Science solves problems in order to enlarge human experience, or to make it possible for man to meet his more primitive difficulties by dismissing them almost wholly to automaticity. Science is untrue to itself if it merely holds man to the continual repetition of the procedures carried through an original scientific investigation, or does not constantly liberate him for meeting larger challenges as he expands his interest and increases his skills. Astrology is definitely unscientific if it puts men in bondage to its routines, making them afraid to move except under the "proper influences." It most certainly is a part of the modern intellectual age in its graduation from magical practices—the sense of continual necessity to make compromises with the environment at every step of life—when it equips man with an understanding quite nondependent on any use or knowledge of astrological aspects in what then become the lesser or automatic details of experience. If the greater efforts of a given career gain a real ordering in the light of the cosmic cycles, petty routine partakes of the universal alignment by simple necessity. Man learns from experience, and an astrology which denies him this right to "grow in wisdom," rather seeking to make him "consult the stars" for those acts well within the normal capacities of everyday simple judgment, is pure magic and thus far removed from scientific ideals.

It is a question whether any astrological student attempts to find the proper "planetary influences" for eating, taking a bath, or catching the bus on his way to work; certainly not for going to sleep or getting up. In primitive life, when food had to be hunted and caught, and when these basic operations of existence involved supreme personal risk, astrology might have been of very great service. But as judgment becomes more commonplace, facing

LOCATING THE QUESTION

little or no element of danger in this sense, it is increasingly impossible to find any rectifying guidance in the great heavenly cycles. The whole drama of human evolution is the success of higher organism in dismissing lesser functions to an automatic stage, or in bringing the problems of conscious selection to larger and more social relationships. This principle is clear enough when it comes to such acts of existence as taking a breath, although breathing can become a problem in the exceptional case of asthma, or even sleeping when an individual is troubled with insomnia, and so on. What is not yet revealed clearly in the astrological literature is the unsuspectingly naïve goal still accepted by many astrology students, namely, the attempt to use the planetary aspects and places as a guide in these petty routines of everyday life.

Thus a businessman may be asked to consult his "directions" or erect a horary chart in connection with every business decision he is called upon to make. Here the real distinction between "magic" and "science" is brought out. The former seeks fundamentally to provide an escape from responsibility, the latter attempts to generalize experience, and thus make possible a greater acceptance and administration of responsibility. If magical practices are a substitute for normal human judgment, astrology made the basis for such a substitution is taking a step backward towards medieval superstition. The proof of the matter here is the fact that astrologically conducted enterprises of this sort are often notoriously unsuccessful. The advocates of various "systems" based on astrology, in the field of speculation, do not ever seem to become rich; indeed, not often respectably comfortable. A businessman who attempts to use horary astrology for his normal day-by-day decisions is continually blunting his own capacity for judgment until, despite the aid to his decisions afforded by planetary analysis, the continual depreciation of his judging faculties results in a lesser net competence than if astrology were never brought into the matter at all. The same result follows from an intemperate resort to spiritualism, or to any other form of guidance which diminishes man's normal self-responsibility.

Astrology demands a crisis in experience as the basis for any possible competency in horoscopic analysis, and this has to be created for the purposes of the analysis if it does not exist otherwise. As a result, a natal delineation of the life is of little worth if this life as a whole is not seen against a dramatized potential of some sort. This necessity explains the exceptional effectiveness of reincarnation, for example, as a hypothesis of life's meaning, since it provides a wholly dramatic understratum for the horoscopic survey. The presence of a definite problem is even more vital in horary astrology, since there is not the essentially critical presence of a living continuum provided in the delineation of a native's life. The wise horary astrologer refuses to proceed unless he is consulted on the basis of some real and critical concern of the querent. The first house rules this querent most importantly, therefore, as the continuing source of the problem at hand.

At the beginning of horary inquiry the first house rules the querent, or the basic situation at issue, as representing the entire body of supplementary relationships which do not normally have to be taken into account. It performs its more valuable service in determining the competency of the horoscope, and in ordering the general procedures of horary judgment. This is the first house in the wheel erected for the time of some significant question or act, which is then given its focus at this original ascendant.

The actual or initial astrological map in horary astrology is known as the crisis chart. This "crisis chart"[1] is the normal figure employed by all astrologers since the time

[1] An improved term over "locative chart," employed in the preliminary mimeographed material issued privately in 1930-31.

LOCATING THE QUESTION

of William Lilly, in no whit changed or altered from the standard practice of three centuries. It has been given its special name in order to dramatize the necessity for a concentration of lines of relationship in experience, as the basis for the pattern of potentially co-ordinate relationships in the heavenly cycles. The crisis chart provides the general ground for judgment on the astrologer's part, but it is completely disregarded in its own terms and meaning when it comes to the specific synthesis, or the practical conclusion on one or more given issues at hand.

The exceptions to this are only apparent as in the rare case of a question located in the first house, and the more frequent but special employment of horary art for (1) determining the outcome of actual ventures, or for (2) the "election" of propitious times to act or make a decision. The procedure in these last instances is the same as when the focal house in normal horary judgment lies in this initial "first" or ascending section of the heavens.

When a question is located, according to the principles put down in this chapter, the house ruling the specific project or issue is considered the "first" in the limited case of the immediate judgment to be made. This is illustrated in the sickness of the cousin's baby, located by the ring-around-the-rosy technique in the seventh rather than sixth house of the crisis chart. As a consequence, there may be many "first" houses in any one original wheel, and in order to prevent any confusion over these distinctions, the basic figure just as it stands, but with the house ruling the specific issue becoming the ascendant, is considered a separate wheel for each inquiry, or is the "judgment chart" [2]

[2] An improved term over "distribution chart," employed in the mimeographed material.

for the purpose of each particular problem brought to an astrologer for analysis. The numbering of the houses in the case of the cousin's baby would therefore be as follows:

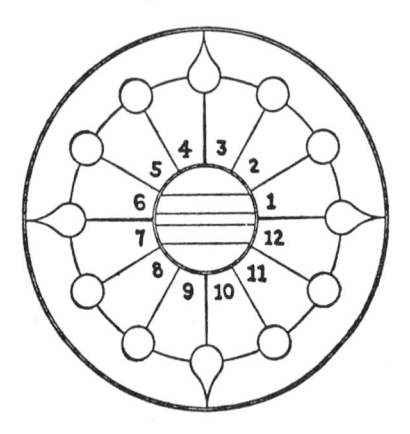

It will be noted that the wheel of the subordinate or judgment chart is not turned around to place the "ascendant" of the particular matter at its familiar position at the left hand. This would mean copying the entire chart. Often, however, a neophyte will find it a help to his perspective if he will turn a wheel around, to put the secondary ascendant in the usual position, even if then he has to look at figures upside down.

Horary astrology exhibits a duplication of nomenclature, with houses numbered from one to twelve in an original wheel, and also in each of the separate considerations for which the original figure is used. Thus the "first" house of the crisis chart in the case of the cousin's baby is also the "seventh" in the judgment chart of the baby's illness, and it might be a "fourth" in a matter concerning business, and so on. This leads to no particular difficulty in actual practice. The distinction is merely in reference, not in any actual division of the heavens, since the ring-around-the-rosy technique never calls for the establishment of a separate wheel; that is, a true horizon corresponding to the cusp of that house in which a problem is located, and other cusps quite at variance with the crisis set. In consequence the terms "first house" and the others may refer to different segments in the equatorial mansions for a given moment, but the context will always identify the reference. In the present chapter, the description of the houses is primarily of those in the crisis chart. Attention is given to the role of the first house in the judgment chart in order to clarify the broader meaning of the astrological "focus," which is the basic indication of any first house anywhere.

The best of the more recent textbooks on horary astrology may seem to give much more specific significance to the first house of the crisis chart than admitted here, but any differences are superficial, due to the greater dependence of a more recent generation of horary astrologers on the modified natal procedures. Thus the question concerning "health" is traditionally assigned to the first house, although when the inquiry becomes specific, as in connection with a definite ailment, it promptly becomes a sixth-house matter. "Health," in other words, is revealed as no more than the general capacity for doing things, or indulging desire, and so is the essence of what has been given a far more incisive analysis in the foregoing pages. General questions regarding location tend similarly to place themselves in the fourth or tenth (sometimes ninth or third) house as they become specific and more definite. The individual practitioner ordinarily needs to watch the first house only to make sure he does not attempt judgment on matters which are not yet sufficiently at a focus in point of crisis, or which are not yet sharpened adequately in their pertinency to the querent, to guarantee a measure of scientific accuracy in his conclusions.

The public attitude which largely prevails towards astrology at the time this book is written is, most unfortunately, a demand for spectacular judgments and procedures, more along the lines of magic-working than any scientific analysis of probabilities. When adequate statistics are used as the basis for a verdict on some particular matter, the expectation will be realized within a high degree of accuracy. Similarly, when astrological judgment is based on an equally careful estimate of probabilities within the limitations of analysis, an equally high accuracy of results may be obtained. However, just as statistically a single instance has no reliability at all, so the specific case in astrology may be at any time a complete exception to general expectation, and the wise astrologer well knows that he can promise nothing but a "probability." He may heighten his reasonable expectation by insisting on a real problem as a ground for any judgment, since the existence of a chain of consequences in experience can usually be co-ordinated to sharper astrological indications. If he attempts to meet the public demand for a magical omniscience, however, he faces inevitable embarrassment; and thereby makes no contribution to the advancement of horoscopy. Actually the fact that astrological judgment fails occasionally to "work" is evidence of the validity of astrology as a science of probabilities, rather than the reverse, and perhaps the best of all possible ammunition for disarming criticism.

Even more serious, in astrology's problem of winning a greater public respect, is the tendency of too many textbooks to contribute to the temptation towards a "showing-

LOCATING THE QUESTION

off" on the part of the practitioner unschooled in the ways of the world. Thus magic-loving people often demand that the astrologer look at a horary chart, and then convince the querent of the wonders of astrology by successfully guessing the nature of the question about to be asked. The degree to which this really can be done is one of the true marvels of astrological practice, but it presents only a degree of probability, such as is reliable to an exceedingly limited extent. While "astrological," it is guesswork based on half the ground materials—that is, the mere horoscopic figure without any account of the situation within which it takes on meaning in the special case of the querent—and it is particularly unhappy guessing because of the variant meaning of words and phrases to different minds. The astrologer who is willing to approach the charlatanry involved in this magic-mongering may remind himself that his "misses" are unimportant, and that his "hits" will be more than compensation because of the extra extent to which he may be able to exploit them, but his attitude is that of the old-time medicine man, and his contribution may be to one of the sad chapters in astrology's considerably checkered career.

Traditional horary astrology has assigned "length of life," as well as "success" or "personal prowess," to the first house. Here again are general considerations which, with the identification of any personal crisis, tend to assimilate themselves into the special focus of other houses. There is a special technique for measuring a life's span of years, but this is part of the natal method in horary art. It will be explained in Chapter Thirteen. Otherwise the consideration is the same as "health." The matter of success in life, or the personal abilities and capacities, is brought down to practical application in the pertinent context of the moment through the judgment chart, but it is also possible to approach the personal dynamic in general fashion through the static evaluation afforded by the natal methods; that is, by an over-all consideration of the querent's state of being as this is focused at the ascendant of the crisis horoscope.

Another type of question often assigned to the first house is whether an individual is at home, whether he is alive, or where he may be found. These matters become secondary to the main statement of any problem put in the dynamic form suggested in the present volume, and whatever salient information is required will be yielded through the proper tracing out of the relationship lines. After all, the idea is not whether a person is here or there, but whether he can be counted on in some certain respect. However, there are special cases when the information is required in the more static relationship, and the details can be worked out through the natal methodology which is postponed for later consideration.

The greatest initial point of confusion among unskillful horary astrologers results from their failure to distinguish properly between the first house and the other eleven. Because of this, the basic purpose of the present chapter is to dramatize the principles involved, so that no student or professional ever need allow mere words or phrases to mislead him. Instead he will always see the dynamic relationship which astrology actually measures, at all times and in all situations; whether it be natal, horary, mundane, or any other branch of the stellar science. Thus the tenth house rules "business," but this means business affairs involving a social group, i.e., living and active relations with other individuals who exercise authority and who demand the assumption of responsibility. A "business" wholly owned by the querent, however, in any matter that con-

LOCATING THE QUESTION

cerns it as a whole, or in any matter that is not one of administering authority over others, is ruled by the first house. This explains why the medieval astrologers placed a "ship at sea" here. The proposition is the same as the case of any enterprise asked about, or considered through any wheel erected for a moment of inauguration, change of policy, and the like.

The Second House

The second house in general represents the fluid and dependable resources of the querent or native, or of the issue at hand, or of the matter inquired about. Most commonly this means personal possessions, such as wealth, money and the like. It may indicate either cash and easily negotiable securities, or else more intangible resources such as rights, royalties, investments and other legal or moral degrees of ownership in whatever may be called on, in one way or another, to produce funds—whether in the normal course of life or in emergencies—and so establish or stabilize credit and provide needed or desired expenditures or disbursements. This does not include realty, land leases, oil and mineral rights, or anything in which ownership is either theoretically permanent or wholly speculative, although the house does show the funds utilized for real estate manipulation and speculative transactions. Primarily it reveals the momentary liquidity of personal finance in general, charting individual means in the rhythm of acquiring them and using or losing them.

There is not only the original second house, but every house around the wheel is a "second" from the one preceding, and as such it will indicate the essential resources or reserve potentiality of whatever the preceding house in question may rule. When the details of an individual's total means become specific, the special rather than original "second house" gives the astrological indications. An example of this, familiar to every astrological student, is the eighth-house designation of "legacies"; that is, money and finances which fundamentally derive from another person. Most particularly the eighth, in this connection, shows the status of a partner's funds, and this has important consequences which must be expanded when that house is examined in detail. If the more personal resources, whether cash or legal interests, are focal in a given problem, they are located in the more specific houses which better describe their full lines of relation. This is on the same principle by which matters focused at the ascendant are moved to other points in the distribution when a more clear-cut analysis is desired. Thus royalties from literary properties would be found, for exact analysis, in the tenth house as the "second" of the ninth—which is the ruler of "books and publications"—and so on.

Because each house is a "second" from the one preceding, it becomes possible to describe the meaning of all houses through a simple sequence of steps in resource around the equator, either from the eastern horizon, or from the four angular points. This affords an introduction to the houses which, at the beginning, is easier to grasp than the more important triangulation of relations presented by this text in Chapter Four, and in consequence it has been made the basis of exposition in the beginner's book of the present series.[3] In the more subtle refinements of horary art this factor of the "resource potential," as the meaning of any house in respect to the one preceding it, permits an almost unlimited ramification of any problem or matter about which inquiry is made. Thus every detail

[3] *How to Learn Astrology,* a smaller manual in this series of textbooks that has preliminary mention in the foreword of the present volume.

LOCATING THE QUESTION

of money as such rests in a second house (whether in a crisis or judgment chart), but this reveals the general question; and the exact potentialities, with a more incisive analysis of the main issue, might need a further distribution.

As a hypothetic case the querent, finding that the given money situation is satisfactory in reference to his main objective, might want to know whether actual cash would be available, or whether he would have to finance some payment in the future. This at once raises the matter of "resources" in a differing aspect, and it is answered out of the next house, or the second from the given "second." Theoretically the regression can be kept up almost indefinitely, as in the further problem: "Then I will get the payment all right, but it will be in the form of a check, and will I be able to cash it without difficulty?," requiring the second house of the "second from the second."

The horary astrologer seldom encounters such an attentuation of straight financial details, but he will sometimes face difficulty because a special house, made focal in some matter by the ring-around-the-rosy technique, has already been used for an astrological judgment. Rather than assuming that the new problem must thereby have an interpretation identical with the one already located in this house, he may have "recourse" by moving on to the next or "second" house, or even to a second or third "next" one not as yet involved in analysis. This particular procedure is of great value in the consideration of multiple questions, covered in Chapter Fourteen.

The medieval astrologers described the practical indication of the second house very cleverly in their phrase "movable things," since it gives an excellent picture of the essential barter idea which not only lies at the root of the house meaning but also represents the very foundation of "money" itself as a social institution. Realty or established "wealth" seems the same thing as money to the modern mind, solely because cash and securities appear particularly stable in an industrial world. However, when it is seen that a dwelling is a dwelling and that a farm remains a farm—under conditions of both depression and inflation, as well as between these extremes—whereas financial exchange reflects every economic fluctuation, much of the difficulty in making the distinction will disappear. The second house fundamentally, at all times, shows "things" which can be put to immediate use. This comprises whatever can be inventoried, dispatched here and there, or traded; hence stocks of goods, supplies and all sorts of loose possessions. Even clothes are included, to the degree they take on social rather than personal significance, or represent financial means; and especially ornaments, jewelry and "personal belongings" in the familiar but somewhat indefinite sense of that term.[4] All these things are the paraphernalia of direct self-strengthening in man's ordinary personal and everyday experience; they are the definitely at-hand adjuncts to a functioning personality.

The older astrology again offers a happy descriptive term in saying the house rules "assistance," which may even include living aids when they are used without any conscious consideration; that is, in a wholly impersonal way, under those circumstances where no supervision or responsibility is required. This is in distinction from servants, shown by the sixth house; from individuals linked in a direct or tête-à-tête co-operation, indicated by the seventh; from the

[4] Note, however, that "clothes" in every utilitarian sense are shown by the sixth house, and that when jewelry or ornaments take on a fetish or talisman quality, or are significant in a special way to personality—other than through their intrinsic or barter value—they are ruled by the fifth.

LOCATING THE QUESTION

specially bred, trained or otherwise-dignified agents of a completely personal sort, such as children or ambassadors, revealed by the fifth; and so on. The assistance received through the second house is always help in the completely literal sense that money, fluid properties and the like are unqualifiedly useful in any given situation. Because of the potential of this "assistance," when it is properly effective, the house has long been said to rule personal liberty. It charts the general total of those resources which enable an individual to choose or act, or to maintain and sustain his own existence, without leaning on any other participant in the social world where he finds himself.

From the deeper or philosophical point of view it reveals basic "reserves" as the means for alternative movement or selection in any self-extrication from a given predicament, and it is very essential that this factor be distinguished from the elements in life which are the more or less mechanical tools and instruments for action and decision; that is, which operate through the application of the energies of self to other things and to other people, or through the "accidents" of an individual's larger situation among other people. These sociomechanical instruments are ruled by the third house when they are inanimate, by the sixth when they are individually organic agencies, by the ninth when they are intellectual instrumentalities, and by the twelfth when they are phases of the social organism or are what are designated popularly as psychic and psychological factors in this same general category. "Instrumentality" in the detached or mediate sense is thus revealed as a cadent-house idea, or as an employment of contributions out of the past, whereas self-resource, in one or another aspect of its non-mediated potentials for experience, will be seen to be the persisting basic significance of the succedent-house group to which this second belongs.[5]

The artificial economic structure of modern civilization is responsible for much astrological confusion over this matter of money, so that it is safer to avoid any mode of description, in phrasing questions or describing problems, which tends to make anything of a financial nature a reality on its own account. Thus a favorite old question with fortune-tellers and their clients is, "Will I be rich?". At once this raises the matter of meaning. What does it imply to be "rich"? Obviously nothing except an unusual personal liberty, an economic freedom which, while certainly a second-house matter, is yet too general an idea to have any real individual significance. The horary astrologer can satisfy his client by dealing directly with this matter of psychic elbow-room, and predict its achievement easily and in a short period of time when the chart gives such an indication. He may then be eminently correct, and yet what seems "riches" from the perspective in a situation of distinct limitation may prove quite the opposite as soon as the client achieves the promised degree of liberty. When that individual proceeds to attempt the further self-expression of which he has dreamed, he finds himself with resources wholly inadequate according to his enlarged view. The astrologer was right superficially, or in an immediate verbal sense; but wrong, according to any real conception of relatively illimitable means.

Major difficulties are apt to arise in connection with the idea of "debt." It must be remembered that debt is credit, even if at a more or less frozen stage, and that, irrespec-

---

[5] The distinction of "past" versus "future," as used for the cadent-succedent indication of the equivalent "social-instrumentality" versus "self-instrumentality," is a much more simple idea, and so is made the basis for general exposition. It has the further merit of avoiding any confusion with the dichotomy of self and group as employed for the spatial rather than temporal "division of labor" provided by the horizon and midheaven meridian, respectively, in the analytical mechanism of the houses as a whole.

tive of which party is debtor or creditor, the situation represents a joint interest in given resources. Here are aspects of financial involvement which only have meaning when they are taken in connection with the more fundamental relations to which they give an instrumentation. The consideration of money as such, or of whatever may be its equivalent for the moment, belongs in the second house of the crisis chart when the immediate issue is a matter of assistance to action or support for decision; as in cases of concern over the amount or availability of individual means, or of worry over some detail in the fluctuation either of value or pertinence in personal possessions or movable goods. Hence the desire to eliminate a money obligation, whether of self to another or vice versa, belongs here whenever it actually is the wish for a release from pressure, or for gaining freedom through a general mobilization of resources. Most cash transactions, however, are indicated by the second house of the judgment chart, as already explained. Thus borrowing or loaning money is a form of partnership, shown by the seventh in exactly the same way as contact with thieves, and the actual funds are then charted by its "second" house, or the eighth of the crisis chart. Any speculative project lies in the original fifth, with the subordinate financial details in the sixth, and so on.

The Third House

The third house charts all elements of pure depersonalized instrumentality in life, including movement or communication in all direct forms, every sort of otherwise personal relationship which fundamentally can be taken for granted, and the total of those normal conveniences of existence which can be described as the automatically employed "tools" of the body or consciousness. As a result the house has far more definite or specific rulerships than any other of the twelve, although the principles from which these are derived are neither many nor complex. Of first importance, at this point, is the sharp line of distinction from every indication of the second house. The "resources" of a given person or situation are elements which essentially are consumed in their use. Money is spent, and valuables are traded. Any accumulation is to develop an increased potentiality for later employment. Irrespective of the form they take, possessions are at all times a manifestation of loss and gain in furthering the specific ends, or countering the specific compulsions, which have come to the forefront of attention in a first-house focus. The third house, by comparison, is adjacent to the fourth angle and has its most direct relationship to end-values, or the emphasis on a sustained rather than a developing side of the given person or matter. The house shows what may be employed in a tool function rather than expended or manipulated on the pattern of money or possessions; i.e., that which in itself is not greatly affected by the use to which it is put.

The most accurate term including all these indications is "environment," or the simple complex in which anything lives or occurs. This excludes whatever takes on specific importance, but reveals the significant whole of everything else in a totality of convenience to life and experience. The house, by revealing this general matrix in which something is expressing itself, charts what medieval writers have designated as "change in general." This means all the moving around which is of no striking or special signifi-

LOCATING THE QUESTION 159

cance, and includes what has always been described as "short journeys," together with the minor adjustments that constitute the normal routine of life and that remain at the background of consciousness because they, of themselves, are never a critical issue. There are continual occasions when the immediate constitution of the environment becomes the basis of a problem, so that questions will be located here no less than in the other houses. However, as in any inquiry, the bringing of analysis to a specific point may tend to place the focus at some further point around the wheel. The problems located here are characteristically the cases of failure in routine operation, disappointment in relatively trivial expectations, and inadequacy in the taken-for-granted performance of some normal function.

In general practice, the simple dynamic idea of tools, with the more static concept of conveniences, will provide the most clear-cut definition of "pure instrumentality" as the third-house indication. This means such obvious agencies as hammers, saws, pencils, pens, pots, dishes, tables, chairs, typewriters, gadgets of all sorts, fans, bells, and what not. It covers such personal things as combs, brushes and appliances for physical comfort, as well as powders or salves, boxes and trunks, and all universally-employed civilized "conveniences." It includes paper and string, bath fittings, towels and soap, electrical appliances, devices for light, heat and ventilation, and practically every detail of the home, except the heavy furnishings and the house itself. It embraces the public utilities such as water, gas, electricity and telephone, the telegraph and radio, the press and periodicals, all of which are widely enough used to be a general convenience, or a commonplace of the environment where they are available. In the same category is ordinary transportation, such as streetcars, busses, rail and air transport—to the degree such can be comprised under the head of commercial facilities accessible to everyone—and also the highways, streets, walks, terminals and loading platforms they must utilize.

At the other extreme, also indicated by this house, are the private conveyances which are wholly taken for granted as individual conveniences, such as automobiles, bicycles, motorcycles, boats, sleds, and so on. An occasional exception to this is an individual's motorcar, when it becomes personalized and sets up a relationship of particular or intimate concern, the psychological interaction such as exists between a rider and his mount. In such a case an automobile, like a horse, would be put in the sixth. A complete exception to the third-house rule of gadgets is found in the case of toys, and the materials of play or paraphernalia of games, which are used to articulate a definite self-expression; thus becoming entirely symbolical in any practical sense, and so always described by the fifth.

The third house includes all other people who participate in the activities of a given context, but who yet are not brought to the focus of attention sufficiently to have any actual personal significance to the querent, or in the immediate issue at hand. Thus the third not only describes the blood relations, apart from parents and children as already pointed out, but it rules all "neighbors" in the sense of other dwellers in the block, boarders in the house, guests in the hotel, tenants in the apartment, and even fellow workers in the office, passengers in the train or bus, and such examples without end. It comprises the special

LOCATING THE QUESTION

aggregation of people in sects, or in a fellow-conformity to particular social habits. In all these cases, however, these people remain shadows, or mere passing details of a general environment, since they have no permanent place in an individual's home background through ties of blood. They must be located in other houses the moment they take on specific importance, since the third rules only the convenience of contact, never the person as such.[6]

It has taken the modern *Gestalt* or organismic psychology to dramatize the fact that an individual commonly permits most factors in his general environment to melt away into the general ground or field of his experience, only bringing out selected characters or details for a place at the forefront of his attention, or in the real circumstances of his situation. What the average non-psychologist fails to realize is that his incidental blood relatives—his brothers and sisters immediately, and then his more remote connections with cousins, aunts or uncles, and the like—are also entirely shadowlike in the normal course of affairs. Thus a brother is "unchangeable," presenting the constancy or dependability of another or "fellow" child in the general environment, as long as he is ruled by the third house. There is always the continuing content of this passive or taken-for-granted side of "self," in these near-ties of family, that prevents any special sharpening of the experience known with other people under equally intimate circumstances. Here are the particular relationships which are dismissed into the general background of self as a contributing factor in maintaining the more active "partnership" potentials at the seventh, and in reaching out beyond the possibilities of present ties in friendship at the eleventh.

[6] Thus a brother or sister as an employer is found in the tenth in all employer-employe relationships, and only in the third to the degree action and response can be held to a strictly "convenient" brotherly or sisterly character, and so on.

The most important function of an environment is to instrument the interweaving relationship of its various conveniences, and this has the most objective form in communication, comprising the telephone, the telegraph, the radio, the newspapers and all periodical literature, as well as letters, messages and all modes by which intelligence is shared or given its useful and general application. Everything in connection with the practical, more-or-less automatic administration of a detailed civilization belongs here, including delivery or transport, merchandising or distribution, on through practically every minor ramification of business; that is, the operations which from the point of view of any given horary or natal chart are entirely taken for granted. Files and filing systems, stockrooms, and the like, are all included, together with all so-called white-collar workers who fail to stand out as individuals, or apart from this general environment of modern commercial life.

Nothing is quite as extraordinary in the astrological literature as the confusion over the meanings of the cadent houses, particularly the sixth in its distinction from the third. Here the difficulty arises in a verbal literal-mindedness, which compresses nearly every practical operation of human society into the notion of "service" and "servants." These, with "sickness," are the commonly accepted sixth-house rulerships, but they are increasingly unfortunate terms with the ever-pyramiding specializations of modern civilization. "Service" as a word originally described the definite attendance of an inferior on a superior in a simple community of personalities who were aware of each other, or who shared experience, across a line of social demarkation. This is the astrological significance of the word in

LOCATING THE QUESTION

connection with the sixth house, identifying both the giving and receiving of this special sort of attendant effort.

With the industrialization of society, however, the idea of "utility" has been added to the word, almost reversing its indication, and making it mean primarily the availability or convenience of serviceable factors. This obscures the fundamental relationship by which circumstances are able to articulate the continuing deference one personality must show to another on the lower levels of experience, in an all-important contrast with the straightaway, "present" or critical relations to a superior—or of a superior in his administration of authority—at the tenth house. The greatly expanded utility or "convenience" function in circumstances, exalted by a definitely commercial culture, is at all times a strict third-house designation.

The proper assignment of indications here will remain clear if it is remembered that the sixth house is the supporting element in the circumstances of authority, which has its focus at the midheaven, and that the third is the similar sustainment in the affairs described by the opportunity for any direct attack upon the problems of the moment, centered at the descendant. The sixth shows the background operations involved in maintaining the distinction of self among others, and it never reveals anything other than a relationship of group difference. Even sickness, as a matter of fact, is an accentuation of one person's right to demand special treatment from his fellows. Contrariwise, the third charts the underlying background functions involved in a self-mobilization for an activity of self-integration, and it never rules anything other than the entirely opposite and complete subordination of all group distinctions to an immediate convenience. The sixth-house "servant" does his work as something wholly directed to an "uplift of the ego" for the individual he serves, while the "service" which, in the sense of utility or convenience is found in the third, offers a sustainment in circumstances which at no point is a reassurance to personality in any socially conscious sense but, instead, is assistance given some effort directed towards a momentarily nonsocial goal.

Thus it is no longer possible to lump all workers in the sixth house, if astrology is to reflect the actual industrial civilization in which it finds itself. Attention instead must be given to the function performed by each of these. Where the contact is through conscious personality-difference, the subordination of one man to another is a sixth-house matter, but where this human touch is offhand, taken for granted, or a detail of the ramifying conveniences of modern life as such, the "inferior" situation of anyone has no astrological meaning in the immediate case, and the "service" is relatively automatic or third-house.

Clerks have always been assigned to the third house because of their "genteel" calling, or a respectability which avoided social penalty in the days when the middle class rose to dominance, and created the businessman's world of the eighteenth-nineteenth centuries. This rulership only holds now in the sense that a clerk fulfills a role of convenience. As a "worker" with "rights"—the desire to unionize his trade, to compel a wage scale and obtain fixed prerogatives—he is no different from the ironworker or electrician, found in the sixth house with its fundamental consciousness of social discrimination, and of individual barriers to be overcome in a society shared with others. The functions described by the third are at all points acquiescent, happy to melt into the background and to cloak any lack of distinction in obscurity. It is from this point of view that the "useful arts" have been placed here, rather than with the definite handicrafts in the sixth.

These "useful arts" show the finer skills of modern life as they are pushed back into a secondary role, and are thus

LOCATING THE QUESTION

denied all recognition as any true expression of personality. They comprise precision work in the use of highly developed tools or special machines whenever it is artistic responsibility wholly restricted to utilitarian ends, that is, denied all individual recognition. While the long-recognized and sharp line of cleavage between the "fine arts" and "commercial art" has tended to disappear in actual life, with the best of artists now commissioned to do advertising posters, magazine covers and book illustrations, all work of this sort on the routine level, as a meeting of assignments in full anonymity, remains in the third house. Editorial and manuscript work are placed at this point according to what may seem to be much more obvious logic, but the principles are precisely the same. It is only when the sketching, painting, drafting, writing, etching or highly skilled use of ideas and tools in the production of objective results is experienced primarily as self-expression, demanding for itself the acknowledgment of its effort as creative, or as stimulating rather than convenient to others, that the rulership moves to the fifth (or on to the seventh, in the very exceptional case).

The third house not only rules all these instrumental factors as separate details, but charts the whole activity of the environment as such in a very general sense. This means the performance of all the mass functions that may be taken for granted or left shadowlike in a civilized existence, as illustrated in all the background rhythms of modern life. More specifically it indicates the conveniently available places for routine group activity, including meeting halls, lodge rooms, churches, clubs and general means of assembly for strengthening the necessary instrumentalities of society as such.[7] This ramifies out to include not only fellow participants in given impersonal experience, but also the type of activity carried on in these commonplace aggregations. Thus the older astrologers place singing in the third. This does not imply the top-flight concert artistry of the seventh, nor the exuberant self-expression of the fifth, but rather an individual participation in effort of a community-conscious sort. Group worship, together with the pageants and feast times surviving from an ancient world, are included in this environmental activity, except as they move into the fifth as entertainment.

However, since the lines of distinction may become very thin in cases such as this, it is evident that the same occasion may have a varying implication to different participants; so that one individual will be undergoing a third-house experience while another at his elbow is in some process of fifth-house realization. It has already been emphasized that astrology gives the functional indication at all times, and that the rulerships in the horoscope go according to the meaning of events and relations to the native or querent. Hence all the personal third-house identifications are of the "other fellow," and the clerk, as an inquirer, appears of necessity in the first, while his "work" as an employe is ruled, of course, by the sixth.

It must be remembered, in this connection, that man's general environment is fundamentally integrative, providing the means by which his experience is held in a functioning unity, almost automatically. This means that the

[7] These must not be confused with the places where individuality is sharpened, or where the group as a whole is a convenience; in specific example, the schools and the facilities for amusements and sports, ruled by the fifth.

LOCATING THE QUESTION

third house rules those things which tend to make events intelligible, whether as a result of definite communication or as an indirect consequence of the simple or taken-for-granted group routines. In other words, meaning is given to every necessary factor that supports the matter brought to a specific focus at a particular time. The horoscope charts man as he responds naturally to the shifting situation in which he moves or has his being, and as he conforms to its pattern or seeks to alter it, so that this house, in natal astrology, is said to indicate the "lower mind"; which embraces the whole area of habits, automatic responses and judgment below the level of reasoned analysis. In horary astrology, therefore, this means the operation of all agencies which carry the materials or substance of habitual response and conditioned reaction, i.e., communication, not only in the form of letters, the telephone, and so on, but also in the particular item communicated as distinct from the means of conveyance; and as apart from its significance.

Here is the "news" of the medieval books, or the "rumors" by which attention is drawn in one or another direction by the environmental orientation. A very common query brought to horary astrology concerns the validity of some word or message. "Is it true?" In other words, what will be the result of accepting the given information, and acting on it? This is a wholly legitimate third-house matter because, although the query is vague and overgeneral, the circumstances yet present an issue; the problem arises because no normal or definite basis for act or choice is available. The taken-for-granted nature of things comes into momentary question.

Because the third house so essentially rules things and agencies, the young astrologer is apt to focus his analysis on the surface rather than deeper reality, and fall into the errors to which considerable attention has already been given. Thus a common question, "Has the letter been received?" is really a desire to know what the response will be. The letter obviously has been received if there are any direct consequences from sending it, whereas, if nothing happens as a result of the writing, the matter of its receipt or nonreceipt is of little importance. Any academic side issue which fails to represent a line of real relationship remains a completely non-dependable detail in horary astrology. Hence the similar and familiar query, "Is the rumor correct?" is seen to approach the matter from an exterior center of relationship, and to be again an attempt to analyze reality in a vacuum. What this querent wants to know is not the truth of the intelligence, actually, but the potentialities of possible change in some given situation. If he will ask about the results of the action he contemplates, in response to the "news," he will have valuable guidance. In both cases, of course, the questions remain in the third house but they are sharpened, or put into a proper form.

The house not only rules the "common intelligence" of the environment as it becomes a matter of interchange or communication, in the loose and everyday social sense, but also as man's knowledge is gathered together or placed in one or another handy form, to be taken for granted in a more specific way. This particularly suggests manuscripts and books as the more or less stable basis of communication, and at once reveals a minor confusion concerning what in a strict sense are "textbooks," as an adjunct to the school routines and learning processes ruled by the fifth house, and what are "books" more on the basis of non-ulterior or simple informative content. They can represent the creative labor involved in their preparation and production—whether (1) in the simple self-expression of this same fifth house, (2) in the "fine arts" of the seventh, or (3) in the synthetic or scientific organization and philosophizing of the ninth house—but for the most part they are inanimate instrumentalities. The whole matter of books is simple enough if it is remembered that they are ruled by the third house only as they are conveniences, or as they may be taken completely for granted. The use of subordinate conveniences in their preparation, such as the typewriter—or even the stenographer if she is machinelike and impersonal enough—and of the basic materials, such as paper and the like, is also indicated here, but all personal, creative or critical activity belongs elsewhere, of necessity.

The psychological "conveniences" in the totality of selfhood are as much a matter of instrumentality, or of "tools," as anything else in these various categories of the third house. Hence it is correct to give it rulership over all personal "skill," as well as whatever practice or rehearsal is involved in maintaining the skill and so keeping it sufficiently sharp to be "convenient"; that is, taken for granted. Obviously any such rehearsal or practice of personal competence, however, when a detail of original development and learning—or when a pleasurable self-expression, even if no more than a psychological uplift—belongs in the fifth house. What the third shows is the basic "adequacy" of self as an integral part of its whole complex.

Environment must thus be seen as a phenomenon of interaction, from any competent psychological point of view, and the house not only reveals those elements external to the self which the self can count on in various details of the everyday business of living, but also those capaities in the self on which the exterior environment no less can depend as constants in the individuality it builds into its own effective whole structure. All these factors are assigned according to their actual significance, or by the way they act, rather than according to any external or abstract definition or classification. Every single case, in consequence, must be taken on its own merits.

Even the line of blood relatives is not to be traced out too literally, according to inflexible rule. Thus brothers and sisters are such through the family experience, and not the legal or genetic niceties, unless the status before the law of an exact blood tie is an issue in point. In such an instance the precise relations can be traced out by the ring-around-the-rosy technique, but ordinarily half-brothers and sisters, or those by adoption, are treated the same as any others. This principle operates also in connection with distinctions among children by marriage or adoption, and so on.

A common but wholly unnecessary straining at definition is found in the matter of "short journeys." The most widely established rule is to put any stay "overnight" in the ninth house as a "long journey," but this is often modified, as in the suggestion to include all traveling not in excess of three days. Actually the distinction is between routine moving about which is taken for granted, such as the trips of a business executive or salesman, and travel which provides an extension of horizons: a change in the life's frame of reference, an adventure stimulating the imagination, or an absence from the accustomed sphere of experience of an extent or duration sufficient to make it impossible to pick affairs up again in any totally taken-for-granted fashion.

Horary astrology in past generations has probably been employed more often for the recovery of lost articles than for any other purpose, and this introduces the problem of

LOCATING THE QUESTION

that crisis or issue which cannot be located properly by house, in advance, due to the querent's lack of adequate information. If the type of inquiry provides a choice of houses in which the focus can be placed, the selection of location in the crisis chart becomes the beginning of horary judgment, since the decision results from the degree to which one out of several houses best fits the facts as known. In other words, one among the possible houses may have a much sharper correspondence than the others to whatever facts are available, and this very correspondence is important light on the matter.

It must be understood, first of all, that a lost article differs from a lost person. Thus a strayed child is found by using the fifth house, or whatever other one indicates the youngster in question, and a missing marriage or business partner is located from the seventh, and so on. Articles that can be "lost" are primarily the paraphernalia or instrumentalities ruled by the third, and they are always located at this point as long as no personal involvement moves the rulership elsewhere. Fundamentally the house reveals the misplacing of something as a detail of the degree of convenience, availability and adequacy of those "things as tools" which it shows, primarily. If the question of a lost article is located here, the necessary implication is that it is only "misplaced," i.e., "lost" in the most simple or ordinary sense.

If it has been "hidden," however—that is, if the querent has put it out of place for a specific purpose—then the question belongs in the fourth house as ruler of "hidden things" or privacy *per se*. Because any other person secreting an article would be unknown to the querent, the general location of these hidden things has to apply; hence the fourth house retains the indication as long as such another person has no purpose beyond depriving the querent. This would be true if the motive were fun, mischief or malice. However, if the article has been taken or secreted by someone with the intent to possess it, or use it for himself, then the loss becomes a matter of "theft," and is placed in the seventh house.

The second house has been seen to have a special significance in establishing a sequence of relations around the horoscope wheel, and by the same token the particular implication of each house in order as a "third" from the proper preceding one—exactly as it is a "second" from the next in order in each case—is even more important in the everyday interpretations of astrology. The meaning of the houses as lying successively "second" to each other is a simple enough realization, and one which helps in understanding the fundamental rulerships of each. While the basic implications may be worked out similarly in a succession of "third" relationships, that idea is in no way as obvious or useful for explanatory purposes, although it is important and should be understood.

Thus it is comparatively easy to see that the original third house of any chart, as "environment," is the larger manifestation or further application of "resources"—i.e., that as a new "second" from the true second house, it shows the basic resources of personality expanded in the larger dimension, where personality can take things for granted—but it is not at all equally easy to realize that the fourth house of any wheel is similarly the "environment" of the second, or is the special taken-for-granted complex in which the resources of personality, quite apart from personality itself, automatically make use of themselves; that is, constitute a private environment or "eminent domain"

LOCATING THE QUESTION

for those things which personality can recognize as contributing uniquely to its own special self-sufficiency. This is one way to describe "home," or the fourth house at root, but it is a notion altogether too inherently philosophical for the average taste. However, the idea of any sequence of "thirds" can hardly be better expressed than in this identification of the process which continually sets up special closed systems of interest in chains, or gives the succession of things which can be taken for granted in separation from each other despite their relationship together. The concept is exceptionally difficult, but it is too valuable to be ignored by any real student.

The fact that his brothers and sisters live in absolute independence from the native's own personality, even while in close association with him, provides a far more vital realization than the metaphysical acceptance of such family-linked souls as those who have been brought to this close association in the past; who now are merely contributing, each in the case of the others, to the opportunity for a similar tie with still different souls in the future. However, both perspectives reveal the third-house function on this animate level as the usefulness of personality to other personality by indirection, through a commonly experienced stability in self-containment. Brothers, sisters and all the blood connections here represent aspects of relation which, more than anything else, can be trusted in their contribution to the general welfare in the immediate environment.

The whole idea of astrological house sequence can be summarized in fairly simple terms. Thus, whenever a consideration is placed in a given house, the adjacent house in order reveals its next potential. Any third house, in relation to the first, always represents the more remote resource idea, or that which can be taken for granted in a regression away from the focal point or issue. This gives the idea of sequence among things or entities which have independent existence on their own account—such as brothers and sisters—and in the technique of ring-around-the-rosy the third-house association provides chains of relation of this taken-for-granted or self-independent sort. The house rules brothers and sisters collectively, together with the neighbors, relatives and the like. But sometimes it is important to know something in connection with specific brothers or sisters, when it becomes necessary to trace out the sequence among them. The older astrologers discovered long ago that in such a case the third house itself ruled the first brother or sister, and then each successive third house the next in order of any brothers and sisters in question. Hence the first of these would be found in the third house of the crisis chart; the second in the fifth house; the third in the seventh house; the fourth in the ninth house; the fifth in the eleventh house; and the sixth in the first house.

The special technique by which it is possible to identify more than six brothers and sisters in this fashion has been explained, through recourse to the second from the third, or fourth house, for a seventh member of the series, and so on.[8] If there are more than twelve members of a sequential series, a narrowing of the consideration or an elimination of factors is necessary. However, even six factors of real significance are seldom encountered. When there are six brothers and sisters, the sixth is ruled by the same house as the querent, and this may require an adjustment. Actually, the querent is one of the children in the line, and the theoretically correct point of view would give him a house

[8] See p. 153.

LOCATING THE QUESTION

along with the others in the proper sequence. This means that he would appear in two places, in his twin capacity as querent and one of the given sequence, and it is possible to eliminate him from the latter, exactly as deceased brothers or sisters may be ignored in the given chain.

The procedure here depends on the particular significance of the relations, whether the querent looks on his relatives as separate from himself or as including himself in the issue of moment. Commonly the third house is taken for the oldest brother or sister, with the fifth, seventh, and so on, assigned down the line to the youngest. In instances where the ages are not available, or where the order of the brothers or sisters is not known definitely, the third house refers to the one of principal significance in the given matter, with the others concerned then placed in the houses according to the order of their importance. If this cannot be done, they can be assigned according to their connection with the particular problem, that is, considering when each in turn comes into the picture. This last ordering may be either in the experience of the querent, or in the knowledge of the astrologer. In some few cases, where only brothers are concerned, any sisters may be ignored—or vice versa—and when classification presents any difficulties because of a varying status of relationship, then blood relatives should come first, in order of directness, followed by connections which are the result of marriage or adoption in that succession.[9]

These general principles apply not only to brothers, but also to children. Thus the fifth house rules all the chil-

[9] Other blood relatives, such as uncles, aunts and cousins, when it is necessary to distinguish them, are traced out similarly, but somewhat more elaborately, through their actual connections, as suggested on page 137.

dren in a given case, collectively, when there is no reason for distinguishing one from the other, or any one child when the personal affairs of that child only are under consideration. When several children are involved in contrast with each other, or it is necessary to trace out some relationship which makes a distinction among them, the fifth house rules the oldest child, the seventh the next, then the ninth, eleventh, first and third. Chronological age again is the ideal determining factor, but an order of concern may be employed exactly as in the case of brothers and sisters. Here the question of those who are deceased becomes a little more important in practice, but the best principle is to ignore them if they are not included in the consideration by the querent himself. In other words, if the one who appeals to horary astrology for a solution to some problem is sensitive to the former members of a sequence, then they will be marked in the astrological figure, and must be taken into account. Sometimes children are lost prematurely, or born dead, but the procedure remains simple because the astrologer includes the child whenever the mother considers him in the sequence of her offspring.

A difference in technique for charting sequences is necessary in those cases where the members of the sequence can only come into the life successively, or where any newcomer displaces a predecessor. Here there is no common linkage in a separate self-sufficiency, but a direct personal tie of the sort which has yet to be subjected to final analysis in this chapter. However, the exposition of the sequence relation follows better here, as an exception to the general rule for concurrent ties in intimacy, than as a detached explanation put in at the later point. Thus marriage in gen-

LOCATING THE QUESTION

eral—or in the case of any particular individual, whether a first, second or any other partner—is indicated by the seventh house. But when a marriage partner is lost as a result of death or divorce, and another one is taken, in any problem involving a comparison or conflict between them, the sequence operates by moving to the opposite house. Hence the first wife is ruled by the seventh, the second wife by the first, the third wife by the seventh again, or by the eighth in recourse, and so on.

By the same token, in any similar case where a critical differentiation is necessary, an actual mother is ruled by the tenth, a stepmother by the fourth and a second stepmother by the tenth, or the eleventh in recourse. There is, of course, no necessary or even probable astrological distinction between remarriage following death and a new marriage after a divorce, although the latter may not have a church sanction. The single striking variance from these principles would be in the few corners of the globe where plural marriage is approved, socially and legally. In such lands the type of sequence would follow on the pattern of brothers and sisters.

The Fourth House

The fourth house identifies the reserved and ultimate or inner focus of any person or matter at issue, as in distinction from the ascendant, which reveals the practical or outer point of identity, realization and crisis. This nadir angle has therefore been described as the point of final recourse; it is man as he is completely cradled in a social complex. It is the parent of final appeal, usually the father. In the most simple terms it is "home," in which aspect it charts the place of safety or retreat. It presents that special aspect of general situation which has become irrevocably private or "hidden." Here is no real or fancied detachment from experience, however, but only the greatest possibility of self-gathering in some phase of daily living. The house discloses both the conscious and subconscious reinforcement of any critical issue in its own unrealized and often concealed foundations, sometimes taking destructive form as superstition. This subjective or more fundamentally spiritual "position" or self-certainty, whether of an individual person or of a critical situation in its totality, when seen on the practical side, is a day-by-day complementary interaction with the very evident social requirements and responsibilities shown at the midheaven angle.

Thus the permanence of resource or recourse, which is the "end of the matter" in the long-familiar phrase of the older books, is to be understood in two ways, namely, as representing that which in the present moment or particular relationship so partakes of the element of the ultimate that it is beyond change, and also as revealing that which by the complexion of the total relations at issue is inevitable in some practical or immediate sense. More simply, this means both those things which will not change at all, and those which are changing so surely that the given process of "change" itself cannot be altered. "Home" is absolute in both aspects, since it always provides an unquestioning retreat and stands against all real interruption to achievement and growth. Here is the strength of the family line, the support of a blood inheritance or tradition as established in the "name" rather than in the more individual or unstable "reputation" indicated by the tenth.

LOCATING THE QUESTION

An important philosophical caution must be sounded at this point against any acceptance of "changelessness" or "inevitability" as anything but relative, outside the immediate context. Thus a man is "changeless" as a human being, in a certain true sense, as long as he remains alive. He promptly becomes something else at death, however, so that "he" can then be taken as a body launched on a process of decay, as a soul which begins a metaphysical existence in "other worlds," and so on. By the same token a fall from the top of a high precipice presents the "inevitability" of falling, but only until the bottom is reached. It is possible to bring other ideas into the inevitable category of such a case, including death to the victim, and bereavement for his relatives, but the term "inevitable" becomes meaningless, a mere academic description, as soon as the given event is completed. What all this implies in astrology is that the factors of certainty become "uncertain" whenever the consideration is sufficiently enlarged. Moreover, an understanding of the principle is a prime requisite in any mastery of horoscopy, either in the horary or natal arts. The nadir angle reveals "inevitability" as a practical boundary of expectation in the given case, but never as any absolute about which nothing can be done through a properly broadened perspective.

The fourth house is the "end of the matter" in the sense of identifying whatever remains a literal "constant" within the present limits of a given problem or crisis in experience, and it comes to have its most important role in horary interpretation, through the ring-around-the-rosy technique, by revealing certain practical aspects of this "final" limitation. Thus the astrologer has a clue to necessities behind the matter at hand when he takes the nadir angle in comparison with the seventh house which, by contrast, shows the "opportunity" or the more definite and immediate outcome of act or choice. It is apparent that the traditional indication of the "end of things" means their dismissal to certainty, on the analogy of the third house which most simply charts whatever common conveniences have been or can be dismissed to automaticity. According to the same mode of description, the second house is a "dismissal to usefulness," and the first an equivalent "dismissal" to the crisis of momentary or particular significance. In the case of the fourth house the "dismissal" has special reference to what has already been done or established, but it is fatal to permit any idea of the "past" to dominate the meanings assigned to the house. True, it rules cemeteries, monuments, memorials, and all permanent tributes given to people and events of yesterday, but this is only as a detail of sentiment. What is actually disclosed is the surviving influence of these various elements in the "present."

Much more important, at this point of perspective, is the rulership over parks, gardens, estates and all the final "special dedications" of general environment by which an individual of lesser fortune enjoys privileges normally accessible only to those of great wealth. The house no less indicates these things when privately owned, since their practical value remains the same, but the astrologer does not as often apply his art to people whose home reaches "estate" dimensions. The common man is at "home" in this respect in community parks and public facilities. Even when these are but "semi-public," requiring a fee for their use; or privately owned, although made available generally; or completely private, but open in one or another way for the use or enjoyment of a single individual; the astrological indication is unchanged because the horoscope

LOCATING THE QUESTION

discloses things as they act or function, not as they may exist in an academic, legal or theoretical sense.

The full extent of the details comprised in the institution of "home" is determined by their meaning to the individual or group whose home it is. Anything that has place in these private quarters, and that is "sentimental" at root, is indicated by the fourth house, but whatever is merely "convenient," and quite taken for granted, will be found in the third. Here, as throughout the distribution of astrological rulerships, the understanding and attitude of the client, primarily, and the conception of a situation and of the significance of its component elements by the astrologer, secondarily, will determine the placing. Many apparent contradictions will dissolve if care is used in thinking through these lines of relationship. Thus the excellent book on horary art by Robert DeLuce, listed in the bibliography, gives automobiles to the fourth house,[10] while this manual assigns them to the third. Unquestionably a man's car may be a place of ultimate resort for him in a psychological sense, without any necessity that he actually live in a trailer, or "house on wheels," but the present text views motor vehicles as generally more a convenience to modern life as a whole than as any provision for the inner relaxation and spiritual strengthening of particular individuals. No two astrologers or students can be expected to stand in perfect agreement on all points, and this volume seeks only to point the way, as broadly and generously as possible, without freezing any practitioner's point of view, and thereby destroying his real usefulness to his clients. However, it should be noted that, no matter what mode of perspective is adopted, the astrological relations remain consistent within the structure of the wheel. If a rulership is assigned with any logic at all, the chart will always distribute it.

[10] On the view that vehicles are the means or tools of locomotion, and that the fourth house is the second of the third

The fourth house, as the ruler of property, basically indicates realty, and it charts any "estate" as an inheritance or a financial foundation, but in no case movable goods, cash reserves or easily negotiable wealth. "Property" here may be owned by the querent, or he may have only the use of it. The latter case is more usual in modern life, so that a man's house is indicated whether he has any title in it or merely pays rent. However, the rented home is only indicated when it is a place of domicile, and the rulership never includes the sections used in any part for business, although buildings owned, whether embracing the living quarters or not, are assigned here in the instance of "income property;" that is, when constituting an estate, or included in a person's financial foundation.

Commercial or industrial premises *per se* are ruled by the third house as long as they are a taken-for-granted convenience—i.e., not primarily created as part of the business "capital"—and places of amusement, by the same token, since they are subordinated to self-expression, are indicated by the fifth. The mere location of any given activity, when not brought to the forefront of attention in any degree of distinction from that activity, is always described by the same house. The moment any necessity arises for distinguishing the premises from the situation as such, they obviously must be seen as an instrumentality of some sort and assigned to houses according to their given import. Thus, when the place of residence is compulsory—i.e., is not under the control of the person who does the residing, as a penitentiary, hospital, or other institution administering any degree of confinement—the rulership of the building or quarters as an agency of external ordering

LOCATING THE QUESTION 183

is in the twelfth, although the room, or even the bed which constitutes the recourse or retreat of the individual, is still the private "home" factor shown by the fourth.

Real estate is ruled by the fourth house when it involves the manipulation or adjustment of permanent values, but broad realty exploitation such as subdivisions, new communities, the sale of land in many parcels and all such speculative enterprises are primarily a matter of the fifth. Note, however, that the real property itself, apart from the problems of its exploitation, is still shown by the fourth. Buying or selling against an expected rise or fall in values, whether realty or anything else, is speculative in fundamental fact, and so again a fifth-house activity. When a house is occupied on the rental basis, the landlord is located in the tenth, just as, when it is owned, the community body or sovereign entity and entities to which taxes have to be paid are likewise indicated by the midheaven. When the home is in a two-family dwelling, an apartment, a flat, or even a room in a boardinghouse, the charting of the "home" as such is through the fourth, with the owner or proprietor located at the tenth. If the personal life is highly institutionalized, as in a modern hotel with its particular and exaggerated conveniences, any actual limitations arising from the large-scale organization will be revealed by the twelfth, but the many special services are no different from those provided by domestics in the ordinary sense, and located always in the sixth.

The administration of any property by the owner is centered at the tenth house, as far as any details of management are concerned. This is true whether the owner is the querent or not, and whether he has any special relation to the inquirer or not. Simple inert property as the source of personal income remains at the nadir angle, a point already brought out, but the second house rules any problem concerning the effort to increase rentals, decrease vacancies or in other ways produce a larger financial return. Tenants as such are placed in the sixth, irrespective of the purpose for which they occupy their quarters, as are stewards, or those who are put in subordinate charge of any property in order to take care of it; that is, to keep it from deteriorating rather than to create income out of it.

An important detail of fourth-house rulership is natural resources, such as minerals and any other valuables found on and under the ground in a natural state, including precious stones and metals, peat and coal, oil and gas, timber and whatever else might be discovered by prospecting or exploring; together with such derivative legal entities as rights of way, riparian rights and the like. The distinction on the one hand is from negotiable securities and movable goods, found in the second, and on the other from the act or process of prospecting, exploitation and development, shown by the fifth. Mortgages, deeds of trust and realty certificates of title belong here if the ownership is for the purpose of definite use, either for residence or as income property, but they must be put in the second if held or gained for purposes of manipulation; that is, profit from trading securities rather than using property.

When certain knowledge of potential underground or geographically remote wealth is gained, the indication belongs to the nadir angle, where the rulership is vested in an original or wholly potential state of affairs. This is the house as it charts "hidden things" in general, i.e., untapped or completely elusive resources as well as protected or stabilized reserves. The term "natural resources" includes everything in that category, whether privately controlled or lying in the public domain.

The idea of "home" has a group as well as an individual meaning, so that the nadir angle reveals men and their homes taken collectively but intimately as the community, or homely units such as villages, towns and cities in special contrast with the county, state or nation shown at the midheaven. This not only means the "community" in a static sense, but also the present condition of the more intimate group affairs on the natural or strictly impersonal side of social reality, which in one practical way identifies the weather and all specific manifestation of nature's forces such as volcanic eruptions, earthquakes, storms, floods and disasters of any sort. Here the "end of the matter" ramifies to include any broad devastation or group impoverishment resulting from war and revolution, as well as the exceptional case of gain from any of these things.

The Fifth House

The fifth house has been seen to be fundamentally the place of self-discovery, or the simple overflow of self. This on the constructive side is pleasure in every form, ramifying into the development and enjoyment of talents, and on the destructive side including prodigal self-expenditure, ranging from dissipation to speculation. The basic expansion of self-realization is revealed not only in these particular modes of individual expression but in the entire learning process, comprising the psychological activity of acquiring knowledge as well as the complete structure of education in the form of teachers, schools and all the direct paraphernalia of instruction. The self-distribution embraces actual creativity, whether children in the literal sense, or symbolical "offspring," such as inventions and the tangible models or other representative objects which instrument any given talent.

The particularly personal paraphernalia and acts of self-expression are placed here, from the talismen and "fetishes" of the consciousness provided in infancy by toys and dolls or in adulthood by jewelry and adornments, to the activities of self-indulgence; especially sex relationships outside the marriage tie, and all forms of overstimulus to the senses. The house shows the tentative choices in formal courtship, and every sort of suit intended to persuade others towards some sort of more definite acquiescence. The ramifications of pleasure include amateur and professional categories, hence both individual, spontaneous or unorganized and group, large-scale or conventionalized activities. Ordinary play or normal self-relaxation is indicated, together with all recreative hobbies. In the artistic field this means everything short of that utter mastery of a medium which as a "fine art" goes to the seventh house, or of the commercial routine and uninspiring use of talents which belong in the third.

Recreation may be largely on the mental plane, in a devotion to cards, chess and such games, or it may exercise muscular as well as other skills in swimming, hiking, ball-playing, golf, tennis, bowling, billiards and similar interests. Spectator or wholly passive amusements are indicated, as attendance at the theater or the athletic stadium. Participation as an amateur in recreational activities may range anywhere from the corner-lot baseball game to special efforts for championship status or recognition of excellence in the individualistic competitive activities of the order found in boxing, swimming, tennis, golf, track meets, and the like. Indulgence in professional or semi-professional sports, even if the remuneration is a basic motive, and if the actual effort approximates very hard work, is located in the fifth because of the necessary "appeal to the gallery," seen or unseen; that is, the sense of special self-satisfaction following on the demonstration and refinement, before the world, of definitely individual capacities proved in open competition. Rulership only moves to the seventh house in the case of definite "contests," or strictly person-to-person opposition where the whole well-being of self is challenged.

The field of professional amusement, taken in the narrower sense, comprises the theater, motion pictures, radio, opera, concert stage, circus and the carnival activities at fairs, amusement parks and such places. Here the fifth-house rulership embraces the actual performers before the public, and the producers, writers and technical assistants who do definitely creative work. Neither in these activities, nor in the organization of professional sports and amateur contests, however, are any officials or workmen included when their tasks are of the order already described as falling in the other houses. Stagehands, property men, electricians, ticket takers, box-office men, ushers, and all strictly adjunct duties here are no different from other normal or relatively routine vocations. The actor, whether on the stage, before the camera, or facing a microphone, has by contrast a task of creative originality on the occasion of every performance. The musician—as well as composer, arranger and orchestra leader—remains in this category at all times. The designer of the scenery ranks as an artist, exactly as the initial creator of stage business, sound or electrical effects, and so on.

The fifth house, as the indicator of speculation, embraces simple gambling as well as long-chance investments, and any query is located here, in connection with the money risked, if the expectation is centered on extravagant or more than fair gains, and is accompanied by the conscious or subconscious realization of the high chances for loss or nonreturn. Hidden resources, of the order revealed by the fourth house, especially gold or precious metals and oil, are never themselves charted by the fifth, but prospecting for covered wealth of this sort, whether journeying into undeveloped country, staking others for such a search, or financing the actual digging or drilling, comes under the head of speculation. This is true even in the case of that exceptional operator so skilled that he seldom fails to "strike paydirt." The more common or polite forms of gambling are found in the area of activity usually known as "investments." When the factor of safety is subordinated to the idea of an increase by manipulation in the capital, or given stake, the investment becomes speculative. Any possession of "inside information," making a move of this sort practically certain, does not change its essential nature, nor the house in which it must be placed. The principle already put down is that when the motive is an increase in the capital value of the resources, the fifth

LOCATING THE QUESTION

house rules, but that when the motive is safekeeping, or the simple intelligent administration of resources, the matter remains in the second.

The "education" ruled by the fifth is the process of learning what is already known and organized by society, and so does not include "research" in the sense of a special or institutionalized enterprise, although any individual creative discovery is charted by the house. The distinction here is first of all between naïve insight, or the sheer creative genius of man, and the determined attack on some given problem which is always the nature of simple "work" as indicated by the sixth. More importantly, however, the fifth house discloses the benefits gained, by the individual himself, through experimentation and growth. The sixth, by comparison, reveals the advantages he gains for himself by his adjustments to the people and things around him.

The idea of continual effort to refine the skills of selfhood—i.e., man's capacity for an uninterrupted tentative outreach into his personal potentialities—develops a curious positive value which is expressed on the negative side in the old books as "strength in resistance." This is an individual's ability to continue a course despite pressure upon him to move in some other direction, or what in more simple terms is the basic persistence of his own primitive desires. The fifth house thus charts the individual's particular gift for doing things entirely according to a private dynamic, or shows the extent to which he will be true to himself. Hence his tendency is to bend others to his will, or to raise up those who will perpetuate his own efforts. This means children, and all the symbolical offspring of self, of course, but it also identifies direct agents and chartered agencies, or those through whom a situation is approached by proxy. These are ambassadors, in the literal sense, and all individuals who act wholly as agents or legates for another. The distinction is from the stewards of the sixth house, who are given responsibility and real latitude in making decisions, since these people are a derivative manifestation of "children" as essentially the replica or extension of the parents. Every child, in this sense, is an ambassador, whether the youngster or his parents "will or no."

The ancient astrologers were much concerned over the possibilities of children, with all of the related questions concerning a wife or a mistress, and irrespective of the fact that the desire might be to have children, or to avoid them. Most of these questions in the later medieval technique involved a static condition, or an effort to make horary astrology reveal a statement of fact apart from its context. It must be remembered, in connection with any question of pregnancy, that the child, biologically speaking, is a parasitic organism without direct functional relationship to the mother, despite the intimacy of association. The not uncommon question, "Am I pregnant?", in actual horary practice is usually unsatisfactory, as a consequence. The inquiry, to have scientific dependability, must be based on an analysis of the results that may be expected in the case of some given act or decision.

There is much additional detail of interest at this point, however, and it is important to recognize the limitations as well as the power of astrology. Thus an older astrology concerned itself with a great welter of detail in connec-

LOCATING THE QUESTION

tion with childbirth. Would there be twins? The question is, in practical fact, what would the coming of twins mean to a given querent. "Twinning" is a definite inherited trait in human genetics, and any astrological judgment really should be supplemented by a knowledge of the family traits represented by the two prospective parents, although the astrological mechanism is capable of reflecting this within the limitations of the significance to the querent. Of this same cloth are the questions concerning the sex of an expected child. In a present age, where the elements of masculinity and femininity are so thoroughly scattered through both actual sexes, the results of the average query are disappointing, simply because the meaning of the birth of a boy as against a girl, or vice versa, is not sufficiently an issue to provide the ground for a dependable analysis.

The location of a lost child has been identified as a matter proper to the fifth house, in the discussion of misplaced articles under the heading of the third. This was a typical example of rulerships explained in advance of the detailed analysis of a particular house given later in the text. Little is gained by mere repetition, since the summary of indications for none of the houses, whether here or in Chapter Four, can be complete. The arrangement of the exposition is for the purpose of revealing the twelve houses in their full functional implication, first in terms of that general over-all distribution which ramifies through the triangulation relationships (Chapter Four), and then in the light of the sequential progression of basic idea from one to the other in order around the equator (the present chapter).

An exceptionally full index permits any student, practitioner or investigator to find easily, throughout the book, all possible points in any special reference. Any attempt to draw these materials together on some arbitrary or verbal basis, such as to put everything to be said about the fifth house in some one place, would not only entail endless repetition but might also contribute to an extensive confusion. This is true because the rulerships of the houses, considered as mere words or phrases out of all particular association with experience, are often meaningless in any practical sense. This is the weakness of the tabulation at the end of the chapter. Perhaps astrology can be said to be a more basic "language" than the English or other medium of speech used by the astrologer.

The Sixth House

The sixth house has been found to have its primary rulership over the adjustments that must be made by each individual as he creates his social place in life, or as he works to maintain or improve it. This not only indicates the process of readjustment as such, but the need for it, or maladjustment in general. Thus it embraces every activity in which anyone participates as a conscious misfit. "Business" ordinarily is focused in the tenth, but some unsatisfactory situation or experience of personal disattunement may be much more real than the actual body of pertinent relations, and the activities become drudgery instead of an exaltation of self in the commercial or professional world. What the tenth house always shows, in this connection, is the general community of organized trade, or the total social stability with which the individual may co-operate for his own advantage. His part in any administration of the group's powers, or in any exercise of his

LOCATING THE QUESTION 193

own social position, is indicated by the midheaven angle, but his struggle in any particular aspect of his own relation to such superior necessities is revealed by the sixth.

Distinct from these problems of adjustment in social difference are the individual or particular acts and details of trade, that is, the moment-by-moment conduct of business affairs by equals among equals. If they are not mere routine, to be taken for granted, and are not actual work directed by others or imposed on others, they are found in the seventh house, as a response to opportunity. What the sixth really charts, therefore, is the basic call on men for an expenditure of effort in the adventure of living, so that the house may be said at the outset to comprise hard work as such, as well as overstrain and unusual or not particularly gratifying employment of the energies, together with all the adverse consequences. It is here that the rulership embraces sickness which, in a literal astrological sense, means the mobilization of the self for some special or pressing need. What is usually known as the "sickness" is in reality that composite of symptoms by which nature seeks to make its adjustment within the organism. Sometimes these are sufficiently commonplace, or experienced broadly and regularly enough, to have special names, and therefore to be met without any distress of mind or difficulty in act. Examples are the ordinary phenomena of hunger, thirst and fatigue, or factors in experience which do not require astrological analysis until some situation produces a distinct abnormality, or raises a genuine problem.

As has been pointed out, the sixth house rules food products in all aspects that cannot be taken wholly for granted, from labor in their production to work connected with their preparation and serving. Food is the foundation "service of supply" for the everyday needs of man, and it provides the lines of relationship through farms and farming, the whole structure of distribution in a myriad of details, and all individual chores and responsibilities which bring plant and animal products from the retail market to the table. Here in the main are those organized contributions to a continuance of civilized existence which deal primarily with problems of continual adjustment, and which set up the constant necessity for effort of the sort usually described as "hard." Clothes, as well as food, are covered in the process. Servants and attendant services are focal in the sixth, provided they cannot be taken for granted; that is, dismissed to mechanical convenience or psychological automaticity. Thus the farmer's pump, while functioning properly, may be placed in the third; but no part of the direct cultivation process. His house will be found in the fourth, but not his fields when considered apart from his legal title to them; unless, indeed, he leases them for oil and changes their function.

Sickness is the typical representation of society's "service of supply" in connection with the abnormal needs of people, embracing not only individual incapacities but also whatever may characterize a group of a section of the country as the basis for necessary changes to be made. This category in its broadest designation means the "climate" of a given situation in time and space, not only as the common characteristics of a particular arrangement of land, air and water—encountered at a certain latitude on the globe, and so providing a complex of natural forces

LOCATING THE QUESTION 195

which man must take into account—but also the general group well-being, together with efforts to achieve it through regimentation and social "projects," or the "climate" of health, political relationship and psychological fulfillment. The sixth house here reveals the background of revolution, agitation and all similar potentials or actualities of social upset, short only of the open conflict ruled by the seventh.

It also indicates the measures society must take against these symptoms of group maladjustment, in the form of all "services of safety." These include the military arm in every aspect of army, navy, air forces, marines, coast guards, militia both national and local, and hence the police, fire, sanitation and other instruments of community adjustment. There are occasions when it may seem difficult to draw a line between these agencies and the taken-for-granted and definitely similar factors of third-house rulership such as water supply, gas, electricity, telephone and the like, but always the true taken-for-granted services represent an individual escape from responsibility, while the sixth house consistently shows the emphasis, in each person's case, of his need to exert himself in order to meet a responsibility on the one hand, or to shape his life and efforts, on the other, to fit into the limitation which his social place impresses on him as a duty.

The analysis of sickness, in the narrow or individual sense, involves many special considerations to which later attention must be given,[11] although inquiries which do not demand supplementary diagnosis (of the sort requiring medical competency of some degree) may be handled as

[11] See Chapter Seventeen, p. 399.

any other problem in horary art. The house rules both the trouble in the organism, and the healing methods employed to ameliorate the difficulty, whether these measures constitute "medical" or some other form of treatment. The special skill or competency of the physician as an individual is ruled by the tenth house in his own horoscope, or in a horary where his fitness is questioned, but the act of consulting him, or any other professional person, is located in the seventh. A doctor's prescribed regimen is shown by the sixth house, as is the patient in all cases where the ailing individual is not the querent. The recipient of professional advice or counsel, as the one who is "served," is placed here in the personal charts of any professional counselor, although only in connection with these specialized services. A physician, lawyer or astrologer, dealing with any individual otherwise, locates him according to the nature of the momentary relationship. Thus, when the matter involves a personal dispute, the house is the seventh, and so on.

The sixth shows all strictly healing services as such, and so nurses, X-ray operators, masseurs and any similar technicians who act under professional instructions. It comprises everything utilized to preserve health, as in contrast with healing agencies. This includes food, already considered, and especially clothing taken as covering rather than adornment. Questions about wearing apparel are infrequent, usually arising out of a practical concern. Clothes are only to be located in the fifth when they become an instrument of vanity or perhaps supply a healthy psychological "pickup." Appurtenances of the home above the taken-for-granted or gadget stage, or those factors of everyday contribution to individual welfare which require detailed attention—and become the basis of necessary at-

LOCATING THE QUESTION

tention as the price of the service they give—belong in the sixth. Table and bath linen, together with all bedding, are house essentials which must be washed, ironed, repaired and distributed as a most important detail of home labor, second only to the preparation of food and the care of clothes. The heavy furniture such as beds, tables and chairs in particular, and definite chore-creating agencies as stoves and furnaces, are examples of service, designated by the sixth, as in contradistinction to the nonexacting conveniences established in the third.

Sometimes it is difficult to distinguish sixth and tenth house rulerships from each other, but the midheaven angle always reveals the exercise or possession of an authority which is self-responsible, and so cannot be carried back or appealed to any higher agency in the given case at hand, while the sixth always shows a mediated service, or an administration of a social necessity in which some other individual or group has a very definite and immediate concern. Thus the nurse with a child in her exclusive care is ruled by the tenth house in that youngster's chart for that period during which she exercises, by proxy, the normal authority of the parents; even though at the same time, in terms of her general relationship with her charge, she is a servant shown by his sixth. The matter would be more important if the youngster were left with this woman for some years, when it would be simple to consider the "nurse" as a "foster mother," but the state of affairs is no different even though temporary.

The vital realization here is that the tenth house, in a given astrological case, does not go back of the *de facto* situation. If the nurse is in charge for the moment, there can be no recourse to the mother. Hence a vice-president identified at the tenth is acting under circumstances when his superior has nothing whatever to say or do in the given reference. "Authority" in the sixth is action under circumstances when a superior jurisdiction is also a factor in the case, either possessed or deferred to; the important point in the indication of stewards, foremen, tenants, and the like. All labor is performed in a context that gives it value by sharing responsibility; therefore the effort as such never goes to the tenth house unless it is, in a sense, effortless because wholly self-sure or individually responsible.

A distinction between "labor," and the "struggle" of a more creative or less outwardly shaped nature, is between activities subordinating the individual to society, and a self-expenditure which psychologically liberates him. The former is placed in the sixth when at the forefront of consciousness, and in the third when wholly automatic or a matter of simple "environment." There are no exceptions to this principle. Creative struggle, on the other hand, in its unorganized form and through its efforts at self-discovery, is primarily indicated by the fifth. As it gets power, and begins to achieve social recognition and so call out a group response, it becomes a direct contest, in psychological terms, between self and not-self. Here is the actual experience of tête-à-tête relations at the seventh house. Professional excellence, which of itself implies no expenditure of effort, and is ruled by the tenth, calls for a skilled application of energies beyond the self-discovery stage of the fifth, and so presents what of necessity is this seventh-house co-operation, best illustrated by the actual professional activity of the physician, lawyer or astrologer.

LOCATING THE QUESTION

All the possibilities of sixth-house rulerships can hardly be put down in any rigid classification, but a suggestive list would include unskilled labor at the lowest point in the cultural scale, and then proceed to industrial or mechanical workers of every sort, both the employes of big corporations and the various service men in the community at large. These may be working for wages or be in business for themselves. On the less industrialized or mechanical side of life there are janitors, cooks, maids, butlers, doormen, gardeners, porters, messengers, companions and an interminable number of similar employes of the middle and upper classes, together with the people trained to perform a distinctly personal service as barber, hairdresser, manicurist, chiropodist, masseur, seamstress, dressmaker, laundress and others without limit. Rulership tends to slip off into the third house when the operations are taken for granted, and this is more apt to happen in connection with office routine, merchandising or white-collar work than in industry, manufacturing or personal-service lines. While the clerks, salespersons, demonstrators, manikins, messengers and other callings of mercantile business are less sharply "labor," the handicrafts and all the more characteristically "one-man business" enterprises represented by the druggist, restaurateur, tavern proprietor, haberdasher, tailor, cobbler, bootblack, laundryman, small storekeeper generally, and even the personnel of the larger groceries, or meatmarkets and chain stores, are almost sixth-house of necessity. This is not only because they touch food, clothes and the necessities of life, but because their sense of service to others is immediate or at the fore in their own consciousness.

The most automatic of routine work can be very personal at the moment of performance, and so lie in the sixth, but most fundamentally the rulership goes to this house when there is a pride of performance in the actual operation, or a sense of success in pleasing some other person. Even the woman who directs her servants will find them real to her, or hold them out of the third house, only by her sense of accomplishment through their particular direct effort. No "servant," however, can be placed in the third house by horary art, since the very fact of the query, or the personal relationship, denies any dismissal to automaticity, or to the status of a "thing." The principle illustrated in this case will explain the inclusion of "small animals" in the sixth, and especially the horse which a man rides and directs, the dog whose special senses he puts to work in a particularly characteristic intimacy, and so on. In a reverse application of the same fundamental relationship an individual will so personalize his automobile, or some piece of machinery he uses, that it becomes a true "servant" to him, and is located in this house. Also the enslaving heavy machinery used in industry, and the worker who operates it, are designated by the sixth.

Whether simple or sixth-house social effort is paid for on salary or by wages, or is a matter of commission, or is given without remuneration, is a distinction which makes no difference in the astrological rulership; although these factors may be of wide importance in a given problem. Work unrewarded in money is tendered for other coin, such as vanity or political advantage. When the endeavor is to coax more work out of less effort, or even to get the rewards without any effort at all, the indication of the effort as such—or what is offered in its stead—still lies in the sixth. The commonest form of this "substitute energy" is found in what the old books term "magic," or what in

LOCATING THE QUESTION

modern terms is mostly the manipulation of the significance rather than the substance of things. Actual occult magic is charted by the sixth, of course, including all the procedures of New Thought or metaphysical healing no less than the legerdemain of operative magic *per se*. In the infrequent cases where this surviving medieval magic is effective, and the many where there is sheer hocus-pocus, the problem is the same, namely, the short-cut achievement of some specific desired result, and hence it is effort expended in the sense of this house.

An important modern form of "magic" is advertising or general propaganda, and this must be seen in distinction from the personal or unorganized cajolery of the fifth house, and the equally personal but more straightforward effort to counsel others, ruled by the eleventh. Some effort has been made to consider this essentially modern method of promotion as the development of reputation or fame for certain given articles, and so place it in the ninth house, but this would only follow in the case of a chart erected for the commodity advertised, or in connection with some problem of its good name. "Advertising" as a form of work or effort is a technique for compelling others to action irrespective of the merits of a commodity. With this fundamental idea on the part of an advertiser, whether he admits it or not, the attempt is to ride over any natural reaction the public might have in the given case. Thus it is impossible to reason that advertising is a form of communication, and hence ruled by the third, no matter what third-house mediums it employs. It acts at all points to break down any taken-for-granted attitude, even if it does seek to set up that very thing along some other predetermined line as an end-result. Individuals in the advertising field, of course, are classified as any other people, entirely according to the nature of their specific work.

The use of force, natural or otherwise, for compelling the action of others, up to the point it is met with counterforce in actual conflict—whether the forces be physical, psychological or mental—summarizes the sixth-house activities at the extreme of their "servant" rather than "service" function. This has expression on the constructive side in labor unions and protective associations, and on the destructive side in aggressive political and military dictatorships, in socioeconomic or intellectual repressions through the propaganda or advertising techniques of modern civilization, and also in that domestication or enlistment of other living creatures with which civilization had its actual beginnings. Here is included every living creature that man can handle with his own hands, and so properly embracing pets of every description.[12] Hence strayed animals are located in this house.

The Seventh House

The seventh house is important because it indicates the major relationships, in joint interest or equal status, of people and things linked together in any immediate crisis or problem. This means all direct partnerships and contracts, such as in marriage or business, and also the equally direct contact in opposition represented by disputes, contests, warfare and conflicts of every sort, whether in enmity

[12] However, birds other than barnyard fowl, domesticated ducks, captive songsters, and the like, are normally placed in the ninth, because of their especially free movement. Carrier pigeons are ruled by the third.

LOCATING THE QUESTION

or friendship. It is the tête-à-tête tie between a thing and any other thing, which either represents and advances or else denies and prevents a given consummation, whether in a transient or permanent situation, and whether the foreshadowed outcome is desirable or otherwise. Thus the house shows the immediate outcome of any act or effort, through the result of the given impact on individuals, groups or even inanimate factors whose presence, approval, activity or even discomfiture or elimination is necessary for the particular achievement.

The basic idea is simple co-operation, of which the commonest manifestation is marriage, and the greatest number of problems assigned to this house in horary art are concerned with marital difficulties. It identifies both intended and actual mates, and charts the conditions under which men and women make or fail to make their "heavenly union" on earth. Business associations of the same intimate sort are analyzed by the identical technique, and the more temporary "partnerships" of professional or expert consultation are included, as well as all instrumentalities of legal and commercial as well as personal co-operation, such as contracts. The rulership ramifies out to embrace contractual relations between social entities of a political no less than corporate sort, or the treaties among nations. In this sense the countries become "allies" as a form of partnership, but not in any degree subordinating one to the other as is the case of second-house "assistance." [13]

On the destructive side the seventh house is not only the inimical focus in the relationships or complexities of momentary pertinency, but is also the promise of trouble as

[13] Sometimes designated as the role of an "ally," and put in the second.

a threat or warning, or the occurrence of trouble in an oblique or totally unapparent tie to conditions at hand or problems at issue. Thus it includes thieves and thefts, and locates stolen articles as well as describing any malefactor of whom the querent is a victim. It identifies strangers, as well as fugitives in a general sense, and reveals the significance of their appearance, whether for good or evil. The house is thus quite impartial in disclosing the reciprocal activities of life as both co-operative and unfriendly, and in showing competitors and competition as both menace and stimulation or opportunity. It fundamentally indicates the critical focus of a general potentiality in any question or crisis, or the immediate concern of everything else in general with that matter which has been brought to the point of consultation or conference.

The house has very great significance in the business world because it charts the normal activities of a commercial "give and take," or indicates the nature and value of specific opportunities. While the second shows loss and gain, or the ebb and flow in resources, the seventh rules buying and selling for the purposes of making a profit. This means trading in the most general sense, except where the operations are purely taken for granted. It comprises any direct contacts with people as a whole, rather than individually, or embraces the entire field of "public relations" in distinction from advertising. By the same token, it is the house of the entirely generalized impact the exceptional person is able to make on everyone else, collectively, as in the case of the fine arts, or those extraordinary achievements by which certain personalities are able to offer themselves to their fellows in an esthetic

LOCATING THE QUESTION

partnership of appreciation and illumination. The house rules the art itself, both the skill and the product, when it reaches this abnormal degree of excellency.

All legal action is placed in the seventh house, including the lawyers on both sides; but with the judge taken as an umpire and located in the tenth, and with the jury, if one is used as a counseling body for determining the facts, assigned to the eleventh as the special "resource" of the magistrate or legal jurisdiction. Where settlement is without the aid of a judge—i.e., "out of court," by agreement of the attorneys—the tenth-house jurisdiction of the state is simply inactive. The decision, as rendered by the judge, with or without the advice of the jury, is a seventh-house matter in all cases where the "suit at law" is recourse to legal procedures for an arbitration of difficulties; that is, where it is not a case in which the state or community has acted to bring the individual to account in some way. In the rare instance where it is necessary to differentiate between the attorneys for the plaintiff and defendant in a lawsuit, the querent's legal representation is found in the normal position at the seventh, and the opponent's lawyer or lawyers are identified by the first.

In cases where a querent faces charges brought against him as a violator of the law, or of group regulations, the state is involved. If the matter goes to court, the judge is still found in the tenth, and the jurors as an advisory body in the eleventh. A jury with executive power—such as a grand jury or a coroner's jury—takes on judicial power as the representative of the state, and like a judge is placed in the tenth. The decision in criminal cases, or in matters of damage or injury where the state is the plaintiff, is located in the fourth house. The attorneys remain in the seventh, or in the seventh and first. The courtroom as the chamber in a building is described by the twelfth, the institutional convenience or the taken-for-granted facilities of the state, but the court procedures—or legal practices and customs as a representation and administration of morality—are in the ninth. The law of the statutes, or society's codified regulations, is indicated by the eleventh; i.e., the resource of racial authority, and man's attempt to control history by shaping human objectives.

The two functions of "law," entirely separate at root, are not clearly distinct in the average person's mind. The result is that the ninth house rulership of custom, or the ordering of life out of past experience, is not properly distinguished from the eleventh's indication of social goals or ideals as these become the basis of legislation, or constitute an effort to improve the present and mold the future. The latter house fundamentally reveals the conscious activity of men in examining their values, and in enlarging their capacity for co-operation with other human beings, while the former discloses those obligations to background and the living tradition of the race by which life, in its deeper aspects, remains dependable. "Law" as a matter of morals and ethical discipline of the individual is always a ninth-house matter, but "legislation," or the intelligent effort of the community to improve its social resources by rule and regulation, is an activity necessarily found in the eleventh.

When an attorney is the querent in legal matters the seventh represents the issue over which he is concerned, and the outcome is determined according to the usual technique. His client, however, like the patient of a physician, is given to the sixth house because, in the consciousness of the lawyer which the crisis chart reflects, the case in question is a proposition pressed by himself. The fact that it is for another's interests is not pertinent. All other rulerships remain unchanged, even in action for violation of the law. In the rare instance where the astrologer is consulted by the prosecuting attorney in government litigation, the defendant of course is described in the seventh. No other complication of human relations possesses the possibilities of confusion to equal these legal relations, but the newcomer will have no difficulty if he remembers that the descendant angle focuses the basic point of attack, showing both the individual or group opposed to the querent, together with every representative of these opposing interests basically, and also that whenever it is necessary to differentiate between such parties and their legal representatives, the recourse is to opposite houses—or perhaps ultimately to houses adjacent thereto—exactly as in the location of successive marriage partners or parents.

In any contest, from common sports with a friendly background to the all-out effort necessary in war, and whether between individuals or groups, the seventh house of the crisis chart always indicates the other party; or whoever is a threat to the rights, standing or record of the individual or group in some particular respect. This is the normal horary point of view, and it must be distinguished carefully from the "inaugural" chart erected for the exact time of a challenge, or an event which can be taken as such. Thus in a horoscope for the moment the contender for a title challenges the champion, or a nation declares war, the first house rules the challenger, or the aggressor. Where a querent in straight horary art, however—when legitimately entitled to ask a question because of responsible concern in the chain of events, or the possession of real power to make a decision of importance in the situation—

inquires about the probable outcome of a conflict, the first house remains the point of personal contact or interest, that is, the home team, local contender, or native country, irrespective of which took the initiative; and the seventh rules the opponent.

The Eighth House

The eighth house has been presented in its function as prime indicator of the potentialities of the soul or inner side of life, an idea which is usually expressed by the older books as "regeneration." This means, most simply, the independent resources of the general opening presented in a given crisis, or the personal side-returns to an individual or group as the result of direct co-operative contact with others. In an important way this charts the capacity of man to produce, within himself, those changes which enable him to fulfill his more remote potentials for self-unfoldment; together with his anxiety or concern in the matter. Thus the house shows wherein the querent will be able to meet whatever necessities are requisite in the consummation of a certain opportunity. While this includes all conformity to pertinent larger ideals, of course, and represents the definite acts or decisions by which a religious realization is possible, it actually comprises no more than the ultimate ordering of man's own self according to the ideals of himself to which he holds, together with all his struggle towards this end. It also indicates any failure in this respect, and so any retreat to a lesser self-realization. Thus it is said to be the house of death, either in the sense of any absolute loss of reality, or else of that inner and

LOCATING THE QUESTION

psychological realization of real rewards in self-discipline which, in a practical way, is a dying out of old limitation and a reawakening into some new and challenging self-expectation; i.e., the process by which life gains a larger meaning. Here it is said to reveal "new cycles."

The idea of regeneration is not very well understood by the average man. This is not a phenomenon by which the individual becomes a better man than he was before, since he "is" what he "is" in any case, if he is to continue to remain the same "he." Any true change is merely a matter of a better organization or presentation of facets of self which certainly have been in existence, and must remain in existence, whether brought to a focus in the present or pushed back into the sustaining potentiality of the past. Growth is an expansion in experience, not in unconditioned being, and a man is only "regenerated" when he begins to live according to the pattern put down for him by people or agencies other than himself. Thus, the Church accepts him as "saved" or "regenerate" when he begins to live according to the moral ideals for which the Church stands. Contrariwise, a secular or frankly atheistic point of view would regard him as salvaged from a welter of "superstition and outworn beliefs" if he were to do precisely the opposite thing, and begin to live according to the humanistic and collectivistic morality coming into fashion with a different social age.

The idea of "death" also requires sharpening for astrological purposes, since it is not an experience of the person who dies but rather is a cancellation of his total existence as far as a given context is concerned. The decease of other people is not an eighth-house matter in the original crisis chart, and there is never enough difference in this complete change of cycle brought about by the physical cessation of the body's organic existence, as long as the horoscope lacks a frame of reference in which to place such a cessation as an experience, to make "death" distinguishable in a literal sense at any time. Hence death cannot be predicted by astrological means alone, with any scientific dependability.

The eighth house, however, provides the relationship of a "one remove" from opportunity at the seventh, and hence includes any or all experience in or beyond the normal dimensions of life, important in special cases where the phenomena of spiritism are brought to the horary astrologer. Thus it includes all direct contact with "spirits" or discarnate entities, or all practical reach "beyond the grave" in any true actuality of experience in connection with the delimitations of "death."

The house becomes exceptionally important in horary astrology as indicator of the other fellow's money, or of general finance as in contrast with the financial conditions of some particular individual or situation. It shows money relations with competitors, as well as their finances in very broad terms. It includes the gain from liquidation, suits at law and the like. In embracing the funds of others, it reveals legacies or entirely indirect income in contrast with the normal or controlled receipt of money. It describes wills, and all legal provisions concerning the disbursement or handling of funds pertinent to a given matter, together with frozen or restricted financial resources as in contrast with the liquid ones indicated by the second house. Thus it comprises trust funds as a form of restricted legacy, or supervision put on money or resources by the self or others. The only exceptions to these disbursements beyond the control of the native or querent—and so located here—are life insurance and annuities, which belong to the ninth because the return is based on actuarial figures instead of earmarked capital. The eighth house essentially reveals money as a social agency, the most powerful in human history, for compelling the beliefs and acts of some individuals according to the desires and designs of others, or as a sort of compulsory "regeneration."

The Ninth House

The simplest of all approaches to an understanding of the ninth house is to realize that what the third covers in an objective everyday and detailed fashion, the ninth indicates in a more personally subjective or remote way. Thus it might be said to comprise everything that can be described as rooted in or dependent on the taken-for-granted "ideas" of existence. Fundamentally it rules the operations of rationalization and intellect, all abstract thought processes, and every self-projection to a distance. It has been presented commonly as the house of mind, considering the third in comparison as the ruler of habit; or as the house of "higher mind" in contrast with "lower mind" as the third. It includes whatever operates directly or indirectly in connection with some generalization out of experience, and so is the focus of vicarious act and decision.

This capacity to make touch with remote reality, complementing the employment of the third house instrumentalities, which are always near at hand, becomes the effort to handle distant things objectively, and the house therefore shows all personal relations with foreign countries, all traveling or shipping to far places, especially over the oceans, and all surmounting of any separation in time or space; that is bringing everything in the world to the service of a given interest, through intellectual act or the inner and individual enlargement of experience. Here is the root accomplishment of science and books, or the organization of knowledge so that its component parts are interchangeable and can be shared universally. What is implied is more than the third-house library or laboratory, the physical paraphernalia of immediate experience; it is rather the sharing of the broader and illimitable relationships of experience. Hence the physical "book" of paper and ink is third-house, but the content is ninth. Writing in the sense of putting the words on paper is third; the creative organization of words and phrases is fifth, or perhaps even the seventh in the case of extraordinary genius; while the inspiration and the basic or dynamic manipulation of ideas are ninth.

The house thus primarily rules the inner world of mind, or what in a general way may be termed consciousness. This can mean an inner sensitiveness to the meaning of events, which is evident as conscience. It can be the codification of standards or a wide subjective participation in the enduring worth of experience. It then becomes values, morality or the sense of justice as that universal law of fellowship which realizes the integrity of inherent human rights, and makes them superior to the convenience of any one class or privileged group. Consciousness thus sets up the special realm of standards which in its usual form is known as religion. While the third house shows churches and all routine or public procedures of worship, the ninth indicates private prayer or faith, as well as any ritualization of personal experience with particular ethical impli-

LOCATING THE QUESTION

cation. It reveals patriotism, and that assimilation of values to some particular individual which is recognized as fame. Here the distinction is from honor, which is position in life and so ruled by the tenth. "Fame" is the report of a person, or what is said about him, and on the destructive side this can be notoriety or a very ephemeral notice. The house rules the clergy, and all people in religious work, as well as individuals specifically concerned with the moral supervision and guidance of society, such as agents of justice, truant officers and those who are not the mere policemen of the sixth, or the investigators and detectives of the twelfth. The ninth thus identifies what each individual has to face among his fellows, by way of consequences out of his own past way of life, and also by way of the requirements arising out of the group's past experience, which take form in "common law."

As the third house rules the mere communication of notions or rumors, the ninth shows any ordered thinking about things, and the presentation of such in "science." The medievals made it the house of knowledge or wisdom; i.e., the positive and personal realization which leads to the attitudes, prejudices and presuppositions of an individual. Since it also implies his sensitiveness to larger or remote ideas, the ninth indicates inspiration, visions, prophecy, dreams, and the whole psychic life in its more healthy form of everyday impact. Maladjustment, or any chaotic or formless condition in this inner realm of sensitiveness is, by contrast, revealed by the twelfth, because such is the result of outside compulsion, or the failure of consciousness to adhere to its own certain inner promptings. Compared with the third house, which charts change in general on the objective side, the ninth shows specific ideas about change, or plans actually in process for making changes. Thus it not only indicates conformity to values, but the lack of this right-ordering of act and decision, or the tendency to nondiscriminating as well as intelligent act. It therefore comprises the liability to accident, as well as those actual mishaps of the purely chance sort which express man's inner relationship to remote or unknown factors.

This element of hazard in the ninth house, especially in connection with long journeys, involved many risks in medieval times which are not known or at least not realized today, with the result that many older questions concerning factors of wind and storm are now meaningless. Moreover, weather as such is a fourth-house question because it is man's most direct or primitive touch with natural forces, which in an industrial age are only infrequently a menace or concerned with human well-being on the personal level. The modern world of experience is more consciously controlled, and civilization reaches out to remote places by artificial means. Of these, the corporation or purely legal "body" or entity is the most important example. Whereas once the favor of nature was sought as aid in spanning the globe with the threads of commerce, now the "company" or incorporated body is the agency for long-range control in life and trade. Any connection with corporate matters, if not in the form of the relations to a company taken or acting as an individual—that is, as an employer, employe, contractual agent or partner, and so on—is shown by the ninth.

The older books are filled with questions concerning socioreligious and political matters, such as success in get-

LOCATING THE QUESTION

ting an appointment, i.e., a "living" in the age when a church position gave security and an abiding social place, or a government office which provided the same necessary sinecure for the average layman of intellectual, artistic or scientific aspirations. In modern times this interest is reflected by the types of security provided by a purely commercial civilization, taking principal form in schemes of insurance and retirement income; quite distinct from the legacies, endowments and trust funds of the eighth house. Life insurance is not to be conceived primarily as "saving," which would be ruled by the second, or as capital frozen so it cannot be hypothecated, an eighth-house matter, but rather as a means for giving financial or negotiable value to past experience, or providing an extra or "corporate" accumulation of worth in the personality. Here is a factor akin to the skills which, located in the third, provide a wage differential, and to the knowledge or wisdom, indicated in the ninth, which is a basis for salary distinctions on a higher level. Fire and other insurance is a further refinement of the corporate function by which risk is transferred to the larger entity, the dependable "environment of the other." Any funds realized from insurance, or put into insurance, are a second-house concern, however.

Dreams and visions were an important detail of ninth-house affairs in a prior generation, but any interpretation today of waking or sleeping fantasy requires exceptional skill because the substance of dreaming is taken very lightly, except by the psychoanalysts. As a consequence the subject matter of the dreams may have less conformity to intelligible pattern because of this diminished interest or expectation. The publishing business is placed in the ninth as an agency for the general diffusion of knowledge, a necessity which emphasizes the fact that the root distinction between the third and ninth houses is not literal "distance" but rather is the specific relationship as opposed to the general. Thus thinking embraces the world at large, willy-nilly, while a book of paper and boards can only reach one person at a time. The enlargement of learning as a whole belongs here, but not instruction, even in college, as long as it conforms to set requirements. While teaching is ruled by the fifth, and propaganda work by the sixth, dissemination of intelligence in new fields, by lecturers as well as writers, is the special province of the ninth. All the inner creative work of a rigidly disciplined science, such as ordered research or theoretical investigation and its background of carefully organized intellectual analysis or philosophy, is a ninth-house indication.

The Tenth House

The tenth house has been identified as the basic manifestation of honor, or the general recognition by others of any individual, group or matter to which consideration can be given; and also as the pertinent or effective authority in any given area, thus including the immediate superior administration of political power in city, state and country, and the active heads of any type of group from fraternal to business organizations. Hence the house shows the public status of anything, or its commercial and industrial effectiveness, as in contrast with any immediate concern over some crisis or problem, (the condition of things

LOCATING THE QUESTION

as indicated at the ascendant). If the first house is the personal focus of any matter, the tenth is the focal interest of the group. This means that the latter reveals what encouragement may be expected from superior authority, or what will be accepted as authoritative; hence it represents good will, general or established credit, and every possible manifestation of honorable condition among men, even to a nobility or aristocratic class, together with all efforts to establish prestige, and any failure to gain or hold it.

The house has been seen to identify magistrates or administrative officers in the sense of those who carry out the will of the group, as well as everyone who issues orders to which the individual must conform; and not only these individuals, but also the sociopolitical entities for which they speak, that is, the states or provinces, the corporations or associations, and the other organized "communities" in which the individual may happen to function.[14] The tenth has been found to designate superiority in general, and so that one of the parents to whom the child from the first yields the most necessary obedience, usually the mother. It charts the ambition of the native or querent, as his dynamic and direct relation with superiors, or in contrast with his more subjective visualization found in the eleventh.

The Eleventh House

The eleventh house reveals generalized objectives, or those "hopes and wishes" in life by which man reaches out ahead of his given opportunities in tentative and imagina-

[14] Note the distinction here from "corporate agency," a ninth-house activity.

tive fashion, thereby validating his desires. It also identifies those who assist this process of self-discovery by being well-disposed towards the individual in question. It not only includes these "friends," but any act of friendship such as the amateur or gratuitous advice which anticipates the organized or professional counsel indicated by the seventh. This, in principle, comprises the whole import of the eleventh. The important detailed observations that have to be made on the twelve houses are increasingly found put down already, in connection with earlier distinctions, and it is necessary again to remember that an ample use of the index alone will disclose all the salient considerations pertinent to each.

The general rulership over "legislation" by the eleventh has been described. This covers the process as well as the product, and so indicates Congress or Parliament, legislatures and city councils, boards of directors, aldermen, and so on; together with lodges and clubs when engaged in a self-administrative or deliberating function rather than in their more normal fifth-house role. When such a body is the sovereign authority in the land, as the House of Commons in London, it has its administrative role in the tenth. A bicameral congress or legislature, shown as a whole in the eleventh, has its chamber with the more definite veto power in the tenth, in connection with any given problem requiring representatives and senators, Members of Parliament and Lords, and the like to be analyzed separately.

The Twelfth House

The twelfth house has been described as ruling institutions, or that psychological organization of life which may

LOCATING THE QUESTION

be constriction or sustainment, either physical or subjective in nature. Here is ground on which the individuality, as ruled by the ascendant, is able to function. For better or worse, it is the reservoir on which the first house draws subconsciously, or instinctively, as in contrast with those resources in the second house which it puts to use directly. Hence the twelfth comprises all the hidden and unsuspected or surprising factors of immediate pertinence in a situation. It shows the possibility of escaping from bondage, and the circumstances under which an individual may get at his own psychological handicaps. Here is not only literal escape from confinement, but a proper release through governmental agencies, such as reprieve, parole or pardon. In the reverse aspect, it charts any situation relative to an escaped prisoner, or a malefactor at large, and includes the work and person of a detective.

The house not only shows hidden enmities on the part of others, but the particular undercurrent or the set of temperament which is responsible for these enmities; or which tends to call them into being and strengthen them. The old books list all the destructive things—envy, malice, habitual misery, criminal impulses, self-betrayal, upset, worry, mourning, regrets, the contemplation of suicide, and any surrender to fearful and self-destructive thoughts —but fail to point out that these inner sufferings contribute to the building of spiritual resources in life, since they enhance the sensitiveness which can always be given a better direction. Individuality is institutionalized here, or is dismissed to that psychic automaticity which is at the root of human character, and the house shows the unrealized potentialities of whatever is found at the ascendant.

The twelfth describes investigating agencies, together with the possibilities for getting at the real root of any matter at issue. Thus it indicates the loose ends of things, or factors that cannot be brought to a head easily or immediately, such as the hidden status and power of private enemies. It shows animals beyond normal control, usually the large ones that no one man can handle; but also all wild creatures that have to be caught or killed because of the damage they do.

Two old-time-favorite blind questions, still brought to the horary astrologer, are handled in the eleventh and twelfth houses if he is willing to entertain them, namely, "Will I get my wish?" in the former of the two, and "Will what I fear come upon me?" in the latter. These are rephrased, to become, in order, "What will the result be of proceeding on the assumption I will get my wish?" and "What will the result be of ignoring the fear that is disturbing me?"

LOCATING THE QUESTION

SUMMARY OF HOUSE MEANINGS

The First House

The querent, the question or the problem at issue, the focus of things

All definite projects and enterprises that may be the basis of inquiry

Any organization, group, company or legal entity acting as a person, or treated as capable of acting as a whole on its own account

The basic continuum of anything, simple selfhood, personality or the ground of personality

"Accidents" as events in general, the ground of experience

The masses, public health and well-being in general

Any indeterminate matter asked about, doubt or concern in the abstract

Infancy, early environment, pre-adolescent immaturity

The availability or general location of a person

Length of life as the chance to do things, personal prowess

A ship at sea, any enterprise with which communication is impossible

The challenger or aggressor in conflicts and contests, the home team, the local contender, native country

The Second House

Money as liquid and available resources, cash and all forms of negotiable securities, including realty instruments

Personal possessions as the symbols of loss and gain, receipts and disbursements, personal finance, current credit, debt

Individual means as reserve potentiality, personal resources, freedom in expenditure, state of riches or poverty

Rights, royalties, shares, interests and nonspeculative investments

Direct assistance from others; assistants other than partners or inferiors, where no supervision or responsibility is involved, allies in this sense

Efforts to increase income or rentals, liberty as freedom to act

Movable goods, stocks on hand, supplies for consumption or sale, all tokens of exchange, simple barter as opposed to buying and selling for gain

Jewelry as wealth, clothes as possessions of value or available for trade

The "second" in a duel

The Third House

All taken-for-granted and relatively trivial conveniences of modern life, gadgets, light tools, supplies as other than tokens of value

Environment in general, neighbors, fellow men and women at work and in normal activities as long as they remain shadows

Brothers, sisters and all blood relatives in general, except parents and children

Communication of every sort, conversation, writing as apart from authorship, letters, telegrams, cablegrams, telephone, radio, press, periodicals, books as objects or instruments of information, messengers, carrier pigeons, manuscripts as such, libraries

News, facts as intelligence, rumors, misrepresentation, gossip, idle talking, all immediately pertinent information, the climate of opinion at any point in time and space

Common everyday activities requiring no conscious attention, habits, reactions, routine movement, superficial change in general, objective mental conditions, ingrained prejudices, simple rehearsal or practice, all trivial or automatic personal skills

General community conveniences, utilities as in contrast with services, electricity, gas, water, steam, transportation of every sort, delivery facilities including mail and express, auto-

LOCATING THE QUESTION

mobiles and all refinements of carriage, private conveyances

Commercial facilities, useful rather than creative arts, automatically employed tools whether physical or psychological, failure in routine operation, simple inconvenience, trivial disappointment

The premises of everyday activity as a taken-for-granted background, business quarters, meeting halls, lodge rooms, churches, retail outlets, streets and traffic arteries, terminals and platforms

Lower mind, editorial work, white-collar functions, clerks or impersonal instruments of convenience

Mass functions, group singing, special environments in the culture, sects, general community enterprise

Misplaced articles, routine movement, shifts within the usual compass of activity, short journeys

The Fourth House

Home, soul, safety, rest; privacy and private grounds, immediate place of residence or domicile, spiritual security

Group co-operation with the individual, available group facilities, parks and preserves, museums and galleries, estates and gardens both public or private, public facilities in general, special privilege in particular, all great public endowments

Foundations in general, the womb, family honor and reputation, background and tradition, roots in the clan or race, old things, the end of the matter, the grave or tomb, cemeteries, monuments, old age

Inheritance as a total estate, any usufruct, realty owned or used, natural wealth such as minerals, oil, timber, game and all pioneer resources, stabilized or secreted reserves, hidden things in general, realty instruments as investment, rights of way, riparian rights, group wealth and impoverishment

Self-rehabilitation as in contrast with self-regeneration, the wholeness of self, ultimate self-gathering, end values

Reserved or inner focus of a matter, purely private experience, final resort, remote consequence, tributes to achievement and the root sentiments in life, superstition and secret beliefs

The community as experienced at first hand, villages, towns, cities

Community whole experience in weather, earthquakes, disaster, cataclysm and devastation generally

Father as the remote-link parent

Court decision in criminal cases

The Fifth House

Pleasure, simple self-expression, prodigality, dissipation, living costs, speculation, gambling, self-wastage of every sort

Creativity, simple talents, offspring in every sense, children, childbirth, invention, models

Personal discipline, schools, the process of learning, teaching, textbooks and paraphernalia of instruction, personal experimentation, dilettante effort, tentative contact for an immediate consideration

Amusements, opera, concert stage, theater, motion pictures, radio as entertainment rather than communication, places of amusement, circus, carnivals, fairs, community gatherings that cannot be taken for granted, recreation, hobbies, games, toys, dolls

Professional entertainers, actors, musicians, professional writers, composers, artists, directors, performers of every sort, stunt people, together with amateurs in all these lines

Sports of every sort except formal contests, including competition in which individuals are free to take part, athletic events as both spectator and participant interests, all paraphernalia of sport, places of events, stadiums and athletic fields, professional and amateur players

Conscious and basic self-persistence, strength in resistance, private dynamics and primitive desire, risk and foolhardiness, immaturity in real or protracted adolescence, self-discovery

Extravagant loss and gain, exploitation of realty and natural resources, confidence men and tipsters, prospectors and those who "grubstake" them, speculators generally

LOCATING THE QUESTION 225

Naïve insight and instinct, symbolical objects as talismen and fetishes, clothes and ornaments for vanity and display, courtship, suit paid to others to win their support, promiscuous or irresponsible sex relationships, master or mistress and paramour

Ambassadors, legates and "personal representatives" as a projection of self rather than a steward or associate, charters as rights given to others to fulfill some special function of self, power of attorney, proxies

The Sixth House

Service as attendant effort, servants as attendants, common routine as a stimulus to effort or a handicap to be overcome

Sickness, maladjustment in general, the basic relation to superiors and inferiors through joint responsibility, the fundamental effort in aligning the self to a situation

Regimentation or group discipline, sheer labor or drudgery, work with heavy tools or under conditions of exceptional risk, overstrain, struggle for place in society, necessary concessions to immediate circumstances in daily duties, social disparity as a personal problem, misfit business or non-distinctive vocation, underprivilege in all aspects, organized labor, social welfare movements

Handicrafts, small personal business except as an employer, all personal service vocations, repair men, mechanics

Employes, clients, patients, tenants, stewards, agents, caretakers, watchmen

All therapeutic activity, the regimen in illness, healing measures of any sort, nurses, X-ray operators, masseurs, technicians

Military and political dictatorship, army, navy, marines, coast guards, militia, police, armed guards of any sort, firemen and uniformed public servants of any description

Domestics, butlers, chauffeurs, maids, valets

Food and clothing in every useful aspect, farms and farming, distribution of perishables, food markets and marketing, state and county fairs in other than their carnival aspect or sports features, husbandry in all branches, domesticated or "small" animals, pets of every description, strayed and lost animals.

Wholesale in distinction to retail outlets

Cooking, sewing, domestic chores, personalized operations on machines, essential furnishings and furniture, stoves, furnaces, linen, bedding, clothes as covering and comfort

Routine of research, revolution, agitation, magic, propaganda, advertising

Climate in general, as distinct from weather

The Seventh House

Direct co-operation with others, partnerships of every sort, marriage, immediate contact with equals, joint activity, simple sharing of experience, opportunity, common-law ties of men and women, tête-à-tête relationship in general, all contracts and treaties

The astrologer, professional consultation, lawyers and legal action, the State's Attorney or Public Defender, strangers in contact

Direct competition, in friendship or enmity, title contests in sport, war, business or trade in any specific case at issue or crisis, buying and selling for profit, thieves and thefts, fugitives, stolen articles

The immediate outcome of events, particularized interest, compass of action, threats and warnings, promise of trouble, the other party in contests or disputes, the individual or state challenged or attacked

Fine arts, artists of especial renown, all extraordinary achievement

The Eighth House

Death, sadness, new cycles, disappointment with self, re-establishment, regeneration

Conformity to external ideals and standards, subjective self-refinement, potentialities of soul, "karma" as a catalytic, anxiety, worry directed to a given end

The psychic life in its subjective isolation, spiritism, spirits, necromancy, enchantment, obsession

Wills, legacies, minor inheritance, personal endowments in money, the independent resources of an opportunity, general finance, frozen resources and trust funds other than insurance.

The Ninth House

Man's "higher mind," thoughts and thinking, reason and rationalization, knowledge, science, language as comprehension, consciousness, conscience, values, morals, customs as distinct from habits, the ethical sense, capacity for implication and attribution, philosophy, religion, cultivated and disciplined insight, maturity as self-balance, generalization and abstraction, taken-for-granted ideas, vicarious act and decision, inspiration, visions as an ordered psychic capacity, the creative manipulation of ideas, metaphysical competency, basic view of the world, faith and expectation as distinct from specific hopes and desires, dreams, prophecy, the psychic life in its objective anchorage

Projection of self to a distance, long journeys, fame as distinct from honor or as the spread of personal report, notoriety, foreign countries and places, books as content rather than objects, universalized fellowship, patriotism

Ethical responsibility, individual consequences of past act, liability to accidents, hazards from natural phenomena, consideration and conscious analysis of change

Common law or the restriction on the group out of its past, court procedures and legal practices as juristic custom, agents of justice with discriminative powers as truant and probation officers, the clergy and religious workers as discretionary administrators of the spiritual law, incorporated entities or corporate organization as a delimitation of group responsibility by law

Organized security through group distribution as in insurance, retirement income, social security under the government, fire and damage insurance of all sorts, appointments and "livings"

Group distributions of intellectual goods as in publishing, lecturing, and agencies of enlightenment in distinction from mere teaching, the planning and theoretical direction of research, practical science and scientists, subjective intellectual discipline, wisdom in general

Transportation to a distance, usually taken as shipping in contradistinction to land portage

Birds other than pets or domesticated species

The Tenth House

Social place, honor, position, authority, dignity

Employer, superior, ranking higher officer at any level of life, magistrates, the active heads in any enterprise

Governmental units to which anyone is subservient, whether the nation, state or smaller entity; the group interest in general, the police power of the state in particular, the judge in court, any arbitrator or arbitrators, a jury as an executive body, the sovereign power as in the House of Commons, any legislative body in connection with its veto power over another body of lesser dignity

Ambition in general, prestige, established credit as a general potential, nobility, aristocracy, distinctive vocation, profession, trained skills on the higher levels of recognition, disciplined capacities of every essentially superior sort

General supervision of life, the pertinent higher reference in any issue, over-all inspiration, social refinements as such, the mother as the close-link parent

The public state of things, business or trade in general, effective action in group affairs, good will and whatever articulates it, the zenith in experience, the most fortunate situation

Administrators of property, proprietors, owners, landlords, managers

LOCATING THE QUESTION

The Eleventh House

Friends, acquaintances, casual ties with others, experience at the expense of others, generalized potentialities, idealized projects, purely vicarious experience as in contrast with ordered intellection, imagination when undisciplined

Objectives in general, counsel and counselors, plans prior to action, hopes or wishes of a tangible sort and their valuation, tentative contacts for a remote consideration, intentions of every kind, remote contingency, caution and forehandedness by instinct, friendly help

Legislative activities and bodies, enacted "law" as in contrast with the traditional "law" of custom and tradition, the jury as a counseling body, congress, parliament, the state legislature and city council, boards of directors in general

The Twelfth House

Institutionalization of life and temperament, hospitals, municipal and state welfare agencies, clinics, emergency shelters, confinement, restraint, penitentiaries, prisons, jails, insane asylums, reformatories, concentration camps, detention homes, rehabilitation agencies, protective custody, escape from bondage, reprieves, paroles, pardons, escaped prisoners

Unrealized potentialities of anything immediately at hand, psychic automaticity, loose ends in general, subjective maladjustment, uncontrolled inner experience, basic inadequacies of self, inner or psychic turmoil, consciousness at the chaotic stage

Psychological sustainment as well as restriction, hidden and unrealized or surprising factors in experience generally, inhibitions and their mastery, spiritual resources, unexpressed devotion, unsuspected help, subconscious guidance.

Hidden enemies and enmities, envy, malice, misery, criminal impulses, self-betrayal, mourning, regrets, suicide, worry as simple fretting, unexpected misfortune, fear in general

Detectives and investigators, courtrooms
Wild creatures at large, animals beyond control or that constitute a threat or damage property, "large animals"

the method of horary interpretation

CHAPTER EIGHT

THE YES-AND-NO TECHNIQUE

THE most important elements in a genuinely successful horary astrology, whether practiced by the professional or amateur, are speed and certainty of operation. This is especially true when a problem is analyzed for someone present in person. The average individual is impatient, and does not enjoy sitting in expectation while the practitioner is busy with figures, or is lost in a brown study. Any adept at horary art has learned to begin the diagnosis of a given situation almost immediately, even if he has to depend on generalities at the start.

This matter of the psychological impression made on the client, however, is the least important reason for the use of fast and sharply defined methods. The human mind is essentially fluid, ever shifting its attention here and there, and judgment from a horary chart, which from its very nature must be exceptionally specific, is apt to become quite uncertain instead, if the mind is given too much opportunity for vacillation, or response to less pertinent and inconsequential side issues. What takes place in horary analysis is akin to photography, when the blurring of images on the negative by moving objects before the camera is defeated by an extra concentration of light rays admitted through the lens in an exaggerated shortening of time, permitting the picture to be sharp. The most effective horary technique sets up a definite schedule of invariable procedures, and the successive possibilities for the quickest and most incisive answers are examined first. Complications are taken up in the order of their complexity, and are found significant as they arise. The astrologer never finds himself floundering around in any questionable grasp of a particular situation. Rather he moves from step to step under a procedure where no move is ever waste motion.

A very sharp differentiation must be made between natal and horary astrology, since the failure to recognize this is the greatest barrier to any real proficiency in horary art. Nothing here implies that the latter form of analysis is a separate kind of astrology, or that the stars and planets, the motions of the earth and heavenly bodies, are viewed any differently by the one branch in comparison with the other. What makes the two modes of approach distinct is the fact that natal analysis is concerned primarily with the totality of affairs in the individual case—that its emphasis is on the whole life of the native, even in examining a very specific problem—whereas the horary attack is upon some one special or critical focus in relationships as this is drawn out in a definite separation from the totality of all things, that is, as some point at issue in experience is clarified in its own immediate pattern of events. Horary astrology examines momentarily independent potentials, as an aid to intelligent choice or action; placing the emphasis upon the situation rather than the individual. It contributes to a real effectiveness in problem-solving by narrowing the focus of relations to some crisis at the forefront of experience.

William Lilly demonstrated the essential technique in any judgment on a horary chart, but the later astrologers who built on his work increasingly assimilated natal meth-

THE YES-AND-NO TECHNIQUE

ods to the clear-cut procedures he inaugurated, and this confusion has come to dominate the literature on the subject. Indeed, he himself failed to make the distinction sharply enough for those who might not look behind his literal aphorisms to detect the striking originality and genius of his approach. As a result the present text must overemphasize the fundamental principles, in order to make them clear, and to exhibit their meaning in their own basic terms. This necessity is responsible for what, to some, may seem an exaggerated deliberation in unfolding and distinguishing the step-by-step process. However, the presentation is strictly a return to Lilly, in the sense of a faithful reconstruction in modern terms of his remarkable "organum" for the analysis and solution of everyday problems.

The first step in this horary art is the employment of what has come to be known as the "yes-and-no technique," a procedure by which fully half the possible questions in this branch of astrology can be answered almost immediately, and with a high predictive accuracy. It enables the professional to operate with lightning speed. It equips the amateur or newcomer with a means for handling enough real inquiries in actual practice, even at the very beginning of his study, to "learn by doing." He may develop a confidence in himself, and in the powers of astrological analysis, long before he need familiarize himself with more complicated details, or attempt any attack upon the more difficult problems brought to the regular practitioner.

The essence of the yes-and-no technique is simplicity itself. If the significators of a desired or intended act or decision on the one hand, and of the immediate consequences of such an action or decision on the other—that is, the planets ruling the two houses in question, in the most simple case a given one and its opposite—come to a favorable aspect between themselves, the answer is "yes." If these significators form an adverse aspect to each other, conversely, the answer is "no." If they do not form any aspect, either favorable or unfavorable, the answer is superficially indeterminate, and in such a case it is then necessary to go further in analysis; that is, the problem is shown to be too involved for a direct "yes" or "no" to be given.

In employing this yes-and-no technique, the conjunction, sextile and trine are taken as "yes," and the square and opposition as "no." Only these five of the six aspects recognized by Claudius Ptolemy (fl. 2d century, A.D.) are normally employed in horary art, as has been stated. The sixth, the parallel of declination, has a special usage, to which a later chapter is devoted.[1] As already explained, these aspects are never taken primarily in the fashion of natal delineation—as they are found at the time for which the wheel is erected, either exactly or "within orb"—but instead they are considered only as any given planet is able to move forward in the zodiac (i.e., in a counterclockwise direction) without crossing the boundary line into the next sign, and to make the aspect exact with some other planet (not ascendant, meridian, cusp of any house, node of any planet or any Arabian part, at this stage of procedure). This may be a movement of almost thirty degrees in the extreme case, and it is always counterclockwise even when the moving planet is retrograde (due to the fact that the turning of the whole heavens is involved, at this point, not actual planetary "motion"[2]).

[1] See Chapter Fifteen, p. 385.   [2] Explained further on p. 239.

THE YES-AND-NO TECHNIQUE

In the recommended phrasing of horary questions, the form of statement has always been, "What will the results be of" some definite action or choice. It is obvious, therefore, that the words "yes" and "no" are not to be taken literally. If a client asks an astrologer "What will the results be of taking the trip to Canada?," the "yes" means that they will be favorable, and the "no" that they will be adverse. This is as far as the amateur or beginner may be able to go. In actual practice, naturally, more information will be desired than the mere fact that the proposed move is good or bad. However, it is decidedly advantageous to know even the bare circumstance that the matter inquired about has a "green light," or a red one. Extra details are determined by the supplementary procedures through which judgment is formed on more complicated problems, or which are employed in cases where the primary indication is less sharp. Attention will be given to these, step by step, in the course of the exposition through the following pages.

When the question is placed according to house, in accordance with the principles of rulership outlined in the prior chapter, the lord of that house is taken as the significator of the query, and the lord of the opposite one as the corresponding significator of the immediate outcome. This, of course, means the first and seventh of the judgment as in contrast with the crisis chart, but the distinction between these two wheels need not be made when the straight yes-and-no technique supplies the required solution for a given problem. Often the aspect set up between these two planets will provide everything necessary in satisfying an inquiry under this first, or most simple, of horary procedures.[3] Thus money questions seldom require more than the simple yes-or-no reply, since all that is wished is knowledge of the favorable or unfavorable potential. If a querent asks, "What are the results of investing my savings in this security?," and the answer is "yes," the person is encouraged to go ahead and do so. If the answer is "no," he is warned to find a better place for his funds. Moreover, in problems such as this, it makes little difference which of the two significators completes the aspect in question. In other words, the ruler of the matter can move to the planet ruling the outcome, or vice versa, with no important distinction to be made; a fact which is not at all true in more involved situations.

It is very essential to remember that events are not predetermined or irrevocably set enough in advance so they can be "predicted," except to the degree that the "present moment," in the largest possible sense, is extended over a considerable period of time. Thus the whole life of a given individual is a "present" of such a sort, with fixed characteristics which definitely predict the consequences of action. Every normal judgment in life is based on this fact. The practical joker who gives the "hot foot" to a man of choleric disposition actually "knows" he will lose his temper. The individual who forgets an important anniversary is in no way "surprised" when his overemotional or sentimental wife is hurt, and bursts into tears. All of life's affairs participate, to a varying degree, in what may perhaps best be called the "extended present moment," or the exhibited momentums or tendencies in things that are char-

[3] In the example chart at the end of the chapter (p. 263) the answer to the question above, about the trip to Canada, is "yes." Every suppositional case used in the immediately following pages is traced out similarly and in detail, for the benefit of the novice and amateur, in the explanations immediately following this illustrative horoscope.

THE YES-AND-NO TECHNIQUE

acteristic enough to be dependable. Horary astrology operates, as a strict science of measurement, by providing a mechanism for charting the sensitiveness of the human mind to these dependabilities in experience.

Horary analysis particularly indicates the focus of the "present" complex or crisis because it is fundamentally an "astrology of the houses." It operates primarily through a distribution of relationships in the celestial equator, or in the heavens as they are presented by the turning of the earth on its axis. Both motions of the earth are required in any branch of astrology; but natal delineation, concerned with human life in terms of years, is principally developed on the basis of the earth's annual movement; while horary technique, dealing with more immediate events of shorter duration, is based upon the earth's twenty-four hour rotation. Hence the actual progress of the planets through the zodiac is completely disregarded, except in secondary methods. What actually happens when planets are said to form an aspect in normal horary analysis is that the heavenly sphere carries the position of one to the place of another. In other words, the sphere's motion distributes the momentary motionlessness it has gained in the focus of a given crisis. The planet of more dynamic influence is the one which describes a given relationship out of the place to which it "moves," or from that section of the heavens which turns to the point occupied by the planet at the moment of query or crisis.

Literally, the zodiacal degree at which the aspect is exact turns clockwise to the place where the significant planet was found, but it certainly is easier to speak of the planet as "moving," in what then becomes its normal direction of motion through the zodiac, counterclockwise from the first point of Aries, through the sign into Taurus, and so on around through the circle. By the same token, the positions of the planets, more accurately measured in right ascension by this equatorial rotation of the whole sphere, are indicated in geocentric celestial longitude; again because it is easier. The slight differences in a movement even of thirty degrees are of no significance in anything but the most precise work, such as is yet to be pioneered by the horary astrologers. In time the use of right ascension rather than longitude may become universal for the horary wheel, but the relation of planets to houses remains a zodiacal mediation, since these bodies have their own motions in the ecliptic circle. Horary astrology does not eliminate the zodiacal factors, but subordinates them to equatorial distribution and motion; as illustrated when retrogradation and interception are ignored in all primary technique.

The fact that a planet is retrograde is significant, but only in a supernumerary sense. Thus in the yes-and-no technique the answer is still "yes" or "no," whether a planet is retrograde, intercepted and badly aspected by the other planets, or direct, well-placed and finely aspected in every respect. Indeed, this is probably the proper time to put down, in italics, the most important of all practical rules for horary astrology.[4]

Nothing in a horary chart is to be considered, except as it is pertinent to the immediate question.

The factors in the chart are only to be interpreted as they are necessary for a question. In most routine yes-and-no cases it is unnecessary to pay any attention whatsoever to any of the other planets, or any of the other relations in the chart. In the cases where supplementary information is desired, that information promptly brings these other factors into pertinency, of course; but they are not to be taken ever as having any indication, in any respect whatsoever, modifying the original yes-or-no judgment. This

[4] This should be taken in conjunction with the general principle italicized on p. 126.

THE YES-AND-NO TECHNIQUE 241

sharpness of consideration, buried beneath the overspecific putting down of aphorisms in the older books, even by William Lilly himself, is nonetheless the real secret of Lilly's own horary genius, and that of everyone who has really understood his method and duplicated his results.

Probably nothing is harder for any astrologer to realize, if he has gained his first proficiency with the natal horoscope, than this important horary application of philosophy's familiar "Occam's razor." Here is the basic logical principle that it is sheer incompetent thinking to bring in factors of consideration before they are necessary. Thus a surveyor will use a tree across a river as a marker, and for this purpose the condition of the tree is utterly unimportant, provided its general appearance is such that it can be described clearly. If a line is to be thrown across the stream, however, the tree must then be viewed as something to carry strain or resist the drag of weight; making sure it is not a dead stump that would at once pull out of the ground, or not a sapling that might break, but rather a firm trunk with healthy roots. Its condition then becomes necessary knowledge. If real permanence is demanded, such as a fixed anchorage for a suspension span, a tree is probably of no use whatever, and a stone or concrete foundation may be required at the spot the tree has occupied.

This parallel to an astrological situation is hardly exact, but it may make clear how a planet in the most simple form of yes-and-no judgment is no more than a "marker," to show where the rulership of a certain house is focused in a given system of relations. Whether the planet is direct or retrograde, it is still this mark of the focus, no more and no less. The same Occam's razor must be used through all astrological details. Corresponding to the planetary complex, the life situation charted by the horary wheel must be treated with the same competent sharpening of analysis in an economy of relations. Thus the question of funds to invest will serve again as an example. The "yes" or "no" is a matter of favorable or unfavorable results to be expected as the result of a given act of investment or trusteeship, and this may be equally "favorable" if the money is entirely the querent's own to use as he wills, if it is tied up with direct restriction of some kind, or if it is involved in any of a myriad of more remote ways.

Natal astrology reflects all these side issues, which is at once its weakness and its strength. Horary art is also both helped and handicapped, depending on whether or not its techniques are properly employed, because by contrast it definitely does not indicate or reflect anything outside the immediate center of interest, or the rigorously narrowed point of crisis. All this, of course, philosophically and psychologically, is merely the essential distinction between an approach to life on the yearly or more ordered perspective, as distinct from the daily or wholly transient and almost completely unconditioned point of view. While it is foolish to assume that any event of a man's life may be omitted from the totality of his whole experience or his continuing individuality, it is equally nonsensical to deny or neglect the faculty possessed by all conscious creatures for separating the experience of the moment from everything else, and for living it entirely in its own terms. This is creativity *per se*, the direct experience of free will.

Natal astrology charts the first of these essential perspectives, that of the totality in potential, as an approach to a psychological mastery of life, and horary astrology the second.

The Classification of Questions

A considerable modification in the yes-and-no technique is brought about by the difference in the various questions that can be asked, or the divergent problems and events

THE YES-AND-NO TECHNIQUE 243

brought to the horary astrologer for analysis. This makes it necessary to classify the various types of inquiry in some detail, and sets up a first classification on the basis of a distinction between the option and the non-option proposition.[5]

An option question is the simple and basic form of inquiry in which the individual is able to go ahead "according to plan," if he is encouraged; or to refrain from proceeding, without any penalty whatsoever, if the outlook is unfavorable. It already has been pointed out that what is revealed by a horary chart will hold as valid or dependable in so far as the conditions of the inquiry remain in existence. These conditions, in the case of any genuine option, are theoretical, or are predicated upon the querent taking the given option, and therefore nothing at all is to be deduced from any of the details of such a chart when the option is dropped.

The yes-and-no technique operates when the inquiry lies in the non-option category, but in a modified fashion. Here is the situation where a querent has already acted, or made his decision, as illustrated in the question, "What will be the result of my action in signing the contract yesterday?" Actually there is a considerable difference of opinion over this sort of query, whether it should not be treated under the technique of elections; with judgment made on the basis of a horoscope for the actual moment of signing, or deciding to do so. The procedure is not necessary, even when the exact time is known. Obviously the regular horary method alone is available if no record has been made of that moment. Due to the psychological struc-

[5] This had its preliminary exposition in Chapter Six, where attention was drawn to the non-option query as a problem of orientation.

ture of the mind itself, both techniques should never be used in the same case, and by this same token no question should ever be made the basis of more than one horary chart unless some change in the situation justifies the reexamination. In exactly the same way that the Bill of Rights will not permit the state to try a man twice for the same crime, so the psychological "bill of rights" makes it exceedingly unethical to harass the mind by calling for a mere confirmatory judgment, thereby prejudicing the mind's accuracy of sensitiveness.

There is no difficulty in the case of a non-option inquiry if the answer is a "yes" because in such an instance the act or decision is approved, and the querent is given what he mostly desires, a reassurance which enables him to proceed along the chosen lines with a maximum of self-confidence. Where the answer is "no" the problem is very real, because the pertinent initiative now lies in the past. What is here indicated, therefore, is a necessity to change the situation as a whole by bringing the matter, if possible, into another frame of reference. The horary chart obviously holds its implication in these non-option questions much more definitely than when the direct initiative still lies in the hand of the querent. It takes on a momentary but marked similarity to the natal figure in the fact that while the pattern is indicated as definitely established, or beyond change in its own terms or complex, the use to which it may be put will permit wide variations. The definite procedures necessary in changing a general frame of reference are revealed by supplementary or subordinate modes of horary interpretation, to be explained at a later point. The amateur confronted with a non-option "no" at this stage will

THE YES-AND-NO TECHNIQUE

simply have to counsel a careful resurvey of the situation by any querent, with a fresh attack upon the issue and its solution, and perhaps a further horary inquiry as a result.

Another classification of questions is between initiative and non-initiative matters, which are never to be confused with the option and non-option distribution. This second classification is illustrated by such a question as "Shall I take the position if it is offered to me?" There is an option, so that the yes-and-no technique remains simple, but the option is contingent on what someone else does. Horary astrology never shows the potentials of a remote contingency with any dependability, except through the agency of some more immediate set of relations. This fact makes it impossible to treat this matter as an ordinary option query, or to obtain a "yes" or "no" reply, without taking the contingency into account on the one hand, and the necessity to act or make a choice, if the issue arises, on the other. Actually the possibility of the matter coming to a head, and compelling a decision, is itself a crisis in the experience of the moment. It requires a set in consciousness which will be an adequate enough anticipation of the outcome to make all adjustment in understanding both intelligent and satisfactory. What makes the inquiry of importance to the querent is the possibility that he will be offered the given opportunity, with whatever degree of immediate upset or disruption of perspectives that may be involved, and the horoscope fundamentally charts the potentiality of self-reorientation as an event in immediate experience. This facing of possibilities requires choice, irrespective of the fact that the end-result may be either action or attitude, either objective or subjective realization.

The technique presents no difficulties, despite the fact that a new dimension is added to the yes-and-no relationship. The affirmative or negative indication still reveals the results of the action taken, that is, the consequences of exercising the option or not doing so, but in addition there is the factor of initiative, or the question whether the querent will have the opportunity to exercise the particular option or not. This is revealed by the distinction between the two planets, in the yes-and-no aspect, as "applying" and "separating." The one which must move forward in the zodiac, to make the aspect exact, "applies" to the other in astrological language, and becomes of first or dynamic importance. When the lord of the house that rules the question is this applying planet, the initiative rests with the querent. When the lord of the opposite house applies, the initiative rests in the hands of others.

If a problem belongs in this classification, the astrologer is at once equipped to give advice of wider latitude, and to be of much greater real service than in the case of the more direct or simple option. When a "yes" is indicated, with the initiative in the querent's hands, he should not only accept the position to be offered, but he also should take positive action to precipitate the offer; that is, he should demonstrate his interest by calling on key people, by doing preliminary survey work of some sort, and by moving in all possible ways to build up and strengthen the projected situation. On the contrary, when the answer is "yes," but when the initiative does not rest with the querent, he should be advised to accept the position if it is offered, but he also should be urged, very emphatically, to let the proposition alone, to refrain from "stirring up the

THE YES-AND-NO TECHNIQUE

animals" or trying to hurry the key individuals in any way. This does not mean pretending to have a positive disinterest, but merely a rigorous care not to attempt or to take any initiative whatsoever.

The "yes" judgment in the simple option inquiry, and the "no" judgment in those option questions where the point of initiative must be taken into account, represent the most clear-cut indications to be found in horary art. The former is an unqualified "green" light, with no further information either necessary or valuable, while the latter is an absolute "red" signal, suggesting that the matter should be terminated or put out of mind completely. This is easy to do if the initiative rests with the querent. If the power to act lies with the other fellow, however, then the inquirer must be set in mind to parry any overtures, or to counteract any lack of action on the other's part, in such a way that no hard feelings are created, and no needless complications are encouraged.

The third great classification of horary inquiries includes the problems which, rather than a proposition of simple choice relative to a given straight option to act or decide, or an equally simple choice as this is contingent on an initiative yet to be exercised, are always the choice between two definitely distinct options. Here is the very important either-or type of question. It is illustrated by the query, "Shall I go to Florida for a vacation, or remain here to plan that new business campaign?" The amateur astrologer must use exceptional care to distinguish between this form of inquiry, and the straight option which a seeming "either-or" matter becomes whenever the alternative is not positively under consideration. Indeed, it is not bad practice to insist that both projected lines of action be believed to be of equal importance by the querent, if one is not to be discarded as a mere device for dramatizing the negation of the other. Thus a man might think of wintering in California, and ask, "Shall I go West, or remain on the job?" This remaining on the job, of itself, is an unimportant detail because it makes little difference to his business whether he goes or not. In his mind it is what he has left to do, his recourse if he should decide to forego the trip.

On further examination of the querent who contemplates the California visit, it might develop that his whole interest is really one of health, and the problem is not of deciding which of two things to do, but rather determining the probable results of the only choice which would represent any positive·action. Staying home, in his case, simply means doing nothing about his health, because he has exhausted his ideas for remedial measures to take in his normal or accustomed environment. In the other illustration, the querent is actually torn between two calls upon him. There are definite reasons for joining his family in the South, as he always has done, and there are equally valid considerations for giving his attention to important developments in his business. It is the best technique when in doubt, however, to treat any question of this sort as a straight option rather than an either-or type. The latter must always arise in a situation which places an individual upon the unmistakable prongs of a dilemma.

The yes-and-no technique in the either-or question is utterly simple if a "yes" is indicated. The decision between the two options is then given by that one of the two planets which is applying to the other by favorable aspect. As

THE YES-AND-NO TECHNIQUE 249

lord of one of the two houses involved—that is, either as against the opposite—the applying planet represents the best alternative of the two possibilities which the pair of houses designates.

What becomes a matter of more advanced or complicated procedure now is the location of two different matters in their significant houses. It should be obvious that to place the options in the crisis chart independently of each other would be to ignore the relationship between them, and thus destroy the basis for a yes-and-no judgment. Matters of this type can be handled separately, each given an analysis and judgment on the basis of its own merits; with the querent thus helped to make a choice between them on the basis of his own mental balancing of the advantages and disadvantages shown for each. Such is the procedure in "multiple questions," but it is not the same direct help which the either-or query, under the yes-and-no technique, provides for the individual who faces a real dilemma. Only when the horary wheel refuses the yes-and-no indication is it proper to assume that the dilemma in question is more apparent than real. Then recourse to the other modes of analysis is entirely proper.

The astrological problem here is the location of divergent lines of action, as the possibilities of choice, in the opposite houses that must be identified for the primary yes-and-no judgment. In most cases there is no difficulty because the human mind usually expresses its "either-ors" in terms whereby one is the cancellation of the other. In the two illustrations used so far, the alternatives are Florida or California and home, and the opposition is not obvious. This is also true in such queries as "Shall I go fishing with my wife, or build the boathouse with my son?"—a typical week-end triviality—and "Would it be better to have my operation, or take my chance to play Nora in the revival of 'The Doll's House?' "

A genuine opposition actually exists in the houses whenever the alternative becomes a true issue in experience, and the skilled practitioner is always able to trace it out. Thus, in the case of the summer activities of the preceding paragraph, the primary basis of rulership is neither the alternatives of companionship nor the difference in energy expenditure, but rather the mode of enjoyment on vacation, or a fifth and eleventh distinction, while the conflict of health and business in the life of the actress is at root the impediment that each becomes to the other, hence requiring a knowledge of the particular urgency precipitating the crisis.[6] For the sake of surety in horary interpretation, therefore, these refinements of exceptional instances must be covered by practical rules such as will serve the amateur or beginner whenever he is unable to identify the deeper lines of connection to his satisfaction.

First of all, in an either-or query, the option mentioned first is the basis of house location unless there are positive reasons for making it subordinate. In other words the astrologer, when in doubt, follows the set of the querent's mind. Secondly, the basis is (1) the option which requires the most positive action, or (2) the one which if accepted will represent the broadest adjustment in immediate circumstances, or (3) that one of the two which seems to be pressing the most imperiously for decision. "How can business be in the third house, opposite to the 'long journey' to Florida?," a new student might ask. In this case the querent confronts a change in pertinent relationships from near to remote factors, which is the root of the conflict in his mind, and the third-house rulership of his "business" is correct because, in this special contrast, the matter comes under the "taken for granted" category. The rulership of

[6] The more detailed explanations follow on p. 265 ff.

THE YES-AND-NO TECHNIQUE 251

the houses in either-or analysis is never descriptive of the issues as they exist, each in its own terms, but always as the characteristics of each come momentarily into opposition in the querent's experience. It is extraordinarily important in horary art to remember that the indications are always in the special set of the moment's meaning. Everything depends on the emphasis supplied by the question itself, together with whatever supplementary information is available.

Thus the man called to go to Florida, although he asks, "Shall I go South, or stay home on business," may be found to have in mind, "What will be the results of sacrificing my wife's plans for the season at Miami Beach, if I stay here to get this new business merger going smoothly?" At once the focus of the question is in the tenth house, with Florida revealed, in any true sense of the word "meaning," as a matter of home, or the fourth. If the business is an opportunity, to be located in the seventh because not yet established in the tenth, the Florida obligation becomes a personal matter of more individual upset at the ascendant, to parallel the more directly personal emphasis established at the seventh.

The ability to make these distinctions correctly marks the difference between the tyro and the expert in horary work, but the occasional practitioner or amateur can avoid all difficulty, and escape every possible chance for misinterpretation, if he will be careful to phrase his questions properly. The queries in the preceding paragraphs have been left in their natural form, to exhibit their either-or characteristics, but before analysis they would each be turned into the "What would be the results of . . ." formula, at once facilitating the house location of the "either" as against the "or." While the options must be of equal weight in the querent's mind, one of them will always be found dominant in its demand for decision or in the degree to which it presents an idea of change and difference, or represents the initiative in the creation of the dilemma in the first place.

The either-or query is only valid under the yes-and-no technique when a "yes" is shown. In the case of an adverse aspect, formed by the lords of the two opposite houses which represent the alternatives of option, the primary indication is a denial of either alternative as advisable. However, a very important distinction arises at this point. Primarily a "no" in this form of question means not so much that either or both of the possible ways of acting must be taken as essentially bad, but rather that an inadequacy of perspective or judgment is represented in the particular either-or situation. It may be that subsequent or more detailed judgment would make both suggestions inadvisable, but this does not necessarily follow; and it must never be given as a definite opinion. What is shown in the case of a "no" answer in this technique is that something is wrong with the either-or. The querent must be sent back to think through his problem again. Thus the man who feels he is torn between his Florida vacation and the needs of his business may be making a martyr of himself. Possibly he can do both, going to Florida a little later or earlier, or "commuting" back and forth.

The sequential-option query is the least simple form of the yes-and-no technique, quite rare in practice, and to be distinguished very sharply from the analysis of multiple questions. It is, of course, the circumstance of more than two options, but only when there is both an equality of

THE YES-AND-NO TECHNIQUE

importance or desirability in the querent's realization of their potentials—so as to create the necessary trilemma, or tetralemma, and so on—and also the same direct or immediate relation among them which establishes the validity of the more simple either-or inquiry.

As an illustration, a businessman has four salesmen, from among whom he must promote one to the position of sales manager. He feels unable to do an intelligent job of selection because, while one man has a splendid record in the results he produces and is liked by the trade, he somehow antagonizes the other salesmen. The second individual is a splendid man in every way normally, but he has emotional weaknesses which cause him to get involved in serious difficulties from time to time. The third candidate is an ideal executive, and would be able to handle the sales force superlatively, but his own personal results are poor, so that while he is liked his judgment and advice are not respected. The fourth possibility has no less a puzzling combination of points in his favor and against him, since he is temperamental in a way that upsets everyone.

The executive, in his tetralemma, cannot turn to his associates in the business for advice, because he knows they play politics and will not consider the men on their merits. At length he consults an astrologer. The four options have to be distributed around the chart. Salesmen are ruled by the sixth house, even sales managers as well as sales-managers-to-be when they are employes considered for promotion by their superior, and the four men are taken in the usual sequence form of six-eight-ten-twelve in the crisis chart, as already explained in the prior chapter. Since more than two factors cannot be distributed through the two terms of a yes-and-no relation, what becomes necessary is the establishment of what amounts to four exactly similar simple option questions: "What will be the results of promoting so-and-so to sales manager?" The sixth house and its opposite give the "yes" or "no" in respect to the first man considered, the eighth and its opposite in respect to the second man, the tenth and its opposite in respect to the third man, and the twelfth and its opposite in respect to the fourth man. The order in which the men are taken follows the rules for such sequences, here probably the succession in which the querent presents them (which may be the way they have placed themselves in his own mind, or their seniority with the company, or any other convenient criterion).

The great sharpness of normal yes-and-no judgment is lost here in this approach to the method of multiple judgment; since the final advice depends on a balancing of minor testimonies, separately derived. When there is a "yes" for one man only, there is no difficulty, and he is recommended. If there is a "yes" for more than one, then the recommendation goes to whichever is indicated by the strongest aspect. When any of these aspects are formed by a planet moving less than three and a half degrees, the "strongest" is the one requiring the least movement, whether a trine, sextile or conjunction; when the aspects are formed by planets moving more than three and a half degrees, a trine is the strongest among them, then the sextile and finally the conjunction, irrespective of the distance the applying planet has to move.

It is possible for the same pair of planets to be the indicators for two of the candidates, in which case the man indicated by the applying planet is accepted as the better choice. In the exceedingly remote contingency that indicators are of equal strength by these rules, if one is retrograde or intercepted it is taken as weaker. Interception is a mark of greater weakness in horary astrology than retrogradation; but neither of these factors have any further significance at the present point in analysis. When all other differentia fail, the planets themselves rank in order of horary strength as follows: Saturn, Jupiter, Mars, Venus, Mercury, sun and moon.

THE YES-AND-NO TECHNIQUE

In every explanation of horary questions this far in the chapter, a possibility of complete freedom in act for the querent has been assumed. There is a final class of queries arising from a situation of conflict, or the case where a clash of interests between one individual and another—or between an individual and a group—is such that the mutual involvement does not leave either party free to act, unless within narrowed limitations and except in co-operation with the other. This is the reciprocal-option. It is in many ways the most difficult of all problems to which horary astrology brings assistance, even though not as complicated as the sequential options. If the querent proves to be interested only to the extent he has an actual choice, then the simplest way to handle the matter is to center attention upon some pertinent phase of the matter where he is able to move, thus converting the query into an ordinary option of the types already suggested. Occasionally the initiative in the given crisis will seem to lie completely in some other person's hands, and if there is adequate relationship to the querent to justify horary inquiry at all, the inquiry can be handled inversely by a consideration of that other person's option, according to the usual procedures. Such an individual is then considered the opponent in the given set of circumstances, and identified fundamentally through the seventh house. This method of analysis through an opponent is one of the least advisable of procedures, however, for several important reasons. Primarily there is danger of misinterpretation. In the case of the "yes" the effect is the same as a "no," since it is a "yes" for the other fellow, and vice versa. Moreover, there can be no certainty that the act or attitude of one who holds the power of choice in a relationship which, of itself, is a definite limitation on the freedom of the querent, is unchangeably antagonistic enough at root to preserve a state of fixed opposition through every shift in the situation, and so give astrological reliability.

A psychological factor that operates against any true dependability, in these attempts through horary astrology to get information on matters of inadequately direct concern to the querent, is even more definitely a handicap in any effort to analyze a given situation through another person with whom the tie is competitive or generally inimical. This is the underlying "wishful thinking" that must of necessity give the substance to all inquiry. It is psychologically impossible to ask a question out of any ultimate background other than pure self-interest, even if this is most minimized by social training. The element of wishful thinking, in the course of normal option queries, is an asset, since it is an important part of the energy that goes into the solution of the problem. However, when curiosity is removed from any practical or immediate relation to self, the accompanying or unsuspected mental "drive" loads the whole machinery of intellection on the side of a subjective or abstracted desire, and judgment notoriously tends to reflect this inner leaning. Here is the whole basis of psychoanalysis, as well as all the spectacular detective work done with psychological techniques, and so obviously the most important single reason for avoiding any analysis through the view or option of anyone whose interests are momentarily or permanently opposed to the querent's own.

The reciprocal-option question, in phrasing and in general structure, roughly parallels the straight option and its normal yes-and-no indication. Examples are, "What will

THE YES-AND-NO TECHNIQUE

be the results of my title bout with the champion?" or "What is the outlook in my suit over the water rights?" These questions are distinct from the non-option inquiry, however, because while preliminary action has been taken, irrevocably, the real activity is yet to come, and it is the joint activity of two opposing parties. When the many problems of this sort are not handled from the times of actual events—the signing of papers, filing of suits, commencement of hostilities in a shooting war, and so on, under the technique associated with "elections"—the interpretation is on the pattern of the either-or query, because two distinct people or parties are involved; but with the special modifications of judgment necessary to take account of the lack of real option in the cases of both the querent and his opponent.

Here is the type of inquiry ideally represented by many athletic contests, which are carried out under definite rules and cannot be canceled by any single party except by forfeiture of any title he may have, or other serious consequences. While participation in most races, tournaments and the like, in contradistinction to this contest between two parties, provides the chance to withdraw with perhaps no penalty, such events afford no parallel to problems in the reciprocal-option class. Lawsuits and warfare, however, reveal the other and important extreme where the side that quits thereby surrenders its rights and perhaps even its liberty without a struggle, and so faces the type of unthinkable action which hardly represents an option. This form of practical consideration is encountered by horary art in divorce, personal quarrels of many sorts, feuds, and all strange or "intimate" ties of human malice.

A "yes" for the querent in a reciprocal-option question —that is, when the planet indicating his interest, following the procedure of the either-or interpretation, applies favorably to the planet of opposing interest—means success in his effort to achieve a desired end, and is a valuable encouragement, while a "yes" for his opponent means that defeat or discomfiture may be expected. The "no" for himself is a little more promising than a "yes" for his opponent, since it shows a situation more capable of response to change, or to a new dynamic. However, it reveals a probable continuance of the difficulty, or of the whole unsatisfactory state of affairs, until something is done about it on the creative side. The opponent's "yes" is a sharp challenge by contrast, and like the case of the non-option negative, it calls for effort to modify the entire complex of relations, thus weakening or defeating the adverse option held against the querent's interest.

Here is a much more difficult problem than in the straight non-option case, because the inimical factors there are the generally inert conditions of some social or economic environment, whereas an active opponent or enemy in this situation seeks to injure the querent, indirectly if not otherwise. Breaking down the structures of relationship which conspire to defeat the free option of an individual is most simply a disarming procedure, such as making peace by finding and offering some kind of an acceptable compromise, or by uncovering and enlisting new strength to counteract an opponent's favorable advantage. Sometimes the fight can be abandoned at one point with the idea of taking it up to better advantage at another; although this is apt to be a risky procedure. Occasionally it

THE YES-AND-NO TECHNIQUE

is possible to curry favor with the other fellow, on the unholy principle of, "If you can't beat him, join him!" Most fundamentally in issues of this sort the call is for an oblique attempt to reorder the whole life situation, since it has come to a crisis for the querent. He must turn to other resources, and in general seek to destroy the option against him by upsetting, as far as he is able, the whole complex that maintains it. The supplementary procedures in horary art, to which a proper recourse is had for further advice in every instance of the sort, will give the definite suggestions for everyday procedure.

People of high moral sensitiveness deny the right of any one individual to attack the situation of another as a means for improving his own. They reject it as the law of the wolf pack. Astrology puts down its all-important dictum as "Mind your own business!" No one by horoscopic means is to go afield from the relationships actually pertinent to the immediate issue in the life of some native or querent. In a sense this is a corollary of the Hippocratic oath of a true astrologer. The problem is whether the inside knowledge provided by a chart is to be employed for the injury of another, even if he is an enemy. Does the need to upset an unfavorable situation justify the deliberate use of destructive force? The answer, of course, is in the negative.

What is required is not the necessary enforcement of any particular results in another life, but only a change in the import of a complex of relations; first of all in meaning and potentiality, and only then in whatever actual development must perforce accompany that transition. The fact that others may come along in this change of the situation, whether with destructive or constructive results in their case, merely demonstrates this fact of their "coming along" to be a convenience in their own personal development and experience. The native or querent is seeking extrication from that which, of no use to him in the light of his conscious desires, has revealed its more unhappy value to him in an unsuspected degree by the extent to which he is enmeshed in it. He seeks to eliminate such a factor in its relationship to his own affairs, but not necessarily of itself in respect to others, and it is his capacity to accomplish this end in varying reference that is particularly revealed by any astrological chart.

Alternative Indications of Yes-and-No

When the two planetary significators of a matter and its outcome do not form a major aspect in a horary chart, recourse in general has been said to be to the subordinate techniques, or to ways of interpretation which progressively regress towards a consideration of the whole figure rather than the sharp and definite lines of special interest. This means that horary art, as it finds itself inadequate in particular instances, retreats and finally disappears in natal delineation. Of the many techniques of subordinate recourse there are two which remain entirely in the class of yes-and-no judgments. Both are essentially horary practice, as in contradistinction to the over-all methods of natal horoscopy.

In the first of these, working from the fact that the opposite house in any given case indicates the "immediate outcome," and that the fourth house from the ruler of the inquiry similarly shows the more remote "end of the matter"—that is, the potential of the situation in general rather than in particular—the significator of the question may be taken to the significator of this ultimate reconcilia-

THE YES-AND-NO TECHNIQUE 261

tion for a more indirect "yes" or "no," exactly as in the more clear-cut cases taken from opposing houses. The great and important difference is that what is shown is less personal; it is more a matter of a slower and piecemeal adjustment or transformation, permitting the issue of the moment to escape into a larger context. This judgment only has meaning when there is no normal yes-and-no indication, according to the principle of Occam's razor.[7]

The second subordinate yes-and-no interpretation is possible when the question is not located in an angle (more exactly, when the house ruling the inquiry is neither the ascendant nor descendant, and when the fourth house of the question by ring-around-the-rosy is also not the ascendant). A still more indefinite yes-and-no indication can then be given by the relationship between the planet representing the querent, and the one which rules the query. A "yes" means that the inquirer is able to handle the problem, although his immediate procedure or method for doing so is shown to be inadequate or unprofitable. A "no" means that he is not situated to take care of the matter without getting more information, or definitely altering the situation in which he finds himself in respect to the particular issue.

This technique of necessity approaches the problem from a perspective taken on the general or ultimate competency of the querent to accomplish his desire, and at times it is a very powerful mechanism of analysis. Indeed, it has often been made the foundation of attack on all issues arising in horary astrology, in which case the house-and-

[7] Note the analysis of the fourth and seventh houses, in their differentiation at this point, on pages 105-6, 179-80.

its-opposite technique becomes the first recourse and the house-and-its-fourth a second. When this is done, the questions in angular houses are included here, of course, and any duplication of possible aspects is ruled out in the other techniques of recourse. What is revealed by this method is less direct in the light of the immediate query, and therefore it does not give quite as sharp a method to horary art as a whole.[8]

Any yes-and-no judgment through the aspects formed by the lords of houses and opposites is dependent on the relation of Mars and Venus, in the case of two pairs, of Jupiter and Mercury in the case of two more, and of Saturn and either the sun or moon in the case of the final two. When there is a regression to the consideration of the relation between a house and its fourth, or a further regression to the aspects formed by the planet ruling the querent and the significator of the question, any combination among the seven Chaldean planets is possible. This means that the same body may be lord of both the querent and question, with no actual "aspect" possible although the situation is equivalent to a conjunction. Such a result provides a "yes" of a very negative sort. It is favorable, but under circumstances where the querent does not have any adequate perspective on the matter, and so may not be alert to the possibilities involved. He will not profit so much from his direct or positive action as from a general improvement in his own morale, or from a general strengthening of the pertinent situation. Thus further analysis is required, in considerable detail, unless the indefinite challenge has real significance.

[8] An example of its employment is found on p. 118.

THE YES-AND-NO TECHNIQUE 263

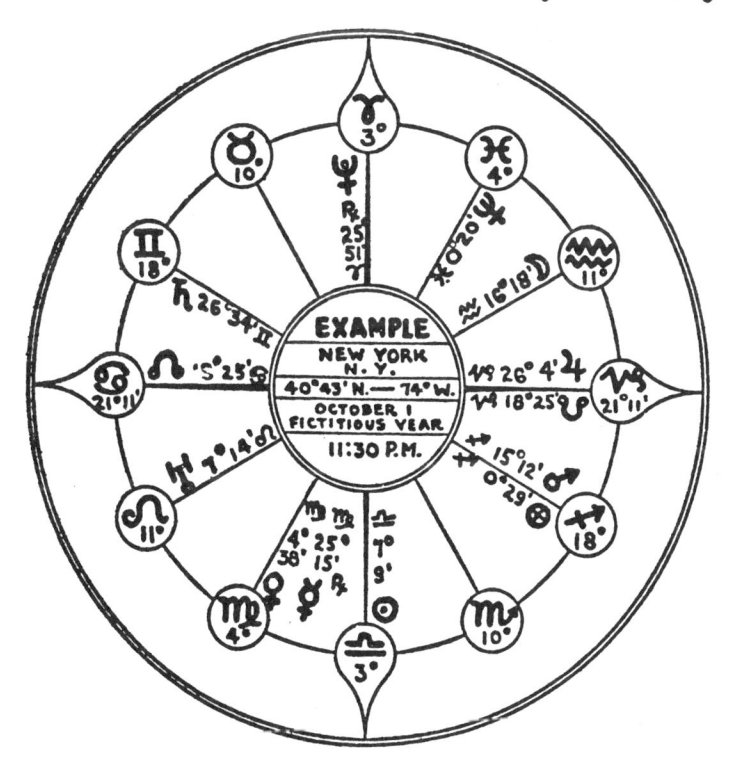

The Chapter's Illustrative Cases in an Example Chart

A trip to Canada (p. 237). This is a simple ninth-house problem, since there is nothing to imply a rulership in the third (i.e., a chance to cross a bridge, as from Detroit to Windsor) and therefore Jupiter as ruler of the ninth is considered in its relation with Mercury, lord of the judgment-chart seventh (the opposite house). Mercury applies to Jupiter by trine, and this gives an unqualified "yes," since no attention is paid, at this stage of any yes-and-no conclusions, to the fact that Mercury is retrograde.

Investment of savings (p. 238). Here is a straightaway second-house inquiry. The sun and Saturn provide the yes-and-no through a trine, indicating "yes"; and the fact that the sun is the planet which completes the aspect is a matter of no significance at this point.

Signing a contract (p. 243). Because it is a seventh-house question, Saturn and the moon become significators. They are trine; hence the client may have the reassurance he needs. Again the fact that the moon is the applying planet has no meaning.

Taking a position (p. 245). As explained on page 139, this is a seventh-house problem. The Saturn-moon aspect yields a "yes." Since this is a contingent option (i.e., an initiative matter), more factors have to be taken into account. Because the moon as ruler of the outcome is the planet of application, the querent must let the opportunity come to him without action or interference on his own part. Had this query been, "What are the results of taking the theatrical engagement, if it is offered me?," the fifth-house placing would have given Mars and Venus as significators, and a "no." In that case the lord of the outcome would be applying in the square. Either the position would not be presented at all, or it would be offered but not advantageously, so that it would be necessary to refuse it in such a way as to avoid future penalties or unfriendliness.

Florida trip versus important business (p. 247). This first develops in an alternative of a move to a distance as against a continuance in the taken-for-granted progress of events, or a ninth-third proposition, with Jupiter and Mercury involved. The either-or dilemma is valid because these planets are trine and, since Mercury applies, the verdict is for staying at home and attending to business. As before, no attention is paid to the fact that the planet is retrograde. On further analysis, however, it turned out that the disturbance in the client's mind was over the fact that his business developments penalized his wife's social

THE YES-AND-NO TECHNIQUE

plans. While the latter were quite subordinate in his interest, the sense of obligation to her was as strong as his own sense of loyalty to his firm. Taking the business in the tenth, and Florida as "home" at this given season, Mars and Venus are the planets involved, and their square suggests that he is not thinking through the matter clearly enough, as pointed out in the main text. However, if the further suggestion that the business call was something new, an opportunity that might be lost if neglected, the seventh and first houses are taken, with the trine of Saturn and moon dictating the judgment, and the application of the latter indicating that his first consideration is his wife, and that he will fare better by risking the opportunity in order to keep his own personal relationships healthy at center.

California visit versus business (p. 248). Up to a certain point this is no different from the Florida matter. However, it turns out to be really a matter of health, and so actually a simple option matter. Jupiter and Mercury are the planets of the sixth and its opposite, and they give a "yes," hence the move is a good one.

Fishing versus carpentry (p. 249). This has been identified as a fifth-eleventh dilemma in the body of the chapter, which means a Mars-Venus relationship, and a "no." Once again an inadequacy of perspective is indicated, and the client must be asked to re-examine his idea of the alternatives he faces. Probably he can give pleasure to his wife, and also get to his boathouse, under some different and much better plan.

Operation versus important role (p. 249). Here is an extreme example of the nonobvious inner conflicts of human alternative. If the surgical attention is taken as primary—because it is mentioned first by the actress, or because it represents the more positive or critical decision, or because it would wholly disrupt her life—the sixth and twelfth houses, ruled by Jupiter and Mercury, are employed for the yes-and-no indication. The application of

Mercury, ruling the opposite house, then calls for accepting the role and postponing the medical care. Contrariwise, if a more careful questioning of the lady leads the astrologer to give primacy to the theatrical opportunity, which as a detail of creative work on the stage would of necessity lie in the fifth house, the dilemma is located under the Mars-Venus square, and its "no" would lead him to demand a new perspective on her part.

An incidental problem for many new students will be the analysis by which the twelfth house, in the first instance, can rule the portrayal of Ibsen's Nora, and how the eleventh house, in the alternative possibility, can show the surgical operation. As has been pointed out on page 171, the selection of location for a given matter is the beginning of horary judgment. The twelfth house is the subjective sustainment of personality *per se*, and in the mind of this actress a success in the revival of the old play would apparently give a psychological "bottom" to everything else she did. Quite probably her projected surgery represents a self-justification, an "uplift to her ego" which balances the visit to the hospital on the scales of her inner esteem. In similar fashion, the eleventh house in revealing general objectives would show the querent's "wishful thinking" in respect to her own physical condition. The dichotomy she here sets up in her own mind shows the projected hospital visit to be a bid for friendly support, a means in some inchoate stirring towards a more active and objective guidance in achieving her goals. The point is not that these implications can ever be forced into the houses, by some sort of "shoehorn technique," but that the linking of alternatives by people in their actual experience—as charted through the house mechanism—is special light upon the real meaning of the various problems they face.

The four salesmen (p. 253). The third man is eliminated at once in the example chart, because the tenth and its opposite, ruled by Mars-Venus, yield a "no" through the square of these planets. The first and fourth men, at the sixth and twelfth houses, are shown by the identical pair, Jupiter and Mercury, and so by a "yes," but by the rules the choice out of the two is given through Mercury, as applying planet and lord of the crisis twelfth. Thus the fourth man is identified as a good possibility. The second candidate is indicated by Saturn and the sun, planets which provide a "yes." This narrows the contest to the second and fourth salesmen because the first man mentioned, when eliminated by the fourth, is also removed from any possibility of competition with the others. The "yes" provided by Mercury and Jupiter on the one hand, and by the sun and Saturn on the other, is by a trine, but the Mercury-Jupiter relationship requires less than a degree's movement for completing the aspect, as against over nineteen degrees in the other case. The retrogradation of Mercury, of course, is a far less detrimental factor than eighteen degrees' difference in original closeness of aspect. Therefore the fourth candidate is recommended.

Title bout and *Water-rights suit* (p. 256). These queries are identical, astrologically, since both are seventh-house matters in a case of direct conflict or reciprocal option. Saturn and the moon are in trine aspect, with the moon applying, so that the querent is favored and may be encouraged to press on to success in both instances.

SUMMARY OF POSSIBLE TYPES OF INQUIRY

    Straight Options
    Contingent Options
    Either-or Options
    Sequential Options
    Reciprocal Options
    Non-Option Orientation

Chapter Nine

TESTING THE GRAIN OF A CHART

SCIENTIFIC accuracy, except in the narrow fields of mathematics, physics and chemistry, is not a matter of fixed quantities or relations, of the sort which are either right or wrong. Rather it is a degree of approximation to expectation. This means it is an approach to an absolute of dependability which not only is never reached, but which has no actual existence. The biological sciences, together with the purely speculative or metaphysical branches of knowledge, do not deal so much with blacks and whites as with grays. They provide a measurement and analysis of things which are found moving or changing at all points, and so are never to be taken as fixed or static except in some very transient compass. Astrology, like any form of psychology or science for the charting and interpreting of characteristic human actions and responses in a physical and social environment, is fundamentally statistical because it can only collect and compare the indications of change in experience. In other words, it has no basic changelessness for its norm. Anything asserted to the contrary remains a philosophical presupposition, no matter what mental satisfaction it may afford.

The result is that a true "scientific dependability" in astrological techniques, in any effort to achieve the greatest possible certainty of expectation, is gained only in part by careful measurement or estimation of the contributing

TESTING THE GRAIN OF A CHART

factors in a given focus of relations. Means also must be found for obtaining a clear index of the degree of certainty itself, such as will characterize the analysis in the given case. Thus an indication in astrology is one thing, and the strength of the indication another. The inadequacy of much interpretation of life's affairs by the stellar art is due to the practitioner's failure to understand this.

It is not enough to find out that a particular horoscope shows excellent chances for a profitable outcome in a financial deal; it is equally vital to know whether the judgment has a low or high degree of probable expectancy. Unfortunately, there are some astrologers who give no thought whatsoever to this phase of the matter. This is the proposition expressed in everyday astrological language when it is said that a horoscope "works" better at some times than at others. What is meant is that the indications wholly derived from the astrological wheel, in respect to a given matter, have a varying degree of one-to-one correspondence with actual events in life, and that the correctness of their astrological import, as a matter of reflecting existing conditions, does not at all necessarily imply an equal accuracy in predicting developments to come.

An approach to the determination, in advance, of the degree to which a horoscope may be expected to "work" is provided in horary astrology, somewhat on the negative side in normal practice, by the four "considerations before judgment;" of which three have been presented, and one of the three discussed in some preliminary detail.[1] Nothing that is now to be said must be taken as depreciating their value in any way, although they are by far the most arti-

[1] See pp. 50 ff, 116, 120.

ficial or mechanical means for indicating the chart's predictive dependability (as in contrast with its ability to establish the correspondence between the astrological factors and the paralleling events in experience). Their primary service is to the practitioner of lesser competence, but they are never ignored by the expert. However, like the famous "inner sign" of Socrates, which could only help him by saying "no" at critical points in his life, they are entirely precautionary—except, of course, when they are made the basis for proceeding in a context of special consideration—and in consequence they are most commonly a means for eliminating the horary figure when its direct correlation to events is significantly below dependability.

It is a logical mistake, with very unfortunate results, if these "considerations before judgment" are seen as something that is fundamentally revealed by the chart itself, or at all akin to the type of indication given when the lord of the question applies by a trine to the planet ruling the outcome of the matter. What they show, rather, is that the effort to identify a significant moment in the case of a given problem is unsuccessful because, in the operation of that general concordance of events which characterizes the universe of experience as a whole, the resulting horary wheel has an inadequate relation to the complex in which the act of choice or decision is to be made (or, if made, is to be seen in its direct potentiality). The proposition is exactly parallel to the impasse in natal astrology when the necessary birth information is unavailable. The deficiency is not in the horary wheel, because it is entirely possible, under proper circumstances, to go ahead. What is wrong is the time of the initial move made to bring the astrological analysis into play. No adequate "time and place" for judgment has been established, and this is not the fault of

TESTING THE GRAIN OF A CHART

the planetary map, or of the details of stellar science, but rather of the particular attempt to focus the problem in the general situation.

Scientific accuracy in every possible field of human knowledge rests ultimately on a very simple proposition. If a certain measure of events or description of relations reveals little deviation from a convenient norm in the past, then the expectancy for future conformity to the norm is high. If a given individual tends to correspond closely to expectation, it is probable that he will continue to do so. Hence past performance, revealed by "testimonials" and "references," is the criterion by which men and women are employed in the social and business world. By the same token, if an individual or his affairs show a close correspondence to some known standard, which has been generalized in the past from the character and experience of all individuals, the chance of continued conformity is good. In the same way, dependable habit patterns are the basis of all refinement of skills among people, by and large, whether in the arts, industry or ordinary social activity; and hence they are the foundation for psychological measurement. Here again, however, it must be noticed that the test of expectancy, or the degree to which a horoscope may be relied on to "work," is not the indications within the chart, but always the one-to-one correspondence between what it shows and what happens in an individual case. Astrology does not indicate or identify "norms," but is itself one form of a "norm" for use in the psychological judgment. Consequently the "considerations before judgment" are a true type of the contributory analysis to be introduced at this point in the exposition since, despite their relative artificiality, they demand a significant "aptness" in any establishment of a horary wheel.

From an entirely practical point of view, the "considerations before judgment" tend to protect the astrologer from chicanery, maliciousness, idle curiosity and simple incompetence. The normal necessity for more than three or less than twenty-seven degrees of the rising sign on the ascendant, indicating whether a horary wheel is "radical" or not, has been found to be an index to the proper maturity of the inquiry. The presence of Saturn in the seventh house, introduced as the second but taken normally as the fourth of these "considerations" (a position which shows an impediment to the astrologer's judgment), cannot be explained in any greater detail until, with the regression to natal methods, the planets are seen in their significance as more than lords of houses; that is, as other than fundamentally the distributors of any pertinent relationship among the matters brought to focus. The second in importance (and third to be presented) of these preliminary standards requires the moon to form a major or Ptolemaic longitudinal aspect before it leaves the sign in which it lies at that significant moment for which the chart is erected. The initial implication in this, a definite lack of pertinent dynamic in the inquiry, can now be expanded to its full import. However, the remaining "consideration" must first be introduced.

What is normally placed third, among the preliminary criteria for a valid horary chart, is the rule that no judgment be made, or else that an added consideration be found in connection with the given query or issue, whenever the moon is *"via combusta,"* that is, placed in the zodiac at any point from Libra 15° to Scorpio 15°.[2] This section of the heavens, known to the ancients as the "burning way" (i.e., the *via combusta*) is now a purely arbitrary

[2] That is, from immediately after Libra 14° 0′ on through Scorpio 14° 59′ but not beyond, and taken quite precisely as a symbolical matter.

thirty degrees. The conventional explanation for the curse on this span in the zodiac, the presence of certain violent fixed stars, is an inadequate hypothesis, since there are other sections of the heavens that may as justifiably be set apart in this fashion,[3] and since the influence of the "fixed stars" in astrology is rather a secondary and perhaps a questionable proposition, at least on the basis of most modern experience. An ingenious and recent suggestion, for which no demonstration seems to be available, is that the "burning way" represented a sort of zodiacal eighth house at a time when the Arabs were making their great contribution to astrology, or when the equinoxes by precession could be supposed to be approximately halfway back in Pisces and Virgo (thus assigning the exact correspondence of the true signs of the zodiac with the arbitrary or familiar constellations to the time of Hipparchus). This would imply a place of spiritual death or universal destruction, but the idea remains highly speculative.

Actually, the explanation is inconsequential, since the convention is established. It has its usefulness as that enforced interruption to the general rhythm of life which is necessary in all activity with any creative potential. The *via combusta* is a symbolical rather than an actual fact, and in consequence a consideration useful only in the more purely symbolical type of astrology, as horary art. It is never employed in natal delineation. As primarily representing a sabbatical interval of withdrawal from the normal course of experience, it most importantly suggests a sort of chaotic reshuffle in the psychological aggregation of self, or a species of cosmic fluxation.

[3] Thus Alan Leo adds the whole of Capricorn (*Horary Astrology*, p. 137).

The practical meaning of the moon in the *via combusta* is an unsettled state of affairs that resists judgment, and that involves a perverse self-satisfaction in the confusion. If the question or problem can be seen, by the regression of perspective, to be an attempt to put such a chaotic condition to advantage, or to make some use of a baffling realignment in the general situation at a time when the lines of specific influence seem to be beyond identification, it is possible to proceed. Such queries would concern the subtle loss of morale in an office or an organization, or the state of a person who, while completely dissatisfied with the existing circumstances in his life, is yet entirely devoid of any idea of what he wants, or what he would like to do. Also there are the cases where something akin to this momentary or even persisting disintegration will exist behind the scenes, and will be verified on investigation, but where the querent is entirely unaware of its existence.

The Lunar Cycle Test

The first procedure in horary analysis, following upon a necessary attention to the "considerations before judgment," makes use of the more positive indications provided by the aspects of the moon. This is known as the "lunar cycle test," and it presents a larger application of the "void of course" concept, in what has become one of the sharpest techniques in all astrology (indeed, much like the yes-and-no procedures in its clear-cut operation). It is most important to note that this test is not properly a detail in the interpretation of the problem at issue, but that it shows—primarily, and at all times—the adequacy of

TESTING THE GRAIN OF A CHART 275

foundation for any astrological judgment. Once an inquiry has been validated by the four "considerations," the employment of this test gives a real indication of the rapport between the horary wheel and the individual querent or problem.

The besetting sin of medieval astrology was the persistence with which well-meaning writers and practitioners insisted on blending factors of analysis into each other, until at times the horoscopic details became as involved in complexity as life itself. Judgment thereby was left as devoid of guiding principles as before the chart was cast. Every failure to hold to the sharp distinctions which astrology makes possible means a blurring of the understanding. The only recourse then is to the "intuition" which, in the terminology of modern spiritism, is little more than a psychometry, despite the fact it is done in the mind and that it makes use of the astrologer's wheel and language. Any effort to cloak this process in the mantle of religion, if not a subterfuge to avoid legal entanglement, is a case of justifying a dependence upon an invisible or remote and unknown guiding principle. No interpretation achieved in this way, whether spectacularly accurate or pitifully incompetent, is ever "scientific," since the processes are not conscious. They cannot be put down for the sake of the record, and they cannot be checked.

No fallacy has more thoroughly ingratiated itself into contemporary thinking than the idea that an increase of factors, or a multiplication of contributing elements, is an aid to clear understanding. "If I knew more about the matter, I could come to a more intelligent conclusion," the unthinking soul will declare. This is true enough in a simple complex, or in a straightaway reference, but when the facts are increased in a climate of confusion, the result is not clarification but perplexity confounded. The schools at last have learned that to add to the "knowledge" of the person without any genius of understanding will merely create an "educated ignoramus." In astrology a voluminous patter of configurations and rulers, of lords disposed here and there, of signs strengthened and weakened, of planets with benign or malevolent enterprises afoot, may indicate astrological erudition with but little or no plain common sense. This latter commodity is the prime essential in life on any level of intelligence, and in astrology it is permitted to function the most efficiently and consistently as the horoscope provides the fewer really pertinent facts of particular significance in a given line of inquiry.

A source of much muddled judgment in horary practice is the conception of the moon as the "co-ruler" of any question or problem. While this teaching presents an important truth, it is an overstress of the moon's function. Every planet in one sense is a co-ruler of everything in which it has any influence, so that the term has little ultimate meaning, but to set up two or more independent significators of equal rank in a horary inquiry is to destroy the basic focus of analysis. The result is akin to the predicament of the man who goes to two physicians, and who is very fortunate if he finds them in reasonable agreement. Behind this and all other "divisions" of indication is the psychological desire of the average unoriented individual to escape from responsibility. The unsure astrologer, like the child who plays his mother and father against each other, wishes to have divergent ways to turn in case of difficulty.

The function of the moon in general is an adjunct rather than a correlative one. The planet has a special importance in horary astrology—and an even greater one in natal or other branches—as the special distributer of the more trivial indication in any given reference; i.e., the public panorama, experience in general. This is because its greater swiftness of motion carries it through the signs at least twelve times as often as any other planet. In directional astrology, or the progressive measure of the natal influences through the span of a life, it conveniently charts the day-by-day developments. Above everything else, however, the moon in horary art shows the particular emphasis of that which, while pertinent, is essentially trivial. This includes normal necessary activities, the passing touch with other people collectively, and the ebb and flow of emotional, reflex and physiological reactions to the general rhythm of the world.

The importance of these trivial or relatively non-emphasized elements in experience is their contribution to perspective. Whatever is an immediate issue is magnified in its relations, and this exaggeration is obviously at once a strength and a weakness. Thus the indication of any broad orientation to life comes through the relatively unimportant factors, because here man is more himself. He is relaxed, off his guard and "different." By contrast, everyone is a hero, or conforms to a standard mold, if the issue is great enough; or if its stimulus carries enough meaning to him. The moon presents the off-side and all-important general rather than specific orientation of a querent or his problem with the given situation. Unless this planet makes a vital aspect before leaving the sign in which it is found, the querent or the key person in the inquiry is revealed as not completely or "honestly" participating in the affair at hand. There is no primary dynamic indication in the horoscope because, in some sense or another, he is playing with life. Since he is toying with reality, it is extraordinarily difficult to help him.

The "lunar cycle test" shows in particular what a moon —in the swing of its function, rather than "void of course" —actually shows in general, namely, that a given individual is effectively or dynamically concerned in the given issue. This is evidence for the dependability of expectation in the given horary wheel. The essence of the test is in the fact that the last major or Ptolemaic longitudinal aspect made by the moon, after it has entered the sign where it is found, together with the next one it will make before it leaves this sign, measure to two events—in the past and future, respectively—which the querent will be able to recognize. The correctness of this indication, in respect to the past event as an immediate testimony, and to the other one for later reference, reveals the chart as one of high reliability; just as its lack of correctness shows the details of expectation to be less dependable (although in all cases the general delineations of the horoscope will remain equally and normally significant). Again, what a horary map reveals is one thing, and the degree to which it may be counted on to "work" is another.

What must be recognized is that the events identified by the "lunar cycle test" are almost essentially oblique, because of the basic nature of the moon; that they will have little or no connection with the matter immediately at issue. Their sharpness in consciousness is due to their unimpededness by any direct connection with the focal perplexity which gives rise to the horoscope, and the moon is able to chart them because the train of consequences in which they have part is steady and towards the forefront of experience. In other words, they do not happen because the moon rules them. Their importance is because the demonstration of correct rapport (with the past, at least) operates to compel a serious attention from a querent, or to impress him enough to call out his real co-operation in connection with the analysis of the main problem at hand. The detailed description of these events is obtained, of course, from elements of astrological indication yet to be presented in the text, and in that respect these observations must of necessity remain preliminary.

At this point a definite terminology is needed for the distinction among charts on the basis of their probable capacity to "work" exactly, in a rather literal sense, as against their contrasting tendency, in the case of many of them, to reveal only generalities of the sort that have little immediate reliability in specific anticipation or prediction. Borrowing from photography, the former may aptly be characterized as fine-grained and the latter as coarse-grained. It is important to be able to recognize or identify the horoscopes which will at times reveal the most spectacularly striking one-to-one correspondence between astrological indications and the events of life, and to take advantage of their "fine texture" with an exceptional definition in any delineation. It is equally vital to realize that when a horary chart belongs in the "coarse" category, the implication is not that it is impossible to help a querent, or to work out the solution of a problem, but only that the interpretation must employ broader generalities, or make allowance for greater individual deviations from normal anticipation. Indeed, the yes-and-no technique, and all the other horary procedures in order, operate as sharply and satisfactorily in the one case as in the other.

If the four "considerations before judgment" are satisfied, either simply or by regression to special indications of high significance, and if the "lunar cycle test" identifies an event in the past of striking but oblique connection to the issue at hand and does so accurately, the testimony is towards fine-graining in the given chart. It is then possible to press on, and to examine additional elements by which a horoscope can be placed in that class with certainty. The factor which ranks next to the moon's cycle, when it comes to testing the grain of a horary chart, is taken from Arabian astrology and is known as the Part of Fortune. This one of many "parts" is widely used in natal delineation by present-day astrologers, and it is a supplementary horizon which reveals the point of direct personal attack upon the basic problems of life. It is sometimes described as the "threshold of success."

The Part of Fortune

Technically, or mechanically, the Part of Fortune is that point in the zodiac which is as far from the ascendant, looking counterclockwise or in the normal order of the signs, as the moon is from the sun, measured in the same way. The easiest method for calculating this "part" requires the expression of all factors in signs, degrees and minutes of celestial longitude. Thus Taurus 6°20′ would be 1ˢ 6°20′, since all of Aries is involved, together with 6°20′ of Taurus. The longitude of the moon is then added to that of the ascendant, and the longitude of the sun is subtracted from this sum, giving the position of the Part of Fortune.[4] Since astrologers are familiar with these signs

[4] The calculation for the example chart on page 21 is as follows:

Longitude of the moon:	2ˢ	29°	48′
Add longitude of ascendant:	6	8	3
	8	37	51
Subtract longitude of the sun:	3	10	24
	5	27	27

This produces Virgo 27°27′ as in the wheel on page 21. Since signs are counted around in a circle their total number of "12" can be added or subtracted whenever necessary. There is no need to do so here.

TESTING THE GRAIN OF A CHART

of the zodiac in terms of their numerical order, it is usually easier to put down the sign according to its number in each case. Thus Gemini 29°48' can be noted as 3·29°48', and so on. Results are exactly the same, because this is merely the addition of "1" to each of the terms for convenience of calculation.

Any of the specific meanings of the houses may at times provide a striking indication through this place of the Part of Fortune, as in the case of an employer in the tenth, a tenant in the sixth and so on. By the same token the ring-around-the-rosy technique may reveal some specially apt clue by identifying a particular aunt or uncle, or by placing a specific legacy in the eighth house. The location of the "part" in the judgment as in contrast with the crisis chart may be exceptionally revealing. On the whole, however, the same limitation must be faced here as in the overenthusiastic demand, of a century or more ago, that a querent's own natal sign and degree be rising when he asks a horary question. It has been pointed out already that this can only happen once a day, and perhaps at an hour which would be distinctly inopportune.

Thus the Part of Fortune is always in the first house while the moon is moving away from the lunation position in conjunction with the sun, or for better than two days; and so on through the other houses for practically all charts. The exceptions to a uniformity of position here are the cases where the signs have special distortion on the house cusps—due to geographic latitude appreciably north or south of the equator, especially when the solstices are on or near the horizon—but this could not afford much variety for any one individual astrologer. Obviously it is impossible for questions concerning marriage, as an example, to be asked only on the two odd days a month. Moreover the professional can hardly shut up shop for the same length of time each four weeks when the moon is *via combusta*. What the Part of Fortune actually shows is the general pattern of the current interest in which the individual has his existence. As a matter becomes more and more socially oriented, or as a problem becomes more and more finely grained in the horary chart, this conformity to Solomon's "time and place for all things" is accentuated.

SIGNIFICANCE OF THE PART OF FORTUNE IN HORARY ASTROLOGY

First House The inquiry concerns self-interest, either a threat to continued well-being, or a necessary choice between divergent lines of responsibility.

Second House The inquiry concerns decisions to be made over possessions, or some necessary adjustment in fundamental security.

Third House The inquiry concerns the convenience of things, superficial change, or the burden of relatives and side issues.

Fourth House The inquiry concerns home affairs, the father, or ultimate responsibilities, including real estate and hidden potentialities.

Fifth House The inquiry concerns direct and speculative self-expression, or matters of children, talent, and organized amusement.

Sixth House The inquiry concerns practical or worldly reorientation, including sickness and all personal services given or received.

Seventh House The inquiry concerns transient or permanent one-to-one relationships, as an equal, with situations and people, for good or ill.

Eighth House The inquiry concerns the effort or need for escape from one complex of experience to another.

Ninth House The inquiry concerns simple but remote and abstract matters, such as are demanding action, decision or growth.

Tenth House The inquiry concerns the achievement or maintenance of a place in life, perhaps involving professional problems and critical issues of authority, superiors or the mother.

Eleventh House The inquiry concerns unrealized objectives, or tentative and casual associations and relationships.

Twelfth House The inquiry concerns problems of detachment or external limitation, troublesome divisions within the self, or hidden obstacles and stimulations.

The most important correspondence, however, is symbolical or oblique, contributing to a fine-grained horoscope in the same way as the "lunar cycle test." The general rhythm in everyday life cannot be denied. While business goes on according to its regular pattern each week, and machinery must operate through all working hours impartially, there is nonetheless this swing of the lunations, and the variations in experience charted by the seasons and the cycles of the great planets. By and large this latter rhythm is the "meaning" as against the outer and commonplace "routine" of life, and the horary astrologer comes to discover, as he develops any refinement of analytical skill, that there is an invariable underlying flavor to questions asked in the first days of a new moon, and that the Part of Fortune shows the deeper psychological implications of problems which may have quite a different cast to the querent. The result is that he may not often be able to impress the stranger by looking at the "part" and exclaiming, "You are worried about your wife!"—unless he intends to sensitize some gift along the psychic order, and frankly enter the ranks of the charlatan, that is, become the type of fortune-teller who wishes to startle and bleed rather than stimulate and help his clients—but he will do other and far more wonderful things.

Fine-Grained Correspondences

The fine-graining of a horary chart is further indicated by an almost infinite ramification of details in which the correspondences between the astrological and the life factors may be very close, and there is really no adequate way to give these possibilities a scale of importance. Most of them are never mentioned in the course of the present text. They might include the coincidences in the outstanding features of horoscopes erected at different times for people particularly connected with each other, or linked in some given experience; or the duplication of significant patterns of the natal chart in the horary, such as a prominent square or opposition similarly placed, or the emphasis of the same outstanding degree in both figures. Naturally the determination of testimonies in this general class must remain an individual proposition, dependent upon the given astrologer's particular skill, as well as his opportunity for observation and comparison. What remains to be covered in the present chapter are those special items of astrological significance which have a broader or more general usefulness, and hence can be summarized for the newcomer or amateur, and be re-emphasized for the more experienced student or practitioner.

TESTING THE GRAIN OF A CHART

Attention already has been given to the necessity that the horary ascendant, in some degree, must describe the querent or the problem. It has been seen that for the major part this need not be any duplication of a natal horoscope, but only an adequate suggestiveness such as will enable anyone to recognize the person in question from the indications in the horary wheel. There are general or broad descriptions afforded by the signs, as these may be found on the horizon, but more reliable indications of appearance are provided by the planets, as one of these may be the significator of the querent, and lie in another sign. Moreover, in much of horary art, the planets by their own indication as well as their place by sign, will be descriptive of other individuals of importance to a given query. Hence the tables to follow may be used for both purposes. Where the correspondence tends to be exact or striking, additional testimony is given to the fine-graining of the chart.

These indications give tendencies only, or the broadest sort of generality. In a previous generation the localization of astrology in England, and in a section of America largely settled by British stock, made it possible to be more specific in the delineations of appearance. The "descriptions," as they appear in the older books, are of little use in an age where the lines of racial and blood distinction have been widened with every generation, especially through the recent developments in world history. On the symbolical side of indication, as in horary art, any standardized approach to problems which are found generally in a hybrid social context will have to wait on some millenia of shakedown and stabilization in the lines of human genetics. There may never be another situation com-

GENERAL DESCRIPTIONS BY SIGNS

Aries	Lean, lusty, dusky
Taurus	Short, full, swarthy
Gemini	Tall, tight, sanguine
Cancer	Low, round, sickly
Leo	Large, full, ruddy
Virgo	Slender, square, clear
Libra	Tall, slender, sanguine
Scorpio	Squat, corpulent, muddy
Sagittarius	Full, fleshy, ruddy
Capricorn	Dry, narrow, dark
Aquarius	Squat, square, clear
Pisces	Short, fleshy, pale

GENERAL DESCRIPTIONS BY PLANETS

Mars	Taller, more active
Venus	Shorter, softer
Mercury	Thinner, fussier
Sun	Fuller, more self-centered
Moon	Thinner, more moody
Jupiter	Fuller, more open
Saturn	Taller, more moody
Uranus	Taller, eccentric
Neptune	Smaller, abnormal
Pluto	Thinner, impressive

---

parable to the time and land of William Lilly. The need for almost an overgeneralization is found in every department of description, although at points to a lesser degree. The designations can merely be held as closely to the traditional concepts and terminology as remains at all practical.

Some general observations may be made on supplementary and general suggestions given by the planets as they become the indicators of various individuals in a horary chart. Sometimes the sun and moon, together with Mars, Venus and Mercury, will indicate a younger person, and the planets Jupiter, Saturn, Uranus, Neptune and Pluto, an older one. The more exact scale of age is indicated fundamentally by the order of the planets' orbits, the sun taking the earth's place in the fourth position, and the moon put first and so used to represent the center of things, or the sun's actual position in the solar system.[5] These details must never be confused with the regular astrological indications of the planets, but may only be employed when the planets are significators of individuals in the yes-and-no technique of horary art, or in its direct modifications.

Distinctions of sex are less sharp than age, because a masculine indication might identify a woman acting in a masculine or dominant role, and vice versa. Where such an indication is valid, the masculine planets are the sun, Mars, Jupiter, Saturn and Uranus, and the feminine ones are the moon, Venus and Neptune. Mercury and Pluto are indefinite or hermaphrodite, an indication in astrology which seldom has pathological reference—that is, to any actual abnormal possession of both male and female characteristics—but rather tends to show either immaturity or a sort of androgynous universality.

American pragmatism has popularized the idea that a man "is" what he "does," and it certainly is true that one of the simplest means for identifying an individual, or

[5] This is the so-called "Chaldean order."

describing him so that he can be picked out of a group or context and thus be revealed in some particular aspect of importance, is to have some indication of his customary vocational activity. The following tables are useful whenever a planet in horary practice becomes the significator of some special person. The planetary indication is normally primary, although the sign may be the most significant when anyone is a passive agent. The houses, which here refer to the crisis chart only, never the judgment wheel, show a subordinate or contributory suggestiveness in all cases.

VOCATIONAL RULERSHIPS FOR HORARY ASTROLOGY

Table One

Mars	Pioneering, leadership, finance, building
Venus	Practical life sustenance, beautification
Mercury	Creative work, all types of transmission
Sun	All born superiority, inherited opportunity
Moon	Public services and relations, normal routine
Jupiter	Professional talent, earned reputation
Saturn	Public administration, building on experience
Uranus	Exploitation of self, forced reputation
Neptune	Exploitation of public, exaltation of fantasy
Pluto	Exploitation of nations, utopian enterprise

Table Two

Aries	Leadership, exploration, achievement by conquest
Taurus	Manufacture, construction, supply of daily needs
Gemini	Merchandising and all commercial art expressions

TESTING THE GRAIN OF A CHART

Cancer	Counseling, teaching and instruction, home industry
Leo	Administration, discipline and exercise of authority
Virgo	Skilled work with hands, routine detail, research
Libra	Public office and duty, politics and esthetics
Scorpio	Analysis and inspection, technical skill, mechanics
Sagittarius	Mental or professional expression, official activities
Capricorn	Negotiation, assembly, organization, institutional work
Aquarius	Abstract science, specialized education, planning
Pisces	Literature, interpretation, promotion, religion

Table Three

First house	Promotion; success through ideals
Second house	Finance; success through consciousness
Third house	Bookkeeping; success through detail
Fourth house	Domesticity; success through integrity
Fifth house	Art; success through pleasure
Sixth house	Labor; success through effort
Seventh house	Opportunism; success through alertness
Eighth house	Science; success through analysis
Ninth house	Publication; success through knowledge
Tenth house	Administration; success through public life
Eleventh house	Politics; success through connections
Twelfth house	Investigation; success through obedience

Nothing in astrology is as consistently unsatisfactory as the traditional geographic table,[6] but there are yet times

---

[6] To make matters worse, there has been widespread disagreement over its detailed assignments, all through the nineteenth and twentieth centuries. The form here presented represents an attempt at a reconciliation of views.

THE CONVENTIONAL RULERSHIP OF GEOGRAPHIC AREAS

Aries — England (general), Wales, Germany, Denmark, Syria

Taurus — Ireland, Poland, Soviet States, Persia, Afghanistan, Irak

Gemini — United States, non-French Africa, industrial England, Belgium

Cancer — All tropics, Scotland, Holland, Australasia, Pacific islands

Leo — France, French Africa, Italy, Czechoslovakia, Arctic-Antarctic

Virgo — Anatolia, Balkan States, Greece, Switzerland, Atlantic islands, Jerusalem

Libra — China, Japan, Tibet, inhabitable Siberia, Siam, Indo-China

Scorpio — Norway, subject racial minorities, Jews, British "Dominions"

Sagittarius — Arabia, Hungary, Yugoslavia, Spain, Latin-America (not Mexico or Brazil)

Capricorn — India, Burma, minor national groups, Mexico, Baltic States

Aquarius — Sweden, Finland, Teutonized Slavs, Nomads, free black-browns

Pisces — Portugal, Brazil, domiciled aliens everywhere, colonizations

---

when the indications are sharp, in mundane astrology even dramatic; and there is no adequate substitute, unless it is the still-theoretical distribution of zodiacal rulership around the globe in geographic bands determined by terrestrial longitude. When there is an overlapping of rulership, the indicator of the smaller or "contained" area will prevail. At times the indication will be strictly suggestive,

TESTING THE GRAIN OF A CHART

as the location of a planet in Virgo affording a neat confirmation of something in connection with Bermuda, or even Staten Island in New York City. More obliquely, Virgo's rulership over Greece might offer a very striking clue in some artistic or philosophical project. By the same token, effort in connection with tulip bulbs or the development of rubber might be shown by Cancer. A theatrical producer considering the production of an Arabian extravaganza would find the place of a significant planet in Sagittarius similarly significant, and so on.

Once in a very long while a horary indication will give a clue to the name of some significant person. This usually refers to the Christian or given name, or to that one of many names by which he is habitually called. Some practitioners may not have use for the chapter's final table, throughout a whole career, but it is an interesting part of horary astrology's paraphernalia.

PLANETARY DESCRIPTION OF THE NAMES OF MEN AND WOMEN

Mars	Generally a clear-cut name of the Latin or Romance type, short
Venus	Generally a musical or ornate name of the Greek type, longer
Mercury	Generally a conventional name common in the family or nation
Sun	Generally a name taken from nature and suggestive of vitality
Moon	Generally a name of special significance, of magic implication
Jupiter	Generally a definitely regal name, of universal suggestiveness
Saturn	Generally a name of great dignity, Anglo-Saxon or heroic

Uranus	Generally a name that is very descriptive, and highly startling
Neptune	Generally a variation or distortion of some other familiar name
Pluto	Generally an impersonal name which identifies some group relation

Chapter Ten

THE TIME MEASURE

Any astrological determination of the nature and probability of events to come is incomplete without some indication of the time at which they may be expected. In a natal horoscope the time measure is based fundamentally upon one or more of several systems of "directions," or "progressions." All of these are the result of a correspondence by which a degree in one kind of motion equates to a degree in another, either exactly or approximately. Thus a day stands for a year, as does a mere four minutes by the clock. In addition there are the "transits," or a timing of events through the relationship between the actual positions of the planets in the heavens and their places at the moment of birth, as shown in the chart. The "return" of the sun or other planets to their original locations in the horoscope has significance, and all these various measures have special ramifications which indicate the moment of an event by the corresponding consummation of a planetary relationship.

The time measure in horary astrology is normally of an altogether different sort, since it is not based on the movement of any of the ten planets, but rather depends entirely on the turning of the heavens around the earth each twenty-four hours. There is a rough parallel to "primary directions," wholly a matter of diurnal motion in natal horoscopy, but in horary art the event is not timed by a

294   HORARY ASTROLOGY

correspondence between two sets of cycles, as in directions, but by the quality given to a planet's "motion" through its situation in the horary wheel. This is a scaling of the psychological potentialities in a given duration, with various kinds of experience represented by different units of time. It is quite a simple matter in life itself. A more entrenched reference in reality means a longer continuance in the given set of relationships. This is the factor of pertinent stability, or "endurance," which is brought to the forefront in horary analysis.

It is because of this symbolical or "creative" measure of time in horary astrology, which charts the strength of a given purpose or momentum in events, and shows this as a projection forward in some self-sustaining phase or complex of experience, that certain rules of procedure are absolutely essential to reliable results. It has been pointed out that the horary wheel only holds as a valid basis for analysis as long as the original situation is left unchanged, or as the querent maintains the set of mind and attitude from which inquiry has arisen. The time measure is thus an indication of potentiality, and not the manifestation of a reality which must be faced of necessity, as in the case of a natal horoscope. This potential, or time-that-may-be, is real once it is accepted and put into experience but, before the act or decision, it is no more so than the "day" in a man's mind when he dreams of fishing, since it may not come to pass, or indeed the "year" when he contemplates a lease he must sign if he moves his residence. He may go to work on some "nice little job," instead of taking the day of recreation, and thereby substitute a "week" in pertinent reality, and so on.

Time units, in a charting of the pure potential or in this analysis of experience on the vicarious rather than actual side, are not any more artificial than those which mark off everyday life on the clock and calendar, but they are always an indication of possibilities in some matter's free agency; never that revelation of the circumscribing total situation which they become, once they are irrevocably ticked off in the actual flow of events. They predict an actuality of "time to come," if the chart is sufficiently fine-grained, but only because the potential has a "time's worth," never because hours, days, weeks, and so on, have any reality of themselves, that is, any existence without attachment to the objects in experience. It is to emphasize this more dynamic or creative nature of time that the horary astrologer always properly insists on having the full content of inquiry stated in the form of question before he takes the focal moment from his watch, and erects his astrological wheel. It is for this reason that the wise practitioner does not attempt to interpret any matters brought up as an afterthought, unless they are obviously inherent in the basic query. This explains the basic demand in horary analysis that various phases of the original inquiry be located in different houses, so that each, with a separate judgment in the general technique, will be illuminated by its own particular durational potential.

Horary time measure consists of two elements, the unit of the measure itself and the number of the given units. Both are derived entirely from the aspects, or from the symbolical motion of a significator to the point of exact relationship in the particular case. The number of degrees the motion covers is the number, by wholes and parts, of the units. The place, by house and sign, of the planet so taken as moving, determines the nature of the units in question. Sometimes the planet may cross into another house, in completing this movement, but only its original place is considered. It cannot leave the sign, of course. If it is a significator in more than one connection, so that the house alters its quality from one judgment chart to another, the unit value likewise changes. Every inquiry stands on its own foundation, in other words, and the classification is invariably on the basis of the judgment rather than the crisis wheel. Here, of course, is where the matter of the particular planet applying to the other becomes of consistent importance.

The houses are scaled counterclockwise, or in the "practical" direction of view, running successively through angular, succedent and cadent rhythms which, in the theory of horary analysis, represent progression from more transient and surface considerations to a complex potential, or towards one less easy to alter according to individual convenience. The signs are placed in sequence similarly, but clockwise to give a complementary reflection of the more "general" or theoretical direction in perspective, running successively through cardinal, common and fixed rhythms which in turn show the deepening involvement of a given potential in the sustaining racial or group norms.[1] The time units are those familiar to human experience in actual events. The seconds and minutes are too short for much meaning in single cases of duration, hence they are omitted. A table is constructed as follows, to show the joint testimony of the houses and signs:

---

[1] This is the distinction among the signs according to "quadrature," which is explained on p. 350. Newcomers who are not acquainted with the sign distributions, through a familiarity with natal astrology, will need this much of the classification in order to make use of the horary timetable:

Cardinal signs	Aries, Capricorn, Libra, Cancer
Common signs	Pisces, Sagittarius, Virgo, Gemini
Fixed signs	Aquarius, Scorpio, Leo, Taurus

THE TIME MEASURE

THE HORARY TIMETABLE

	Cardinal signs	Common signs	Fixed signs
Angular Houses	Days	Weeks	Months
Succedent Houses	Weeks	Months	Years
Cadent Houses	Months	Years	Indefinite

The use of this table involves little or no difficulty, provided the astrologer remembers that the house values are always determined by the judgment rather than the crisis chart. The first hypothetical case in the earlier chapter is the trip to Canada.[2] Since it is a simple-option inquiry, the original ninth house becomes the focal first. The "yes" is given by Mercury, which lies in the crisis third but the judgment seventh, that is, the place of "opportunity" for the matter asked about. This planet has to move a little less than a degree to complete its trine to Jupiter, and since its place is in an angular-common combination of houses and signs, the time for taking the trip is shown to be a little less than a week. This would be a significant confirmation of the plans made by the querent, if he had thought to leave about that time, or would provide an additional detail of advice, if he were inclined to hurry off too precipitously or to delay too long for his best advantage.

Rather frequently the time indication in a horary analysis yields a figurative or directly symbolical rather than literal indication. The next illustrative case used in the text, the question about the advisability of investment in a

[2] See pp. 237, 263.

given security,[3] provides a "yes" through the trine which the sun, ruler of the crisis second in the example chart, makes with Saturn, lord of the opposite house. The sun's position in the particular judgment wheel is in the third house, creating a cadent-cardinal time unit. It has to move better than nineteen degrees which, by the table, signify months. Here is a period of nearly two years, hence the curious result of introducing the duration factor is that the astrologer's judgment is almost exactly reversed. In other words, it is a good move to make the particular investment, but in nineteen months! However, no deficiency in horary art is revealed, but rather its exceptional powers of analysis; which are actually dependent on this fluidity of meaning, or the many variant ways in which an implication may be given. The time equation is only to be taken literally when it "makes sense," or has an immediate and practical value.

In the inquiry about the investment the indications of a good move are clear enough, and they are correct in every basic respect. While the results are satisfactory enough, therefore, they are nonetheless short of reasonable expectation. Thus it might turn out that the funds while safe would be frozen, and that any ultimate returns would have to wait until well towards the close of the second year. Here is an excellent example of the supplementary information which a horary wheel reveals constantly in the hands of a skilled practitioner. It makes no difference, of course, whether the client is told, "It's a good investment if you make it in nineteen months," or "It is a good move, but it will tie up the funds, and you will have to wait nearly two years for your returns," since the essence of the help given the querent in either case is assuring him that he is on the right track, although he is not yet acting in his own interest to the greatest possible extent. A "yes" in horary astrology is not unlike the expression, "You're getting warm!," used in the children's game when the

[3] See pp. 238, 264.

searcher moves in a promising direction. The finer techniques, in thus distributing or expanding the affirmative indication without branching too far afield from the pertinent consideration, are developed with experience. Such supplementary deductions are never a matter of actual modification or contradiction, but are rather an amplification of the yes-and-no judgment in a very fundamental fashion. Although presented in a separate chapter, they are an essential part of the technique itself.

The next development of practical time-indication is in connection with the non-option queries, as illustrated by the example of the man who signed a contract, and consulted his astrologer only after committing himself.[4] The reassurance given by the moon, moving to its exact trine with Saturn in a little over ten degrees and so signifying ten years through its succedent-fixed situation in the judgment chart, testifies simply to the fact that the favorable consequences of the contract may be expected to endure for a decade or more. If it so happened that this ten-year term had some particular implication to the querent, however, that fact would dictate the import of the judgment, since the horary interpretation—here as always, and so consistently differing from natal delineation as already explained in detail—is directed according to the actual activities or dynamic factors in every given case.

In questions of the contingent-option sort the meaning of the time factor is even more definitely shaped by the surface facts of the situation at issue. Thus the example problem of the querent wondering whether to take a position, if it should be offered him,[5] shows the same ten years as in the preceding illustration. The period here has an entirely different meaning, however, probably with a psychological rather than literal import. The astrologer must tell his client that he is in too much of a hurry, or is taking too much for granted. "You will be very wise if you act

[4] See pp. 243, 264. [5] See pp. 245, 264.

precisely as though the offer would not come to you for ten years yet." In other words, the possible neglect of ad interim opportunities and responsibilities might even tend to destroy the very chance for the opening coming to the querent. The assurance of the consummation he desires could defeat him, despite the astrological testimony, by encouraging him to "count chickens" in advance, and break the whole set of consciousness on which horary art depends. This affords a neat demonstration of the call a horary counselor faces, to use everyday common sense as a dependable or scientific substitute for any mere psychism which would ever lie, of necessity, outside his conscious control.

The factor of control is employed with equally illuminating results in the either-or queries. Thus the case of the alternatives, represented by the Florida trip and remaining home to meet the demands of business,[6] presents the same ninth-third indication as the question about going to Canada and so shows the time factor of a little less than a week. In other words, the testimony in such an astrological location of the matter would be, "Make your decision at once; do not keep everyone upset, and your own mind in a turmoil." However, if the interpretation is centered on the business, to give a tenth-fourth identification to the dilemma, the "no" of Mars and Venus would mean eleven years, and so once more provide an instance where a rather meaningless long span of time is testimony to a static condition which must be approached from a new point of view; thereby supplementing the conclusion already reached from the "no" judgment. Contrariwise, if the matter proves to be the problem of taking proper advantage of an opportunity, then the seventh-first indication of the almost equivalent ten-year period simply confirms the judgment derived from the yes-and-no relation, in another way, and says, "This opportunity will be hanging around indefinitely, and you are losing nothing by refusing to sacri-

---

[6] See pp. 247, 264.

THE TIME MEASURE

fice your personal peace for the extra profits you hope to make."

When the similar dilemma between the California trip and business affairs is taken in the sixth, as suggested by the analysis,[7] the move of Mercury to Jupiter, again in an angular-common combination, yields the "less than a week" which sends this client on his way to the West Coast at once.

The indication of ten and a half months in the example of the exceptionally trivial inquiry, the dilemma of the man who did not know whether to go fishing or work on his boathouse,[8] is a case where the time element becomes merely "indeterminate length." It is again a confirmatory clue to an inadequate sense of present or immediate realities.

The illustration of the actress,[9] if taken from the health angle, provides the time of "less than a week" which suggests that she should accept the part promptly. If the fifth-eleventh identification is accepted, the resulting "no" produces the indication of an "unintelligent" time once more and is, as in the preceding paragraph, the call for a reexamination of the whole problem.

The hypothetical instance of sequential-option inquiry, provided by the problem of promoting a salesman to the manager's position,[10] properly uses the time measure for the fourth man only, on the principle of Occam's razor already explained in detail. The "less than a week" indication suggests action at once, on the pattern of the several foregoing paragraphs.

The astrologically identical queries, as far as the first steps in a yes-and-no judgment are concerned—the title bout and the water-rights suit[11]—reveal their essential difference in the detailed ramification of interpretation brought about by the time indication, since the "ten years" in the case of an event of a fixed date is an implication of

[7] See pp. 248, 265. [8] See pp. 249, 265. [9] See pp. 249, 265.
[10] See pp. 253, 266. [11] See pp. 256, 267.

the stability or enduring results to be expected, following on the event, whereas the same decade, in the example of the suit at law, is a warning to the querent that while things are working out in his favor, his action is not decisive or vital enough in the pertinent circumstances to assure him of any immediate or really definite settlement. In this latter instance the factor of the long interval will mean success in a given present step of the battle, but with every possibility that the issue may have to be faced all over again. By the same token the ten years might mean delay, advantageous to the querent now, and with the issue brought successfully to a real conclusion in the future.

Horary "time" at all points is a symbolical factor, except most fortuitously and incidentally. This might be expected, since it charts the meaning of a sequence in events and not any bare cycles of existence apart from all pertinent context. It shows the capacity for enduring the given set of relations, or the self-sustaining momentum of some particular situation. In other words, it is an approximation or a psychological correspondence. Hence the charts for actual events—the "inaugural horoscopes" erected for the time of an occurrence rather than for the moment of a query, or the "elections" by which favorable moments are selected in advance—can never employ this mode of time measure. They operate not out of the creative approximations of judgment itself, but through the more literal matrix of experience where natal methods must prevail.

CHAPTER ELEVEN

PLANETARY DYNAMICS

THE first "rule of logic" in horary judgment is that nothing can come into the consideration, legitimately, except through a tangible line of relationship to something already brought forward by definite connection with the querent or problem-at-issue. This means a step-by-step regression from the original ascendant, but only as a specific need arises to meet some particular inadequacy in the factors available for analysis. No recourse can be had to any house other than the first or seventh; to the position of any sign upon any house cusp; to the place of any planet, symbolical point or node in any given sign or house; to the aspects between any planets or groups of planets other than the fundamental yes-and-no indication; or to any additional astrological element of any sort; except as some pertinent fact in the problem under examination can be identified with each detail of the expanded relationship. It is exceptionally necessary to avoid gratuitous assumptions in horary decisions, and a rigorous adherence to the rule of logical progression will make it easy to do so.

It might be objected that the whole process of determining the grain of the horary chart is a violation of this principle. The "considerations before judgment" and the "lunar cycle test" may seem to be a case of very real attention to side lights and subordinate issues. The difficulty here is a purely surface and meaningless contradiction, because the concern with any factors in the "expectation of accuracy" is a matter of rectifying procedures, not of direct analysis or prediction in the matter at issue. However, the same astrological elements that are of such very great use in the estimation of a chart's graining are exceedingly valuable in the major inquiry, whenever the yes-and-no technique proves inadequate. Up to the present point the planets have appeared only as significators, with no distinction made among them on the basis of their own fixed or root astrological meaning. The single exceptions to this have been the recognition of Saturn as an adverse influence in the analysis of the astrologer, when it is found afflicting the seventh house, and the use of the planets together with the signs to contribute suggestive or brush-stroke descriptions of the particular individuals they might indicate in their significator function. It is this latter function, now to be demonstrated more specifically, that has so large a part in determining the grain of a chart.

Whenever it is necessary, in the more detailed delineation of a horary chart, to regress from the simple yes-and-no technique, the ten planets at once take on a larger degree of characteristic distinction. Nonetheless, even in this first step towards the use of natal methods, these bodies themselves are still neutral—they remain significators primarily—since what they show here through their own astrological nature is entirely a matter of supplementary indication. In other words, any given planet is taken into consideration because it is the lord or ruler of a certain house although, with the expansion of interpretive art, it also describes some person who is a key figure in the affairs of that house, or who administers or controls the course of that department of affairs in the actual life situation of the querent. This role of the planets has been given a full but preliminary outline in Chapter Nine.

At this stage in analysis the planetary aspects also take on an individual character, as in natal delineation. Horary art confines its analysis to the six Ptolemaic relationships at all times, and of these the parallel has been reserved for later consideration because of the different manner in which it is formed and measured; it is essentially supplementary at the present point in the ordering of procedures. The other five have been defined, but have been assigned no meaning other than the simple "favorable" indication of the conjunction, sextile and trine, and the contrasting "unfavorable" testimony of the square and opposition. When it comes to the contributory relationships in human problems—where no one single line of direct act and consequence is charted—they necessarily have implications which make them quite distinct from each other. They now represent man's activities as "different in kind," since they express the modes of functional co-operation in life. They are no longer primarily good or bad, or distinguished as merely co-operative and non-co-operative in the superficial fashion of a yes-and-no judgment.

The following table shows the root significance of all six major aspects, in both the natal and horary branches of stellar art.[1] The first aspect made by a significant planet is the normal basis of judgment (except in the yes-and-no

[1] With the distinction, already emphasized on p. 119, that in natal delineation the aspects are taken as the planets in question are within proper orbs at the moment a chart is erected, whereas in horary technique the aspects are taken as a planet may be moved to the exact point of relationship counterclockwise in the zodiac without crossing the boundary line of a sign.

technique, of course, and also in cases where other aspects can be identified in contributory relationships).

THE MEANING OF THE MAJOR ASPECTS

Conjunction	0°	Emphasis, or co-operation in simple convenience
Parallel	0°	Same (more subjective, measured differently)
Sextile	60°	Encouragement, or co-operation in friendliness
Square	90°	Construction, or co-operation under compulsion
Trine	120°	Momentum, or co-operation in a common vision
Opposition	180°	Awareness, or co-operation in direct rivalry

The first procedure in regression from the simple yes-and-no judgment is when a "no," given by that mode of analysis, calls for further deduction and additional detailed advice on the basis of the given wheel. This may be illustrated through two of the example cases described in Chapter Eight. Thus the position anticipated by the querent on page 245, if classified as "theatrical," puts the focus in the fifth house and makes Venus the fundamental significator through its application to the square of Mars. This means that the latter planet, in Sagittarius and the second house of the judgment chart, describes some person of outstanding importance to the querent in the matter. According to the tables provided in Chapter Nine,[2] Sagittarius would suggest an individual of full proportions, inclined to be rather fleshy and ruddy, but Mars would make him more

[2] See pp. 288 f.

slender and active than the sign expectation. By the three vocational tables he might well be identified as the financial man in the theatrical venture, with the result that a key to the whole difficulty may be found in a business rather than artistic consideration.

It is impossible, of course, to carry out these threads very advantageously in a purely suppositional situation—out of all relations to the facts the querent would normally supply in his precise identification of the horary implications—but at least it can be seen that the problem in this imaginary instance might be the salary demanded by the actor, and it would be possible for him to have his agent, as the result of the astrological insight, make a more modest offer or suggest some other concession to prevent his complete dismissal as a possibility, which outcome is indicated by the sharp "no" in the original technique. This sort of penetration to underlying factors, not at all evident on the surface of a given problem, is the particular genius of horary skill. In this hypothetical instance the actor might have had a degree of encouragement from the director, the author or friends that would have blinded him completely to the obstacles raised far behind the scenes in the business office.

The same "no" is given by Venus and Mars in the case of the man who is expected in Florida, and is held north by business developments, but the aspect is seen in different fashion because Mars is found in the ninth house of the judgment chart. The fundamental description of the important person would be the same, as far as sign and planet are concerned—and these, of course, are generalities which must be particularized by the querent—but now the ninth-house placement suggests an individual symbolized by a "publishing" or "scientific" rather than "financial" function. It might develop that the querent was being misled, or carried away by distant and remote vistas, not only failing his wife and his social obligations thereby, but heading for disillusionment and even definite loss according to the exact potentials he would be able to identify from the astrological lines of suggestion.

In these two cases the first major aspect made by Venus is the square to Mars, which also is the basis of the "no" judgment. In many instances this would not happen, with the result that the key individual would be shown by the initial aspect the planet makes. If this were a conjunction, sextile or trine he would be someone able to help in changing the situation, rather than the person who in a real sense is the obstacle in the given matter. More than one planetary relation may be employed in this fashion when a second one to be formed is given a secondary importance, and so on in order.

The regression towards natal techniques becomes much more vital in cases where neither a "yes" nor a "no" are indicated by the horary wheel. The specimen horoscope on page 263 offers no possible case of this, but the example chart now presented is so arranged that the yes-and-no will fail to operate, according to all primary procedures, no matter what sort of query is taken for illustrative purposes. Thus a querent might ask about the results of a trip to the Argentine. Saturn, as lord of the ninth, and the sun, as ruler of the opposite house, are unable to make any of the five major aspects employed by the yes-and-no judgment. Saturn, however, applies by a sextile to Venus, situated in

PLANETARY DYNAMICS

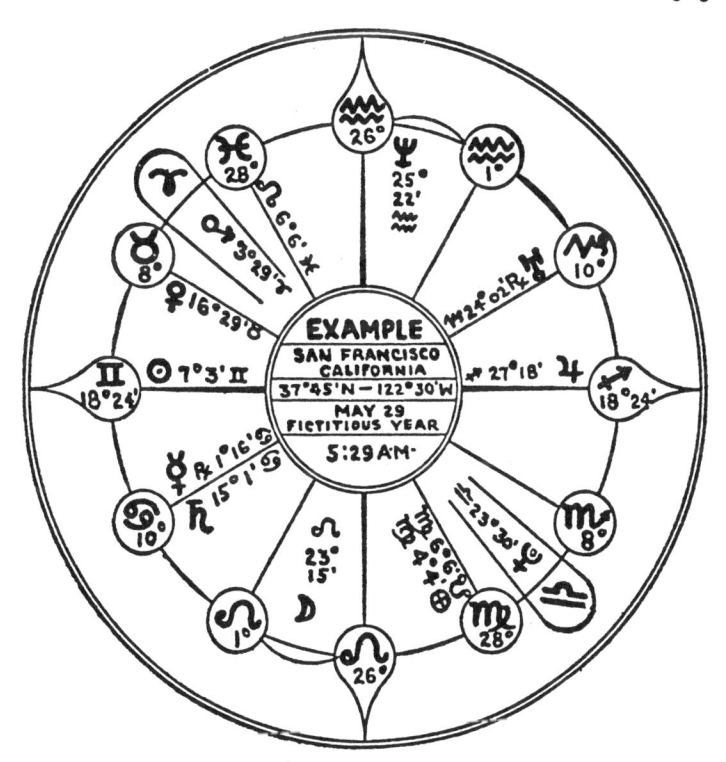

the fourth house of the judgment chart, in Taurus.

This identifies an important individual who is short, full and swarthy, with the shortness of his stature exaggerated if anything, and one who is rather pudgy and soft. He probably is concerned with the practical supply of everyday needs in the business of human "necessities," whether on a large or small scale. The sextile indicates that he will be helpful in the given issue and, if desired, the horary timetable may be employed—in this detail of interpretation as well as any other true horary technique—to obtain an idea of the probable moment of development. Here Saturn, the significator, is in the judgment chart's sixth house in Cancer and the aspect therefore shows six weeks (a month and a half) as the time contact can best be made with the key party, a fact which may well suggest the proper dating for the trip itself.[3]

Thus the first steps, in the transition from strictly horary to natal methods, are a continued use of the planets as significators, but in their relationship to other planets, much on the pattern of procedures outlined for the lunar cycle test.[4] An increasing knowledge of the astrological elements is required, since they yield the pertinent side lights on horary problems whenever the yes-and-no judgment and its modifications prove insufficient. At this point, in consequence, it becomes profitable to consider whether any planet, as it signifies or describes some particular person or matter, is retrograde in the zodiac, or is placed in a sign intercepted by the houses.

Retrogradation is a phenomenon produced by the fact that the planets lie in a horoscope, not as viewed from the center of the solar system—or in their "correct" positions according to abstract celestial mathematics—but as seen from the earth or according to their actual motions in man's experience.[5] Since the earth also moves in its own orbit, as a mechanical fact, it "overtakes" the other bodies at times, in one way of describing it, and so causes them, as measured from this globe, to move backwards in the zodiac. In general the circumstance that a planet is retro-

[3] Note carefully that the moving planet gives the time, and the body to which it moves provides the descriptions.
[4] See pp. 277 ff. [5] The rationale of this has been presented on p. 38 f.

grade means, in both natal and horary astrology, that its action is essentially more indirect or subjective. When the significator of a given problem fails to give a yes-and-no judgment, the fact that it is also retrograde is an indication that action to be taken, under the guidance gained by this regression to other methods, must be more sensitive to the undercurrents of the general situation, and must have a greater sympathy for the sensibilities of other people involved. Otherwise any accomplishment is hampered by its own precipitateness.

Mercury is retrograde in the example chart on page 309, and this is not unexpected in a case where the yes-and-no judgment is impossible, since the planet represents the querent irrespective of what question might be asked, showing him to be inadequately self-ordered in his efforts and not properly sensitive to the conditions around him. If the query should be concerning the results of opening an amusement enterprise, Mercury is also significator of the project at issue. No tie can be established with Jupiter, lord of the opposite house, and the first aspect made to any other planet is a square with Mars. The latter body would then describe a significant individual, quite possibly the key person opposing the enterprise. His physical appearance would be suggested by the combination of Aries and Mars, and his place in life by these two factors, with the added significance of their location in the judgment horoscope's seventh house. The retrograde situation of Mercury would show that the matter itself was presented with no real appreciation of the circumstances in which it would have to function, or with too little steadiness or depth in the idea and its execution. The querent, advised of these factors, would then be able to attack his problem of changing the whole general set of affairs, and perhaps be helped to move on more sure ground towards his ultimate success.

The position of a planet in an intercepted sign is of much less importance in horary art, since place by house alone is so much more significant than in a nativity. Most simply, a sign is "intercepted" when it does not lie on the cusp of any house, that is, when it is entirely embraced within a house, and does not have contact with either boundary. This means that its function, together with that of its lord in respect to itself—and also the functions of any planets it may contain—are sometimes completely subordinated to the major issues of the given problem. Action taken, or decision made, under the leading of a planet in this case, must be examined carefully to make sure that the factors involved are correctly understood; or that they are properly and honestly represented. Any person described by a planet in an intercepted sign in horary analysis is apt to be found caught up in his own prejudices or preconceived notions, or to be essentially unreliable in the particular set of circumstances.

Mars is intercepted in the chart given on page 309, so that the unfriendly individual, in the hypothetical instance just described, would be strongly established in his own way of thinking, and thus not brought around very easily to listen to any reasonable presentation of facts. If Mars had been the significator of the inquiry, as in some question about sickness in this particular example wheel—when, of course, no yes-and-no indication is possible—the situation would be seen to be one of distraction, lack of ordered relation to life in general, and perhaps broad disintegrating tendencies. A first suggestion by the astrologer, in such an illustration, would be a firmer mind or attitude, a more determined effort to meet the problem and find an effective therapeutic agency. Since the first aspect made by Mars is the sextile to the sun, in this wheel, any sixth-house matter would have the encouragement of an individual described by the Gemini-sun combination, with the supplementary indications of the seventh house, and this would be a steadying influence in some one respect or another.

Somewhere along in the course of the unfolding developments in horary technique, when the clear or sharp lines of the yes-and-no technique have to give way increasingly to the methods of general synthesis which always characterize natal delineation, the amateur or neophyte may begin to wonder if he is not getting into a mass of potential ramifications far beyond his immediate competency. The horary professional at this point actually brings in all the wisdom of his long experience with every type of horoscope, something far beyond the person of little astrological background. However, the step-by-step exposition employed in the present text will equip even the beginner with a greater measure of guidance than he may ever suspect. The nature of horary deduction is such that even the illimitable materials of genethliac analysis may be sorted out, arranged in an order of convenience, and used in the consistently logical narrowing of the consideration to the point of pertinent crisis.

All that has been added to the yes-and-no method, thus far, is the means for describing the persons and activities of those who have a contributory relationship to any matter at hand, through a consideration of (1) the sign containing the planet made significant by an aspect, (2) the nature of the planet to which the aspect applies, (3) the implication of the aspect itself, (4) retrogradation and interception, together with (5) additional indications regarding age, sex, occupation, geographical location, and type of name. This sort of somewhat specific information becomes possible when the lines of direct relationship are traced out through the planetary dynamics by a logical deduction of the step-by-step order, since each detail is validated in turn and the whole pertinent situation can then be uncovered through its self-consistency.

The Indications of Personal Involvement

The next forward move in this more complex horary analysis is the use of the planets to identify, not people or characters, but rather potentialities of action. Here the chart shows specific lines of conduct, such as will help the querent accomplish his desires. There are two factors in this expansion of indication, based first on the added insight given by the planet which is the significator of the matter, and secondly on the suggestiveness of the other planet—or planets, in the occasional instance—with which it makes aspect. Whenever the yes-and-no is inadequate, and any description of people concerned in the given issue is an insufficient clue to means for meeting a given issue, the planets can be specialized further to show the querent what he can do by his own attitude and understanding. Here the horary wheel becomes the "little horoscope" of the moment in a very pregnant fashion.

Jupiter and Saturn in general always represent the ties with other people on the basis of equality, or the association of peers in normal experience. Jupiter is a protecting and Saturn a challenging influence, so that Jupiter is the bodyguard and Saturn either the criminal or that person who while "within the law" is yet a threat to some particular desire or project. Conversely, in the same general sense, Saturn is the law, or any calling to account or bringing to justice as a consequence of mistakes, whereas Jupiter is liberty, or the escape from penalty, together with the seemingly undeserved rewards of life. These relationships summarize the two functions as expressed in given individuals in the most simple objective form. Jupiter primarily is always the friend, and Saturn always the enemy.

The sun and moon in general always represent ties with other people on a basis of inequality or effective difference, that is, associations with superiors and inferiors in everyday life. The sun is the ruler, the magistrate, the governor or mayor, the executive in business, and so on, while the moon is the clerk, the servant, the repair man, the child, and the like. The sun is always the representative of fame on the one hand, and of display or ostentation on the other; or of those who either exalt the individual or force him to acknowledge the special worth of someone else. The moon is the inferior person who caters to his "betters," or seeks to depreciate them; as well as the individual with the "common touch" who seeks to express or justify it. If the sun is the giver of fame, the moon is the bringer either of notoriety or nondistinction.

The six remaining planets, in contrast with these four—where the practical status of individuality is more or less an issue, or where the appreciation of personality and the sense of individual worth, esteem and power is always in question—indicate the more impersonal or transitory relationships with people, especially as individual identity has little or no significance.

Mars and Venus in general always represent associations with others in casual or momentarily convenient fashion. Mars indicates force, and therefore activity, virility or potency of any sort; as an individual makes it manifest or brings it to an issue. This involves personality, but "personality" *per se* is subordinated to the social consequences of the given activity. Venus reveals love, romance and whatever gives satisfaction to the senses, as this is especially dramatized by some significant individual; but by someone only seen in the idealized form. While Mars and Venus, in the older tradition of astrology, always indicated individuals according to sex—Mars a man and Venus a woman—this is obviously too literal an interpretation of Mars, which is aggressiveness or action, and of Venus, which is receptivity or reaction and emotion. The indication of romance or pertinent intimacies of relation is through the houses in horary astrology, not the planets, and these planetary descriptions, in the subordinate or regressive details of horary analysis, show the essential participation of side rather than main relationships. Mars identifies a person who is stirring things up in some contributory fashion, and Venus one who is drawing off the initiative of others, as they are concerned in the problem at hand, by satisfying them, calming them down, or turning their interest in other directions.

Uranus and Neptune in general are not to be taken as basic indicators of people in horary astrology, although both, at times, may be very significant in describing individuals who are completely alien in the given situation. Uranus identifies an eccentric person, or one who is anarchistic in temperament or intentions and is acting in total disregard of others. Neptune reveals a person who misguidedly or maliciously seeks to submerge or discourage all real individuality, and so to reduce human personality to some common denominator selected by himself.

Mercury and Pluto in general are mental planets which, when they indicate individuals in horary astrology, usually identify people not at all directly concerned with the querent or the critical situation. They represent, rather, either a direct counterinterest or else an abstract intellectual concern which has to be aligned with the main objectives in some way. Pluto, like Uranus and Neptune, is of course only exceptionally the indicator of actual personalities.

In the example chart on page 309, a query concerning an investment would make the moon its significator. This planet's initial aspect is a sextile with Pluto. This moon,

PLANETARY DYNAMICS

as the conscious inferior, suggests an effort on the querent's part to keep pace with his social betters, while the sextile shows he is attempting to get assistance, that is, "co-operation in friendliness," from agencies which by Pluto are revealed as totally disinterested, or as merely encouraging him idly. Here is a more detailed confirmation of the judgment on the situation through the lack of a yes-and-no indication, thus more superficially described as without adequate foundation. If the question were concerning the results of a contemplated change in business policy, the significator would be Saturn, and its first aspect the sextile to Venus already noted in another connection. The nature of the inquiry does not suggest the judicial Saturn. The sextile's revelation of the querent's effort to get help in some project rather suggests that what he has in mind is unwittingly, if not otherwise, a species of sharp practice. Venus, in its helpful capacity, then could be a distracting agency which is diverting him entirely for his own good. These are hypothetical interpretations, as so often before, but they illustrate the procedure, and show how fundamentally simple it is for those who master the astrological elements.

The Indications of Special Instrumentality

The planets, as very occasionally the indicators of things rather than persons, reveal the instrumentality of some special mechanism, or organism, which to all intents and purposes acts as a person. Thus Mars might identify a machine, such as a typewriter or an automobile, and **Venus** could represent the goods on the shelf in a store. Mars here shows instruments that can be used to surmount obstacles, cut Gordian knots and make various materials available for immediate use. Venus shows things corresponding to the inner resources of self, so that, most importantly, this planet is the basic indicator of money, literally and symbolically. Indeed, this special role of Venus is the most singly important indication of any one planet in all astrology.

Jupiter, in a very broad way, indicates things which are dynamic, encouraging, and inclined to strengthen health and purpose, whereas **Saturn** rules objects and entities that are static, disheartening, and inclined to dissipate energy to no account.

The **sun** indicates those things in life by means of which the self is able to feel stable, or to maintain its interests without direct attention. The **moon,** contrariwise, indicates any possible phase of the tides or instabilities in experience, as well as whatever drifts to self to nourish and replenish its substance.

Uranus indicates unexpected obstacles in both their discouraging and stimulating aspect, whereas **Neptune** indicates those things which threaten to engulf the interests of self, whether for its benefit or its hurt.

Mercury describes intellectual or physical objects which impede the smooth running of affairs, leading to exterior or superficial confusion, and **Pluto** shows objects of governmental and community importance, such as divert individual effort into alien channels.

The Indications of Contributory Events

It is important to make a very sharp distinction between individuals identified and described by the planets in horary astrology, as well as the more general agencies or even inanimate and tangible objects of significance in the given case, and actual events or special situations which are of a subordinate sort, although definitely contributory to the main problem or issue. Here the regressive technique of

PLANETARY DYNAMICS

horary analysis exactly parallels the procedure in the "lunar cycle test," and the considerations here supply the needed factors for a full employment of the methods given their preliminary outline in Chapter Ten, and needing no special illustration at this point.

Jupiter indicates any event which is primarily an opportunity, with the group interest proving to be the same as the individual's own; whereas **Saturn** rules some event in which this same group interest operates to the disadvantage of the individual, and compels him to make some adjustment to meet it.

The **sun** indicates an event in which the individual is called upon to put his best foot forward, if he wishes to profit from it; while the **moon** rules an event in which he gains publicity and is taken out before people, no matter whether he is on his good behavior or not.

Mars indicates an event where there is liability to accident; and **Venus** one with a certainty of satisfaction or consummation.

Uranus indicates an event that encourages or supports original and intelligent action; and **Neptune** one demanding some unwilling conformity to a strictly group requirement.

Mercury indicates an event of an irritating or awakening sort; and **Pluto** one that tends to show an individual betrayed against his own interest.

The Indication of General Direction

Within some very marked limitations, that restrict the detail of technique to rather fine-grained charts for any real dependability, the astrological directions of the compass are one more type of general planetary-pointing with an important and valid place in horary astrology. The compass directions are of value primarily in the identification of lost articles, strayed animals, and the like, but at times, when the graining makes it possible, the indications apply in the "lunar cycle test."

THE ASTROLOGICAL COMPASS

Houses	Direction	Signs	Direction
First	East	Aries	East
Second	E. N. E.	Taurus	S. by E.
Third	N. N. E.	Gemini	W. by S.
Fourth	North	Cancer	North
Fifth	N. N. W.	Leo	E. by N.
Sixth	W. N. W.	Virgo	S. by W.
Seventh	West	Libra	West
Eighth	W. S. W.	Scorpio	N. by E.
Ninth	S. S. W.	Sagittarius	E. by S.
Tenth	South	Capricorn	South
Eleventh	S. S. E.	Aquarius	W. by N.
Twelfth	E. S. E.	Pisces	N. by W.

These traditional indications have come down to modern astrology from several centuries of use, and they are another illustration of that principle in rulership used by the medieval pioneers, namely, that when a set of relations is projected one way through the houses, it is taken in the other through the signs. The simple reversal in direction of sequence, encountered in the horary timetable, here takes, against the mere progression in compass points for the houses, a "geographic location" of function in the signs through triangulation, or an emphasis of triplicity as at root a deeper "pointing" of existence itself. Thus all fire signs partake of the nature of "east," modified in each subordinate case by the squaring axis, and so on. The complicated schematism makes these compass directions difficult to learn. Because they are used infrequently, few astrologers find it advantageous to memorize them. What

PLANETARY DYNAMICS

should be understood is that the house directions have the basic or literal application to actual facts, while the signs provide a more symbolical or psychological indication.

The practical difficulty, when both tabulations are used, is that a planet in the first house is only occasionally in Aries. Thus, referring again to the example chart on p. 309, it might be desired to find out where a certain superior officer, indicated by the sun, was to be found in terms of geographical location relative to the querent. This planet is in the twelfth house of the crisis wheel in Gemini, and to tell the client that he was east-south-east, west by south, would be almost sheer nonsense. If the house indication, however, is taken literally, and the sign as merely the psychological contribution, the meaning of the contradiction becomes "to the east, southwardly, and not very far."

Chapter Twelve

THE JUDGMENT CHART

It may be well to point out again that the distinguishing characteristic of horary astrology, in comparison with the other branches of stellar science, is its primary dependence, in the measure of events, on the distribution of circumstances through the houses. The planets for the major part, except in the regression to natal methods, are only significant in a very neutral fashion as lords of the houses; that is, as significators of given matters brought to an astrological designation, or rendered subject to analysis, by their location in the houses. The signs, because of this emphasis, remain even more neutral; becoming little more than the convenient means for charting the relative positions of the planets, the house cusps and various parts or nodes in the wheel. The exceptions to this broad principle —most commonly marked in the "considerations before judgment," the "lunar cycle test," the measure of time, and the designation of compass directions—are a matter of recourse to additional factors of orientation in judgment.

The "guiding principles" in any true science are not of value because they achieve a pretty nicety; indeed, the most significant fact in nature is the wide manifestation of "sports" and "exceptions to the rule." Whenever a structure of understanding, a supposed "law of nature," operates without deviation of any sort, the scientist at once

THE JUDGMENT CHART

suspects it. Hence the rigorous delimitation of techniques in astrology is not because these separations are themselves of importance, or because they are "real" in any abstract or philosophical sense, but because they are useful in developing both a better understanding and a more effective accuracy in astrological practice and exposition. Every branch of stellar psychology employs methods arising out of the genius of some other one, and it is interesting to note that the mode of analysis summarized in this chapter has been the outstanding contribution of horary method to natal interpretation. The significance of the position in which the lord of a given house is found—first in that house, and then in each of the other eleven in turn—is the basis of tabulations which were exceptionally popular during the first quarter of the present century.

The fundamental horary technique provides a judgment founded on the logical consequences of varying relations among the houses, determined in each special case by the aspects made by their lords. This becomes the yes-and-no procedure, with modifications which in the regression to natal methods have their climax in the "planetary dynamics" of the preceding chapter. The point of view in the step-by-step outline of procedures is essentially positive, throughout these developments of a pattern for analysis, since the conclusions reached are nearly always founded on the movements of a planet in some dynamic distribution of its significance. The corresponding negative perspective—to the degree that it is a consideration of over-all conditions, and that they are taken more or less in their pertinent totality—is a very definite adoption of the natal perspective. However, because the factors are still the planets as significators, acting completely in their neutral or true horary function, the determination of the "statics" or inert potentials of a particular query or problem is almost as thoroughly an original or non-regressive horary procedure as the yes-and-no technique itself.

There are two stages in the charting of the house interrelationships at this point. The most familiar to the general practitioner—and by the same token the one that reveals the pertinent status of affairs more practically, and so becomes the most useful—is the consideration of the place by house of the significator in the given matter. When any house contains its own ruler, the testimony is ideal in horary art because it can be said that the querent has full control of his situation. The germ of the solution for the problem is available and potent in and through the situation itself. The position of the significator of a matter in a house other than the one ruling the inquiry means that this other house has control over the querent's immediate concern, or the difficulty at issue, and that an appeal must be made in one way or another to whatever person or set of circumstances is identified at this other point.

What is here revealed, in contrast with a yes-and-no judgment—but only valid when the horary wheel for the particular inquiry fails to yield an adequate yes-and-no delineation—is a definite limitation which must be faced. Here are terms to be met, either a hindrance or else a potentialty to be turned to account. In other words, whatever is not shown as effective by a pertinent aspect between significators is of necessity activated by another and essentially alien dynamic; and the consequences are exactly the same as in the case of the direct "no" indication in a non-option matter, namely, the need for an attack upon the whole set-up of affairs, and for establishing the pertinent circumstances in an effective and satisfactory frame of reference. This analysis of the statics of a given matter provides the essential clue to any possible realignment of the general life situation; it is an important and profitable mode of regression to a broader consideration.

There are two ways of proceeding in this first of the two stages in the "static" interpretation of house interrelations. One is by use of the crisis chart, and the other is by reference to the judgment wheel. Thus the lord of a question concerning action contemplated with a child, a fifth-house matter, found in the original first in the example horoscope on p. 309—in a hypothetical case where no yes-and-no aspect exists, and where the original seventh house identifies a marriage partner with whom the querent is having trouble—indicates that the youngster's affairs are safely in the control of the parent who is making inquiry. Here is analysis by the crisis chart, giving information which shows what may be attempted safely in countering any dynamic adversely effective in the issue. The querent may stand his ground firmly. By the same token the significator of the child, in the terms of the judgment chart, is in the ninth house of that wheel and, by reference to the tabulations following, it can be presumed that the difficulty in large part might lie in the motives and moral capacity of the child. Perhaps the youngster is too inclined to a solipsistic attitude, insisting that his own immature conscience be his sole guide; he may be looking more to remote and phantasmal than immediate and practical criteria.

There is a certain fixity of relationships between these two horary wheels, since they are really the same houses of the same chart in a mathematical or astronomical sense. When a fifth-house question is asked, the position of the significator in the first of the one means that it is also always in the ninth of the other. Rather than a conflict of testimony in any possible instance, the invariables of this sort are a confirmation of the universal concordance in experience. A philosophical analysis of the illustrative case will demonstrate this because, when self-expression is dominated by the dynamic of a very focal self-realization in the general view of any crisis, the result is that this self-expression in the specific judgment is always under the necessity of a particularly sharpened interaction with its own past or moralized and intellectualized experience. The emphasized distinction made here between the crisis and judgment wheels is to afford an organization for the logic of the matter, equipping the practitioner or student with a set of terms for the houses in each special connection.

This should not be objectionable. Life commonly changes names with any real variation in function, so that the postman in a vocational category is the deacon in the church, and the tiler in his lodge. While he is "Mr. Smith" to most people he is "Bill" to his cronies, "dad" to his children and "darling" to his wife. It is only when these convenient and shifting designations become metaphysical realities, or are no longer seen dynamically in their origin, that anyone is ever confused.

The second of the two stages in charting the house interrelations is a consideration of the planets contained by each of the houses in order. When such a planet is the lord of the house in question, the significance is apart from any house-against-house tie; since it has already been shown that this fact reveals a pertinent and effective potential of integration in the affairs ruled by that house. In every other case the indication, as a natural corollary of the more fundamental perspective already outlined, is that the house controls, or can control, the affairs of those others of which such planets are the rulers. This of course concerns contributions to the matter at issue, or subordinate factors that may be put to use; but never the basic statics of the focal house.[1] An example of the procedure can be taken in the hypothetical fifth-house query about the results of the action contemplated with the child of estranged parents, used for illustration just above. Since three planets are found in the houses they rule, Mercury in the judgment ninth, Jupiter in the judgment third and Venus in the judgment eighth,[2] the importance of the child's ninth-house mental attitude or *motivation* is reemphasized, and the practical or opportunistic *discretion* as shown for the third by the tabulations to follow, together with the broad *acceptability* of the project as a new cycle in the youngster's life revealed by the eighth, are strengthened over the other nine houses. Not only is the matter shown to be in the querent's control, through the place of the lord of the query as such in the crisis chart, but the three emphasized houses also affirm, in the judgment wheel, the convenience of whatever superficial contributory factors may be needed and the strength and practicality of the projected new orientation as such.

The houses other than these and the focal first are of less significance, but they can be brought into the analysis

[1] Hence a case of "mutual reception," when each of two houses contains the ruler of the other, does not alter the pertinent emphasis of the matter inquired about; although it does reveal a subordinate reciprocal interest of possible value, which may be worked upon with advantage.

[2] Note that Mercury is in a house it rules, but not a sign, and that Mars is in a sign of which it is lord, but not a house.

with considerable profit. The ruler of the *fluidity* or resources of the matter (second) is in the place of *pertinence* or opportunity of the judgment wheel (seventh), indicating that these resources can be employed successfully only as they contribute directly to the execution of the proposed plans. The lord of this *pertinence* is in the house of *discretion* (third) or the strengthened indication of the convenience of everyday facilities in the move. The *strength* or "end of the matter" (fourth) in judgment-chart terms has its significator in the judgment tenth, so that the *prestige* sought in the projected change for the child must be maintained firmly to assure the successful outcome of the issue. Since Saturn also rules the *versatility* (fifth) and *distribution* (sixth) of the project, every personal recourse in the matter must likewise be shaped to the larger or over-all view that gives real dignity to the project, as well as to each special effort in a practical adjustment for the needs of the enterprise. The lord of the *prestige* (tenth), which controls three houses in this way, is found in the judgment eleventh, so that the enlarged conception or broader view of the child's future, or the visualization of measures needed to develop his greatest potentials, are dependent on a real *promise* or very definite plan and set of objectives. This house, in its turn, together with the place of *dependence* or underlying psychological unity and self-organization (twelfth), are subordinated to the judgment eighth, or the *acceptability* which gives the one all-important emphasized description of this projected new cycle for the child.

In order that the widening technique of judgment from the interrelations of the houses (to the explanation of which this chapter is devoted), may be as clear as possible, the consideration has been held to a use of the planets in their pure significator function. However, it is obvious that the planetary "dynamics" presented in connection with the graining of the horoscope, and especially expanded in the preceding chapter, may be employed as

THE JUDGMENT CHART

supplementary factors in the judgment chart as such. The same principles apply as in the crisis wheel—in the case of which they have been outlined—and it is only necessary for the horary astrologer to keep his lines of significance clearly defined.

HOUSE RULERSHIPS IN THE JUDGMENT CHART

Focus The first house of the judgment chart indicates the focus of the matter. This fundamentally is little more than the location of a given problem or question in its general matrix, so that the most important role of this house is to give a special subordinate importance to other factors when their particular significators are found here.

Fluidity The second house of the judgment chart indicates the fluidity of the matter, or what fundamentally is the self-possessiveness of the elements which are at all focal in the inquiry. This means, in a practical way, the stock of energies on hand, or the particular availability of resources for any very special call to be made upon them. It is a measure of the lack of inhibition on which to count when and if the querent or key individual moves to the solution of his problem.

Discretion The third house of the judgment chart indicates the discretion of the matter, or the general capacity for intellectual or useful reaction to the needs of the special case. This is not a drawing on inner or private reserves, the fluidity of act and understanding revealed by the preceding house, but the entirely practical and even opportunistic employment of whatever lies at hand. Here is the possibility for avoiding unprofitable involvement in nonessentials while able, at the same time, to turn anything to account the moment there is a purpose to be served.

Strength The fourth house of the judgment chart indicates the strength of the matter. This is the ability of the querent or key individual to anchor himself in his own tradition or background at every point in crisis. Here is where he is found to have the steadiness of underlying attitude, or the sense of ultimate values, which will be deeply grounded enough to serve him for a foundation in any change of policy, or for any reorientation of effort, as this becomes necessary in the solution of a given problem. The house reveals that influence of the inner life which makes him reliable at any point in a changing world.

Versatility The fifth house of the judgment chart indicates the versatility of the matter, or its potentialities for holding to its own way of going, despite extraneous influences. This is the pure resourcefulness of individuality, not in the way of drawing on inner reserves but as a cleverness in finding every phase of development in events a means for the discovery and exercise of new possibilities along some given line of effort. Here is the fertility, creative capacity, or general pregnancy of whatever lies at focal issue; not a mere use of things as they are.

Distribution The sixth house of the judgment chart indicates the distribution of the matter, or the querent's capacity for directing effort directly to its own ends; and for balancing immediate needs against pertinent obligations. At this point the key personalities of the inquiry are revealed according to their gifts for sustained interest in a task at hand, for ability to obtain a faithful performance of duties from others, and for a willingness to make sacrifices in contributing to the goal of the moment. Here is where simple individual differences are brought into contrast, and found to be worthwhile by direct experience.

Pertinence The seventh house of the judgment chart indicates the pertinence of the matter, or its degree of immediate and one-to-one relationship with the general situation in which the given problem has arisen, or in which the particular project has been conceived. This is the straightforwardness through which a maximum of co-operation can be gained, and it is especially the determined act of the sort that refuses to compromise itself to please opposing influences. The degree of real aptness of anything in direct and salient contact with anything

THE JUDGMENT CHART

else, or of the actual pertinency of anything in a critical point-to-point relationship, is shown at this angle.

Acceptability The eighth house of the judgment chart indicates the acceptability of the matter, or what meaning the querent's act or decision, or the emergence of the special problem, is apt to have in general for other people. Here are also the contributions to the solution of the given difficulty, as these may be expected from others or from life at large, or the broad potentiality of a reorientation or a new cycle in affairs as this represents a new strengthening of the larger situation in which the particular issue has been sharpened.

Motivation The ninth house of the judgment chart indicates the motivation of the matter, in response to the mass or group ideas contributory to the general critical issue. This shows the degree to which the querent can think clearly, or to which the central figures in the situation can hold a proper over-all view of things. Here is where it is possible to escape the persuasion of confusion, and develop an ordered concept of the larger frame of reference and its possibilities.

Prestige The tenth house of the judgment chart indicates the prestige of the matter, or its power to maintain an advantage and capitalize on reputation and human respect. This indicates the extent to which group effort can be commandeered, or to which the necessary authority to act can be compelled from those who possess any power in the given case. Here is the capacity of key people in the critical situation to meet the requirements of any and all superiors.

Promise The eleventh house of the judgment chart indicates the promise of the matter, or its imaginative potentiality. It shows both the possibility for continued enjoyment or utilization of any preferential position in the given crisis, and the degree of effective vision available as an encouragement to a continued effort in solving the difficulty. Here is the moral energy that comes from sensing the approval of others, or from having their good counsel.

Dependence The twelfth house of the judgment chart indicates the dependence of the matter; primarily the underlying psychological unity of the pertinent factors in a given case, as an organic sustainment of the mood or momentary set of personality. This reveals the intangible elements of co-operation in the critical situation, together with the undercurrents tending to obscure the clear lines in any special issue. Here is the subconscious "excess baggage" of the mind, the very valuable "oblique intuition" to which attention must sometimes be given before a difficulty is entirely settled.

It is important to note that all the indications of these houses in the judgment chart have been described on the positive side, because they come into significance only as the presence or rulership of a given planet gives them a marked dynamic. However, the emphasis on any particular aspect of circumstances is obviously in terms of a plus or minus, and the latter potentiality may be sufficiently sharpened in consciousness to appear fundamental, or more "real" than the actual potentiality. This is especially true when any planet comes out of its neutrality, in a regression to natal techniques, to express a privative function. In such a case Saturn, which in the example chart on page 309 has a second-house placing, might indicate the situation of loss or inadequacy of resources no less than the effective possession and utilization of them. "Fluidity" is just as much what it is when the flow of these literal and immediate potentials is momentarily against the interests of self. Such an interpretation, of course, is a matter of additional regression in analysis, justified by details of the widening consideration.

The highly subjective nature of the judgment chart must be kept in mind at all times, whenever it is used in analysis. The special perspective on the given problem, which it affords, is gained through the distinct pattern of that matter's own potential. It is of value only as it is used to delineate the positive procedures to be employed by the querent, that is, the key person or group in a particular issue, in an attack on that general social complex which, for one reason or another, has been permitted either to crystallize in an unfriendly set against some given project or desire, or else has been helped to instrument or strengthen a positive opposition. This does not mean that these psychological elements are at all intangible, but only that they are entirely initiated and maintained, in their potentiality for good or bad, by the human activities and interests which, as they have come to some measure of crisis, have been made the basis for a horary wheel.

Supplementary Procedures

The judgment chart, in a regression to natal methods, may be employed for a full delineation of the given problem on the pattern of a life analysis, and any partial move in this direction may be taken by a practitioner, as has been suggested; all to the degree he is able to obtain dependable results. When a supplementary Part of Fortune is used in the judgment wheel, it must be specially calculated; that is, the longitude of the moon must be added to that of the cusp of the house of "focus" instead of the original ascendant, in order to obtain the sum from which the longitude of the sun is subtracted in obtaining its position.

A modern innovation, which proves curiously effective at times in both natal and horary astrology, may be added to these techniques as another means for analyzing the statics of any given matter (through either the crisis or judgment chart). In the same way that the lords of the houses reveal the points around the zodiac where the affairs of each house in turn are definitely limited, hence the direction in which the agencies for their control must be sought—the planets "exalted" in the houses (that is, of course, in the signs on their cusps) will conversely, in a directly opposite manner, reveal how (through a more subjective or inner magic of the circumstances it rules) each house containing a planet may find both a special outlet for its own interests and a particular under-cover co-operation with its ends, in that area of experience which is described by the house in which the planet is exalted. The possibilities of this added interrelationship among the houses particularly parallels and interprets the multiactivity of a mechanical civilization, with its highly stratified social structure, and in consequence the three new planets are employed in this technique, together with the dragon's head and dragon's tail or the nodes of the moon which, as a matter of the step-by-step presentation adopted for this text, are introduced in the following chapter.[3]

THE EXALTATIONS OF THE PLANETS

Aries	. Sun	Leo	. Neptune	Sagittarius	. Tail
Taurus	. Moon	Virgo	. Mercury	Capricorn	. Mars
Gemini	. Head	Libra	. Saturn	Aquarius	. Uranus
Cancer	. Jupiter	Scorpio	Pluto	Pisces	. Venus

[3] See p. 363.

the ramifications of horary art

CHAPTER THIRTEEN

THE USE OF NATAL METHODS

THE distinguishing characteristic of natal astrology, in contrast with strictly horary procedures, is its primary emphasis on the planets instead of the houses. Thus the actual geocentric movements of these ten bodies in the zodiac, rather than their symbolical "movement" in the celestial equator as brought about by the earth's rotation, is made the basis of analysis. While horary astrology fundamentally narrows the consideration to some one more or less straight line of action and consequences, natal delineation primarily broadens its survey to discover and exhibit the over-all possibilities for a whole life. This amounts to a more direct concern with the different kinds or phases of cosmic force which, collectively, make up the solar system.

The celestial energies are manifest through every detail of physical or psychological existence, and it is the job of astrology as a whole to chart these in their significance to human personality. Whether the planets themselves are the source of the heavenly forces in any or every part or whether they are merely bodies which indicate, like objects afloat on an ocean, the course of the energy streams—that is, the stresses and strains within a closed system of cosmic activity—is always a metaphysical question, and so of no immediate importance in horoscopy. The continual interaction of dynamic relations in the general field of being is the basis for any pattern in experience as a whole, and the delimitation of this in a natal horoscope, by the ten "planets" of astrology, provides an intelligible ordering for each individual identity, and so permits in turn a highly reliable prediction of probabilities in human affairs.

The astrological revelation of a life's total potential is given its orientation, in any competent interpretation of a personal nativity, by employing the planets, all ten together, in a determination of the "temperament type." They are then taken singly or separately, as a next step, and used to trace out the relationships of the underlying temperament to experience in detail. Two screens of analysis are provided by the houses and the signs, which exhibit the particular and general ties, respectively, that link the one person with other people and with his world of events. The "planetary dynamics" of natal art depends on the basic differentiations among these bodies. In other words, their own intrinsic connections with each other—which will reflect subordinate systems of energy in man himself—become distinguishing factors in psychological measurement and create the "planetary departments."[1]

The houses provide a thorough differentiation of those complexities which make up man's immediate experience.

[1] These consist most simply of the sun and moon as vitality or organic integrity; Jupiter and Saturn as the soul or psychological self-sufficiency; Mars and Venus (together with Mercury) as the socioeconomic instinct for self-protection and superficial aggrandizement; and Uranus and Neptune (together with Pluto) as the conditioned capacity for response to community values and group objectives. These departments have been employed, without designation as such, for outlining the significance of the planets in the horary "dynamics," pp. 314 ff. A full description and demonstration of the natal methods, of necessity treated here in the briefest summary, constitutes the author's preliminary manual or his *Guide to Horoscope Interpretation* and his larger or companion volume in the major series of texts, *The Essentials of Astrological Analysis*.

THE USE OF NATAL METHODS

They constitute almost the entire fabric of horary astrology in consequence. The signs, as the corresponding screening of general or relatively absolute potentialities, have a minimal importance by comparison, not only in questions and problems of the moment but when natal methods are employed for horary interpretation. They reveal the points at which various elements of background stability become of importance in some particular case. They do not do this through the dynamic interrelations among themselves, on the pattern of house indications, but by contributing special significance to the planets and the house cusps.

It is obviously impossible to present an adequate survey of natal astrology in this single chapter of a book devoted to another branch of the stellar art, and the reader without background in the genethliac delineation must of necessity supplement his study here with work in other texts. The purpose of the presentation at this point is twofold. The first objective is guidance for the professional in adapting his experience with nativities to the exigencies of horary interpretation. The second goal is to blaze the way for the neophyte or amateur, so that he may shape his further investigation and practice to the best advantage by possessing a clear idea, in advance, of the principles he will employ as soon as his own skill permits and his need of the moment dictates. In the meanwhile he can decline to give any judgment beyond that point where he finds himself over his depth in astrological potentialities.

The first step in a full regression to natal methods in the analysis of a question, or a querent's problem, is to determine the basic pattern or "temperament type" of the given wheel. Here the parallel to horary point of view is still very marked because the planets remain entirely neutral; in other words, the indication is identical no matter which particular ones of the ten bodies may constitute the configuration.

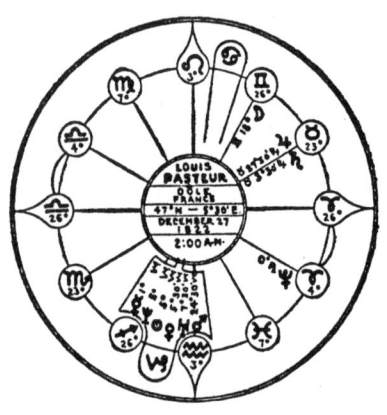

A technical distinction must be made between the overall patterns of a horoscope, which reveal the general classificatory "types," and the "focal determinators" which, by contrast, disclose the outstanding individual differences among the myriad of possible planetary arrangements. Purely as a matter of graphic convenience, an example of the latter affords the best introduction to the whole philosophy of the former. This is the rather common stellium, or the grouping of four or more planets in some one house or sign in a horoscope.[2] It is a configuration which gives a special emphasis to that special house or sign, or both, quite apart from the indications of the particular planets

[2] At least two of these must be other than the sun, Mercury and Venus. The recent increasing currency of the alternative term "satellitium" is somewhat unfortunate, for the reasons pointed out by the author in *The Guide to Horoscope Interpretation*, p. ix.

THE USE OF NATAL METHODS 341

through their house and sign positions. The case most familiar to astrologers generally is the chart of Louis Pasteur, a striking example. Here obviously the concentration of influences is in one section of the wheel, and this general emphasis of necessity was reflected in the temperament.

The Over-All Patterns in Temperament

The horary practitioner, in any use of natal procedures, must realize that there are two principal ways in which the planets [3] may be distributed around the astrological wheel. This fact sorts all horoscopes into two main classes. The special significance of any given one of them follows first of all from the class to which it belongs, then to its distinctive character as a member of that class. In other words, two broad factors go into the determination of "temperament type," and the initial one of these is the degree of simple concentration, or of wide and even distribution, shown by the planetary places around the zodiac.

When the planets are all spaced more or less evenly around the wheel, or have a corresponding fairly even distribution through any fractional part of the whole circle— such as a two-thirds, a half or a third segment—the problem or question is characterized by a basic singleness of direction; the matter at issue is shown to be functionally

[3] Again it may be well to point out that by "planets" is meant, at all times in this text, the ten bodies whose positions are given in the various ephemerides. In recognizing both the effective horary cycles, and these fundamental patterns of any horoscopic figure, no account can be made of planetary nodes, Arabian parts, or house cusps. These are supplementary factors in astrological analysis, and the procedure may be seen to be logical when it is realized that the configurations to which first importance is given are those having an actual existence in the heavens, that is, those which represent real complexes in a definite energy system.

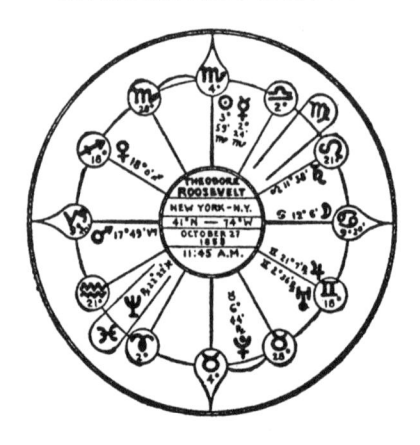

self-sufficient in its capacity to act and react according to its own private nature. This is the more simple and generally more usual state of affairs, illustrated by the three example horary charts on pages 21, 263 and 309. The first of these has the planets spaced fairly evenly through an approximate two-thirds section of the wheel, and the two others reveal a relative evenness of planetary positions around the entire zodiac. Natal astrology has found it convenient to establish four basic differentiations on this scale of measurement, illustrated by the horoscopes of Theodore Roosevelt, Henry Ford, Helen Keller and William James, as a distribution in order through the whole wheel, a two-thirds part, a half and a third section. These are, respectively, the "splash," the "locomotive," the "bowl" and "bundle" types of natal delineation.[4]

---

[4] Fully analyzed with six other examples for each type, together with the seven illustrations for each of three other types to be cited, in *The Guide to Horoscope Interpretation*; where also the authority for each particular horoscope is placed on record.

THE USE OF NATAL METHODS

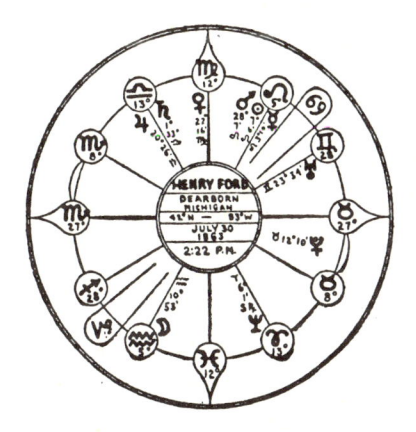

From the politician to the philosopher, down through intermediary stages shown by the industrialist and the courageous blind woman, the successive moves from an open involvement in affairs of every sort to a more and more self-centered interest in special and narrow matters is a most valuable scaling of over-all significance.

The second of the two broad factors entering into the determination of "temperament type" is the less simple state of affairs, and hence it is a distinction which is much more difficult to take into account, and to understand. The more unconditioned or "single" approach to life described by the even placement of planets in single zodiac segments (of which, of course, the whole is one) must be accepted as the normal state of things because anything else is essentially a deviation, and this "normal state" will have to be assumed whenever the astrologer lacks the experience or insight to see into the potentialities of a more complicated psychological pattern of relations.

344   HORARY ASTROLOGY

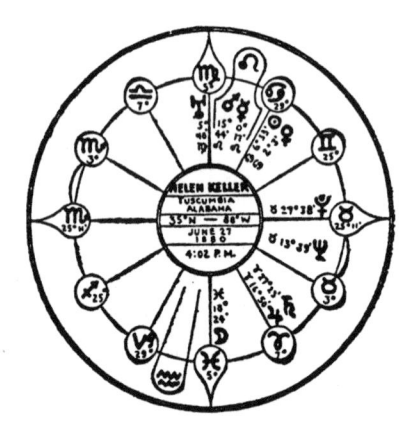

The non-single and more conditioned situation in a life, or in some matter at issue, is indicated when (1) the planets are divided into easily recognizable or sharply defined groups, or when (2) they are not inclined towards any regularity of spacing in whatever section or sections of the zodiac contains them. This reveals the fundamental dependence of something on its relation or tie to elements other than itself, and there is a clue here, in horary art, to some opportunity or encouragement definitely exterior to the focal or original interest. The extremes of possible planetary arrangement, within this second of the two great classifications, range from symmetry to asymmetry, and are illustrated on a scale of differentiation provided by the horoscopes of Karl Marx, Lewis Carroll and Algernon Swinburne as examples of the "seesaw," "bucket" and "splay" types of natal technique.

The most simple case of arrangement is the division of the planetary places in two opposing groups, which is sym-

THE USE OF NATAL METHODS

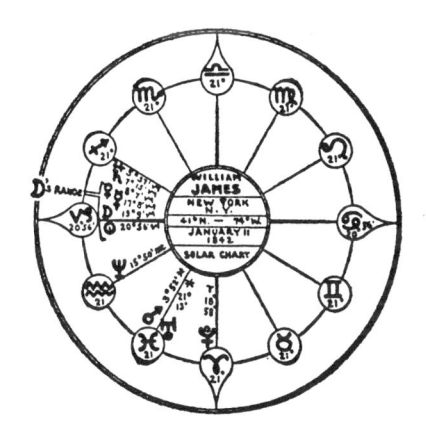

metrical as they tend to be even in number and to lie at definite counterpoints in the zodiac—showing an unimpeded tie of functional co-operation between some one phase of life and another, either achieved or inflexibly demanded—and asymmetrical as they are, contrariwise, increasingly uneven in number and not primarily at opposite sections of the circle. Because there are two criteria involved in this scaling, the progressive (1) unevenness of number and (2) tendency to fail in marking clear lines of opposition, they act concurrently but separately as a clue to a net diminishing fluidity of capacity in the expression of the pertinent general genius of the group, and as a clue also to an increasing and important emphasis on the development and expression of a highly original and more particular potentiality.

Thus Marx was far more the product of prevailing currents in philosophy and economics than a pioneer in any strictly creative sense, while Swinburne was the end-result of little other than the almost anarchistic stirrings of his own private consciousness. What must be seen, however, is that both men, and Carroll with them—when taken in contrast with the other general group—were to no degree as direct or single, as individualistically untrammeled in their life and activity.

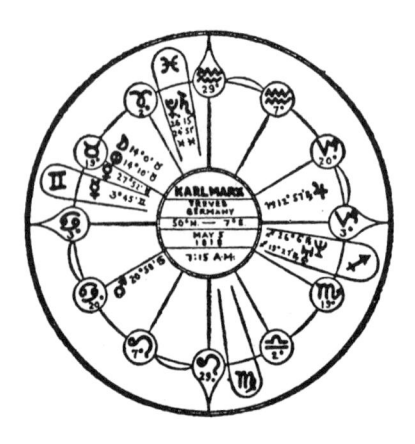

The Patterns of Individual Difference

The age-old determinators of focal emphasis, by which natal astrologers have recognized and encouraged the individual capacities of men, have been introduced in this chapter through the stellium, of which other examples are found in the charts of William James,[5] Lewis Carroll [6] and

[5] This is a "solar chart," with the sun's place taken as the horizon and the "houses" merely a twelvefold division of the heavens in lieu of true equatorial houses; a common recourse of astrologers when the hour of birth is unknown. It is impossible to tell, therefore, whether this is a stellium by house as well as sign, as in the case of Pasteur.
[6] By house, but not by sign.

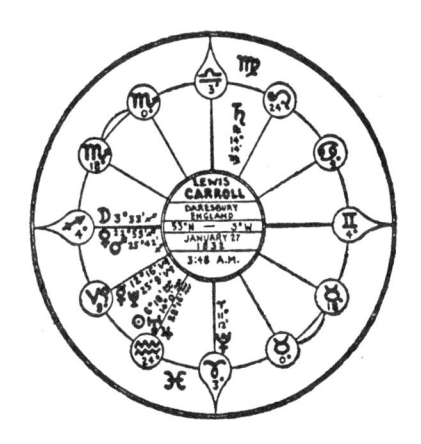

Algernon Swinburne.[7] There are many more of these "focal determinators" than can be presented in a brief summary, but all the principal ones may be identified for the sake of any newcomer into this special company of astrological devotees.[8] Thus it may be noted, in the horoscope of Lewis Carroll, that a single one of the planets lies in the southern hemisphere. Here is a phase of the all-important "hemisphere emphasis" which can be used so effectively as a springboard for the beginner's first dive into horoscopic waters,[9] and again it is a recognition of the planets in their neutral functioning. When all ten lie above the horizon, the indication is an "above the earth" situation, with a contrary implication in the reverse case. When they all are east, by the same token the events tend

[7] Effective in his surviving influence but not in his own lifetime, since Pluto's presence is necessary to establish the stellium.

[8] Given the more thorough exposition in *The Essentials of Astrological Analysis* as already suggested, and with full explanation of the whole horoscopic rationale in the author's *Astrology, How and Why It Works*.

[9] Employed in *How to Learn Astrology*.

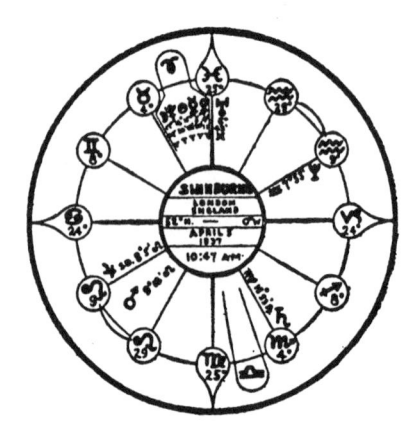

to be "rising" or more subject to the initiative of the native or querent, whereas a complete placing in the western hemisphere indicates a more necessary general conformity to the accident of the moment, the existing drift in developments.[10]

Any one of the four hemispheres is similarly emphasized by the position in it of one planet only, which is then known as a "singleton," illustrated by Saturn in Lewis Carroll's case.[11] This always means a special stress of events in the given hemisphere; in particular accordance with the genius of the one planet. Carroll won a world-wide reputation of a very much "above the earth" order, but there was the oddly Saturnine twist which gave it little repercussion into his own personal life as a staid mathematician and which made his "Alice" a remarkably critical and incisive

---

[10] Helen Keller is a dramatic case of the last possibility.
[11] The balance of weight here puzzles some neophytes, who forget that the "lost sheep" and not the "ninety and nine" always provides the focus of attention in life generally.

THE USE OF NATAL METHODS 349

portrait, on the satirical side, of his age and section of society. Here is another way, in consequence, by which a planet may be brought to focal importance in a horary chart; demanding that it be taken into special account in the supplementary planetary dynamics.

A single planet may also become a focal determinator, and demand this preferential consideration in horary analysis, through its position in its own sign under those circumstances where any section of the zodiac of which it is lord will be found to contain all the other planets also, or else those of the others which in their succession—to as many removes as necessary—are rulers of the remaining bodies. Here is the "singleton in disposition" exhibited by the example horary charts on pp. 21 and 263, and by the horoscopes of William James and Henry Ford. In the last of these four cases the sun holds Mars and Mercury in Leo with itself. Mars, as the lord of Aries, "disposes" of Neptune. The Mercury signs contain Venus and Uranus, and the Venus signs, by a next remove, take care of Saturn, Jupiter and Pluto. Saturn, at the end of the chain, brings the moon into line. The emphasis of a given planet here is even stronger than in the hemisphere singleton of the house structure, since the life is stimulated in whole rather than partial areas.

The other determinators of focal emphasis, among the particular group of those with front-rank importance in any horary resort to natal methods, establish a functional stress in the zodiac—that is, the planets themselves are completely neutral—and these may be examined more effectively in connection with the enlarged horary significance of the signs themselves.

The Special Indication of the Signs

The fundamental distribution of the zodiacal factors in all astrology is on the basis of quadrature and triplicity. The origin of these distinctions is in the relation of the house circle to the ecliptic.[12] Beginning with the three "quadratures," the four cardinal signs, constituting the first group, are those created by the impact—directed positively or in a counterclockwise direction—of the house point of view in the zodiac. They are the most practical four, out of the twelve, and they always indicate a primary concern with the issue at hand. By the same token the common signs, established just behind the equinoxes and solstices—or the negative and clockwise direction of house impact—are more inversely or subjectively concerned with practical issues. This fact makes them the most personal four, of the twelve, and they always reveal a basic interest in people and in human relations. The fixed signs, quite removed from house contact, are the four with only a theoretical relationship to everyday life; hence always showing an activity centered in ideas and values. It must be clear, of course, in connection with this, that these distinctions represent extremes, or the possibility of domi-

[12] The signs of the zodiac, because they have such little direct significance in horary astrology, have merely been identified on page 54 as an expression of man's experience with the "seasons" of the year. More technically, the two points where the celestial equator intercepts the ecliptic are the spring equinox, known as Aries 0° in astrology, and the autumnal equinox, known similarly as Libra 0°. The points of maximum distance between the two circles, are the summer solstice, identified as Cancer 0°, and the corresponding winter solstice, which is Capricorn 0°. The signs are established at these four focal points in the same way as the houses, that is, by a fourfold triangulation in a scheme of trisected quarters. Position relative to the points is "quadrature," while each triad of signs is known as a "triplicity."

THE USE OF NATAL METHODS

nant slants and attitudes. It cannot be said that a person born on November fifteenth—i.e., with his sun in the fixed sign Scorpio—is only an "idea," or that he is in any way incapable of a very practical concern over what goes on around him; moreover, the sun is only one of ten planets.

The triplicities, in comparison with the quadratures, differentiate a characteristically internal or subjective rather than external or objective type of human reaction. Fire signs indicate a fundamental interest in the identity of self, or in the purely self-centered effort of individuality to further its own affairs. Water signs identify a basic response to universal factors, or the world-wide aspect of things. Air signs, which like fire are equinoctial in their origin, reveal any man's determination to substantiate, validate and justify his self-interests. Earth signs, which are solstitial like the water group, show a fundamentally practical turn to further the immediate availability of everything; to establish the right to use, share and spend humanity's resources in every way.

Natal astrology, in its approach at all times to an overview in analysis, properly gives a very real importance to the "focal determinators," because they yield a quick and highly accurate insight into the native's predominant cast of character as it has its expression within the wholly general "temperament types." The simple preponderance of planets in a quadrature or triplicity, six or more in the one and five or more in the other, reveals an exceptional development of the characteristic reaction tendencies. None of the three example horary wheels exhibit this phenomenon, since they have been arranged to show the widest possible distribution of interhouse relations. The horoscope of Algernon Swinburne, however, shows seven planets in fire signs, that of Louis Pasteur eight in earth, and that of William James six in earth; while the latter two, in addition, provide an illustration of quadrature preponderance with seven cardinal planets each.

In the case of triplicity, considerable significance may be attached to the absence of planets in any one of the four elements. The horary examples again do not afford an instance, but Louis Pasteur, Lewis Carroll and Henry Ford are characterized by the lack of water; Algernon Swinburne by the lack of earth; and Helen Keller by the lack of air. This means that life for these people has been largely given its form, in their own consciousness, by a very positive demand upon them to develop or manifest the reaction typical of the element in question. This negative emphasis of triplicity in a horary chart would have the same indication in some special reference to the question asked, or the issue at hand, whether on a personal or a quite impersonal basis.

Sometimes two or more planets in opposition to each other will be squared by another planet or planets, creating the cosmic cross of the T variety, and occasionally the squaring planet or planets may also be opposed to establish the X cross or grand square. This is an emphasis of quadrature, exactly as the corresponding grand trine, with three or more planets linked around the circle at 120° intervals, is an emphasis of triplicity. The horary wheel on page 21 has a T cross in fixed signs, and the one on 309 not only another fixed T cross but also what might functionally be considered the same focal determinator in predominantly cardinal signs, if Jupiter is seen

THE USE OF NATAL METHODS 353

completing the necessary aspects from Sagittarius into Capricorn. This sort of configuration is meaningless in horary astrology, however, because no planet can be taken across the line of a sign. Moreover, it has little implication as a focal determinator in natal astrology because any quadrature or triplicity emphasis as such is diluted. Examples of the T cross in fixed signs are found in the horoscopes of Algernon Swinburne, Henry Ford and Theodore Roosevelt; and in the latter case there is also a T cross in common signs. The chart of Henry Ford has a wide grand trine in air signs.

The further application of this horoscopic "preponderance" is of little worth to horary practice because it represents too great a degree of refinement in over-all indication; it tends to obscure the more direct lines of immediate significance with which the astrologer must attack the immediate problem at issue. The horary importance of the signs, in consequence—apart from the qualities and elements—arises from their sharpened individual indications. These have been traditionally expressed through the symbols by which they are known, such as the ram in the case of Aries. This does not mean that a person with his sun or ascendant in that sign will necessarily look like a ram (even when the astrologer's imagination is good) but that the temperament is symbolically typified by this aggressive or butting animal. In modern times the stellar scientists have found it more valuable, by and large, to express the characteristics through traits of character or leading tendencies in temperament, especially when it comes to considering the planets other than the sun by their places in the signs. This has led to the development of a special series of keywords in which "aspiration" rather than "butting ahead" (or the literalistic "pioneering") is learned for Aries; and so on, through the twelve.

Many practitioners encounter real difficulty in their employment of these and other keywords because they fail to realize that a term to have functional significance need not necessarily imply an idea of work or action, that is, be "verbally" dynamic. Language would be more effective if it had words for all the various shadings in life's continuous subject-object distinction, but then the dictionary would be swollen indeed, and only pedants would be able to talk, at least correctly. A case in point is "equilibrium" for Libra, which superficially seems a wholly static notion. However, it takes far more energy, and a much more difficult species of work, to maintain selfhood in its varying complex at the autumnal equinox than to flail out with swashbuckling freedom at Aries, since Aries knows little necessity to hold a place of steadiness in change. No set of keywords can be perfect in even the least respect, and ultimately an astrological insight gives them more meaning than the dictionary. Primarily these functional or psychological typifications of the signs are designed to express the idea of the basic pliability in each potential context for some given planet.

Of additional distinctions among the signs which are occasionally illuminating in horary interpretation, one is the difference between those of short ascension, Capricorn through Gemini, and of long ascension, Cancer through Sagittarius, so classified because of the foreshortening of the winter signs as compared to the summer and due to the same factors which produce the seasons themselves (that is, which bring the zodiac up over the horizon at greater and lesser speeds, respectively, despite the fact that the earth's

KEY TABLE FOR THE SIGNS OF THE ZODIAC

Aries	♈ Ram	Cardinal	Fire	Aspiration
Taurus	♉ Bull	Fixed	Earth	Virility
Gemini	♊ Twins	Common	Air	Vivification
Cancer	♋ Crab	Cardinal	Water	Expansion
Leo	♌ Lion	Fixed	Fire	Assurance
Virgo	♍ Virgin	Common	Earth	Assimilation
Libra	♎ Scales	Cardinal	Air	Equivalence
Scorpio	♏ Scorpion	Fixed	Water	Creativity
Sagittarius	♐ Archer	Common	Fire	Administration
Capricorn	♑ Goat	Cardinal	Earth	Discrimination
Aquarius	♒ Water-carrier	Fixed	Air	Loyalty
Pisces	♓ Fishes	Common	Water	Sympathy

---

rotation is constant).[13] Any emphasis of the latter group—that is, Cancer, Leo, Virgo, Libra, Scorpio and Sagittarius—is an indication of developments which have a more natural and solid nature, unhurried but at all times subject to change, whereas the other six signs, taken collectively, show a more artificial and faster operation of things; often illy considered, going off "half-cocked," bull-headed and not subject to adjustment to the same degree. Thus the older nineteenth-century astrologers taught that things bought under the influence of the long ascension signs, or Cancer through Sagittarius, can by and large be sold or traded to advantage.

---

[13] Note that this distinction would be reversed in horary charts erected for places south of the equator, although the general implication of the signs goes unchanged since—in any practical psychological sense—the experience of individuals in the Argentine, Australia and so on is essentially "northern hemisphere" in its concepts and its mode of attack on the problems of life.

There are many conventional and long-established "special qualities" of the signs, which are of uneven and often very questionable value. The most important of these appear in the following tabulation, which is made from Wilson's dictionary.[14]

SPECIAL QUALITIES OF THE SIGNS

Signs	Quality
♈ ♊ ♌ ♎ ♐ ♒	Masculine, Fortunate, Diurnal
♉ ♋ ♍ ♏ ♑ ♓	Feminine, Unfortunate, Nocturnal
♈ ♉ ♊ ♋ ♌ ♍	Commanding, or Northern
♎ ♏ ♐ ♑ ♒ ♓	Obeying, or Southern
♉ ♊ ♌ ♍ ♐ ♑	Changeable
♈ ♉ ♌ ♐ ♑	Bestial, or Fourfooted [15]
♈ ♉ ♋ ♏ ♑	Hurtful
♈ ♎ ♏ ♑ ♒	Violent
♊ ♍ ♎ ♐ ♒	Voice [16]
♈ ♉ ♌ ♑	Hoarse
♊ ♍ ♐ ♓	Bicorporal (according to one view)
♊ ♍ ♐ ♒	Human [16]
♋ ♏ ♓	Fruitful, and Mute
♌ ♏ ♓	Broken, or Mutilated
♊ ♐ ♓	Double Bodied (or Bicorporal)
♊ ♎ ♒	Sweet, or Whole
♊ ♌ ♍	Barren
♌ ♏ ♒	Strong
♋ ♑ ♓	Weak
♈ ♌ ♐	Bitter
♉ ♑ ♓	Crooked
♈ ♉ ♑	Ruminant
♌ ♐	Brutish, or Feral [15]
♈	Luxurious

[14] Wilson, James, *A Complete Dictionary of Astrology*, London, 1819; reprinted at Boston, A. H. Roffe & Company, 1885.
[15] The last half of Sagittarius only.
[16] The first half of Sagittarius only.

THE USE OF NATAL METHODS

A different sort of "quadrature" distinction is provided by the position of the signs in the actual quadrants of the zodiac, with a general influence as shown in the following table.

THE SEASONAL NATURE OF THE SIGNS

Spring signs	Aries, Taurus, Gemini	Mental
Summer signs	Cancer, Leo, Virgo	Domestic
Autumn signs	Libra, Scorpio, Sagittarius	Productive
Winter signs	Capricorn, Aquarius, Pisces	Serving

The Special Indication of the Planets

The planets not only have their fixed implication, or the meaning which applies to each of them in every appropriate connection, but also an acquired "nature" as in contrast with their "significance;" that is, an indication over and above what they may reveal as pertinent significators, or may show through their focal positions in any determining pattern of a chart. This purely artificial or special nature is known as "planetary dignity," and it is a detail of horoscopy which was immensely popular around the turn of the century, or until the rise of what at once proceeded to call itself "modern astrology." The acquired planetary natures are of two sorts. Those which are the result of the situation of these bodies by sign are known as "essential dignities," and those which result from the positions of the planets relative to each other, and to the houses, are known as "accidental dignities."

The most important essential dignity is when a planet is placed in the sign of which it is lord, according to the table of rulerships given on page 117. It is then said to be in its "house" (an unfortunate but long-established use of the term, since "house" here refers to a sign). When a planet is in a sign opposite one it rules, it is said to be in its "detriment." Of the signs of which the planets are lords, one gives a greater dignity than the other and is said to be the "joy" of its ruler. In the case of the sun and moon, which have only one "house" apiece, the single sign is said to be their "joy" also. The joys of the other five planets are Mercury in Virgo, Venus in Taurus, Mars in Scorpio, Jupiter in Sagittarius and Saturn in Aquarius.

When a planet's "house" contains another planet it is said to "dispose" of that other one, and it is then increased in dignity at the other's expense, a point of occasional importance in comparing the strength of the two bodies, and of constant value in looking for the "singleton in disposition." Sometimes two planets will each be in a sign ruled by the other. This "mutual reception" dignifies both.

The second most important essential dignity is the position of a planet in the sign where it is exalted. These exaltations have been given on page 334, and they are elements that come close to the designation of questionable importance in all but the exceptional case. If the planet occupies the sign opposite its exaltation, it is in its "fall."

The third essential dignity, in the old astrological hierarchy, is the position of a planet in a triplicity with which it has particular sympathy. The sun and Jupiter are given the rulership over fire, Mars is made responsible for water, Saturn and Mercury are associated with air, and Venus with the moon is linked to earth.

The further essential dignities of medieval astrology are those by which the planets have special relation to irregu-

THE USE OF NATAL METHODS

lar fifth parts of a sign designated as "terms," and to the even third parts known as "faces" or "decanates." The tabulation follows, and it is a question if the distinctions have any validity at all. A modern revision of the faces, pre-empting the designation of "decanate" in the newer astrological literature, has come into an increasing favor, but with no more really adequate explanation than can be given for exaltation, triplicity (as a dignity), term or face in the older sense. The medievals considered a planet out of all dignity as "peregrine," or quite unable to operate with effectiveness.

TABLE OF MINOR ESSENTIAL DIGNITIES

	Triplicity Day Night	Terms [17]	Faces [18]
Aries	☉ ♃	♃ 6 ♀ 14 ☿ 21 ♂ 26 ♄ 30	♂ ☉ ♀
Taurus	♀ ☽	♀ 8 ☿ 15 ♃ 22 ♄ 26 ♂ 30	☿ ☽ ♄
Gemini	♄ ☿	☿ 7 ♃ 14 ♀ 21 ♄ 25 ♂ 30	♃ ♂ ☉
Cancer	♂ ♂	♂ 6 ♃ 13 ☿ 20 ♀ 27 ♄ 30	♀ ☿ ☽
Leo	☉ ♃	♄ 6 ☿ 13 ♀ 19 ♃ 25 ♂ 30	♄ ♃ ♂
Virgo	♀ ☽	☿ 7 ♀ 13 ♃ 18 ♄ 24 ♂ 30	☉ ♀ ☿
Libra	♄ ☿	♄ 6 ♀ 11 ♃ 19 ☿ 24 ♂ 30	☽ ♄ ♃
Scorpio	♂ ♂	♂ 6 ♃ 14 ♀ 21 ☿ 27 ♄ 30	♂ ☉ ♀
Sagittarius	☉ ♃	♃ 8 ♀ 14 ☿ 19 ♄ 25 ♂ 30	☿ ☽ ♄
Capricorn	♀ ☽	♀ 6 ☿ 12 ♃ 19 ♂ 25 ♄ 30	♃ ♂ ☉
Aquarius	♄ ☿	♄ 6 ☿ 12 ♀ 20 ♃ 25 ♂ 30	♀ ☿ ☽
Pisces	♂ ♂	♀ 8 ♃ 14 ☿ 20 ♂ 26 ♄ 30	♄ ♃ ♂

[17] The degrees identify the end of the segment ruled by the planet given; thus Jupiter rules Aries 0°-6°, inclusive, and so on. These are the terms adopted by the original Raphael (R. C. Smith) and most moderns who have given any attention to them. The terms "according to the Egyptians" have some considerable variations, but the general idea and basic arrangement are the same.

[18] The more modern system of "decanates," taken from Hindu astrology, gives the first third of each sign to itself, the next equal part to the following sign of the same triplicity, and the remaining section to the other member of the same group. Thus Aries would be taken as Aries-Aries, Aries-Leo, and Aries-Sagittarius in significance, and so on.

This doctrine of "dignity" represents the effort of astrology, at the depths of its most superstitious period, to set up a scaling system by which to judge the comparative worth of the celestial bodies. In effect it sought to achieve what today is available in much more satisfactory form through the pattern analysis and the focal determinators. Nothing justifies any complete abandonment of the cumbersome method, however, since it must be remembered that it can produce results. Now an astrologer seldom employs the essential dignities and debilities—unless the house and exaltation on the one hand, and the detriment and fall on the other—but he may well know them all.

The accidental dignities have never been as definitely established as the others, and there is no real agreement as to which ones to consider—or in what order of importance to take them—since they are seldom used. Present-day practice always gives special significance to (1) the elevated planet, or that one of the ten nearest the tenth-house cusp on either side, and (2) the rising planet, or that one which while below the ascendant (between the ascendant and the fourth-house cusp) is nearest the horizon. Properly a planet is not "elevated" unless it lies in the ninth or tenth houses, and not rising unless found in the first or second.

Further "accidental dignities" are admitted by most old-line astrologers when (1) a planet has preponderantly favorable aspects, when (2) it is placed in an angular house, w (3) it is oriental or on the eastern side of the chart, when (4) it is swift in motion and when (5) it has wide declination. Such a body is swift in motion when, at the time used for horary analysis, it is moving at more than its average speed in the given twenty-four hours. This can be determined (in the case of the bodies whose motion is appreciable enough to permit such a dignity) by comparison with the following table. By wide declination is meant position south or north in excess of seventeen degrees.

THE MEAN MOTION OF THE PLANETS

	°	′	″
Moon	13	10	34
Mercury	0	59	36
Venus	0	59	36
Sun	0	59	12
Mars	0	30	48

The planets gain an important accidental dignity, under the more modern over-all view, when they are prominent in the focal determination of the chart. This is particularly true when one of them is singleton in a hemisphere. When they tend to aggregate in tight groups, or to form pairs around the chart, they are dignified to the extent their arrangement in these knots is with nearly exact aspects.

On the other side of the picture are the "accidental debilities," as when a planet is retrograde or intercepted. An important case is when it is "combust," or within 8°30′ of the sun.[19] Combustion was said by the ancients to mean that the given activity was diverted into the general purpose or deeper motive lying behind the issue of the moment. However, in this tradition, if the planet is "within the heart of the sun," or within less than 17′ of exact conjunction, it is "cazimi," and highly strengthened.

Somewhat akin to "debility" are the specific impediments to desirable aspects which horary astrology takes into

[19] Mercury is excepted, however, in traditional horary practice.

account when resorting to the zodiacal motion of the planets, or using natal procedures entirely. Thus it is necessary for one body to make a certain aspect to another, in order to bring a given relationship to consummation, but it makes another aspect first instead; or a third planet is able in the meanwhile to complete a different aspect to the second one, and so interfere with the process in a different way. Under zodiacal perspectives, this is a positive indication of interruption or distraction, such as can usually be traced out or identified in considerable detail. It does not necessarily deny the desired outcome, but shows much trouble.

More unfavorable by far is the situation when a planet is about to approach a desired aspect but, rather than completing it, turns retrograde and does not do so. This is the "refranation" of the medievals.[20] It reveals the complete collapse of some project, or the failure of a given effort, due primarily to a lack of adequate preparation.

The practical value of all these dignities, whether essential or accidental—in any modern practice of astrology, natal or horary—is in the rare case where the indications otherwise make it difficult to decide which of two planets is the stronger, and so which factor of life is most apt to prevail in a pertinent clash of interests, or a situation of major conflict. The dignities and debilities of each class have strength in the order they have been presented.

Supplementary Planetary Indications

Natal astrology has a wider general scope than horary in ordinary familiar practice, due to its inclusion of more

[20] Many particular possibilities along these general lines were worked out and named by the older astrologers, such as "abscission of light," "destruction," "frustration," "prohibition" and, on the constructive side, "delation."

THE USE OF NATAL METHODS 363

planetary factors; most particularly the Arabian parts, the various nodes, the minor aspects, and the significant degrees. The "parts" are secondary horizons, created by taking, from the ascendant, whatever distance is found to lie between two planets, cusps or points in pertinent relationship, always moving counterclockwise in the zodiac. Of these, the Part of Fortune (or *Pars Fortunae;* but not just *Fortuna*) is almost universally employed, and its use has been demonstrated in considerable detail.[21]

The nodes, similarly, are secondary ecliptical points created by the intersection of the orbits of the earth and the given planets. Only two are found in the average horoscope wheel. The moon's "north" or ascending node is known as the dragon's head (or Caput), and the opposite or "south" and descending point as the dragon's tail (or Cauda). The former is a point of definite assistance, wherever it is found. It shows a special co-operativeness from individuals or affairs ruled by the house which holds it. It reflects, of necessity, the function of the moon. The tail is a definite impediment in horary art, principally showing the promise or consequence of self-undoing, indiscretion and lack of common sense. All the planets have nodes, which can be used in similar fashion according to the signification that can be given to each of them. They have thoroughgoing exposition in the author's *Mundane Perspectives in Astrology* (not yet available in 1971).

The greater refinement of planetary indication is obtained most commonly by the use of the more important non-Ptolemaic aspects, a table of which follows with the degrees of exactness and general implication in each case.

[21] See pp. 280 ff.

THE PRINCIPAL MINOR ASPECTS

Semisextile	30°	Same influence as a sextile but weaker
Semiquintile	36°	Same influence as a quintile but weaker
Semisquare	45°	Same influence as a square but weaker
Septile	51°26′	An aspect of special obligation or fatality
Quintile	72°	An aspect of special talent or artistry
Sesquiquadrate	135°	Same influence as a square but more uncertain
Biquintile	144°	Same influence as a quintile but more uncertain
Quincunx	150°	Same influence as a sextile but more uncertain

Some horary astrologers in a regression to the use of pure natal methods—and so the zodiacal motion of the planets—continue to use the medieval "assisted aspect" in its two common forms. "Translation of light" is the case where two planets, not legitimately forming an aspect because of wide orbs or a situation in signs that cannot have the proper tie, are both brought into a strong aspect by a third planet, which in a sense thus pulls the more important relationships into an effective significance. Such a mediating planet would describe persons or conditions which may bring about a consummation otherwise beyond hope. "Collection" is a similar proposition when two significators have no aspect with each other, or cannot form one, but both make their next effective tie with a third planet. In such an instance the mediation is passive, since the other two planets provide the active factor, and the help comes through uncovering some other person or factor of pertinent and available significance.

THE USE OF NATAL METHODS

Some fine and deep minutiae of astrological distinctions, with a corresponding real insight into the life situation, are obtained through employing the degrees of special significance. The medieval tradition preserves the "affections" of certain degrees, as a finer measure than the terms, and a table of these follows:

TRADITIONAL AFFECTIONS AND SIGNIFICATIONS OF THE DEGREES

	Aries	Taurus	Gemini	Cancer	Leo	Virgo
Masculine	8 15 30	11 21 30	16 26	2 10 23 30	5 15 30	12 30
Feminine	9 22	5 17 24	5 22 30	8 12 27	8 23	8 20
Light	8 20 29	7 15 28	4 12 22	12 28	30	8 16
Dark	3 16	3 30	7 27	14	10	5 30
Smoky				20	20	22
Void	24 30	12 20	16 30	18 30	25	10 17
Pitted or Deep	6 11 16 23 29	5 12 24 25	2 12 17 26 30	12 17 23 26 30	6 13 15 22 23 28	8 13 16 21 22
Deficient or Azimene		6 7 8 9 10		9 10 11 12 13 14 15	18 27 28	
Increasing Fortune	19	3 15 27	11	1 2 3 4 15	2 5 7 19	3 14 20

	Libra	Scorpio	Sagittarius	Capricorn	Aquarius	Pisces
Masculine	5 20 30	4 17 30	2 12 30	11 30	5 21 27	10 23 30
Feminine	15 27	14 25	5 24	10	15 25 30	20 28
Light	5 18 27	8 22	9 19 30	10 19	9 21 30	12 22 28
Dark	10 21	3 30	12	7 22 30	13	6 18 30
Smoky		24	23	15	4	
Void	30	14 29		25	25	25
Pitted or Deep	17 20 30	9 10 22 23 27	7 12 15 24 27 30	7 17 22 24 29	1 12 17 22 24 29	4 9 24 27 28
Deficient or Azimene		19 28	1 7 19	8 18 26 27 28 29	18 19	
Increasing Fortune	3 15 21	7 18 20	13 20	12 13 14 20	7 16 17 20	13 20

These "affections and significations," which are given by Wilson in his dictionary, but not recommended by him, are explained as follows: "Against Aries are found 8, 15, and 30 in the masculine column and 9 and 22 in the feminine column:—this shews the first 8 degrees of Aries to be masculine, the 9th feminine, from thence to the 15th masculine; from the 15th to the 22d feminine, and from thence to the 30th masculine: in like manner the 3 first are dark degrees, from thence to the 8th light degrees, from thence to the 16th dark, and from thence to the 20th light. The 29th is also a light degree, the rest are indifferent. There are no smoky degrees in Aries. The 24th and 30th are void degrees, the 6th, 11th, 16th, 23d, and 29th are pitted or deep degrees.—There are no azimene degrees, and the 19th degree is fortunate.

"If the ascendant or its lord be in any of these degrees in a nativity it is said to denote something in the native's fortune or appearance corresponding; thus, if in a masculine degree he or she will be more masculine: if in a feminine, more feminine. If in a light or dark degree, more fair or dark; and if in a smoky degree more dun and swarthy, with dull intellect. Void degrees render the native empty and void of knowledge. Deep pitted degrees subject the native to deep marks of small pox or scars, etc., or, according to other sapient gentlemen, they cause an impediment in speech, troubles and disputes in which they are sunk as in a deep pit. The azimene degrees make them crooked, lame or deformed, according to the nature of the sign and the part signified by it, and this they say is the invariable rule. The fortunate degrees, if on the cusp of the 2d house, or if the lord of the 2d be in such a degree, or if Jupiter be in a fortunate degree, the native will acquire great riches and honour; such nonsense as this deserves no comment."[22]

A modern enterprise with very rich promise, still in work and enlisting a considerable number of outstanding

[22] *Dictionary of Astrology*, pp. 25-6.

THE USE OF NATAL METHODS 367

astrologers of reputation in both England and America, is a tabulation of degree characteristics according to the exceptional frequency of various types of occurrence in correspondence with them. The consideration of the fixed stars is related to this research, which means recognizing that the principal ones among them have appreciable value at times, in both horary and natal analysis.

Of much more immediate importance in the general project of which this book is a part—and again an enterprise that has its roots in the medieval tradition—are the symbolical degrees. There are several sets of these, of very mixed value. Those of Charubel have proved exceptionally suggestive.[23] The Sabian symbols for the zodiacal degrees are a wholly original or independent contribution, and a rather spectacular development that has been subjected to long continued and elaborate testing before publication.[24]

The Special Consideration of Life and Death

A matter often not considered within the ethical province of horary art is the length of life, or the probabilities of death, and any consideration given to a problem of this sort requires a considerable regression to natal techniques. At best an analysis of the duration of life is a dangerous detail of astrological work, since it is possible either to frighten or overly assure someone to the point of doing him permanent injury. Moreover, nothing concerning the

---

[23] Charubel (John Thomas), *The Degrees of the Zodiac Symbolized*, London, L. N. Fowler, 1898.

[24] *The Sabian Symbols in Astrology*, by Marc Edmund Jones, a companion volume in this series of textbooks. It contains a full explanation of the rationale of this sort of symbolism, with an account of the origin of this set and an exposition of the ramifications in significance.

cycle of life is fixed in a fatalistic sense, as even Lilly pointed out in 1646. However, the astrologer of sufficient skill and knowledge may gain considerable information; and if he wishes he may keep it to himself, using it indirectly in a way that can be of real help to others.

The determination of the life span in a horary chart is built upon the hypothesis that its events are charted through the houses clockwise or backwards from the ascendant, each house representing a twelfth of the whole. An older generation of astrologers used five years to the house, and the present length of life expectancy suggests six, but a more accurate device is to average the years lived by the closest relatives where all lines are deceased (ignoring accidental and childhood deaths) and to divide this by twelve for the number of years to give each unit. Some greater measure of accuracy is gained by taking the mother and her brothers and sisters for a man, and her father and his brothers and sisters for the generation back, and so on, reversing this in a woman's case. Taking the houses for proper time units in this manner, and proportioning fractional parts of each house as necessary, the points of affliction by the planets to the lord of the ascendant, and to the moon and sun, according to their location in the horary wheel, indicate the critical periods of life. When the lords of the fourth and eighth houses, or Saturn in any case, participate in these afflictions, then a point of possible or probable termination of life is shown.

Inquiry about the length of life belongs in the first house, as has been explained, while the specific examination of any death potentials as such is located in the eighth house. Most commonly a question here will concern the nature of death; or the factors in a situation that might be used to defeat it, or that add to the risk and can perhaps be eliminated. Death, as an event, is never really experienced by the person who dies and, as a matter remote from his

THE USE OF NATAL METHODS

immediate experience, may not be reflected dependably in a horary chart. The pertinent concomitants of death are revealed most importantly through the nature of the planets most involved in the matter by position or aspect. Thus Jupiter, Venus, sun and moon are "good," and Mercury is either "good" or "bad." Jupiter gives an easy or happy death, Venus a pleasant one, the sun a demise with honor, the moon an end with attention-satisfying excitement and Mercury a final passing "according to expectation." On the other side of the picture, Mars gives a violent or unexpected death, and Saturn shows protracted and often painful lingering before the end. These two planets are the especially lethal factors in astrology. Uranus shows an accidental and sudden, and perhaps a unique demise, Neptune a generally mysterious or disgraceful one, and Pluto a death which may be individually insignificant, or some sort of sacrifice to a larger group interest.

The Regressive Implications of Time

The time factor in horary astrology is fundamentally a matter of the symbolical measure, or the prediction of the interval to events from the relations created by the earth's diurnal turning on its axis. With the regression towards natal techniques this becomes increasingly unreliable, so that astrologers turn to zodiacal motion, and in some cases even bring the directions or progressions of the nativity into horary analysis. The traditional primary directions, entirely diurnal in nature, are valueless because four minutes correspond to a year, and the questions and problems of everyday life must have an almost immediate resolution if the astrologer's services are to be of any use at all. By the same token, the employment of the secondary directions of a horary wheel is hardly more satisfactory because of the little zodiacal motion available, even in the moon's case, to become co-ordinate with the immediate developments in some given issue. A syncopated scale has been suggested for these secondary cycles, such as a day measuring to a month instead of a year, but it would be wholly artificial, and devoid of all theoretical justification. Actual recourse is to the transits, and a cardinal procedure in connection with elections—and all other horary work where the normal timetable is unsuitable—is to make all judgment on the basis of these actual movements of the planets in the heavens.

The transiting planets are utilized in two ways, over and beyond their place in the horary wheel itself. The most important of these requires no special exposition. It is merely the normal comparison of the movements of the planets ahead, or on from their positions in the horary chart, entirely on the pattern of ordinary straightaway natal guidance. As aspects are formed by these transiting planets to the planetary places in the given horoscope, they are analyzed according to (1) this aspect, (2) the significators involved, and (3) the general conditions at issue. This gives a time for events to be expected, which is taken from the ephemeris without modification; and it involves no difficulty since the interpretation is in the light of the general possibilities revealed by the chart.

A less obvious employment of these actual positions of the heavenly bodies at the time a horary question is asked —whenever the yes-and-no judgment is denied, or when it proves inadequate to supply any requisite information— is for the purpose of gaining light on the whole issue by a comparison of the moment the problem appears with the

THE USE OF NATAL METHODS 371

current heavenly condition, and thereby estimating the graining of the chart; in this way achieving a larger insight into the meaning of events, not only from the horoscope itself but from the general planetary tendencies. This procedure might be termed the special "consideration before judgment" whenever natal methods are employed, and it makes use of some very simple phenomena. Thus every practitioner can count on the fact that, in general, problems will turn up in a complex which has high meaning in his own experience. He will notice the tendency of certain issues to aggregate, so that on one day three or four in succession may involve finances, whereas on another an equivalent string of romantic difficulties will be presented. At a moment when money seems to be dominant in the minds of all who seek advice, it is a fair supposition that some element of finance might lurk in the background of consciousness in the case of someone worrying about marriage or divorce. Here is the "immediate overtone" in horary practice, and it can be a very sharp and important guide in making sure that the horoscope is given a proper interpretation, and that any advice is made clear and pertinent.

The professional astrologer prepares himself for a recognition and employment of this shifting "immediate overtone" through his daily contact with the ephemeris, and his week-by-week or month-by-month experience with the changing pattern of the planetary forces. In addition to this, he often takes the nature of the day and hour into account. The days of the week are ruled by the planets which give them their names, directly or indirectly in most modern languages, as Sunday by the sun, Monday by the moon,

Tuesday by Mars, Wednesday by Mercury, Thursday by Jupiter, Friday by Venus, and Saturday by Saturn.

The planetary hours are perhaps of greater importance, however, because they change swiftly, giving the superficial tides of experience, and because they chart the impact of the different heavenly emphases through the course of the day. Tables of these may be purchased, or the astrologer may calculate his own. They operate from sunrise to sunset, and from sunset to sunrise, with each of these intervals divided into twelve periods of equal length, but nearly always more or less than sixty minutes. The first hour from sunrise is always ruled by the same planet as the day. The others in order are given to the planets according to the sequence of "Chaldean order"—or Saturn, Jupiter, Mars, sun, Venus, Mercury, and moon—which continually repeats itself. In twenty-four hours this sequence of seven, after three times around, takes three out of itself to start another day at the middle or fourth position. Thus Saturday is ruled by Saturn and begins with the Saturn hour; Sunday is ruled by the sun and its first hour is at the fourth place in the hour sequence of Saturn. Monday is ruled by the moon, which lies at fourth place in the sun's sequence. The basic table of the week is given on the following page.

Matters coming up on particular days are inclined to show an underlying sympathy with the daily rulerships, as a foundation for the immediate overtone. Sunday, which the Christian world has taken as its sacred day, or its weekly Easter, is a point of beginnings, or a getting at that central core of things which is represented by the sun; whether in the spirit of rest and relaxation on the one hand or of self-regeneration on the other. Monday, under the

THE USE OF NATAL METHODS

TABLE OF PLANETARY HOURS

Day Hours; Sunrise to Sunset

Sunday	Monday	Tuesday	Wednesday	Thursday	Friday	Saturday
Sun	Moon	Mars	Mercury	Jupiter	Venus	Saturn
Venus	Saturn	Sun	Moon	Mars	Mercury	Jupiter
Mercury	Jupiter	Venus	Saturn	Sun	Moon	Mars
Moon	Mars	Mercury	Jupiter	Venus	Saturn	Sun
Saturn	Sun	Moon	Mars	Mercury	Jupiter	Venus
Jupiter	Venus	Saturn	Sun	Moon	Mars	Mercury
Mars	Mercury	Jupiter	Venus	Saturn	Sun	Moon
Sun	Moon	Mars	Mercury	Jupiter	Venus	Saturn
Venus	Saturn	Sun	Moon	Mars	Mercury	Jupiter
Mercury	Jupiter	Venus	Saturn	Sun	Moon	Mars
Moon	Mars	Mercury	Jupiter	Venus	Saturn	Sun
Saturn	Sun	Moon	Mars	Mercury	Jupiter	Venus

Night Hours; Sunset to Sunrise

Jupiter	Venus	Saturn	Sun	Moon	Mars	Mercury
Mars	Mercury	Jupiter	Venus	Saturn	Sun	Moon
Sun	Moon	Mars	Mercury	Jupiter	Venus	Saturn
Venus	Saturn	Sun	Moon	Mars	Mercury	Jupiter
Mercury	Jupiter	Venus	Saturn	Sun	Moon	Mars
Moon	Mars	Mercury	Jupiter	Venus	Saturn	Sun
Saturn	Sun	Moon	Mars	Mercury	Jupiter	Venus
Jupiter	Venus	Saturn	Sun	Moon	Mars	Mercury
Mars	Mercury	Jupiter	Venus	Saturn	Sun	Moon
Sun	Moon	Mars	Mercury	Jupiter	Venus	Saturn
Venus	Saturn	Sun	Moon	Mars	Mercury	Jupiter
Mercury	Jupiter	Venus	Saturn	Sun	Moon	Mars

WARNING: These operate on true local mean time, and standard (war or daylight saving) hours must be corrected.

---

moon, is busy with the task of taking up the threads of things again, and it usually carries the atmosphere of a broad public concern over the details of business, such as supplies and the like. Tuesday carries a distinct Mars undertone, with an enlargement in point of view and sometimes a certain breaking out of the pioneer spirit. Wednesday, at mid-week, always has the greatest leaning towards an introspective summation, superficially central in the business of civilization. Thursday, under Jupiter, is the strong expansive day which develops the sense of a week moving to its climax, and it is here that the undertone has its greatest general expansiveness. Friday, ruled by Venus, begins to capture the spirit of the week end, and to give a feeling of culminations, completeness, satisfaction and esthetic realization. Saturn winds up the cycle, and is preeminently the day of measurement in the sense of sports, contests and the like; or of the relaxation into a greater reality.

The planetary hours are always much sharper than the days, but in an application to very trivial or minor things. While in some respects not unlike the planetary days, the hours much more importantly reveal the groundwork of the prejudice or inner and hidden motives which bring the question to be answered, the problem to be judged. Saturn shows things at a critical pass; Jupiter identifies some compelling sense of opportunity; Mars brings out the pressure for decision or action; the sun discloses the dignity of personality asserting itself; Venus reveals some insistent demand for satisfaction or justification; Mercury dramatizes every uncertainty, or stirs up every turmoil in relationships; and the moon signifies the pertinent excitement by which experience is somehow enlarged in its dimension.

An Appendix on Terminology

Many odd terms in the outworn vocabulary of medieval astrology will persist in modern books and articles, due largely to an uninspired copying of older writings. Some

THE USE OF NATAL METHODS 375

of these are altogether too obscure to justify listing and definition, and others are entirely obvious; or are good literary words even if not in everyday currency, such as "matutinal" for the dawn and "vespertine" for evening. A few should be noted, however, for the sake of the individual who wishes a rounded and competent grasp of horary art.

The astrological diagram of the heavens is itself not only known as a horoscope or chart—the most common designations—but also as a "nativity," a "figure," a "map," a "wheel," a "scheme," a "theme," a "geniture" and, of course, a "diagram." The aspects appear somewhat cumbersomely as "configurations," and daintily as "familiarities." A planet's movement will appear as its "inclination," as in reference to the place to which it is moving. The "promittor" is the significator of a given matter in the terms of what it promises to do, and the words are practically synonymous. The "prorogator" and the "apheta" are the "hyleg," or the promittor of life in the same way that the "anareta" is the corresponding significator of death. Planets not in aspect are "inconjunct" (although by an odd development the word has also become synonymous with the quincunx aspect in some literature). As an aspect is exact (in longitude, and sometimes in latitude also) it is "partile," and when very wide it is "platic."

There is a "querent" in horary astrology, and also a "quesited," i.e., the person or thing inquired about. A chart erected for the time a native takes to bed in illness is a "decumbiture." Planets in aspect are "joined to" each other in any case—not the conjunction alone—and if one lies in an evil configuration it is "impeded." Because of their special importance, the sun, moon, tenth house and ascendant have been identified as the "moderators," and because the "lights" or "luminaries"—that is, the sun and moon—took their coloring from the signs according to the medieval notion, they were sometimes called the "passive stars." The strongest planet in the chart—according to all types of "dignity" scaled together—is the "almuten." In the matter of planetary movements and aspects the new moon and full moon are known as "syzygies," with the term also applied to any sort of familiarity at all. The places where a planet changes direction are identified as "stations," and any body within seventeen degrees from the sun, when not actually combust, is said to be "under the sun's beams."

Chapter Fourteen

MULTIPLE QUESTIONS

The first step in all competent horary procedure is to focus any given matter at issue under a single head, as far as possible, and so bring all contributory or extraneous considerations into an ordered line of relationship. The entire analysis of the houses, in connection with the initial location of a given inquiry, has been shaped to help the practitioner or student achieve this end. The ring-around-the-rosy technique usually enables him to get the details of a particular difficulty into some kind of a logical sequence, as a basis for measuring and weighing the probabilities; so that he then can proceed to an intelligent job of prediction and advice. Obviously, however, there are many cases where different problems actually come to a point of crisis at once, and where there seems to be no immediate or genuine relationship between them.

Certainly a man can have sickness to upset his home life at the same time he faces a reorganization in his business. Probably this piling up of troubles indicates a common denominator, but the astrologer has no right to use pure imagination, or resort to guesswork, in order to identify it. The necessary technique at this point is to treat each palpably separate matter as a distinct question, to be answered or judged entirely on its own account. Each should be stated very clearly, or perhaps even written out independently, before the time for the whole combination is taken. It must be remembered that no detail of inquiry can be added after the moment is accepted as significant, if it is in any way an "afterthought"; that is, if it is not a direct and necessary amplification of some factor definitely under consideration. Adherence to this rule holds the general inquiry to its single head even when, so to speak, there are several "faces" on the matter.

The multiple-question technique can be illustrated by the case of a man who asks, (1) "What will be the results in my wife's campaign for president of the Garden Club?", (2) "What will happen if I discharge X and promote Y to his place?", (3) "What will be the consequences of going to Canada next week, as I plan?", (4) "What are the chances of coming out all right if I put ten thousand in Fred's business?"

Obviously distinct matters, these are all part of the general milieu in which the querent is operating, although without any identifiable central core in consideration. Thus his wife might go ahead, to express her own wishes, but she insists upon the guidance of his opinion; and he finds himself with no real basis for judgment. The record of X for this year is bad, but there is a problem of general morale. It happens that this businessman has been successful very largely because of the degree to which he will stand behind those who work for him. X made a magnificent showing the previous season, and may well stage a comeback. As for the Canada trip, this has always paid dividends, if only by developing new perspectives; but general conditions suggest it might be better to stay on the job, since quick decisions are becoming increasingly vital. There is every reason to back up Fred, but ten thousand makes a considerable hole in available cash resources, and business economists insist that there will be a slump in this particular line of effort for perhaps a year or two

MULTIPLE QUESTIONS

ahead; so that every resource may be needed. Ideally a client should come to the astrologer with problems such as these as they arise, one at a time, but if he brings them all at once, the astrologer must have the techniques with which to handle them.

Multiple questions mean a different pair of houses, on one or another of the patterns of yes-and-no analysis, and so a different judgment chart, for each of them. It cannot be emphasized too strongly that the coincidence of two or more matters coming to a head at one time or one place, in horary practice, due to some combination of circumstances, can never justify an identical answer to any among them unless an actual common denominator has been recognized in the given affairs, and the identity of judgment follows upon an analysis of that primary factor. Whatever remains different in experience must be measured through a corresponding astrological distinction. The previous chapters have presented the rigorous methods developed to preserve such a separation, whenever two pertinent relationships have their obvious basic primary identification in the same house, and the procedure is the same in a multiple as in a simple inquiry.[1]

Continuing with the illustration, the wife's club-work project can be taken simply as a seventh-house matter; that is, it remains the wife's activity irrespective of its nature. However, club enterprises of an avocational sort belong in the fifth house, and the fifth from the seventh would put this in the eleventh of the crisis chart.

The discipline of an employe belongs in the sixth, as an irreducibly simple example of locating a matter. What is important here is to notice that it is an either-or proposition, since it is not so much the retention or elimination of X as it is the choice between retaining X or replacing him with Y. The problem is which employe will produce certain necessary results, and what the effect will be on all

[1] See p. 153.

employes if a change is made, under circumstances when the pro and con are both of weight.

The trip to Canada is an inquiry which has its focus in the ninth house, so far not employed in this particular wheel. The possible combinations for locating these multiple queries have been seventh-first or eleventh-fifth, sixth-twelfth, and now ninth-third.[2]

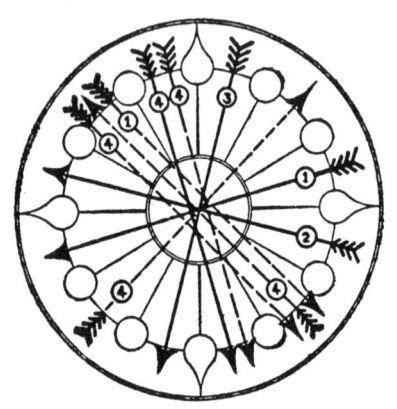

When it comes to the advisability of putting money behind a friend's business, the second-eighth axis is available, and also the tenth-fourth and whichever one of the seventh-first or eleventh-fifth combinations is not used for the club election. There is no difficulty if it is seen as purely a matter of money, the second-eighth, but this is obviously not right. Money loaned to friends is hardly an income investment, but is speculation (fifth) or an act of friendship (eleventh), if not a tacit partnership in a given opportunity or enterprise (seventh). What is primary here? Obviously the relationship to Fred more than any idea of a profitable use for the ten thousand. Normal location would go to the eleventh to identify Fred.

[2] The special chart displays the alternatives graphically, the solid arrows identifying the final place of each query, and the dotted arrows the other possibilities.

MULTIPLE QUESTIONS

This house may have been used for the wife's campaign. To regress to the next one would make the issue at focus in the original twelfth, which is pre-empted for the X-Y matter. However, inquiry about the Garden Club can be made seventh-first as suggested, freeing the eleventh-fifth for this fourth query, as quite the easiest solution.

The relocation of a question, which is the simplest procedure in that case where another matter is already focal in the same house of the crisis chart, is the horary technique which comes closest to the edge of real psychological danger. The best of practitioners, all unwittingly, are ever prone to move here in response to their own wishful thinking; ultimately forcing a horoscope to yield the verdict predetermined by their own inner desire. When it becomes possible to juggle relationships around too haphazardly, the astrological wheel in time loses all real meaning; horary art becomes both incompetent and silly. In consequence it must be understood that any step of relocation is only justified by adding a new factor to the consideration, in conformity with the fundamental astrological principle that every new recourse in judgment must contribute a necessary and pertinent detail of realization to the given issue.

There is, also, a parallel law of general psychology. The fact that an inquiry can be framed is the promise of an ultimately satisfactory answer. The horary practitioner of adequate skill will never admit any lack of recourses, whenever he has need of them. It is always possible, therefore, if a yes-and-no is denied, to proceed by this relocation of the matter. However, here is where a wishful rationalization is apt to be most subtle and unsuspected, and the particular recourse is not recommended in single queries, unless as a detail of regular policy in avoiding an angular-house focus in the crisis chart.[3] The procedure becomes definitely essential at times in multiple-question cases, when it always calls for the anchorage of the given factor at issue in some broader frame of reference.

Returning to the illustration, the astrologer questions his client further about this investment in Fred's business, and finds that it is not really so much a matter of response to friendship, in the usual sense of that word, as it is a strong notion of reciprocity, or a conformity to the code of a certain business group. There was a time some years back in which Fred came to this man's rescue, generously and at some sacrifice. There is a consequent refined sense of obligation which is not so much a matter of money as of social prestige. Fred can go to Jack and get twenty thousand. Other elements come to light and at once it is obvious that this is a tenth-house matter of "commercial politics," and that there is no choice as far as the money is concerned. He must put it up, or "lose face"; sacrificing the particular advantages he has gained. What is actually at stake is whether he may continue "on the inside" with this group, meeting the requirements of association with those whose resources, by and large, are very much greater than his own. With the question rephrased and relocated in the tenth, the astrologer is in a position to be of real help to his client. The fact that he was compelled to dig more deeply in this matter shows the working of the "common denominator," or underlying concordance of events as they tend at all times to compel a proper ordering of themselves.

Multiple questions are limited under ordinary circumstances to six items, since there are only that many pairs of

[3] See p. 132.

MULTIPLE QUESTIONS 383

houses. In the truly unique instance where more queries are involved, the regression must take some special form. A house can only be used again as its relationships are modified. What is now explained is the procedure for cases where the yes-and-no pairs are already pre-empted, and also where those that are available may not be suitable. The essence of recourse is simple enough, consisting of either a resort to natal methods in the second analysis of any house thus duplicated as focal in matters at issue—a technique which needs no further exposition—or else a use of different planetary rulerships. These alternative lords are provided by accepting Uranus, Neptune and Pluto for Aquarius, Pisces and Scorpio, in order. To do so means that analysis must be placed on a strictly modern level of significance, as a justification for taking these new bodies into a yes-and-no potential; but it is nearly always possible to meet this necessity. A further resort to alternative rulerships—little justified by contrast, except in the case of really extraordinary psychological complications—is achieved by using the exaltations rather than the lords of the signs.

In addition to the somewhat common occurrence of the multiple questions asked at a single time by one individual, there is the rather exceptional proposition when two people or more happen to make inquiry at the same identical moment. The possibility of this always seems to distress the layman, as well as the new devotee of horary art. No particular difficulty is involved, but teachers of astrology sometimes demonstrate the answer to any doubts about the general concordance of all experience in a way that dramatizes, neatly, the degree to which the seemingly scattered things of life are yet completely reconciled in cosmic orderliness. Members of a class will be permitted to ask various questions, which are written on the blackboard, and then a horary wheel is calculated for the group of them. The results may have striking accuracy as long as the basic interest of the participants in the exhibition, at the time the questions are put down, is effectively directed to the problems made the basis of inquiry; that is, when those present are not allowed to become engrossed with what is a pedagogical "stunt," and most unreliable when it degenerates into a "show-off." Thus it is necessary for the teacher to keep his group free from any "mind set" or expectation, and he will have the best results if his demonstration comes as a surprise. The professional astrologer, of course, can employ this same technique successfully when various inquiries arrive at the same time, as in a single mail.

CHAPTER FIFTEEN

PARALLELS OF DECLINATION

As ONE of the six major or Ptolemaic aspects, the parallels of declination have a theoretically equal importance with the others in astrology, but they are definitely neglected in actual practice. As a consequence the use of parallels is infrequent in horary art.[1] However, they are very valuable as another recourse in regressing from the yes-and-no judgment to natal techniques, and they certainly should be taken into account whenever the chart is approached from an over-all perspective, or when any complete analysis is made of the five more familiar aspects. They supplement the indication of the others; but should never supplant them, or be given a more primary importance, except when the problem at hand—or the particular frame of reference in which some horoscope is to be considered—has a definitely recognizable correspondence to their special nature.

This "parallel" between planets is established whenever their positions "sidewise," as in contrast with "around-wise" in celestial longitude or right ascension—in the terms of the tilt in the planes of their respective orbits in relation to the plane of the celestial equator—is an expression of a like emphasis in this particular deviation. Less technically, it is the situation when two planets lean out of line in the houses to the same degree; akin to the brake-

[1] See p. 305.

man on a freight train hanging off at arm's length on one or the other side to get a better view while helping spot a car or two in the railroad yards. By this token the parallels represent a state of like position in the effort at special perspective in life, and what counts is the planets' amount of lean; which indicates the pertinent capacity for larger or deeper insight in the particular relationship. This degree of declination is emphasized, and an aspect is created, when two planets share it; or have an identical amount of leaning, whether on the one side or the other. It is position at the same degree of declination, north or south, in astrological language, and as is the case with other aspects, it does not have to be exact to be effective.[2] The extreme orb permitted is a degree and a half, with no more than a full degree allowed for most practical purposes.

No one detail of astrological practice is more puzzling or disturbing to the astronomer, or to the mathematically trained critic of stellar science, than the superficially curious coupling of the non-co-ordinate measures of celestial longitude on the one hand and declination on the other. "Why don't you use latitude for the planet's deviation from its plane of movement, since you indicate the motion and identify the other major aspects in longitude?" The difficulty here is no actual inconsistency, but rather the failure of most astrologers to realize the significance of the distinction they make. The parallel of declination owes its effectiveness in horoscopy to the very fact that it belongs to a different system of co-ordinates. It brings light to any given matter by showing the accidental balance of the planets relative to the plane in which the houses are created, and reveals experience as sharpened in a sort of shortcut potential.

[2] The point of view, of course, is natal, and the consideration of ephemeris rather than the symbolical motion employed on pp. 305 ff.

PARALLELS OF DECLINATION

Those zodiacal relations among the planets which are expressed in the other aspects, or measured in the circle describing their actual motion relative to the earth, chart the underlying pattern of life's activities by the mode of correlation outlined through the preceding chapters. This is one thing. The more personal equatorial relations of the planets, as manifest through the houses, may of course be indicated in right ascension as a supplementation to this, but it would constitute no more than a translation of the apparent positions in the zodiac, and so little additional meaning would be found unless in the very fine special analysis of the type represented by primary directions. To gain the required crosslight on any given matter, in this enlistment of the equator's co-ordinates, it is necessary to have measurable differences of a degree sufficient to have astrological meaning. Declination serves such an end.

Here is not merely the question of getting the perspective represented by a "side" view, since celestial latitude is available for that purpose and is, moreover, co-ordinate with zodiacal longitude in the ecliptical system. Latitude has little implication because its deviations are slight, tending to be nonsignificant, and there is no celestial latitude in the sun's case. Declination, by contrast, reveals the rhythm of the great swing north or south of that plane in which the houses of the horoscope are established in the heavens. This rhythm provides the practical basis for an astrological significance. In addition, the possibilities of bringing one system of measurement in to check the indications of the other is the much more important justification of the aspect, and the real clue to its specific meaning.

It is because parallels are both "latitudinal" and "equatorial" that they offer the maximum contrast to the other aspects—which are "longitudinal" and "ecliptical"—and that in consequence they reveal some supernumerary phase of immediate reference to the ground of experience, and hence chart a particular dynamic of consciousness. Here is what takes basic form in an individual's effort to achieve psychological elbowroom or "living space" in his own affairs.

No distinction is made among the parallels, in the usual technique, on the basis of their strength. They obviously are stronger as they are most exact but, with so small an allowable orb, it has not been found worth while to give any attention to the degree of exactness. There is a growing tendency, however, to take them as more like the conjunction in effect when both planets are in north or south declination, as the case may be, and as more akin to the opposition when one is north and the other south. This indicates, in the first instance, an accentuated stimulus to positive action or decision and, in the second, an impulsion to an equally definite preparation for possible later adjustments.

A minutia of significant details can be worked out—such as seeing which planet applies to the parallel, noting the frequent cases when both move into the relation, and drawing conclusions from (1) the significance of the planet which is the more dynamic [3] in this sense and (2) the fact of its position either north or south—but none of the refinements are employed to any extent, and their indications are not normally of enough consequence to justify the distinctions. A recent tendency to see a more immediately practical or personal implication when a parallel is north—or is emphasized in that equatorial hemisphere of the heavens—and a correspondingly somewhat more theoretical, remote or group concern when it is placed or given its dynamic focus on the southern side, is a judgment of value only in an exceptionally fine analysis.

[3] When two planets move jointly into an aspect, the swifter is taken as the stronger.

PARALLELS OF DECLINATION

The exact point at which parallels of declination should be considered by the horary astrologer, in his recourse to natal factors, is ultimately a matter of taste, since they provide a completely oblique point of view, and one that will fit in at any stage of things. They can be taken in the case where the significant planets in a yes-and-no relation, failing to make any other of the major aspects, yet form a parallel. The rule would then be that "movement" in horary declination would only be from a lesser to a greater degree of declination, either north or south, and that the planet which "moves" to make the aspect complete could not be taken through a greater distance in declination than its actual change while remaining within the sign in which it is found by longitude.[4] In all other instances the method of interpretation would be in accordance with usual natal procedures, modified for horary purposes in the same manner as any other over-all technique.

[4] Since sign and house distinctions are "longitudinal" factors, the horary timetable cannot be employed.

Chapter Sixteen

INAUGURAL HOROSCOPES

Horary astrology includes a very important department of analysis which—since it deals with actual events rather than with questions and inquiries into particular problems or issues—seems at first thought to be almost identical with natal practice. The distinction between the great divisions in the "science of the stars" is not on the basis of the techniques employed, however, but instead is created by the subject matter of delineation. The nativity is always the measure of a living organism, and the horary chart by contrast a mapping of potentials in some one limited complex of experience. Life *per se* must keep on going as it can, whether or no, while an individual's participation in a series of events is more or less at will. A natal perspective operates in a reference of relative necessity, but a horary point of view—to the degree it is valid—is only concerned with choice. The lines may never appear this sharply defined, but they are very real.

Thus a native easily can insulate himself from life, but its relationships exist, behind the scenes. He makes adjustments with his circumstances and shapes his destiny, which may involve an extravagant degree of change and growth, but at bottom he is a continuity· at no time can he actually get out of himself. He expands his own nature constantly, and fulfills his own potential in a myriad of ways —exactly as by intelligent act he makes his world very much the kind of place that suits him—but he never escapes the inevitable on-going of those experiences-in-chain that make him up. Hence natal astrology deals with the universe as a compelling reality in which various surrenders can be balanced with compensatory demands, but in which no clear-cut separation of Self and the All is possible. Here is the malign "fate" of the medievals, as transformed into the wonder-working "character" of modern psychology.

Astroanalysis at this point embraces mundane astrology, or the measurement of influences at work and potentialities available on the world stage, simply because in his national and racial destiny the individual faces existence through the effective totality of its compulsions and permissions on the broader scale. In precisely the same way that a native cannot step out of his own temperament-set, despite the manifold ways in which he may exploit it—and make it the vehicle of an immeasurable success and happiness—so he cannot extricate himself from his actual interaction with the realities of his larger social, national and racial background. The study of warfare, business cycles and all the details of world astrology, is merely an individual horoscopy ballooned up to the dimension of group destiny, and in consequence mundane analysis—together with every medical and every other highly specialized technique for charting the living organism of man as a functioning whole, in a person and in a society; or as "microcosm" or "macrocosm" in the twin terms of Paracelsus—is natal astrology.

Horary art cuts right across the necessary reality of all experience, which is at once its explanation and its justification. Because it fundamentally reveals the potentials of any given act or decision, rather than any necessary proclivity to move in the projected direction, it has been presented throughout this text as the measurement of vicarious or tentative reality. The essence of skill in its use has been seen to lie in the approach to situations as always the complexes of relation which may be adopted or abandoned entirely as they are convenient and desirable, or the reverse. This is no less true if act or decision lies in the past, since experience is not approached here in its totality, but in its immediate possibility; of which not the least is changing the consequences of poor choice. This means that horary analysis is of problems, projects and the day-by-day materials of experience. The mode of judgment is through the acceptance of any issue as primarily an opportunity for choice, through what in its simplest form is the straight question; that is, an inquiry into some problem where the obligations for act or decision have not yet precipitated the momentarily irrevocable choice. Less simply, the practitioner may be called upon to find an advantageous way to utilize the consequences of something already done—rather than to advise what to do *de novo*, as it were—but the essential inquiry is of the same order.

The problems in horary art range from cases not only of uncertainty in choice, and of need to make adjustments consequent on past act and decision, but of the events which comprise the occasions and objects of man's choosing. Thus there is the approach to some problem as a client gives it form and substance in his mind—the more usual horary procedure—and also the attack upon its elements as he establishes these in the actual materials of everyday experience. Here is the special technique where horoscopes for objective events are erected and judged. A new business is opened, a contract is signed or a lodge is organized. The precise hour for anything of the sort can be taken, or put on record, and it provides the astrological map of the enterprise. Because this is hardly a living organism that can be said to be "born" in the biological sense, but is instead a social or economic entity which must remain a construct

INAUGURAL HOROSCOPES

in transient experience, such a wheel is termed an inaugural horoscope to distinguish it from a nativity. It is what is known to older astrologers as a "chart for an event."

Since events have horoscopes in this fashion, and since these horoscopes supply vitally effective guidance at times, it was not long in the early development of astrology before some genius realized that the destiny of an enterprise could be determined effectively in advance by the simple device of selecting a favorable chart, and making the start at the time which produced the given wheel. Here is the fascinating branch of horary work long identified as "elections." The inaugural horoscope may be judged before or after the actual event, in consequence, and it is interpreted in precisely the same way in both instances, since the identical sort of information is desired. The principal difference is that the foundation choice behind the event may be improved when the moment of inauguration is "elected," since any preliminary selection of a "time" can be rejected in favor of a better one.

The election chart is astrology in reverse, and a younger astrologer may find himself under the necessity of proceeding by pure trial and error. Thus a group of people decide to come together on a certain Tuesday evening, to organize a municipal power plant, and it is the intention of the chairman to call the meeting to order at eight. However, a horoscope erected for the precise place and time shows a great amount of unnecessary trouble. The next logical step is to see what improvement can be affected by bringing the group to order at a later hour, or perhaps earlier. This may possibly change the rising sign, since a new one rises approximately each two hours; thereby altering the whole picture. The aspects of the planets obviously remain unchanged through the short span of any given evening, but the rulership of the angles and the import of the houses are subject to radical revision. Failing satisfactory indications by what manipulation of the hour is possible, the meeting can be moved to another evening, or the first gathering restricted to preliminary discussions with an adjournment to a favorable date.

In the case of all efforts to select a "best time" the outstanding limitation is usually the physical one of available conditions. If a fraternity can only be launched at night, and only on a Friday evening at that, and if the organization has to be completed within the span of a month or six weeks at the most, the range of choice is relatively narrow. The question, all too often in an election chart, is not finding an ideal time—granting such is ever possible—but rather selecting an effective moment for proceeding, out of a number of choices which may be none too good at best.

The yes-and-no technique operates to meet the need for reply to a given query, or for the solution in a certain immediate crisis, since it sets up a single line of act-and-consequence for guidance in a relatively simple decision. The question form of horary procedure is preferable whenever this is the desired result of inquiry. The query is then of value because it provides a clean elimination of all side issues for the moment. The inaugural chart, however, faces a much different task. It meets the demand for a more complete or ramified picture of the situation, and necessitates an immediate and complete regression to the natal methods now outlined in great detail. In consequence of this disparity in mode of approach, it is important that the two types of demand on the practitioner be understood very thoroughly. Here is the sort of difference illustrated in the case of a man who first wants to know the result of starting in the drug business, and then wishes to find the consequences of making the specific beginning he has in mind. Thus there are occasions in life when action is best analyzed in outline, and others when it is seen more profitably in a wholeness of detail. Since both the inquiry chart and the inaugural horoscope should never be used together, for the reasons already given,[1] it is wise to see which will serve best in a given instance, whenever the necessary data is available for both and the choice between them is possible.

The horary rather than natal meanings of the houses should be employed at all times in an inaugural chart, for the obvious reason that an event or an enterprise is not a biological organism. The planets and signs should be taken similarly, according to the natal methodology, but with horary implication, as amply illustrated in the several preceding chapters. The measure of time has been discussed in detail, and the reasons given for using the transits in almost complete part for measuring any future developments.[2] While ring-around-the-rosy and the horary timetable have been applied at times to the inaugural horoscope, results are seldom satisfactory because the basis of analysis here is not the fluid or creative capacity of the human mind, as this is encountered in the interpretation of a question.

Much more skill is required for the election chart than the normal inaugural horoscope, simply because the responsibility is greater. If an event has taken place, the wheel shows the pattern of potentials, and there they are, but in the selection of a time in advance it is necessary to

[1] See p. 244.   [2] See pp. 369 ff.

bring the best possibilities into play, with sharp penalties in experience for any failure to do so. The astrology of a former generation gave a very great deal of attention, in consequence, to the general principles to be considered in this form of astrological advisement.

The most simple procedure is to provide a chart with the equivalent of a definite "yes" aspect, quite free from all contributing impediments. There is no ring-around-the-rosy location of the matter in the horoscope of an event, hence this means that the first house should contain no undesired planets, that if possible it should hold advantageous ones, and that its lord should be placed to give a satisfactory pointing to the whole enterprise on two counts; that is, by (1) its place in the houses and (2) its favorable aspect to the lord of each other house in which an emphasis is vital.[3] Attention also must be given to the converse of the requirements, avoiding if possible all affliction to the lord of the first house, or to planets it contains. As far as it can be done, as a next step, the tenth house is treated in the same way, but its needs must remain subordinate to the ascendant.

When unfavorable planets are unavoidably present in key places, it is necessary to make sure that conditions will be able to take advantage of the fact. If Saturn is prominent, everything must be carried out more philosophically; that is, with greater understanding, sensitiveness and depth. If Mars is present, there must be an adequate outlet for human energies, such as clashes in opinion, the jostling of interests, and every give and take of a healthy but primitive situation. Uranus, Neptune and Pluto are not helpful, either by their presence in any key house or by their major aspects to its significator, or to planets it contains. When Uranus is involved, the enterprise to be successful must

[3] With reference to proper orb in zodiacal position, not symbolical motion as in the yes-and-no technique.

INAUGURAL HOROSCOPES

involve sharp originality. When Neptune is prominent, there must be a definite acceptance of some broad social responsibility; i.e., the weight of the world, willy-nilly, must be borne on the shoulders of the enterprise. If Pluto is strong, problems of public relations must be advanced to the forefront of attention, and all concerned must be sensitive continuously to the undercurrents of public opinion. The dragon's tail should not be permitted in the first house under any circumstances, nor should the lord of the ascendant lie within a two-degree conjunction of this point. Otherwise arrangements will be necessary, from the beginning, for an eventual reorganization or realignment of the whole effort.

Planets in the ascendant are dignified because they are rising, and those at the midheaven by the same token are strengthened because they are elevated. In the construction of an election chart, if planets are in the tenth house, those in the ninth may be ignored to a considerable degree. However, with an empty tenth, a ninth-house planet will dominate the midheaven, and it must then be taken into account. The greatest single testimony to a gratifying public success is a good tenth house, and the presence of desirable planets in the elevated or rising positions is almost as strong an indication. The sun, or the lord of the ascendant, is especially favorable in this connection. Next in order in general is the moon, but much depends on the nature of the enterprise, and the relations of the ten bodies in their focal-determinator patterns and as rulers of the various houses. Jupiter and Venus are excellent as rising or elevated planets, although the former may incline any effort towards overstretching itself, and the latter may make any project too self-sufficient or too much inclined to exclusiveness or conservatism.

By and large, in an election horoscope, the places of the planets in the equatorial divisions are the most fundamental influence. The houses which contain them will reveal the circumstances that may be expected at the foreground of development. The place and relations of these bodies as lords of the various departments will chart the possibilities of conscious control and direction in the enterprise. The planetary aspects and patterns will indicate the background or "character" of the project as an integral whole. Thus the most effective technique is to consider the general pattern of the heavenly aspects, since little can be done about this in any short period of time, placing it in the wheel in such a way that the houses have the desired stimulation. Then the suggested chart can be checked through the indications of the house lords.

The astrology of "elections" in some respects is only a half-art, or a syncopated mechanism, if no attention is given to the nativities of the key figures involved in any enterprise. Professional astrological advice presupposes the use of the natal wheel whenever it is available, and to the greatest degree possible in any matter involving the destiny of a life. Horary art is reliable in a very real sense for the immediate but relatively trivial issues of experience, but it is only to be used charily as an actual substitute for a nativity. Thus the horoscopes of the central people in an election should be examined, in exactly the same fashion as the charts of national leaders and the like are employed by mundane astrology.

Chapter Seventeen

SPECIAL FIELDS OF JUDGMENT

The keynote of modern civilized life is specialization, and it is becoming increasingly impossible for any one person to be competent, in any true sense, in more than a very limited number of different fields. Because of this fact the astrologer faces greater difficulties than any other professional counselor, since he is called on to guide the acts and decisions of individuals whose particular areas of experience are often quite alien to anything he has ever encountered in his own personal development. Astrological relations have a universal application, but any intelligible outline of their specific indication depends on a very real knowledge of the nature and conditions which characterize the world of the native or querent. The stars do not change in these varying sections of life, but language does, together with any genuine understanding, to a degree not often realized by the average student. This does not mean that the astrological practitioner is unable to give advice to a carpenter, in respect to some problem of carpentry, but it does make it necessary for him to deal with any technical aspect of woodworking in astrological generalities. He must present the fundamental relationships which apply to all human effort for the moment, and allow his client to find their exact meaning in the special field.

The trouble in this resort to generalization is that the astrologer is only half-armed. He has no means for checking the response of his client, or for knowing whether his advice has the meaning, in the other's experience, that meets the horoscopic necessities. He is throwing altogether too much responsibility back upon the shoulders of the individual who seeks his help. Unless he uses the "language" of this other person he is remote, "abstract" and at times even dangerously detached from reality. His generalities will be given concrete form of some sort in the mind to which they are given, and if he cannot control the essential implication of his counsel he may be responsible for a very serious misguidance. This is especially true if he yields at all to the persistent public demand for a "show-off" technique, which asks the practitioner to operate without the common-sense co-operation given the physician, lawyer and spiritual adviser as a matter of course.

The problem here is illustrated by the difficulty which a trained editor faces when asked to work on a technical manuscript in some specialized field which is foreign to his own private background. He has the full use of authoritative texts, the dictionary and common sense, but he is inevitably handicapped because he knows nothing of the fine nuances of words and terms, and as a result he will fail to notice little inaccuracies which are immediately obvious to the specialist. The genuinely competent astrologer is not only an "expert" in horoscopy, but he has wide experience in the areas where most questions are asked, and most issues are raised. Every new problem of marital inharmony is an old story in most of its details, and this proves equally true through the list of financial difficulties, political jealousies, vocational adjustments, and most common social complications. Certain lines of human relationships, however, which enter into astrological practice very frequently are altogether too technical for a practical mastery by anyone unable to devote his whole time and energy to their demands upon him. The two most important of these are law on the one hand, and medicine in an all-inclusive sense on the other.

In the most simple terms, this means that the practitioner should never permit himself to make a final judgment on any matter involving the advisability of legal action, or of moral decision with potential legal consequences, without consultation with a practicing attorney. It is true that he may well acquire a very sound legal instinct, in time a thorough knowledge of general juristic principles, but the laws vary to a tremendous extent among the forty-eight states; and they are in a constant process of change, with an almost equally continuous interpretation and reinterpretation by the courts.[1] The situation in connection with medical advice is far more difficult, since it involves the possibility of both legal and psychological complications of a very serious sort. Practically every state in the Union has a penal statute related to the practice of medicine, and possessing real teeth—that is, exceptionally heavy penalties—largely due to the prevailing temper of public opinion and the traditional concern of the medical profession over its own prerogatives. The average practitioner or astrological enthusiast does not recognize the breadth of the limitations put upon him at this point. It is generally illegal for him to give even the most simple advice if it can be construed as a curative measure; so that actually he must never even suggest that a client diet on

[1] This reference to the United States primarily is a matter of simple convenience. The applications elsewhere are obvious.

orange juice and milk, take vitamins, drink more water, try a Turkish bath for relaxation, or anything of the sort.

It is inevitable that astrology and medicine, long divorced, will again work together in a closer co-operation, through the specialization which is the commonplace among medical workers; and which is coming to characterize horoscope work. For the present the amount of knowledge and training required for competency as a physician completely bars the astrologer or other outsider from the practice of orthodox medicine; and the legal requirements of osteopathy and chiropractic are coming to be but little less exacting. Drugless therapy, including the naturopath and the herbalist, is given considerable latitude in some sections of the country, but in most states the branches in "medicine" of lesser requirements are prohibited from performing operations, delivering babies or performing full curative functions. While restrictions of this order are sometimes circumvented under the cloak of religion—when special sanction is gained for prescribing diet, using exercises, and employing various specific forms of healing art—this is little more than a subterfuge, of no value to astrological practice. Medical men here and there are beginning to recognize the value of astrology, and the astrological practitioner in any community should be able to find a competent individual, with an M.D. degree and good hospital connections, who is willing to co-operate in the administration of the healing measures indicated by a horoscope.

Medical horoscopy is a branch of natal delineation, and perhaps the most exacting and ramifying of all. The function of horary inquiry is not to provide any sort of general

SPECIAL FIELDS OF JUDGMENT

diagnosis, for which the nativity is an absolute necessity, but is rather to gain some reliable insight into the immediate or general symptoms as these are factors in a situation where action or decision is especially vital. The natal horoscope reveals the nature and meaning of physical and psychological maladjustment in an individual's total frame of reference, whereas the horary chart provides the narrowed but sharpened information that can be an efficient guide in such practical problems as the changes to make in the plans for a given situation as a result of the sickness, the selection of a physician or the mode of treatment, the determination of the altered arrangements necessary when illness is an oblique factor in some given matter, and so on. The principle put down for horary diagnosis of sickness, therefore, is that no attempt is to be made to identify or describe the physical condition of the person involved, in any medical sense, but that instead the effort must be directed to finding direct everyday consequences of the condition itself, as these take form in the activities of the individual in question, and of those concerned with him in the matter.

Horary methods are not changed in any way when they deal with sickness. Inquiry is normally focused in the sixth house of the crisis chart. A wheel may be put up for the time of "taking to bed"—calling for natal methods because it is the chart of an event—but the time of the query will be used to better advantage if it yields a yes-and-no aspect and so indicates the duration of sickness, together with the potentials of cure, the return to business, and so on. The reality of the illness—a detail of importance, since there is so much shamming and self-delusion in connection with bodily symptoms—is shown by the strength of the sixth house, its lord and its contained planets. When there is recourse to natal methods, risk or danger in connection with sickness is shown if the rulers of the crisis first and sixth, or either, lie in the fourth, sixth or eighth; and absence of anything of the sort if these conditions do not prevail.

One factor in natal astrology is of sufficient general importance to be taken into account at all times in any horary analysis of physical and psychological maladjustment, namely, the place of the moon by transit; that is, where it lies in the horary wheel, and where it will be found by ephemeral motion, or according to its actual position, in the heavens at any future time. In general, no operations should be performed and no changes should be made in the mode of treatment when the moon is in the sign ruling the part of the body involved in the illness.[2] These traditional rulerships are shown by the following table.

THE CONVENTIONAL ZODIACAL MAN

Aries	Head and face, brain
Taurus	Neck and throat, cerebellum
Gemini	Shoulders and arms, lungs
Cancer	Chest and breasts, stomach
Leo	Back and spine, heart
Virgo	Abdomen, intestines
Libra	Lower back, kidneys
Scorpio	Excretory and sexual organs
Sagittarius	Thighs and hips, flesh generally
Capricorn	Knees and skin, secretion generally
Aquarius	Ankles and calves, the circulation
Pisces	Feet and toes, liver

When natal methods are employed, the position of the other planets in relation to the moon, their presence in the

[2] Some astrologers discourage action if the moon lies in the opposing sign.

SPECIAL FIELDS OF JUDGMENT 405

crisis first, fourth, sixth and eighth, and their distribution through the whole twelve houses of the judgment chart, are most revealing in the light of the general physiological natures of the planets. Thus the "lights" (sun and moon) are always most concerned with the organs, the sun indicating the possibility of strain and the moon the potential of exhaustion. Mars, Venus and Mercury indicate a tendency to defective functioning in the nervous system, with Mars related to fevers, Venus to infections and Mercury to nerve inflammation. Jupiter and Saturn often show trouble with the glands, Jupiter through overfunctioning and Saturn through underactivity. Uranus, Neptune and Pluto are often linked to mental disturbance, Uranus suggesting a psychological crowding or sense of pressure that leads to breakage and violence of some sort, Neptune identifying fears and illusions, and Pluto revealing a proclivity to an unhealthy or exaggerated dependence on alien and external stimulations, or on the excitement sustained by social malcontent, utopian propaganda and the like.

Chapter Eighteen

THE METHOD OF BIRTH PLANETS

The professional astrologer faces some very appreciable astrological and psychological difficulties whenever he experiences a continual impact of problems for solution. If questions or issues were brought to him intermittently enough, they would fit into a stronger pattern of his own experience, either as a person or a counselor; and it would throw a special light upon them. He would be helped in utilizing the general concordance of events as an orderly frame for his services. Unfortunately the very nature of his profession conspires against him. If astrological judgment were purely physical, he would have no trouble. Thus a dentist can examine teeth all day long, and a physician look at throats by the thousand. Psychological analysis by contrast is creative. The human mind cannot rise to the demand for a continuous novel reconstruction of living situations. As the hours pass, inspiration seems to fail. Even everyday normal insight is apt to become fuzzy or dulled.

A wise practitioner circumvents this creative exhaustion to some extent by a personal life which is as rich as possible; especially by the depth and sincerity of his interest in the cases coming before him. Life then unfolds itself as a tremendously fascinating drama, and he quickens to every change when the curtain goes up to reveal a different setting on the human stage. The astrological procedures themselves do not help him very much, however, if he is at all dependent on horary indications; because his wheels show little change in the course of mere hours. A long working day can only bring a difference of some five rising signs, together with perhaps half a dozen degrees of movement by the moon, at the best. While a general practice based principally on the natal charts will solve much of this difficulty, the judgment of nativities in adequate fashion does not easily fit into the needs of the public in day-by-day interview work. Moreover, a conscientious but hurried consideration of nativities is more wearing than horary work, contributing to a much greater mental fatigue. For this reason astrologers find that for any real success they must use both the natal and horary techniques.

It would be inevitable that long experience with both branches would in time lead to a method of blending their indications for the requirements of professional practice, and the results of this, in terms of the special development of horary art, have been reflected throughout the preceding pages. What remains for examination is an actual combination wheel, both natal and horary in nature, such as offers a special and final recourse to every student and amateur as well as professional practitioner. The interesting fact is that quite a number of prominent American astrologers developed this method independently, and used it, before Evangeline Adams gave it publicity. The essence of the technique is that the natal planets of the client are put in the horary houses, which are obtained in the usual way. The planets are used for their corrected positions, if the nativity has been calculated and is available. Otherwise the noon positions are taken directly from the ephemeris, with the possible range of the moon marked as in a solar or equilibrium chart.[1]

A very common modification of the procedure is to insert the horary planets also, on the pattern of the common practice by which natal, progressed and transit positions will be shown in separate rings of a nativity wheel. This in general is not helpful, because apt to be an unnecessary multiplication of factors and so a violation of the principle in Occam's razor. If both sets of planets are to be employed, they must be made separately significant, or a rectification of each other rather than a contribution to confusion.

The great advantage in this horary use of the natal planets is that every horoscope on a given day of interviews (or interpretations by mail) is not only quite different but that the dynamic pattern of each natal chart, shown entirely by the planets in any case, becomes a factor in the immediate analysis. The horary houses continue to provide that minutia of distribution in day-by-day relations which is of special value in counseling, and the very backbone of horary work. Moreover, the "considerations before judgment" are no longer significant in this combination method, so that every chart of the sort is "fit to be judged." The "lunar cycle test," by the same token, is ineffective. The grain of the chart, or the reassurance of its validity to the practitioner, is therefore determined entirely by the degree of its aptness in the light of the problem at issue.

When it comes to interpretation, the rules are used exactly as put down for the normal horary wheel, in every particular. A start is made with the yes-and-no technique. The horary timetable is employed. Every other detail of method is enlisted, as needed, in its proper place.

[1] This type of "nativity" is illustrated in the wheel of William James on page 345.

A PRIMER OF SYMBOLISM

A PRIMER OF SYMBOLISM

How Do Symbols Operate?

The most familiar form of symbolism, in universal use by mankind from the beginning of time and wholly taken for granted by virtually everybody, is language itself. To permit any functioning of conscious existence it is necessary (a) that a name be given to whatever of tangible or intangible make-up may come to attention in experience and moreover (b) that it be the same name employed in the same way by most of the individuals who aggregate in any type of common group. Verbs as distinct from nouns must yet have names that in their case identify causation or action of potentials of such a nature, following along the lines of the essentially functional naming of all parts of speech. The human groups can range from family or tribe or community or nation on to every accidental gathering of people whether few or many in some possible association of either trivial or vital sort.

As a necessity for the use of language, grammar orders the needed differentiation of reference among various things as primarily nominal or verbal in perspective. This is the basis of all effective realization as essentially of factuality or aliveness, and astrology quite conveniently may be explained as a species of psychological grammar.

Names are the symbols for the most simple manifestation of existence.

An equally common form of symbolism found in as universal use down on into human life of very primitive sort, and no less taken for granted everywhere although ultimately managing to fascinate and then baffle understanding through its more sophisticated development, is simple number. Numbering permits the mind to engage in the counting or reckoning on which everybody relies most completely if perhaps subconsciously in the uncomplicated and practical business of everyday affairs, and this reliance ranges from (a) such familiarities as making change or telling time on to (b) the more mature necessities of self-existence in predicting consequences of act or decision and indeed often in comprehending and executing the most intricate of operations. This species of sheer quantity and quality symbolism throughout reality in general has its origin in the phenomenon of plus and minus. A very direct interrelationship of some and none, or of more and less, is the inescapable bottom fact of all experience.

Such quantitative or qualitative differences, and nothing else fundamentally, are what actually make astrology possible. Here in a fashion is dynamic or verbal in contrast with static or nominal perspective.

Numbers are symbols for the most simple manipulation of existence.

The most vital form of symbolism, when it comes to the task of individuality in (a) recognizing or knowing itself and (b) maintaining or advancing and fulfilling itself among other selves, is in its case so taken for granted that people generally have no notion of its functioning. In consequence and very commonly they may be altogether unaware of what of necessity determines each marked pertinence in their thinking. This is a phenomenon that can be identified and controlled and brought very signally to the service of man in the development of his individual distinctiveness in better self-realization, together with the more definite maintenance of the character that establishes his particular identity among his fellows. Here actually is as important and fundamental a symbolization as name and number, and in the form of conscious awareness it is the important factor of the everyday meaning of whatever happens of a sudden to be pertinent in experience. It is the special significance of all things as each may come to attention in any given situation at any particular moment. Meanings identify the immediacies of reality with which astrology must concern itself primarily, if it is to be of any practical value.

Many difficulties encountered by the inexperienced astrologer, in his analysis of the horoscope, will be found to have their basis at this point. He must realize that the meaning of anything in life and experience is what may come to be attributed, and often in most spontaneous fashion, to the kaleidoscopic elements of everyday actuality. This is true at all times, and under all circumstances. Meanings primarily are always a contribution of particular pertinency, and in consequence they can be exceedingly ephemeral. In other words, by no possibility whatsoever are they ever inherent in anything. They cannot represent an absolute indication, since there is no place for ultimate absolutes in a universe of illimitability. No specific implication can ever be maintained objectively in some unchanging significance of language, or preserved as more than simple symbol. Indeed, and almost obviously, existence itself is never fixed or established once and forever in some overall and purely hypothetical reality of time and space.

Thus what anything means is no less symbolization than name and number, with which meaning never ceases to be conjoined. The human mind of course and because of its fundamental structure must keep a vast array of realities constant in its own abstraction, as a needed scaffolding for its insight. The individual thinker however must recognize such constancy as no more than a norm of convenience, on the basis of which to measure or judge the shifting actualizations of human experience coming continually to pertinence in his consciousness. It is through this mental operation that he is able to comprehend the various phases of (a) situation and (b) eventuation, for his effectual self-realization and self-direction. Self thereby in a sense makes its own world, and must of necessity continue to do so over and over again in its shaping of its personal self-continuance.

Meanings are symbols for the most simple personalization of existence.

Whenever it comes to the utilization of words for (a) the consideration of these same words or their fellows as they have their everyday acceptance in some particular language, in (b) what becomes a special analysis of the structure and condition of this common usage, the procedure can be identified quite conveniently as a resort to metalanguage. What is identified is an extra dimension in the thinking process, and something very akin to it is represented in the preceding threefold preliminary exposition of symbolism. Such a mental establishment of overall perspective has now served its purpose, however, and need not be employed any further. Thus any direct reference to the concept of meaning would actually be to no point, since in a sense nothing else will now be having any attention.

The end of all astrological interpretation is (a) to identify and apply the varying significance of all things in their ramifying relationships to (b) some particular individual person or eventuality. Most simply this is a matter of what they may come to mean with informative specificity in each or every possible pertinence in human experience. Names of course will continually prove to be of high importance, but as in all life this will be relatively in passing or merely because of what they may designate in some pertinent particular in horoscopic context. They become the mental tools of the astrologer in his determination of the nature of the significance of given elements at special moments of self-existence.

Number contrariwise comes forward as perhaps the whole basis of any possible understanding of astrology, and this in a sense has already been suggested. It is entirely thanks to the fact of sequence or successiveness identified first in the motions or movements in a universal and eternal ordering arrangement of the components of a cosmic manifestation, such as in the relatively infinite permutations has a functional stability which the mind can observe and to which it can cling, that the astrological mechanics of delineation are established and perfected.

With the help of the foregoing consideration of the tripartite basics of astrology, analyzed in a metalanguage of sorts, attention can now go perhaps more incisively to the fundamental specifics of horoscopic symbolization of life encountered in personal realities.

What Is Astrology?

Astrology is a technique for establishing horoscopic or personalized meaning in the relative dependability of the celestial movements of the earth and moon and major planets of the solar system. In this way it has long been able to provide a totally impartial screening and ordering of the human lives and events on earth that (1) have their particular existence and pertinent occurrence within the single overall and perhaps almost completely self-sufficient complex of cosmic energy, and that in consequence (2) participate in the inescapable interweaving of the macrocosmic and microcosmic factors involved in any phase of man's pertinent reality. It is assumed that in their differentiations these lives and events can be expected to exist individually, but to manifest themselves in significant parallel with or in conformity to the endlessly varying interrelations in eventuation of the heavenly bodies. This is because these latter are under the same necessity of continuing to be in the one fundamentally self-sustaining gravitational field of the sun.

All such explanation is of course mere hypothesis, but it is wholly devoid of complication since the suppositional microcosm of man and macrocosm of the universe of

PRIMER OF SYMBOLISM

which he is a part can be kept separate in every possible respect. It is a rigid separation that preserves the incisiveness of basic perspective. Here however are symbolical realities that can be identified only in their functional balance with each other and in a purely mental operation. Nonetheless a whole and a part are in this way found in a most effective and detailed mutual revelation of each other. And this, on the earth's side of the polarity, can provide a precise analytical charting of life and its eventualities and thereby contribute to invaluable counseling.

Actually there have been countless hypothetical and ramifying explanations for the possibility of correlating movements in the heavens with human events in everyday existence, and as is true of all metaphysical speculation these may help sustain the mind in its practical and at the best a logical analysis of the vagaries of man's experience. But all the theories of themselves prove nothing, even while they give substance to comprehension and aid every individual to more or less extent in organizing his own insights.

When it comes to astrology the inescapable phenomenon, which can never be explained away entirely, is that in general it works. If its performance is poor or unconvincing in the hands of amateurs who proceed by rote, or of practitioners of inadequate skill in any disciplined or logical analysis, there is yet an ample indication of a very valid potential. Consequently the inevitable superficialities and wild pretensions, that in the course of history have handicapped the refinement of every major science, can be ignored in astrology's case in principal part. A detailed explanation of the factors that have emerged and become the fundamental components of the horoscopy of today, based on the hypothesis of a relatively gradual and wholly empirical origin and growth, constitutes the author's *Astrology, How and Why It Works* as the companion and a foundational volume in this series of texts.

Astrology, as any other form of logical analysis, employs special names as the essential convenience of a technical language. In its case there is an alphabet of symbols that spell out all horoscopic communication. It consists of (a) twelve houses of the horoscope, (b) twelve signs of the zodiac comprising (c) four triplicities and (d) three quadratures, (e) ten generally employed planets of which one is the sun acting as surrogate for the earth and another the earth's own single moon, (f) six major aspects of which one is the parallel of declination almost completely ignored by today's astrologers and (g) eight particular minor aspects. These fifty-five fundamental factors of designation, together with a somewhat similar list of astronomical ones needed for the numerical calculations, must be learned by the beginner as no less necessary than the everyday earlier mastering of the alphabetical characters or letters of his mother tongue as a condition of becoming able to read and write.

Where Does Number Come In?

Astrology in every respect is a manipulation of existence through number. Thus no matter what form this manipulating may take in practical procedures, the operation is always fundamentally a case (a) of a mental or logical freezing or conceptualizing of some given state of numerical interconnections as these come to special pertinence relative to particular inquiry in order (b) to chart some consequent and significant shift or possible shift in the particularized context of relationships with the various parts or wholes of everything else collectively. This sets up the tentative minus-plus as a first step in all astrological logic. Something either is lacking or intrusive. The hypothetical freeze of reality, to be accomplished in the course of the ordering of mind, promptly facilitates the effective symbolization of all the ramifying relations and consequences of the pertinent immediacy. So much for definition bordering on the metalanguage.

In everyday life the procedure is a commonplace of shopping in a supermarket. The price of some particular item desired is fifty cents a pound, and the quantity selected comes to an even six pounds on the scales. The mind freezes the fifty-cent norm, to see by simple multiplication if the economy of the pocketbook can handle the matter or if perhaps less than three dollars should be spent at the moment. This sort of proposition is only more difficult, for an untrained imagination, when the numerical factors are represented by the convenient but almost necessarily pictorial symbols of horoscopic analysis. A question might then be raised. Why describe the process with such a surfeit of terms, and skirt the borders of metalanguage? The answer is that the mind must be brought to a continual recognition of the logical procedure underlying the use of any symbolization of such very technical nature as in any scientific pursuit no less than in astrology. There is far more to this than the mere rigmarole an explanation may seem to be at the start.

There is a different but rather minor difficulty at this

point, however. It can be met typographically perhaps by printing the basic number one in small capitals or as ONE to indicate when there is reference to the technical symbol of perfect unity rather than an identification of the basic unity in counting or a mere numerical differentiation.

The specialized employment of number that constitutes astrology always has a necessary beginning in an identification of some given positive unity coming to individual pertinence in existence, and a realization that this is a case of ONENESS actually established in consciousness by the mental operation. Here is a ONE that in thus emerging into pertinency provides the constant for logical fixation. Thereupon and by necessity it continues to be what it is despite its special relationship of significance with its nonexistence prior to its establishment in the thinking process. It is through the potential absence of itself that it has become knowable. Thus in logic's seeming rigmarole there is a completeness of a fundamental minus in any unity or ONE identified through the plus or more obvious or tangible actualizing of the possibility of itself. Man in general does not exist, but is an imaginative reality dramatized by every individual who gains existence and so becomes logically recognizable. A ÓNE if frozen in the logic of comprehensibility makes possible the examination of any particularized or representative ONE. For everything there is an archetype that is the measure of the potential. Thus astrology measures potentials, in infinite ramification of changeless ONENESS, but only deduces the probabilities of actualization.

There need be no real complication in the intellectual procedure. It is a commonplace realization that inventive genius must comprehend a need to provide an answer to it. Creative contribution is the permutation of a minus into a plus, but what the logician notes and astrology stresses is that the minus persists as an abstraction in its practical fulfillment. What was needful was not cancelled out, but rather was satisfied, and the ideation of the need is the sustainment of the satisfaction. The potential does not disappear in the actual, but in logical fact continues to nourish the actuality. In horoscopy, in consequence, everything not only means what it means but continues to do so. Progressions do not negate any natal indication. It can well be remembered that potentiality is the womb of actuality. Thus when a child is born it permits the particular minus of itself before birth to become the given actuality of itself thereafter, and its birth in no way (a) disturbs the ONENESS of the cosmic illimitability in the midst of which it emerges as a tangible ONE on its own account as well as merely one of its kind but (b) in no respect produces anything additive to the overall total in which its reality is cradled. Plus and minus are essentially the substance of aliveness and the corrective of factuality.

A superficial reasoning is often unduly obsessed with the phenomenon of cause and effect, and an unskilled astrologer delineating a horoscope is likely to view its native as altogether a consequence of the factors exterior or extraneous to the constituent elements of his special make-up that now have converged to produce the natal event. By this manner of thinking, what is cause in the particular instance is effect or the product of a cause behind such as in turn has been effect of cause farther behind and so on back in endless sequence. Moreover, cause is never a single line in what otherwise is a vacuum. Two parents come from four grandparents who come from eight great grandparents. Regression to infinity in causal chain thins out into insignificance very quickly, and the mind loses all incisiveness in its needless bondage to the complexities in which it involves itself. In a more effective understanding, all potentiality is seen as convenient rather than compulsive or as fundamentally an unconditioned concordance with the possible instead of a blind acceptance of what would tend to approach the inescapable.

The negative universality or absolute impartiality of the cosmos, in respect to all the widely varying manifestations of any definite individuality it comes to embrace, is the guarantee that the potential of the child in its newborn ONENESS is equally illimitable in all the possibilities of pertinence in its case no matter how unmanifest these may be at the start. The child's complementary self-totality, that in its turn is the minus or the free potential, remains the invulnerable basis of a microcosmic as of no less order than a macrocosmic self-identity. Little ONE and big ONE are identical in this fundamental generality of their existence. Except in the infinitely regressive perspectives of time and space, where differences no matter how sharpened are only permutations of each other, there can be no differentiation of ONE and ONE. Selfhood through astrological indication can be enthroned in the immediacies of itself, to the end it may master rather than suffer the fulfillment of itself.

Here then is the horoscope as total or universal symbolization in an uncompromising personal relevance. Most fundamentally it diagrams an absolute alikeness or at-one-ment of the universe, and the segment of the universe represented by man as envisioned or realized in the human mind, and thereupon delimits the segment in a temporal and spatial mesh of conscious experience ultimately cradled in the cosmic matrix. Infant and world are taken as functionally identical at the fleeting focus of a moment of birth, since the encompassing minus and the evolving plus are then in perfect balance, and the symbolical location of the event at a mathematical point in the celestial mechanics concomitantly establishes a horizon on the earth and thereby provides the threshold or ground of a personal existence now launched into its experience in time and space relations necessary for self-consciousness.

In logic what is anterior to or consequent on an event in any or all forms of relation to the event is of necessity a one-remove in consideration of the given eventuation, and thus likely to contribute to confusion in analysis unless held in leash in the thinking. Hence gestation is seen as the rehearsal of natural processes in mobilizing potentiality or in bringing the general potential to the immediate service of the specific actualization. What is here a remove in relationship is a contingency in significance, and out of this sort of circumstance comes the ordering of priorities or the establishment of extent of emphasis in horoscopic technique. What lies closest to the moment of virtually pure ONENESS at birth is considered in the varying respects of the directness or indirectness of its space and time de limitations. This will have to have detailed examination.

The illimitable and eternal reality of all that is, of which space and time are a manifestation rather than themselves any sort of creative agency responsible for the cosmic existence, is in practical terms a kaleidoscope of inescapable movement. Nothing ever is still, except as brought to theoretical motionlessness or inert stability within some mind in process of analysis or judgment. Motion as such however, in infinitely varying case, can be brought to pertinence or dismissed to its own business with about equal facility. Man can sleep, and then wake and start all over again in dealing with the problems of his individuality in their immediate exactions. In the measure of days and years he will know this as progress, and the details are best charted in the number symbolizations from any convenient start or restart in his comprehension. He may furthermore reach out from or retract to center in selfhood in everything he does, and this is most comprehensible to him in minus-plus fashion whether in children or dollars or otherwise in his various spheres of influence or responsibility.

The structure of the generally accepted form of a modern horoscope is made possible by the fact that the earth as a solar planet has two fundamental major and concomitant movements. These are of inescapable if not always obviously equal importance to the presence of conscious life on the globe. They are familiar enough through the rhythm of day and night and the seasonal swing between summer and winter, resulting respectively from the earth's daily rotation on its axis on its own account and its annual heavenly pilgrimage around its orbit in its tie with the sun. This celestial circumstance equips the astrologer with the pair of factors he may employ by holding the indication of either in momentarily fixed relevance to what he seeks to know or measure in order to establish the other more dynamically as his basic logical tool of examination and analysis. Everything he does, however indirectly, is a use or adaptation of this primary procedure of the logical freeze of mind at a pole of a dual relationship. Here, most simply, appears the dichotomy of character and circumstances as ever seeking equilibrium with each other.

How the minus-plus balance in pertinence of a ONE against a ONE, in the effective symbolization of number, goes into the structure of a horoscope with turn after turn in application and refinement of technique is considered in essentially preliminary form in the author's *Astrology, How and Why It Works*. Also taken into account in its pages are the numerical evolutions of astrology in the functions of the TWO and the THREE and the FOUR symbolizations embraced in the familiar twelvefold distributions. Along with this is the fractionizing of the circle to create the planetary aspects as distributive phases of the ONENESS of conjunction in contrasting opposition, trine, square, sextile and so on.

Where Do Names Come In?

In astrology the role of names primarily is to provide the delineating mind with an effective anchorage or placement in its own experience for anything of pertinence whenever, in the course of horoscopic analysis, it is necessary to gain and maintain a reliable rapport with the actualities of circumstances as a means for arriving at an intelligent judgment. The establishment of the more fundamental labels for the elements in the creation and interpretation of a horoscope has a logical beginning in the two motions of the earth already identified as the phenomenon that provides the familiar horoscopic structure, and at the start almost of necessity in the axial rotation that defines the faster and in the course of everyday realization the more immediate motion. The projection of this movement of the globe into the heavens, with the apparent result of causing the celestial vault itself to revolve, creates the houses or equatorial mansions of the astrological wheel. These twelve segments of the whole cosmic sphere are not named in any usual sense but are known by number. This fact helps symbolize the very important and special alignment of their horoscopic signification with the more uncomplicated and day-by-day interweaving of purely existential or chance-disposed factors in the commonplace course of human life.

Basic number is thus not only kept at a forefront of attention to indicate the prevailing scope of the more transiently immediate potentials of a personal reality, but also to show the illimitable possibilities of special relation through the simple sequence that is the essence of all conscious experience. Recognizing what is second to any prior taken as a first can be carried out to infinity, as may also whatever has the relationship of any ordinal number such as third or fourth. In the houses of the horoscope this sequential potential provides an invaluable measure of circumstances in their kaleidoscopic unconditioned distribution of individual self-manifestation. The first house delineates personality, but whether of a human being or an animal or a project or a problem is no part of what is

PRIMER OF SYMBOLISM

revealed through this normally primary mansion of the celestial equator. It is established by the totally exclusive horizon of a distinctive and absolute self-existence, or is marked out by any actual or symbolical entity at the point where the heavens arise initially at the moment of birth or event to identify the once and for all emergence into a reality that will remain indisputably private and effective from then on.

The astrological names that are quite the most familiar to the general public are the signs of the zodiac, or the houselike divisions in the ecliptic created by the earth's annual swing around the sun, and these are identified in the skies by twelve out of the eighty-eight constellations or star clusters in the heavens as now of universal recognition. The horoscopic sign divisions have the same names as the stellar groupings that occupied essentially identical celestial positions at about the time of the Greek astronomer Hipparchus, or some twenty-one centuries ago. The clustering is created by perspective from the solar system, and of course may be very different when seen from elsewhere in the cosmos. Astronomically they are a pictorial means for charting the ecliptical or sign rather equatorial or house positions in the sky, and astrologically while not actual entities of any sort they yet through their celestial or own special numerical sequence can be used very conveniently to diagram the individually dynamic function of man as an organism. Here is the less immediate motion of the earth, and hence it can be seen to represent him in his more general individuality. Since he is the mammalian animal that he continues to be in his physical existence, he provides a greater correspondence in that to the archetypal or generalized man established in astrological perspective.

The zodiacal signs are special symbols of as high importance as the horoscopic houses because they provide an essentially individual significance that can be employed as a sort of logical or symbolical mirror imaging of the kaleidoscopic manifestation of chance immediacies measured or charted by their equatorial complement. They reveal the entity quite apart from its immediate circumstances. In practice neither mode of measure is effective ultimately in absence of the other as the needed corrective in any final or conclusive judgment. Man's functions as the living organism delineated in the zodiac are what permits his circumstantial experience in its more strictly individual form, and it is his circumstances of course that facilitate the enlargement or refinement of his organic functioning both physically and psychologically in the expression of his personal character. What of make-up in temperament and skills is thus symbolized in the zodiac is fundamentally identified in human affairs as it is mirrored symbolically in the practical context that permits the manifestation of its constituent elements. The symbols themselves stem from antiquity and as they have survived they are not themselves too suggestive today, except of course as they have gained a special astrological significance. The human tendency to call a man a wolf or a woman a snake represents the process probably operative with similar aptitude of sorts in ancient minds. Character in a horoscopic differentiation can be epitomized with considerable latitude for an interpretive convenience.

In the zodiacal differentiation the relative constants in

human individuality are thus delineated fundamentally as each given person gives them expression, and concurrently faces the tides of chance and circumstance indicated by the houses, in a continuous interchange of relationship that commonly is known as conscious experience. The possibility of charting the interrelation of the separate cosmic phenomena constituting such wholly private eventuation arises primarily from the fact that the earth's celestial equator, in which the house divisions of a nativity are established, serves to distribute the parallel astrological significations in the zodiac by creating the equinoctial points in the heavens from which the signs stem fundamentally. And this corresponds with the way in which the personal or particular horizon determines the horoscopic house differentiations in the equator's case. The two measures are consistently distinct from each other however, with no necessary first-house implication in Aries and no Arian characteristic particularly involved in the ascendant and similarly around the two great circles.

Where Do the Planets Come In?

In their motions the planets employed in astrology provide a needed differentiation of the basic operations in the cosmic order that has its measure in the great circles created by the earth's two major movements in the heavens, and that is dramatized astrologically as a general ONE with which each individual person must exist in logical balance. They can therefore be used to chart activities engendered both by natural or persisting function at large and the everyday or ever-shifting circumstance of more particular pertinence in the inescapable but wholly chance relation they will have for each other. Thus by their conduct in their gravitational field the heavenly globes in their orbits come to be convenient for the horoscopic delineation of (a) the dynamic potentials of selfhood in perpetuating its existence through its experience and (b) the channels of repetitive and characteristic drifts or momentums in the eternal churning of whatever continuing general components may have momentary and particular importance for selfhood in the familiar world of time and space. The names of what were early recognized as the moving bodies in the heavens are mostly borrowed from the gods of ancient mythology, and these give only minor suggestion of the actual horoscopic roles to be identified. Indeed and this sometimes not too helpfully, as in confusing the Greek words Cronus and chronos for the Titan deity Saturn and the phenomenon of time respectively or in the careless association of idea leading a superficial astrology to give the Mars initiative an unnecessarily warlike implication.

As astrological symbols the planets provide a manageable charting of selected pertinent differentiations in human activity, such as distinguishing initiative from enthusiasm or basic attitude from natural drive. This differentiation establishes the operational side of astrology, through which the human individual in the usual course can be dissected psychologically in order to determine what factors of potential selfhood are or may be brought to personal actualization at various points and times. On the one hand this may suggest a requisitioning in essence of the sustaining substance of the cosmic restlessness or kaleidoscopic illimitability of all things through circum-

PRIMER OF SYMBOLISM

stances, or on the other hand and perhaps concomitantly a rehearsal or strengthening of some pertinent phase or phases of the illimitable capacity of self-establishment or what equally in essence has been or can be the everyday manifestation of the conscious individuality.

Analysis may proceed in this fashion from the microcosm of the personal unity or in a reverse fashion from the macrocosm as when in a popular or more superficial astrology the consideration is of the man as buffeted by the course of events in a more impersonal if no less sympathetic view, but one or the other analytic perspective must be maintained rigorously. The advantage of the former is compensation for its greater exactions in leading to more incisive suggestiveness of dynamic understanding and action by the self in its own interest. In either approach to the horoscope, however, it should be remembered that the fundamental arbitrariness by necessity of all symbolization of reality means that any well-ordered rationale of thinking exists always to serve the mind and facilitate human judgment rather than ever managing to represent realities outside the pertinent and endlessly varying experience with them.

The fundamental structure of the planetary symbolism in modern horoscopy includes three planets undiscovered by the astronomers before the late eighteenth century. The special employment of these ten significators in charting the basic dynamics of selfhood in its sheer aliveness, or relative to the continuing unfoldment in existence of the conscious entity once it has emerged into an essentially physical self-sufficiency at the moment of birth, is the basic consideration of the author's companion volume, *The Scope of Astrological Prediction*. What the three newcomers in astrology's enlarged schematism has helped make possible today in a more and more global and an increasingly individualized society, is an effective and over-all symbolization of the basic experience of the whole human race itself in unusually graphic terms. It was of course hardly possible to approach anything of the sort with the original seven Chaldean significators. The foundation for the particular refinement of planetary symbolism characterizing this series of astrological texts is the establishment of the four basic planetary departments as a primary application of the principle of pairs within pairs in a logical organization of the species of successive mirror imaging or dichotomization through which the whole development of symbols in astrology can be seen to emerge.

Thus the ancient astrologers, who at the beginning perhaps were essentially astronomers in a quite proper sense, were most conscious of a contrast between (a) the two lights or the sun and moon taken together and (b) the stars at large generally. Among the latter they came to give attention to those known to them as movable ones, or in their day the five original planets of what slowly came to take form in a definite horoscopy in full separation from astronomy because essentially a symbolical as against a physical or natural science. An observable difference in an annual regularity in contrast with a haphazard geocentric conduct probably led next to the designation of the outer two of the five as greater in significance in comparison with the inner ones and so constituting (c) a special group

PRIMER OF SYMBOLISM 433

on the order of the lights and apart from (d) the three seen of lesser dignity in the earlier scheme.

The names of the aspects formed by the planets in astrology are purely descriptive. They identify important horoscopic symbols of dynamic relationship as types of gravitational stress or counterbalance among the bodies in the heavens such as can be indicated by their positions in their orbits that in turn have geocentric pertinence in the plane of the ecliptic or zodiac. However, mere name as taken only in varying dictionary ramification may prove anything but useful horoscopic symbolization. This is true no less of the common designations for the planets themselves than of those for the houses and signs and all technical factors in horoscopic procedure. Thus no attention need be paid to any variations as Hershel instead of Uranus for the planet, or ascendant for the first house, or quadruplicity for quadrature, or nativity or chart or anything else for horoscope and so on endlessly. Perhaps the simplest way to make the matter clear at this point is to realize that in horoscopy, or indeed in any science where abstractions come to be vital to its functions, an actual and separate and self-sufficient language is developed within the frame and convenience of the vernacular tongue employed by its exponents or specialists.

How Do Symbols Become Keywords?

A cardinal principle put down for the development of the techniques given their exposition in these textbooks, to the end that horoscopy may be refined as a more genuinely rigorous science, was that every horoscopic indication without exception should always be seen meaning precisely no more and no less than what it consistently is taken to mean. Hence, in no possible fashion, should its testimony ever be contradicted or even qualified to the least extent. Symbols operate to trigger the mind to realizations or recognitions of greater scope or pertinence than ever can lie in the mere descriptive power of conventional language, but they may be just as imprecise as simple unordered or spontaneous description. Thus to characterize a man as a wolf or a woman as a snake might be pure prejudice, with little in fact to substantiate such a judgment, and to conclude that a license to practice some professional skill guarantees a possession of impartial common sense could at times have very unfortunate consequences.

In pursuit of the emphasis on preciseness in these texts a considerable number of symbolical terms have been established as keywords. This means that these symbols as far as possible are to be used only under the technical restriction that requires them to have a single and completely unvarying implication in any and every horoscopic context. Obviously such an ideal may never be reached in full, but as any appreciable approximation is achieved there can be a much greater reliability and incisiveness in delineating both the nativity and its progressive potentials. The greatest difficulty in mastering the keyword technique is managing to avoid any undue employment of the same words in their more imprecise or everyday reference, and so in such fashion preserving their functional distinctiveness in a mind schooling itself for the inescapable complexity of the astrological judgment. To have coined a genuinely unique vocabulary for the special purpose envisioned at this point would of course have had no practical justification whatsoever. Moreover, as the precedure here is understood, the trouble in adhering to it tends to disappear.

The actual emergence of the concept of keyword is far from new, but it has had only a limited acceptance as in astrology in connection with the zodiac perhaps most generally. Thus if the term Aries comes to mind, the skilled practitioner at once has something akin to an encyclopedic spread of possibilities of implication flooding into his consciousness, but because of his ever-pyramiding experience there also is a single and fundamental generality that really dominates his thinking and so gives point to the whole complex of differentiation and holds his judgment to what is ever and always and irrevocably the essence of the familiar symbol. His logic thus has in the name a reliable keyword for his rational procedure, and this has long been a common phenomenon for him. But when it comes to capturing the core insight in everyday language, whether for himself or others, it proves the impossibility well dramatized through the whole of these and all other astrological textbooks in the presentation of the zodiacal sign in nonsymbolic fashion or in the basic superficiality of any cold verbal description. The mere name of Aries only identifies the infinitely general horoscopic realization.

What Is the Scope of the Horoscope?

The horoscope is a wholly mathematical ordering of an illimitable and universal symbolism brought to pertinence at a given moment in a particular complex of event.

FUNDAMENTAL SCHEME OF HOROSCOPIC OPERATION

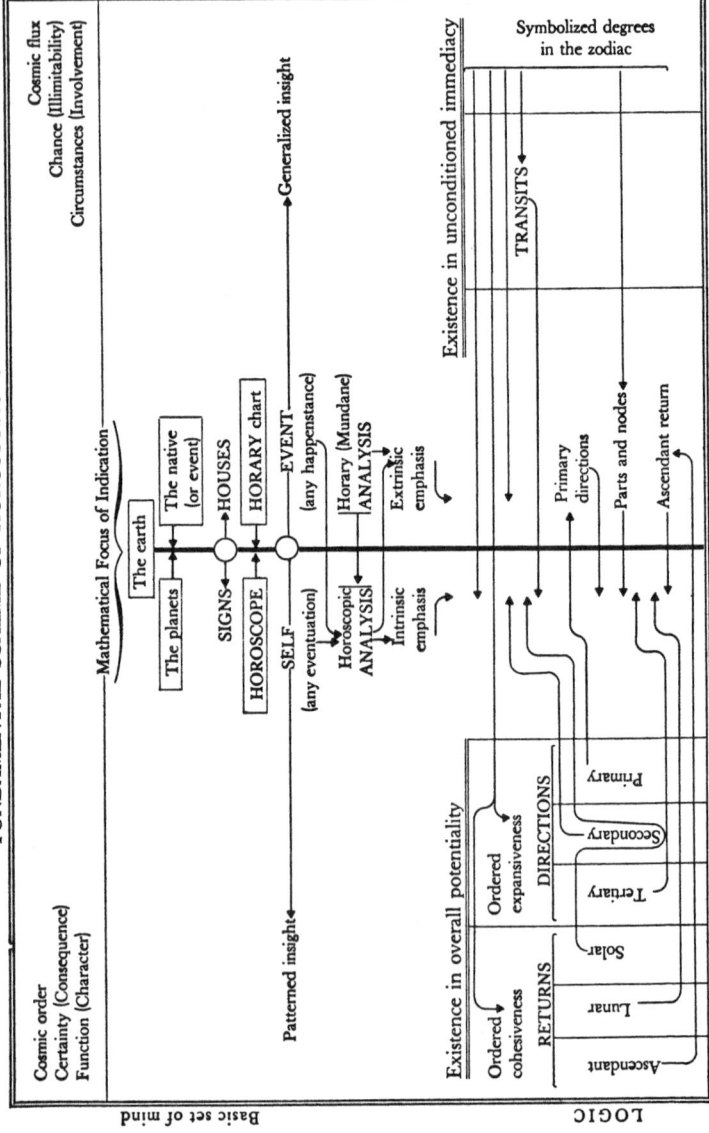

Through its various ways of manipulating number it employs the symbols that have become established as the basic astrological keywords and produces (a) an unchanging and fundamentally reliable pattern of man's widely varying individual character or make-up in its possible fact and its underlying potential and (b) an also possible and essentially illimitable pattern of the unfolding and refinement of every shifting manifestation of detail in the total potentiality in the course of a continuing existence and a conscious personal experience. Here respectively are the basic and dynamic horoscopy to which these textbooks are devoted. All the inescapable components of a living existence are made subject to identification by keyword or especially symbolical name that can be placed in any or every context of immediate or remote significance, as may be dictated by the eventuation of fact or possibility, and in consequence and thereby they can contribute to understanding and an intelligent ordering of act and attitude.

The overall horoscopic schematism can be outlined perhaps best by diagram.

In the manipulation of number or what is altogether the essence of an effective astrology, or in any given instance of concern in the mental operations that lead from any identification of the pertinencies and any recognition of the interrelations of possible or actual sort among them and so on to an effective understanding or judgment, there always must be a fundamental structure of dichotomy in the mind. This has been stressed in pointing out that any analysis is most simply a quite arbitrary denial of all change to some one factor in the particular context, through freezing it in a sense in the thinking, in order to contemplate some equally distinct other single factor in its changing or shifting into or out of pertinency in whatever event or issue has alerted consciousness or triggered attention.

Utterly necessary therefore in any really fundamental scheme of horoscopic operation is a properly flexible pattern of rational orientation to significant dichotomies among their almost illimitable possibility in practical or reliable thinking. Specifically if momentarily they provide the convenient anchor element in the mind's operation at each point as it deals intelligently with the dynamics of transient or enduring significance that can be brought to functional balance with the given anchorage. In this presentation of a universal symbolism the whole core of astrological insight has been found in the interplay of suggestiveness in negative-positive co-operation provided between the two major motions of the planet on which human life has developed. Out of the cosmic or irrevocally primitive polarity of significance thus recognized comes the ever primary and essentially inescapable distinction of signs of the zodiac and houses of the horoscope, or what in their total independence of each other are able to contribute to each other in symbolizing in detail the paradoxical fact of a conscious human individuality.

The human ability to think quite apart from astrology or any particular context presents an utterly primitive dichotomy that is inbuilt in its actuality. This is a dependence on the self-sufficiency in the reasoning process, or the phenomenon of logic on the one side, and its freewheeling creativity in a completely contrasting employment of imagination. These facets of mind correspond to cosmic

PRIMER OF SYMBOLISM 439

order and cosmic flux respectively, and hence in turn to the overall dichotomy of all conscious awareness perhaps best identified as consequence or certainty in balance with chance or illimitability. Here of course are technical symbolizations of very general abstractions or essentially metaphysical concepts that in this presentation of symbolical evolutions constitute definite keywords. In the convenience of diagramming the schematism of horoscopic operation can be seen to be at root a mirror-imaging in the special sense of these pages or an ever-shifting balance that holds character or individual function and circumstances or individual involvement in continuing but ramifying pertinence to each other.

In all this schematic distribution of significant pertinencies the horoscopic symbolism should be found serving two quite distinct purposes. For the serious student and the competent investigator it should help reveal the rationale of the astrological procedures in terms of the psychological necessities that establish them. Here could well be an effective contribution to the most practical grasp of the subject. What is more important is the exposition of the varying ways in which through astrology there can be a furthering of the efforts of the human individual to understand and appreciate himself and thereupon to refine his skills and develop his capacities to the happiest and most enduring self-fulfillment he may desire. This properly adds up to far more than reading the horoscope in a superficial fashion, such as presumes to deduce all the secrets of character by fascinating means from a wheel and its curious marks on a sheet of paper or to predict the events of the future in a frame of fatalistic assumptions. A nativity charts the emergence of an individual in a special reality that has its principal roots in a cosmic order of which the circling heavens are fundamentally a manifestation, and what it facilitates above all else is the potential of a reliable ordering that the newcomer to life may in due course establish in an equally fundamental fashion for the private little world of his own distinctive and conscious existence.

How Is Man Symbolized?

Man is a self-symbolizing animal, which means that each individual not only has an ultimate uniqueness as dramatized in his fingerprints and the like and so is only a single member out of an illimitable number of his kind but very importantly that thanks to the utter spread of all human individualism at core he may be a consistently varying manifestation of himself to himself and to others as differing occasion demands or encourages. At birth he is a helpless complex of totally undifferentiated potentials that ramify out to infinity in their possibility, and in this he duplicates the fundamental characteristic of the cosmos itself in an encompassing illimitability. The ultimate identity of the big ONE and little ONE has already been noted in the phenomenon of human birth where the dichotomy of minus-plus establishes the necessity for the manifestation of the child's particular ONENESS, and consequently creates the horoscope that symbolizes the pertinencies brought to pertinence through the emerging entity's conscious existence.

PRIMER OF SYMBOLISM

The dichotomization can therefore be given a variant form in the mental imagery, and be comprehended either as an unimpeached cosmic order balancing a corresponding cosmic flux that sustains a proliferation of the illimitable oneness of all existence, when this is seen more fundamentally or in overall fashion, or as a ubiquitous and essentially impartial consequence or certainty on the cosmic side sustaining the phenomenon of chance or illimitability in the individual manifestation. Meanwhile the familiar everyday reality, in which any actuality of living human experience becomes possible, must for analysis be examined from the frame of an extreme of fixity or liquidity he can never wholly exemplify. In a particular person's case the necessary anchorage of the astrological mind in its logical freeze of reference must almost by necessity be established in the macrocosmic fixity as the simplest extremism to identify in practical realization. The cosmos for the average person ends up as undisputed order, and mankind for untold ages has symbolized this as representative of a god or divine power to be acknowledged as supreme in some type of religion or its substitute in concepts of an omnipotent natural scheme of things. Man always has and in general still continues to worship or defer to a super-reality of some sort, and thus gain a dependable mental and fundamental anchor for his self-ordering.

In fact of course the infinitely differentiated elements of the macrocosm will have their differences averaged out ultimately, in theoretic substantiation of the supreme ONE-NESS man desires to feel is somewhere in the background of things, and conversely he is happy to take advantage of the parallel phenomenon of cosmic flux or unlimited permissiveness or ultimate unity of differences in his own conscious existence. But while his mind has every freedom of function in dealing with the realities of life on the personal or microcosmic side, of no less and great practical importance to him is the fact that the microcosm which is himself as his private totality must in the dimensions of its own particularity and no less than the cosmos have a basic ONENESS at the logical extreme of ultimate order. In the horoscopic schematism this self-oneness is established in the terms of the individual character, or the pure and independent function of any conscious or self-activating entity or self-propelling eventuality. Standing in balance with the theoretic self-oneness in the dichotomous relation here are circumstances, or the unimpeachably individualized involvements in any or every phase or manner of practical relationships. On this everyday level of man's experience the process of analysis may operate from either side of the dichotomy, as through the symbols centering in the signs or his self-functioning fundamentally or in the houses and his practical and familiar problems as may seem convenient. One or the other however must be taken for the logical freeze. Under psychological guidance, transient eventuality tends to take care of itself, and with purely pragmatic moves to the solution of commonplace problems the individual's personal adjustments are likely to follow almost unnoticed.

In primitive societies man symbolized himself almost completely through language, and about as automatically

PRIMER OF SYMBOLISM 443

as by and large it continues to be at the start in the case of the child. A baby begins to find itself as its response to attention brings reward and thus cultures first and feeble motivation. The fact that much of this seems instinctive does not alter the fact of it. Perhaps the first of learned skills is imitation. In the bosom of family or tribe or community or nation or school or occupation and so on endlessly, man names or identifies and characterizes himself ceaselessly, and thereupon functions in accordance with his progress as it may at times be encouraged or penalized. Meanwhile heredity and environment interweave in and out of each other constantly in the course of his growth. The development and contribution of the special argot employed by oddly disjunctive groups well illustrates the phenomenon of verbal self-substantiation, from the pig latin of an earlier generation of children to the continually shifting terms now adopted by teen-agers.

With civilization however, and especially in its industrialized forms and with almost instant global communication, the self-ordering is in no wise as simple or easy for a particular person who might wish to frame his ambitions and his self-gratifications in a way more rewarding for the type of individuality emerging in a newly evolving great age of mankind. An individual may and perhaps unhappily be far more caught up in inescapable limitations of the older culture and its heritage of some two to three millenniums or so than he might suspect. Class distinctions and mindless prejudices and the like are still no less a factor in the natural gestation and early shaping of human nature. Symbolism in fact can serve deficiency quite as well as dynamic capacity, as when someone of marked ego and consequent achievement remains blind to some equally marked incompetence. This obviously inadequate ordered state of individual self-administration is all too frequently a very definite block to effective horoscopic counseling, since none are so blind as those who cannot see.

Nonetheless a native's difficulty of this sort is easy enough for the astrologer to comprehend, and thereupon to adjust to the special necessities in dealing with it. He must realize that a characteristic of all nature is to hold to the more established groove in each way of doing things, if this can be done. Because of this tendency in the natural world it has been possible to trace out the course of evolution through its untold eons of development. And now recently, in connection with the heart transplants, the general public has been familiarized with nature's dogged determination to brook no basic interference with its processes as in this case through the rejection phenomenon inbuilt in living human tissue. In usual course the tissue of a given individual will accept no grafts, or will not co-operate even for the good of the organism with other tissue at all alien to itself. But what very few people realize is that there is a parallel rejection phenomenon of mind, and that it is equally intractable. Nobody is likely to let superficial prejudice go unrecognized when he sees it, but the astrologer must be particularly alert to a sheer mental inability of a client or indeed anybody else to react intelligently to anything that bends or distorts or threatens his inherent logical structure or his ingrained beliefs.

How Is Delineation Disciplined?

Judicial astrology or the analysis of the personal horoscope was usually learned in medieval times by the apprentice system, as were most human skills of the age, and that procedure in the essence of it remains the most effective course today. It would then perhaps be required that the neophyte live with his teacher, and he very possibly would pay for his keep and his instruction by shouldering what he could of the chores as a member of the family. In any case he would come to know his own horoscope as well as those of all his new intimates and gradually of the regular clients as well, and this with exceeding thoroughness. He probably would sit in on all the daily computations and speculations, and ultimately take his part in working with them. Naturally he would observe at first hand the correctness of prognosis and its errors. Reasoning at the start from his own nativity as a base, his mind would be ordered in a definite growth of capacity to press on in judgment from variables he thereby was able to keep in context. He generally would have recourse in memory of actualities well-realized and similar to the varying astrological factors coming fresh to consideration, and in operating from the continually validated familiar he would in this fashion seldom be unable to expand his insights sufficiently and even quite accurately enough to deal with any stranger details of interpretation. Thus delineation for him was disciplined almost painlessly. He well knew how man could be symbolized.

The whole-view method of horoscope analysis today parallels the earlier type of operation by providing, out of reference perhaps to almost numberless examples, an establishment of relatively sure and reliably typical familiarities from which to build quite as logically to sound delineative conclusions. Thus the identification of temperament types in seven general categories has become very popular as an aid in this approach, as they are seen in simple distinction from or in comparison with each other. The technique of focal determinators provides definitive categories of symbolized familiarity or significance unique in general aggregates of distinctive group diversity. What is thus provided are analytical tools of far greater usefulness for the mind than a twelvefold differentiation of a single planet's zodiacal place in mere normal course as in the sun-sign designations of long popular acceptance but inescapably superficial employment. By the same token the establishment of the activity-facets of self in the dynamic horoscopy is a similar aid in progressive analysis through channels of distinctive difference in human experience, and the embracing and more comprehensive organization of the ramifying possibility of measure through varying perspectives on man's self-unfoldment has been shown by diagram and has exhaustive attention in the companion textbook of this series, *The Scope of Astrological Prediction*. The temperament types and focal determinators and the whole scheme of whole-view organization of the basic interpretation of the nativity have a complete attention in the companion *Essentials of Astrological Analysis*.

In an undisciplined horoscopy the problem of all too many students and even practitioners is the seeming demand at almost any step in delineation that the mind proceed to synthesize an almost impossible host of separate indications. And then too, these often are taken so superficially that they continually tend to modify each other or perhaps virtually cancel each other out altogether. Thus the mind's task would be something only the most sophisticated of computers could accomplish, granted the accomplishment were possible. What avoids the impasse is the point-to-point approach through continuous anchorage to recognizable actualities, as in the now outmoded apprentice system of the medievals or the present-day recovery of its effectiveness as in the methods presented in these texts.

In practical fashion a definite system of priorities is needed for the points to be considered at any moment. Such a procedure however must be worked out fundamentally by the individual astrologer so that primarily it suits his manner of thinking, but it must be fluid enough for an effective and smooth adjustment to any case of obviously unusual factors in counseling. He should follow the example of nature herself and as far as possible always operate in whatever varying manner he has established for himself. But he should be aware first of all and quite consciously whether his approach is from the cosmic order as brought to focus for the particular individual in the nativity, or from the cosmic flux as perhaps charted most characteristically by horary astrology. The diagrammatic *Fundamental Scheme of Horoscopic Operation* could be particularly helpful in his determining of the details of his particular course thereafter.

Diagrammatically his concern always is at midpoint between the conveniently alternate extremes of perspective, and this is represented by the astrological wheel that identifies a native at birth or an issue at crisis. As a nativity it holds slightly leftward or more responsibly in the schematism, or has a priority in terms of cosmic order charted by the signs although this is distributed rightward or toward choice into the circumstances that the houses represent particularly. On page 56 of this text there is a recognition of degrees of freedom in reality, and here in general exposition there is a parallel scaling of additional horoscopic consideration with added factors of consideration to be taken into account very necessarily in delineative detail. In logic this is the matter of significant removes or the proposition for example that in turning to the distribution of character in actual experience is a one-remove in reasoning. Priority in horoscopic procedure can be seen as established in essence or through the diagramming by the columns in the schematism suggested by this exposition of astrology's overall symbolism, or in the move out to the extremes of perspective that can be taken as providing the characteristic modes of fundamental horoscopic symbolization.

Thus the symbolized degrees of the zodiac stand close to the use of pure imagination, and the solar and lunar returns are pure recapitulation of original pattern-ordering in the signs but in complete independence of the equally original houses in their emphasized alignment toward overall order as such. It can be seen that the transits are two removes from the nativity, thanks to their indication of passing chance in circumstances, and hence should have less priority in consideration than the one-remove secondary directions in which the natal planets themselves move if in symbolical fashion to their pertinency in delineation. In primary directions the planetary movements to indication are arbitrary in the same manner as in the time indications of horary astrology, and so these modes of measure are in one-remove from the nativity but on the side of chance in its manifestation of unconditioned convenience.

This sort of diagramming is of course essentially theoretical or metaphysical, and as functioning in the area of hypothesis must as already pointed out be seen as perhaps of the greatest help to man's rational processes but not constituting anything of any absolute or unquestionable or uniquely correct validity. Again it must be emphasized that the astrologer not only must order himself but must himself establish the competence of the astrology he uses. Its justification inescapably remains the effectiveness it demonstrates in very practical and everyday terms.

INDEX TO PRIMER OF SYMBOLISM

Alphabet, astrological, 418
Absolute implication, 413
Apprentice system, 445
Astrology, deficiencies, 417, 421, 439, 446
Astrology, How and Why It Works, 418, 425
Astrology, nature of, 416, 420

Birth, nature of, 421, 422, 423, 440

Cause and effect, 421
Child, SEE birth, nature of.
Constellations, heavenly, 427

Delineation, faulty, (SEE ALSO astrology, deficiencies.), 421
Departments, planetary, 432
Dynamic perspective, 412

Ephemeral meaning, 413
Essentials of Astrological Analysis, 446

Freeze, logical, 418, 425, 437, 441, 442

Grammar, astrology as, 411

Heredity and environment, 443
Hipparchus, 427
Horoscopic operation, fundamental scheme of, 436, 447
Horoscope, nature of, 422, 424, 426, 428, 436, 438, 439, 440
Houses of the horoscope, 426, 429, 438, 442
Hypotheses, astrological, 417

Keywords, 434, 435

Language, (SEE ALSO metalanguage.) 411, 418, 433, 442
Logical freeze, SEE freeze, logical.

Macrocosm and microcosm, 416, 431, 441
Meaning, 413, 415, 421, 434
Metalanguage, 415, 416, 419
Metaphysics, 417, 449
Mind, functioning of, 414, 417, 418, 419, 422, 424, 431, 434, 435, 437, 438, 446, 448
Minus, SEE plus and minus.
Movements, the earth's two, 424, 426, 427, 429, 438

Names, 411, 415, 425, 427, 430, 433

Number, 412, 415, 418, 424, 425, 426, 437

One, and oneness, 420, 422, 425, 429, 440, 441
One, big and little, 422, 440

Perspective in delineation, 412, 431, 447
Planets, in astrology, 429
Planets of recent discovery, 431
Plus and minus, 412, 419, 420, 421, 423

Qualitative, quantitative, 412

Rejection phenomenon, 444
Remove in consideration, the, 423, 448

Scope of Astrological Prediction, The, 432, 446
Self, nature of, 414, 422, 424, 443
Signs of the zodiac, 427, 429, 438, 442
Space and time, their nature, 424
Static perspective, 412

Theory, astrological, SEE metaphysics.
Time, SEE space and time.

Universal motion, 424

Whole-view analysis, 445
Words, function of, 414

main text indexes

INDEX

THE DIAGRAMS

Horary charts, 21, 263, 309
Natal charts, 340, 342-8
The triads, 81, 85, 93, 99

Skeleton of the houses, 69
Houses of cousin's baby, 146
Multiple Questions, 380

THE TABULATIONS

Signs of the zodiac, 54
*Rhythm in house meanings, 80
The ten planets, 116
The lords of signs, 117
Additional planetary factors, 121
The house meanings, 221 ff.
Possible types of inquiry, 267
The Part of Fortune, 282 f.
General descriptions, 286
*The indications of age, 287
*The indications of sex, 287
Vocational rulerships, 288 f.
The geographic rulerships, 290
Planetary name-types, 291 f.
The horary timetable, 297
Meaning of major aspects, 306
Personal involvement, 314 ff.
Instrumentality, 317-318
Contributory events, 319
Astrological compass, 320

The judgment houses, 329 ff.
The exaltations, 334
The signs of the zodiac, 355
Qualities of the signs, 356
The seasonal natures, 357
*Joys of the planets, 358
*Planetary triplicities, 358
*Planetary decanates, 359
Minor essential dignities, 359
*Accidental dignities, 360
Planetary mean motions, 361
*Accidental debilities, 361 f.
Principal minor aspects, 364
Affections of degrees, 365
*The kinds of death, 369
*The planetary days, 371 f.
The planetary hours, 373
*Obscure horary terms, 374 ff.
*Alternative rulerships, 383
The zodiacal man, 404
*Indications of illness, 405

* Embodied in the text, not in tabular form

ILLUSTRATIVE INCIDENTS AND CASES

Actress, youthful, 24 f.
Adolescent in love, 122 f.
Amusement enterprise, 311 f.

Anniversary, forgotten, 238
Argentine trip, 308 ff.
California friends, 14

California vs. business, 248, 265, 301
Canada trip, 237 f., 263, 297
Celebrity taking airplane, 16
Chess player in dry well, 71
Child, quarrel over, 325 ff.
Contract signed, 243, 264, 299
Cousin's sick baby, 237 f., 145 f.

Deal, closing business, 126 f.
Dimensions of trouble, 86

Fishing vs. carpentry, 249, 265, 301
Florida vs. business, 247, 264, 300, 307 f.

Joker giving "hot foot," 238

Libra client in summer, 57
Location of superior, 321

Man facing eviction, 135 f.
Man fearing discharge, 118
Man using friend, 193 ff.

Man with many problems, 378 ff.
Mathematical examples, 110 ff.
Municipal power plant, 393 f.

Oblique suggestiveness, 291
Operation vs. role, 249, 265 f., 301

Position, offer of, 245, 264, 299 f., 306 ff.

Riches, prediction of, 156

Sales manager, clever, 26 f.
Salesman and connections, 24
Salesmen, four, 253, 266 f., 301
Savings, investment of, 238, 242, 264, 297 f.
Sickness, query about, 312 f.

Title bout and water-rights suit, 256, 267, 301 f.
Tree used by surveyor, 241

War, query about, 134 f.
Widow, charming, 28 f.

GENERAL SUBJECT MATTER

Above the earth, 74 f., 347
Adams, Evangeline, 407
Affliction, 121
Ambient, 43
American Astrology Tables of Houses, 42
Angular houses, 78; focus in, 132
Apparent movement, 39
Arabian parts, 363 ff.
Arabs, 273

Ascendant, 43, 65
Aspects, 119 ff., 236, 254, 305 ff., 363 f., 385 ff.
Astral world, 14
Astrological rulerships, functional basis of, 84 ff., 98, 104, 133 f., 140, 161, 164, 166, 180 f.
Astrology, antiquity of, 18 f.; as magic, 141 ff., 148; as psychology, 18, 268 ff.; as re-

INDEX

ligion, 275; astronomical basis of, 38 ff.; basis of meaning, 41, 58, 64, 66 f., 107 ff., 337 ff.; in petty business detail, 143 f.; in speculation, 143 f.; statistical nature of, 26, 66 f., 107 f., 148
Astrology, How and Why It Works, 347

Below the earth, 75, 347
Bible, 23, 138
Bibliography, 33, 36
Bill of Rights, 244, 395
British types, 285
Butler, Hiram E., 110

Cadent houses, 78, 155 f.
Carroll, Lewis, 344 ff.
Cause and effect, 41, 66 f.
Cazimi, 361
Centuries of Nostradamus, 18
Chamber's *Mathematical Tables,* 114
Change, 178 f., 268
Chart, astrological, basis and nature of, 41 ff., 52 ff., 58; form of, 21
Charubel, 367
Clairvoyance, 17
Clockwise vs. counterclockwise, 74 f., 296
Coincidence, 15
Collection, 364
Combustion, 361
Common sense, 276, 300

Consciousness, levels of, 17, 22, 32, 34 f.
Considerations before judgment, 34 f., 50, 54 ff., 116 f., 120 f., 269 ff., 303, 371
Constellations, 40 f.
Convenience, 25
Conventions, 15
Co-ordinate measure, 386 ff.
Corrections for time and longitude, 45 ff.
Co-rulership of the moon, 276
Counting, ancient, 138
Crisis chart, 144, 237 ff., 325 ff.; importance of crisis, 144, 148
Cusp, 68

Dalton, Joseph G., 42
Debilities, planetary, 357 ff.
Decanates, 359
Declination, 386 ff.; wide, 361
Degrees, of freedom, 56; significant, 365 ff.; Sabian symbolizations of, 367
Degrees of the Zodiac Symbolized, 367
DeLuce, Robert, 36, 181
Dependability in astrological work, 268 ff.
Descendant, 69
Determinors, focal, 346 ff.
Detriment, 358
Dictionary of Astrology, 356, 365 f.
Die Deutsche Ephemeride, 42

PROBLEM SOLVING

Dignities, planetary, 357 ff.
Dipper, Big, 39 f.
Directions, 293, 369 ff.
Divinatory Astrology, 36
Dragon's head, tail, 121, 363

Ecliptic, 350
Either-or questions, 247 ff.
Elections, charts of events, 29 f., 55, 57, 125 f., 145, 207 f., 302, 390 ff.
Ephemeris, 42, 46
Equator, 51 f., 63 f.
Essentials of Astrological Analysis, 338, 347
Exaltation, 334, 358
Experience, 16 f., 19 f., 27 f., 29, 52, 63

Faces, 359
Fall, 358
Fixed stars, 39, 273
Ford, Henry 342 ff.
Free will, 71, 91, 105, 126

Gadbury, John, 33
Geocentric longitude, 110
Geocentric point of view, 39
Golgge Ephemeris, 42
Grand square, trine, 352 f.
Greeks, 78
Greenwich mean time, 112; meridian, 45
Guide to Horoscope Interpretation, 338, 340, 342

Heliocentric longitude, 110
Hemisphere emphasis, 347
Hindu astrology, 359
Hipparchus, 273
Hippocratic oath, 259
Horary Astrology (Leo), 36, 273
Horary astrology, as different from natal, 20, 54, 56, 58, 65, 80, 83, 94, 104, 118, 119, 122, 125 f., 127, 132 f., 141, 144, 147, 234, 239, 242, 260 f., 270, 273, 293 ff., 305, 337, 362 f., 391 f., 398, 403, 406 ff.; materials required for, 44; meaning and definition of, 19, 23, 25, 27 f., 29 ff., 34, 37; requirements for, 118 f.; timetable, 120
Horizon, 41 ff., 63, 65
Horoscope, SEE chart, astrological.
Houses, nature of, 50 ff., 63 ff., 108 f., 239 f.; of the planets, 358
How to Learn Astrology, 152, 347

Immediate overtone, 371 ff.
Individual differences, 24
Inevitability, 179
Initiative, 245 ff., 255 ff.
Intelligence, 23
Interception, 310, 312 f.
Introduction to Astrology (Lilly), 36

INDEX

Intuition, 14, 16, 22 f., 133 f., 275

James, William, 342 ff., 408
Jones, Marc Edmund, 36, 152, 338, 347, 367
Joys, 358
Judgment, astrological basis of, 20, 23, 26, 38
Judgment chart, 145 f., 237 ff., 325 ff.

Kant, Immanuel, 79
Keller, Helen, 342 ff.
Keywords, use of, 354

Latitude, celestial, 386 ff.; geographic, 42 ff.
Legal considerations, 401 f.
Length of life, 368 f.
Leo, Alan, 36, 273
Life, organic nature of, 17
Lilly, William, 33, 36, 133, 145, 234 f., 241, 286, 368
Limitation, 71
Litmus paper, 74
Location of questions, 131 ff., 249 ff.
Logarithms, 114
Logic in judgment, 126, 240, 303
London fire, 33; meridian, 42
Long ascension, 354 f.
Longitude, celestial, 110 ff.; geographic, 45 ff.
Lunar cycle test, 274 ff., 303

Marx, Karl, 344 ff.
Mathematics, 18, 37 ff.
Medical considerations, 401 f.
Meridian, 42 ff.
Methods, variant, 58 f., 104, 133 f., 181
Midheaven, 43, 65
Midnight vs. noon, 42, 46
Mind, operation of, 14, 32 ff., 35, 58
Minor houses, 78
Modern Scientific Textbook (Davis), 36
Moment, present, 20, 24, 26, 29 f., 35, 37, 238
Moon as co-ruler, 276
Motions, heavenly, 38 ff., 109 ff.
Multiple questions, 139, 249, 254, 377 ff.
Mundane astrology, 391
Mundane Perspectives in Astrology, 363
Mutual reception, 327, 358

Nadir, 67 f.
Names as functional, 326
Nature of death, 368 f.
New Thought, 201
Nodes, planetary, 121, 363 ff.
Normal curve, 25
Nostradamus, 18

Occam's razor, 241, 275 f., 301, 408
Options and non-options,

128 ff., 243 ff.
Orbs of aspect, 119 f., 236, 386
Organic factors, 17, 22
Orientation questions, 128 ff.

Part of Fortune, 121, 280 ff., 333, 363
Past, in relation to present, 87 f.
Pasteur, Louis, 340 ff.
Peregrine, 359
Philadelphia ephemeris, 46
Philosophy, Grecian, 79; of number, 78 ff.
Photography, 233, 279
Planetary days, hours, 371 ff.; departments, 338
Planets, 107 ff., 115 ff., 123, 276 ff., 304, 341 ff., 383
Polygamy, 96, 177
Positive correlation, 38, 41, 64
Potentiality, 16
Pragmatism, 287
Precession of equinoxes, 40
Prediction, 18, 37
Preponderance, 353
Probability, analysis of, 148; nature of, 37
Professional relationship, 31
Prognostic Astrologer, 36
Progressions, 293, 369 ff.
Psychoanalysis, 256
Psychological fallacy, 94, 132
Psychology, 18, 268 ff.
Psychometry, 275
Ptolemy, Claudius, 236

Pythagoras, 78

Radical charts, 50
Raphael, 36, 359
Raphael's Ephemeris, 42
Reciprocal options, 255 ff.
Refranation, 362
Regression in consideration, 35, 55 ff., 240 f., 260 ff., 303, 381 ff.
Relocation, 249 ff., 381 ff.
Retrogradation, 240, 310 ff.
Return, solar, 293
Rice, Hugh S., 42
Riches, meaning of, 156
Right ascension, 44, 110
Ring-around-the-rosy, 137 f., 281, 377, 395 f.
Rising sign, 57, 59
Roosevelt, Theodore, 342 ff.
Rule of three, 112
Rulership, basis of, 117 f.

Sabian Symbols in Astrology, 367
Science, 18, 23, 134, 141 ff., 268 ff., 275, 322 f.
Sequence, direction of, 296, 320; through houses, 151 ff., 177 ff.
Sequential options, 252 ff.
Short ascension, 354 f.
Sidereal time, 42 ff.
Significator in houses, 324 f.
Signs of the zodiac, nature of, 50 ff., 67 f., 117 f., 296; special indications of, 350 ff.

INDEX

Simmonite, William Joseph, 36
Simplified Scientific Ephemeris, 42
Simultaneous questions, 383 f.
Singleton, 348 f.
Socrates, 270
Solar Biology, 110
Solar chart, 408; return, 293
Solomon, 23 f., 282
South-hemisphere charts, 355
Space, 19, 29, 37 ff., 79
Spherical Basis of Astrology, 42
Stellium, 340
Story, John, 36
Succedent houses, 78, 155 f.
Swinburne, Algernon, 344 ff.
Symbolism, its naive nature, 71 f.; of signs, 353 ff.

Tables of Houses, 42, 43, 46
T cross, 352 f.
Temperament types, 338 ff.
Terms, 359
Time, bases of selection, 30, 32 f., 34 f.; daylight saving, 45; equating of, 293 ff.; horary indication of, 389, 395; mean, 47; nature and importance of, 15, 19, 24, 30 f., 32, 37 ff., 43, 79, 294 f.; notation of, 30; regressive implications of, 369 ff.; selection of, 30, 32; standard, 44 f.; symbolical nature of horary, 294, 297, 302
Timetable, 120
Transits, 293, 369 ff., 395
Translation of light, 364
Triplicity, 350 ff.

Universe, orderliness of, 25, 85 f., 91 f., 126 f., 135

Via combusta, 272 f., 282
Void of course, 120, 274

Wilson, James, 356, 365
Wishful thinking, 256

X cross, 352 f.

Zodiac, 40, 51

THE HOUSE RULERSHIPS

First, 65 ff., 72, 76 f., 80 f., 92, 100, 131, 137 ff., 140 ff., 152, 180, 205 f., 219, 285 ff.
Second, 90 f., 151 ff., 158, 172 ff., 180, 184, 188 f., 203 f., 215, 219
Third, 94 ff., 147, 155, 157 ff., 180, 182, 186, 194 f., 197, 198 ff., 201 f., 211 ff., 215
Fourth, 70, 75 ff., 77, 100 f., 103 ff., 147, 171 f., 177 ff., 188 f., 194, 206, 214

Fifth, 82 f., 90, 94, 154 f., 157, 160, 165 f., 168 f., 171, 175, 182 f., 184, 185 ff., 196, 198, 201, 212, 216

Sixth, 87 ff., 95, 147, 154, 155, 157, 160, 162 ff., 184, 189 f., 192 ff., 206 f., 213, 216, 403

Seventh, 69 ff., 76 f., 91 ff., 96 f., 99 f., 105 f., 131, 139 f., 154, 157, 165 f., 169, 171 f., 179, 186 f., 193, 195 f., 198, 202 ff., 212

Eighth, 103, 152, 157, 208 ff., 215

Ninth, 81 f., 97 f., 147, 152, 155, 169 f., 201 f., 206, 210, 211 ff., 217 n.

Tenth, 65 ff., 75 f., 77, 83 ff., 92, 94, 103 f., 139, 147, 150 f., 152, 161, 177 f., 183, 185, 192 f., 196 ff., 205 ff., 213, 216 f.

Eleventh, 96 ff., 140, 201, 205, 217 f., 220

Twelfth, 90, 98, 101 ff., 155, 182 f., 206, 213, 218 ff.

Acquaintances, 96 f.
Adjustment, 88 f., 192
Advertising, 201, 204
Advice, 218
Agents, 190
Allies, 203
Ambassadors, 190
Ambition, 217
Amusements, 82 f., 182, 186 f.
Animals, 89 f., 200, 202, 220
Annuities, 210 f.
Aristocracy, 217
Army, 89, 195
Art, 73, 94, 164 f., 188, 204 f.
Assistance, assistants, 154 f., 203
Astrologers, 94, 117, 198
Asylums, 102
Authority, 65, 84, 87, 198, 216 f.
Automobiles, 160, 181, 200

Birds, 202
Bondage, 219
Books, 81, 168, 212
Borrowing money, 157
Brothers, 95 f., 160 f., 173 ff.
Business, 75, 84 f., 89, 104, 150, 192 f., 199, 202 ff., 216 f.
Buying, selling, 204

Carnivals, fairs, 187
Cataclysm, 185
Cemeteries, 100 f., 180
Change, 158, 214
Children, 82, 90, 96, 171, 175 f., 189 ff., 191
Churches, 165
Clerks, 164, 199
Clients, 206 f.
Climate, 194 f.
Clothing, 89, 154, 194, 196

INDEX

Communication, 95, 162, 201
Competition, 88, 187, 195, 207 f.
Confinement, 101, 182 f., 218 f.
Congress, 218
Conscience, 81, 212
Consultation, 73, 94
Contests, 88, 187, 207 f.
Contracts, 202 f.
Co-operation, 73, 91 f., 203
Corporations, 214 f., 217
Counseling, 201, 218
Courtroom, 206
Courtship, 82, 186, 201
Cousins, 96
Creativity, 82
Credit, 151
Cycles, 209

Death, 103, 208 ff.
Debts, 156 f.
Deeds of trust, 184
Detectives, 219 f.
Dignity, 87
Disaster, 185
Dissipation, 82
Doubt, 141
Dreams, 97, 213 f.

Editorial work, 165
Eminent domain, 172
Employers, 84
End of the matter, 75, 100, 105, 178 f.
Enemies, 102, 202 ff., 219 f.

Environment, 158 f., 165, 169 f., 172
Escape, 219
Estates, 77, 101, 180
Exploitation, 184

Fame, 201, 213
Family, 77, 101, 178
Farming, 89, 194
Father, 104 f., 177 f.
Fear, 219 f.
Finance, 152, 210
Fine arts, 73, 94, 165, 204 f.
Focus, 141
Food, 89, 193 f., 196
Foreign matters, 211
Friends, 96 f., 218
Fugitives, 204, 219
Furniture, 197

Galleries, 101
Gambling, 188
Games, 160, 186 f.
Gossip, 95
Government, 65, 84, 185, 216 f.
Grave, 76

Habits, 167
Handicrafts, 164, 199
Healing, 196, 201
Health, 147
Hidden enemies, 102, 219 f.
Hidden things, 171 f., 178, 184, 188 f., 219
Home, 75, 100, 173, 178, 185
Honor, 87, 213, 216

PROBLEM SOLVING

Hopes, 97, 217
Hospitals, 101, 182

Ideas, 211
Imagination, 97 f.
Immediate outcome, 105, 203
Income, 182, 184, 210
Inheritance, 101, 103
Inspiration, 213 f.
Institutions, 101, 218 ff.
Inventions, 186
Investments, 151

Jewelry, 154, 186
Journeys, 82, 95, 170, 211 f., 214
Judge, decisions, 205 ff.
Jury, 205 ff.
Justice, 212

Knowledge, 81 ff., 98

Labor, 88, 90, 164, 193, 198 f.
Landlord, 183
Law, 196, 198, 205 ff., 213, 218
Lecturing, 216
Legacies, 103, 152, 210, 215
Legislatures, 218
Length of life, 149
Letters, 95, 162
Liberty, 156
Life insurance, 210, 215
Loans, 157
Location of person, 150
Loss and gain, 91, 151
Lost articles, 170 ff.

Machinery, 95, 200
Magic, 200 f.
Magistrates, 84, 217
Maladjustment, 89, 192
Manuscripts, 168
Marriage, 73, 92 f., 96, 176 f., 203
Masses, 141
Mind, 81, 167, 211 ff.
Minerals, 184
Misrepresentation, 95
Mistresses, 190
Models, 186
Money, 90 f., 151 f., 210 f.
Monuments, 100 f., 180
Mortgages, 184
Mother, 104 f., 177, 197 f., 217
Movable things, 153, 184
Museums, 101
Music, 188

Name, good, 201
Natural resources, 184 f., 188
Navy, 89, 195
Neighbors, 160
News, 167 f.
Notoriety, 213
Nurses, 196 f.

Objectives, 97
Offspring, 82, 186
Oil, 184
Old age, 100
Opinion, 95
Opportunity, 73
Ornaments, 154

INDEX

Pageants, 166
Pardons, paroles, 219
Parents, 96, 103 ff., 177 f., 197 f., 217
Parks, 77, 101, 180
Parliament, 218
Partners, 72, 93 f., 171, 176, 202 f.
Patriotism, 213
Penitentiaries, 101, 182
Periodicals, 159
Personality, 65, 141
Pets, 89, 202
Physicians, 196, 198
Plans, 97
Play, 160, 186
Policemen, firemen, 195
Position in life, 76
Possessions, 91, 151, 154, 158
Pregnancy, 190
Premises, 101 n., 165 f.
Press, 159
Prodigality, 82
Profession, 65, 87, 94, 104
Propaganda, 201, 216
Prospecting, 184
Prowess, 149
Public relations, 204
Publishing, 216

Query, querent, 65, 80, 132, 144

Real estate, 151, 153 f., 182 f.
Recreation, 186 f.
Reformatories, 102

Regeneration, 103, 208 f.
Regimentation, 195, 202
Relatives, 95 f.
Religion, clergy, 81, 212 ff.
Research, 189, 216
Resources, 90 f., 155 ff., 158, 188 f., 219
Revolution, 195
Rights of way, 184
Routine, 95
Royalties, 151 f.
Rumors, 167 f.

Safety, 100, 178
Salary and wages, 200
Salesmen, 253
Schools, 82, 186, 189, 216
Science, 81, 212 f.
Sects, 161
Security, 215
Servants, 88, 194, 199 f., 202
Service, 88, 162 ff., 197
Sex of child, 191
Sex relations, 83, 93, 186
Ships at sea, 150
Sickness, 88, 162, 193, 195 f.
Singing, 166
Sisters, 95 f., 160 f., 173 ff.
Social work, 195
Soul, 76, 101
Speculation, 151, 183, 188
Spirits, 210
Sports, 83, 186
Stewards, 184, 190, 198
Stolen articles, 204
Storekeepers, 199

Strangers, 204
Strength in resistance, 189
Subconsciousness, 102
Success, 149
Suicide, 219
Superior, superiority, 65, 84
Superstition, 178

Talents, 82
Tenants, 184, 198
Theaters, 83, 187 f.
Thieves, thefts, 157, 172, 204
Thought, thinking, 98, 211 ff.
Threats, 203 f.
Tools, 95, 158 f.
Towns, cities, 185
Toys, 160, 186
Transportation, 160
Treaties, 202 f.
Trust fund, 210, 215
Twins, 191

Ultimate relations, 75, 177
Unexpected events, 102
Useful arts, 164 f.
Usufruct, 101
Utilities, 159, 163 f., 195

Vicarious experience, 97
Visions, 213 f.

War declarations, 207 f.
Warnings, 203 f.
Wealth, 151
Weather, 185, 214
Wisdom, 82, 98, 213
Wishes, 97, 217, 220
Womb, 104
Work, 88, 90, 164, 193, 198 f.
Worry, 219 f.
Worship, 166
Writing, 212

Marc Edmund Jones
October 1, 1888 — March 8, 1980

Marc Edmund Jones was an original. He dropped out of high school to go into business and years later he completed his formal education with a Ph.D. in philosophy from Columbia University. He participated in the creation of the movie industry by writing scenarios in the very early days and was instrumental in founding what later became the Screen Writer's Guild. He was a Presbyterian clergyman and served in a parish for five years. He was a philosopher, author of the major work, *Occult Philosophy*. However, most people knew him as an astrologer.

Marc Jones began the study of astrology in 1913. In 1922, working with a psychic, Elsie Wheeler, he developed the symbols for each degree of the Zodiac, which have become known as the Sabian Symbols. In 1923 he worked out his Key Principles of Astrology for use with his regular classes. This base was expanded in the following years as he developed 12 sets of lessons for his students, presenting in mimeographed form a comprehensive but condensed version of a variety of approaches to astrology.

While working on his Ph.D. in New York, Marc came out in the open with his ideas on reforming astrology. Some of the problems he saw in the way astrology was usually practiced included assigning rulership to planets, over-personification of symbols, creation of "influences," unnecessary confusion over the distortion of houses, confusion between signs and houses, viewing the signs as quite set in nature, and taking the zodiac as a mystic conglomeration of heavenly influences upon man to which he must submit.

In his increasing efforts to correct such misunderstandings, Marc Jones traveled and lectured in many parts of the country. In these talks he did not refer to "benefics" and "malefics" in the chart. And he challenged the age-old notion that the power is in the stars, that the chart creates the destiny. Instead, he taught that astrology properly used helps clients see more clearly their own tendencies so they can decide for themselves what they want to do with those tendencies.

Beginning with the period in New York, he produced the series of books which had been projected years earlier as the rigorous presentation of techniques worked out in the mimeographed lessons. His plan was reinforced both by the growing public interest in astrology and by his position as occult book editor for the David McKay Book Company. Eleven astrological books were written and published over the years from 1941-1979. His last work, *The Counseling Manual in Astrology,* had been written and most of the type set at the time of his death, and publication was completed posthumously.

In his later years, Marc Jones was widely recognized for his valuable contribution to astrology, and was customarily and affectionately referred to as the dean of American astrology.

𝓜arc Edmund Jones created a solid foundation for contemporary scientific astrology in his many groundbreaking books and lectures. Methods he developed are integrated into the work of astrologers globally. Within his techniques are comprehensive principles which reach beyond astrology.

The Sabian Assembly implements the philosophical concepts developed by Marc Edmund Jones as the Solar path of initiation, basing knowledge on personal experience rather than external authority. Founded in 1923, the Assembly continues Dr. Jones' dedication to competent rather than superficial answers to the problems of life. To accomplish this the Assembly issues Dr. Jones' weekly lessons for each cycle. New students plunge directly into the flow of lessons all are currently receiving. Regular study groups, conferences and workshops offer opportunities for members to meet and learn together and share significant experiences.

To obtain more information about the ongoing fellowship known as the **Sabian Assembly** write to:

The SABIAN PUBLISHING SOCIETY
POST OFFICE BOX 7
STANWOOD, WA. 98292

The Marc Edmund Jones Literary Trust is devoted to keeping Dr. Jones' books in print. If you want to know more about this program or to contribute to its success, please write to the above address.

3 CLASSICS BY DR. MARC EDMUND JONES

THE SABIAN SYMBOLS IN ASTROLOGY
Illustrated By 1000 Horoscopes of Well Known People
ISBN: 0-943358-40-X Paperback 456 pages

ASTROLOGY HOW AND WHY IT WORKS
AN INTRODUCTION TO BASIC ASTROLOGY
ISBN: 0-943358-38-8 Paperback 448 pages

HORARY ASTROLOGY
PRACTICAL TECHNIQUES FOR PROBLEM SOLVING
WITH A PRIMER OF SYMBOLISM
ISBN: 0-943358-39-6 Paperback 464 pages

THE DANE RUDYAR SERIES

THE ASTROLOGY OF PERSONALITY
A Reformulation of Astrological Concepts and Ideals In
Terms of Contemporary Psychology and Philosophy
ISBN: 0-943358-25-6 Paperback 445 pages

PERSON CENTERED ASTROLOGY
ISBN: 0-943358-02-7 Paperback 385 pages

THE LUNATION CYCLE
A Key To the Understanding of Personality
ISBN: 0-943358-26-4 Paperback 208 pages

for a free catalog write:
AURORA PRESS
P.O. BOX 573
Santa Fe, N.M. 87504